For Phyllis Wise,
one of the great inside
operators who could feel perfectly
at home in Mr. Sam's "Board
of Education," with the
abiding gratitude of her
friend,

FORGE OF DEMOCRACY

The House of Representatives

Forge of Democracy

THE HOUSE OF REPRESENTATIVES

By NEIL MacNEIL

DAVID McKAY COMPANY, INC.   NEW YORK

FORGE OF DEMOCRACY: THE HOUSE OF REPRESENTATIVES

Copyright © 1963 by Neil MacNeil

Library of Congress Catalog Card Number: 63-11721

MANUFACTURED IN THE UNITED STATES OF AMERICA

VAN REES PRESS • NEW YORK

I dedicate this book,
with affection and gratitude,
to my parents

Acknowledgments

To Kennett Rawson of David McKay Company, Inc., I owe a special debt. His interest in this book never flagged and his enthusiasm was infectious. He has edited the entire text, and, with his practiced eye, has spared the reader many an otherwise disjointed or obtuse passage.

It is only just to say, finally, that this book could not have been written without the encouragement and active help of my wife, Laureen MacNeil.

Preface

THIS book is an attempt to define the House of Representatives. In writing it, I have not been satisfied merely to describe the House's great Constitutional powers, to translate into layman's language its parliamentary manuals, and to list the names and deeds of its many members. I have tried rather to portray the House itself as a living political institution. Its Constitutional powers, and the way the House has exercised them, of course have given meaning to the House's existence. Its rules and parliamentary practices have played an important and sometimes decisive role in the House's formal actions. The Representatives themselves have been the elemental ingredients who have made the House's collective judgments. The House of Representatives, however, is something more than the sum total of its legal powers, its rules, and the 435 men and women who are elected every two years as its members. The House, as well, is the product of its own past and traditions. As a legislative assembly, the House has an inner life of its own, shaped by its institutional feelings about men and things. These institutional feelings have taken palpable form in the growth of the House's committee structure, its seniority system, and its hierarchy of leaders. They have taken more subtle, intangible form in the House's almost intuitive attitudes toward its own members, the Senate, the President, and its own function in the scheme of the American government. They have helped mold the great power blocs and coalitions inside the House and to fashion the House's instinctive responses to the lobbyists, the voters back home, and all those who have tried to influence the House's ultimate decisions. I have tried to show the House, in its many facets, as a vital part of the federal government, reflecting the immense complexity and variety of American life.

The materials here printed are partly the distillation of my own daily observation of the House for eight years and of many thousands of conversations with its members. I have also drawn heavily from the rich treasures available to the researcher in the history of the House, the earlier studies by scholars, and the biographies and memoirs of Representatives and journalists, in the belief that only out of an understanding of the House's past could a valid interpretation of its present be constructed.

I am indebted to many persons for help in writing this book, to no one more than to the late Sam Rayburn of Texas, who generously spent many hours explaining to me his own profound understanding of the House. I am particularly indebted also to John McCormack and Joseph Martin of Massachusetts, Charles Halleck of Indiana, Carl Albert of Oklahoma, Leslie Arends of Illinois, Richard Bolling of Missouri, Wilbur Mills and James Trimble of Arkansas, John Byrnes of Wisconsin, Hale Boggs of Louisiana, Gerald Ford of Michigan, Alfred Santangelo of New York, Clarence Brown of Ohio, Paul Kilday and Frank Ikard of Texas, Frank Thompson of New Jersey, Stuart Udall of Arizona, and William Avery of Kansas.

I am heavily in debt to Lawrence F. O'Brien, Bryce Harlow, Richard Donohue, and Henry Hall Wilson, all of whom contributed to my understanding of the President's relationship with the House. Also D. B. Hardeman, William Arbogast, Robert Allett, John Holton, Robert Smart, Leo Irwin, Boyd Crawford, and William Phillips. Lewis Deschler, the Parliamentarian of the House, explained many technical points and kindly read the chapter on the House's rules. To them all, I can only offer my thanks and the acknowledgment that whatever errors may have crept into the text are my fault, not theirs.

Table of Contents

"Here, sir, the people govern."

—Alexander Hamilton

FORGE OF
DEMOCRACY

The House of
Representatives

CHAPTER ONE

The Solemn Assembly

THE United States House of Representatives, as its very name suggests, has acted through the decades of the American Republic as the agent of the American people in the federal government. In the Hall of the House of Representatives, those chosen by the people to represent them have gathered every year since 1789 to decide the nature of American law and set the historic course of the United States. Freely chosen by a free people, the Representatives have had imposed upon them the high calling of synthesizing the discords and the rivalries of a diverse and heterogeneous people, scattered across a vast continent, into viable national judgments. In war and peace, adversity and prosperity, trials and triumphs, the House of Representatives has borne the awesome responsibility of speaking and acting for the American people.

The delegates to the Constitutional Convention at Philadelphia in 1787 created a mixed government of rival branches—executive, judicial, and legislative—to check and balance each other. The delegates deliberately chose to make the House of Representatives the democratic arm of that government to reflect as directly as possible the will of the American people. Indeed, a furious quarrel broke out in the Convention, and raged on through the conventions called by the several states to ratify the proposed Constitution, over the "democracy" of the House of Representatives. There were those who charged that the proposed House of

1

Representatives would be too democratic, and those who complained that it would not be democratic enough. Both groups feared that the House's democracy (or lack of it) would destroy American liberty, either by fomenting anarchy or by imposing a tyranny of its own over the people. The House of Representatives, said George Mason, one of Virginia's great constitutionalists at the Philadelphia Convention, was "to be the grand depository of the democratic principle of the government." [1] Roger Sherman, a delegate from Connecticut argued against creating any such institution. "The people," he told the Convention, "should have as little to do as may be about the government. They want information and are constantly liable to be misled." [2] Elbridge Gerry, one of the Massachusetts delegation, agreed exactly with Sherman. "The evils we experience," Gerry said, "flow from the excess of democracy. The people do not want virtue, but are the dupes of pretended patriots." [3] Gerry had reference specifically to the "democratic" revolt of Captain Daniel Shays in western Massachusetts. James Madison of the Virginia delegation and James Wilson from Pennsylvania not only denied the thesis of Sherman and Gerry, but insisted that no federal government could be created—with any expectation that it would last—unless it contained a democratic branch. A democratic House, argued Madison, was "essential" to any "free" government. It was necessary, Madison said, both because a democratic branch in the government would "inspire confidence" of the people in that government and because a democratic House of Representatives "would induce the government to sympathize with the people." [4] Wilson argued that the government had to be founded, if it were to last, on the broad base of the people themselves. The House of Representatives, he said, "ought to be the most exact transcript" of the whole people, reflecting exactly the people's views and will. "No government," he said, "could long subsist without the confidence of the people." [5] Wilson and Madison won the argument in the Convention: the delegations voted to make the House of Representatives a democratic body, elected by and responsive to the people. The decision, however, was not unanimous. The delegations from six states—Massachusetts, New

2

York, Pennsylvania, Virginia, North Carolina, and Georgia—voted to make the House democratic, but two states voted against the proposal—New Jersey and South Carolina; and another two delegations, those from Connecticut and Delaware, were evenly split on the question.

This, however, did not settle the question. The Constitution had still to be approved by the states. At the state conventions, grave doubts were raised that the House of Representatives was not democratic enough, that with its great legislative and political powers it might "swallow up the liberties of the people." [6] In the New York convention, John Jay and Alexander Hamilton argued against that fear. "Here, sir," said Alexander Hamilton of the House of Representatives, "the people govern. Here they act by their immediate representatives." [7] And what of those Representatives? Would they not prove dangerous to the people's liberties? "Sir," replied John Jay, "I am not fearful of my countrymen." [8] The Representatives after all would be American citizens. In the Massachusetts convention, similar arguments were raised against the House. Fisher Ames went to the core of the matter when he argued that the government itself could not be created without representatives of the people. "Much has been said about the people divesting themselves of power when they delegate it to representatives," Ames said, "and that all representation is to their disadvantage, because it is but an image, a copy, fainter and more imperfect than the original, the people, in whom the light of power is primary and unborrowed, which is only reflected by their delegates. I cannot agree to either of these opinions. The representation of the people is something more than the people. I know, sir, but one purpose which the people can effect without delegation, and that is to destroy a government. That they cannot erect a government is evinced by our being thus assembled on their behalf." [9] Samuel Stillman argued that the very frequency of election of Representatives—every two years—gave solid assurances that those chosen as Representatives would not "seek every opportunity to enslave us." "They who are out of office," he said, "will watch them who are in, with a most critical eye, in order to discover and expose their malconduct, if guilty of any,

3

that so they may step into their places." Besides, who were these Representatives to be? "They are ourselves," Stillman said, "the men of our own choice, in whom we can confide; whose interest is inseparably connected with our own." [10] At the North Carolina convention, Samuel Johnston made much the same argument against the fear that the House of Representatives and the Senate would destroy the liberties of the people. "They are to be bone of our bone, flesh of our flesh," Johnston said. "They cannot injure us without injuring themselves." [11]

A political institution thus created had automatically the rightful claim to a great voice in the operations of the national government. The President, elected indirectly by a select few, and the Senate, then chosen by the state legislatures, could make no such claim, at least in the early years of the American Republic. The Philadelphia delegates, however, went beyond giving the House of Representatives the right to speak for the American people in the federal government. The delegates assigned to the House of Representatives exclusive jurisdiction over three fundamental areas of the government: the power to elect a President whenever a majority of the Presidential electors failed to do so, the power to impeach all federal officials, and the power to originate all revenue bills. The first was purely an emergency power, to assure the continuance of the executive branch of the government. The other two, however, were implicitly the raw power of government. By giving the House of Representatives the power to impeach all federal officials, the Philadelphia delegates gave the House primary jurisdiction to oversee the entire federal establishment. By giving the House the power to originate all revenue legislation, the delegates gave the Representatives control of the national purse, the greatest power of all.

Those powers provided by the Constitution and the political complexion the Philadelphia delegates imparted to the House of Representatives were but meaningless instructions until the House of Representatives itself breathed into them life and significance. In so doing, the House tempered and qualified them in its own way.

Like any institution, the House of Representatives necessarily

4

has had an inner life of its own and an institutional sense of itself. Necessarily, the House could not remain frozen as a static, unchanging fossil, stabilized forever by the strictures of its Constitutional creation. Rather it has been, like a living organism, constantly changing, developing, varying, fluctuating, as it has transformed itself—within the framework of its Constitutional rights and responsibilities—to meet its own needs and those of the nation.

In its inner life, the House has had a mind of its own, filled with prejudices and tolerances peculiar to itself. These institutional understandings and intuitions, often puzzling and bewildering to the outsider, have shaped the decisions of the House and made the House what it has become. Sometimes sullen, sometimes whimsical, sometimes reckless, sometimes cautious, the House has been an institution of many moods and humors. With a seemingly tireless capacity to endure the dry-as-dust tedium of its own enervating procedures, the House has patiently examined for many months the most trivial of matters, and yet has seen fit, within a single afternoon, to speed the nation to war. Frequently boisterous, occasionally violent, sometimes impetuous, the House has lacked the formalized dignity and decorum of the United States Senate. Caleb Cushing of Massachusetts even attempted in House debate in the 1830's to vindicate the uproarious proceedings of the House as a safety valve for public opinion and popular excitements. The House's debates at times have been marked with coarse ribaldry, cruel sarcasms, and biting invective, and at other times with grace, gallantry, and eloquence. The House, reflecting its democratic origins, has had the offhand casualness of a western barbecue, a notable lack of pretense, and the easygoing friendliness of everyday Americans. At moments of high drama or grave decision, the House has become profoundly sober and serious, hushed with expectancy, often austere and somber. A volatile assembly quick to take offense, passionate, and emotional, the House has been at the same time an institution almost maudlin in its sentimentalities. With the death of any Representative, the House has traditionally suspended its proceedings immediately to eulogize glowingly the dead colleague

5

and then adjourn for the day in further token of respect for the departed. For more than a half century, on every January 29, the birthdate of William McKinley of Ohio, one of the House's most beloved members, the Representatives have worn red carnations, McKinley's favorite flower, in remembrance.

However capricious at times, the House has always been deeply committed to its own traditions, willingly bound, for instance, by its own immensely technical rules and precedents. The House has had an intuitive feeling for orderly procedure, for the *regular* order of procedure, ratified by past usage, to violate which has been to offend the House at its most sensitive nerve. Indeed, over the decades the House has compiled almost numberless precedents and procedures that have formed in the 1960's a vast body of parliamentary practice nearly incomprehensible to the uninitiated. These rules and precedents have not only shaped the decisions of the House but shaped the House itself. The rules and precedents cover every possible eventuality, every possible aberration of normal usage, and the presiding officer has had but to impose them to impel the House to perform its appointed tasks.

The House of Representatives, however, has been something more than a group of unpretentious men committed to orderly procedures, for the Founding Fathers at Philadelphia had laid on the House a heavy responsibility. In House debate in 1809, Josiah Quincy of Massachusetts sought to define the House of Representatives as he understood it in its largest meaning. He described the House as "this solemn assembly, the representative of the American people, the depositary of their power, and, in a Constitutional light, the image of their wisdom." [12] A solemn assembly? The delegates at Philadelphia intended nothing less. The image of the people's wisdom? The delegates at Philadelphia had sought, with great deliberation, to make the House of Representatives the political arm of the federal government truly representative of the American people.

The House of Representatives, in Quincy's time, was already noted for its partisan violence. Quincy himself had been disgusted by the petty squabbling of his colleagues, by the uncouth vulgarities of debate, and by the frequently riotous conduct of members

6

of the House. A friend and House colleague of Quincy, Barent Gardenier of New York, in 1808 had almost lost his life in a duel with George Campbell of Tennessee for words spoken in House debate. In 1814, when the United States was at war with England and English troops were marching on Washington, a proposal was made in the House that the Representatives march out of the Capitol in a body to meet the enemy. Speaker Henry Clay declared that he would be sorry to lead such a disorderly body into battle.* This turbulence did not lessen the Constitutional obligations placed on the House of Representatives, nor did it diminish the vast Constitutional powers of the House.

To the visitor in its galleries, the House has always appeared as a confused mélange of unknown men, battling blindly for obscure and even petty causes in a parliamentary chaos. The seeming confusion has laid the House open to the severest criticism. When, in 1831, Alexis de Tocqueville, the French aristocrat, visited the House of Representatives, he found it "remarkable for its vulgarity and its poverty of talent." Other visitors before and after Tocqueville made equally harsh criticisms. The boisterousness of the House offended Tocqueville's sensibilities, and he found the Representatives of such inadequate qualifications to deal with their assigned responsibilities that he believed they actually risked the continued life of the United States government. "On entering the House of Representatives at Washington," he wrote in his *Democracy in America,* "one is struck with the vulgar demeanor of that great assembly. The eye frequently does not discover a man of celebrity within its walls. Its members are almost all obscure individuals, whose names present no associations to the mind; they are mostly village lawyers, men in trade, or even persons belonging to the lower classes of society. In a country in which education is very general, it is said that the representatives of the people do not always know how to write correctly." The Senate, however, Tocque-

* The English did march into Washington and burned the Capitol and the White House. Before setting the torch to the House of Representatives, according to an old account, the English commander, Sir George Cockburn, mounted the Speaker's dais and put this question for a vote by his troops: "Shall this harbor of Yankee democracy be burned? All for it say 'aye.'"

ville immensely admired. "The Senate," he wrote, "is composed of eloquent advocates, distinguished generals, wise magistrates, and statesmen of note, whose language would at all times do honor to the most remarkable parliamentary debates of Europe." The French nobleman accounted for the striking difference between the House and the Senate by the method in which Representatives and Senators were chosen. The Representatives were elected directly by the people, democratically, the Senators by the state legislatures; and, unless the method of choosing Representatives was changed, Tocqueville wrote, there was great risk of the American Republic "perishing miserably among the shoals of democracy." [13]

Confirmation of Tocqueville's impressions of the House's coarseness came from no less an American than Davy Crockett of Tennessee, the bear hunter and braggart who was to die in the Alamo. Crockett served three terms in the House in the 1820's and 1830's. "We generally lounge or squabble the greater part of the session," Crockett wrote, "and crowd into a few days of the last term three or four times the business done during as many preceding months. You may therefore guess at the deliberations of Congress, when you can't hear, for the soul of you, what's going on, nor no one knows what it is, but three or four, and when it's no use to try to know." [14] More scholarly examinations of the House of the 1880's came from Woodrow Wilson, then a young man, and Lord Bryce. To Wilson, the House appeared as "a disintegrate mass of jarring elements." [15] "When you enter," Bryce wrote of the House, "your first impression is of noise and turmoil, a noise like that of short sharp waves in a Highland loch, fretting under a squall against a rocky shore." [16]

The very size of the House of Representatives contributed to the sense of disorder, but often the antics of the members themselves brought public contumely on the House and made the chamber a favorite target for comedians' jokes. When Samuel F. B. Morse in 1842 asked Congress for an appropriation of $30,000 to finance the first real experiment with his electric telegraph, the proposal was hooted at with derision by at least some of the members of the House. The House adopted an amendment

8

to the bill to spend half of the money on making experiments in mesmerism, an amendment later removed from the bill; and the House finally approved the appropriation only after defeating another "joke" amendment to use the money to build a railroad to the moon. In 1846, the gift of $500,000, which had been willed to the nation by James Smithson to use to build what became the famed Smithsonian Institution in Washington, was greeted by some members of the House with outraged chauvinism. John S. Chipman of Michigan expressed his indignation that the United States government would accept this gift from an Englishman, a foreigner, and said it was "a stain on the history of the country" and "an insult to the American nation." [17] In 1950, the House actually voted to cut off all foreign aid to Great Britain until the British Parliament ended the partition of Ireland, a vote that the House, on more sober reflection, later reversed.

The members of the House long have had a poor reputation among the American people. This has been at least partially the result of the notoriety of the eccentric and sometimes outlandish men that some Congressional districts have sent to the House as their Representatives. As early as 1794, there was evidence of the low public opinion of members of the House. "A serious attention to business marked the countenances of the Representatives, who were all very decently dressed," wrote an English visitor in that year, obviously with some surprise.[18] Davy Crockett of Tennessee pursued a flamboyant career as a Representative and there were many others in the history of the House of Representatives almost as picturesque as Crockett: John Morrissey of New York's Tammany, a strong-arm gambler and former heavyweight boxing champion of the world; Jeremiah "Sockless Jerry" Simpson of Kansas, who wooed votes by refusing to wear socks; and James Watson of Indiana, who clattered about his Congressional district in wooden shoes to impress his Dutch constituents. In the late nineteenth century, a Washington correspondent reported that the only political capital of some Representatives was "a dirty shirt, a slouch hat and a shake of the hand." The modern House has had similar instances of Representatives bringing public scorn on the chamber. Periodically,

9

members of the House have been condemned for putting relatives on their payrolls at high salaries paid by the government. From time to time, a Representative has been indicted for federal crime, been convicted of the charge, and sent to jail.

Out of such isolated instances did the House of Representatives suffer in public esteem; and there were others, too. Occasionally, the drinking of whiskey and other beverages has caused public scandal for the House. In the last century, it was not unusual to see Representatives intoxicated on the House floor. Some, before making House speeches, used to "liquor up" for the effort at a bar, long since closed, that was located between the House and the Senate. It was known as the "Hole in the Wall." The House during Prohibition in the 1920's was once embarrassed when a bootlegger, George Cassiday, known as the "Man in the Green Hat," was arrested in the House Office Building while delivering his wares. There were many other reasons, fair and unfair, for public condemnation of the House—the free franking privileges allowed Representatives for their mail, every increase in pay the Representatives have voted themselves, abuse of their stationery accounts, their pensions, the offices maintained in their home districts at federal expense, and even their publicly paid funerals. All were frequently damned as waste and extravagance. So were the travel expenses of the Representatives, whether for trips to and from their homes or for trips around the country and the world. The baths in the Capitol were criticized for their luxury: one Representative, fresh from his bath and clothed only in a blanket, once rushed dripping wet to the House floor to cast his vote on a crucial bill.

As severely condemned as any of the Representatives' activities were their speeches on the House floor, many of which were just read into the *Congressional Record,* or even inserted into the *Record* without being read, so that copies of them could be mailed free to their constituents. This practice actually gave birth to an American word, "bunk." In 1820, during the great debate on Missouri statehood, a Representative from North Carolina, Felix Walker, gained recognition to make a speech. In his Congressional district lay Buncombe County. He planned only to

10

make a speech for the benefit of his voters back home, and he signaled his colleagues that there was no reason for them to stay to hear him. "This is for Buncombe," he said. Soon "speaking for Buncombe" became the accepted term for such provincial speeches, and the words "buncombe" and "bunk" evolved, meaning nonsense.

This public irreverence for the House of Representatives, caused partially by misunderstanding of the chamber and partially by the idiosyncrasies and worse of some of its members, has long grated the feelings of those men of the House who sensed its awesome responsibilities and controlled its great political and legislative powers. These Representatives—and they have been common in every House since the beginning of the American Republic—could only regret the public misunderstanding of the House and they could only hold in contempt those Representatives who failed to live up to their high calling. Such Representatives as neglected their duty or abused their privileges might win a national notoriety, but they could have no standing in the inner life of the House. "I have been a member of the House of Representatives . . . twenty years," Nicholas Longworth of Ohio said in 1925. "During the whole of that time we have been attacked, denounced, despised, hunted, harried, blamed, looked down upon, excoriated, and flayed. I refuse to take it personally. I have looked into history. I find that we did not start being unpopular when I became a Congressman. We were unpopular before that time. We were unpopular when Lincoln was a Congressman. We were unpopular even when John Quincy Adams was a Congressman. We were unpopular even when Henry Clay was a Congressman. We have always been unpopular. From the beginning of the Republic it has been the duty of every free-born voter to look down upon us, and the duty of every free-born humorist to make jokes at us." [19] For Representatives like Longworth, and Longworth was one of the House's distinguished Speakers, the House was something more than a political rally, something more than a raucus, moblike gathering of hack politicians, and service in the House was something more than a mere job. To them, the House was the greatest legislative assembly on earth, an embodi-

11

ment of American democracy, to which, with gratitude and devotion, they could dedicate their lives.

Perhaps most grating of all to the men of the House has been the designation of their assembly as the "lower house" of Congress. Among themselves, they could joke about the matter. Benjamin Butler of Massachusetts, in the 1870's, once so teased Samuel Randall of Pennsylvania at the close of an annual session. "I expect to meet you some day, Butler, in another and better world," said Randall to his old antagonist in the House.

"Oh, no, Sam," replied Butler, "you will be there, as you are here, a member of the lower house." [20]

Representatives long have liked to say that the Senate was the "upper house" of Congress only in the sense that the Senate constantly "upped" House appropriations bills. John McCormack of Massachusetts, elected Speaker in 1962, often argued that the House received the designation "lower house" only because in the original Hall of Congress, in New York, the House of Representatives occupied the lower floor of the building and the Senate the upper floor. In the Constitutional Convention at Philadelphia, in 1787, the delegates repeatedly referred to the House of Representatives as "the first branch of the legislature of the United States" and treated the House first in the Constitution. The members of the House could see that as only appropriate. John Nance Garner of Texas, Speaker of the House in the early 1930's, spoke the feelings of his colleagues in the House when he claimed the superiority of the House over the Senate. "The House of Representatives is not the 'lower' house," he said. "It is the most numerous, but not the 'lower.' In the most important functions of taxes, appropriations, and control of the purse, it is the originating and, therefore, the highest house." [21]

Sam Rayburn of Texas, Speaker of the House for most of two decades, totally rejected the idea of the inferiority of the House of Representatives. Addressing the House in 1957, he expressed his view of the House's importance in the modern world. "This is the highest theater that anyone plays in upon this earth today," Rayburn said. "I must refer again to the tremendous and at times appalling responsibility that falls upon the shoulders of each and every one of us. We must so act in the days to come that we will merit the confidence and the faith not only of our own people but of the people of the whole world, because your country and mine has been challenged to take the leadership of the free world." [22]

The impression of bedlam in the House, more pronounced in its early years than in the twentieth century, has frequently been scarcely more than an outward impression, for the severest criticism of the House through most of its history has been that it was a legislative assembly operating under the most stringent parliamentary controls. Debate, although often violent and bruising, has been for decades strictly limited. The rules of the House, adopted expressly to prevent the seeming chaos, have made the House an efficient legislative factory. The procedures and practices of the House have been revised and refined, again and again, to perfect the House's ability to act, to shape a national consensus, and then to pronounce that consensus in American law. The hurly-burly of the House's sessions have but masked the inner nature of the chamber. With the burden of its immense responsibilities in the operation of the American government, the House has scarcely had time to waste, and its rules and precedents, procedures and practices, have all the while—despite the din and seeming confusion of the members—been moving the House implacably toward action.

The House has always relied on its own leaders to guide its course, the leaders on the House floor, the Speaker in the presiding officer's chair, and the rank-and-file members with special talents and knowledge. This was but natural and was forecast by one of the Founding Fathers of the Republic before the House of Representatives even held its first meeting. "A few of the members," he wrote, "as happens in all such assemblies, will possess superior talents; will, by frequent elections, become members of long standing; will be thorough masters of the public business, and perhaps not unwilling to avail themselves of those advantages." [23] The leaders of the House, from the beginning, have come to power in the House by just that route, described in the *Federalist*

Papers in 1788. They have been chosen by their colleagues out of the ranks of the House, because they were trusted. The House of Representatives, from its earliest years, has had its own appreciation of merit, and it has followed Representatives of merit when making its decisions. "The House of Representatives," Sam Rayburn never tired of saying, "is the greatest jury in the world." The House, Rayburn meant, knew how to test and decide the qualifications of its own members and the recommendations they proposed as the House's judgments. Rayburn echoed a recurring theme throughout the House's history. Frederick Gillett of Massachusetts, Speaker in the 1920's, had expressed the same view that Rayburn reiterated. "This House," Gillett said, "becomes in time a pretty infallible judge of a member's merit. It learns to appraise motives. It discriminates between the modest men who with sincerity are trying to render service and the men who are only working for display and self-advancement. And it is refreshing to note that although the home folks may often be deceived by the fake statesman who is always playing to the gallery, yet here the sincere and industrious and modest man has his recognition and his reward." [24] Champ Clark of Missouri, Speaker before Gillett, described the House of Representatives in much the same terms. The House, he said, "is a poor field for mountebanks, imposters, make-believe statesmen, and empty-pated orators." The House has had mountebanks, imposters, make-believe statesmen, and empty-pated orators, but they have been given short shrift in the House and no control over the House's great political and legislative powers. "I say," said Clark, "there is no such training school for intellectual development anywhere else on earth as the House of Representatives. A man whose mind does not expand there is an incorrigible fool." [25]

A full generation before Gillett and Clark, James A. Garfield of Ohio and James G. Blaine of Maine both gave similar interpretations of the nature of the House's inner life. "There is no place," said Garfield, a distinguished leader of the House before he was elected President, "where a man finds his true level so certainly and so speedily as in the House of Representatives." [26]

14

Blaine, a Speaker of the House, enlarged on the same theme. "There is no test of a man's ability in any department of public life more severe than service in the House of Representatives," he said. "There is no place where so little deference is paid to reputation previously acquired or to eminence won outside, no place where so little consideration is shown for the feelings or failures of beginners. What a man gains in the House he gains by sheer force of his own character, and if he loses and falls back he must expect no mercy, and will receive no sympathy. It is a field in which the survival of the strongest is the recognized rule, and where no pretense can survive and no glamour can mislead." [27]

These harsh judgments of its own members the House has always made, from the beginning in the eighteenth century, through the evolution of the nineteenth century, to the fruition of the twentieth century. Often throughout its history, the House's most effective members have operated in near anonymity to the public at large. They were, however, men whose talents were known to the House; and, in terms of the House's inner life, its institutional reality, that was enough. They had been tested and found fit men to follow. Frequently, ineffective members of the House have won a national notoriety far greater than that of the Representatives whose decisions and judgments have guided the decisions and judgments of the House itself. The House far preferred to follow men who worked diligently and selflessly for the House and the nation. These were the men who have held the real power of the House of Representatives and shaped its fateful decisions. They have plumbed the wellsprings of the House's inmost institutional understanding of itself, its institutional commitment to order and responsibility. These men whom the House has trusted and followed have not been disconcerted or bewildered by the seeming chaos and disarray of the House in session. They have not been mystified by the maze of parliamentary rules and regulations or the methods of using those rules and regulations to persuade the House to act with precision and dispatch. They have not, in the confusion, lost sight of the House's great Constitutional powers and responsibilities. They

15

have not forgotten the solemn obligations imposed by the Constitution on the House of Representatives to represent the whole people and to act for them in the management of the federal government. In so doing, they left their mark profoundly on American history, for they wrote the laws under which the American people have built the strongest and freest nation on earth.

CHAPTER TWO

Rival for Power

THE House of Representatives, claiming its ancient right to speak for the American people and the prerogatives of its Constitutional powers, stood athwart the national government in mid-twentieth century. No law could be enacted without its approval, and in large measure not even the President could initiate new policy in domestic or foreign affairs without paying deference to the views of the 400-odd members of the House of Representatives. Although the House had lost, by a subtle historic erosion, much of its power to initiate public policy and federal law, it retained, in fact had reclaimed, its authority to participate in the government's fundamental decisions affecting the American people in the uncertain, swiftly changing contemporary world.

The American people in the twentieth century confronted a continuing crisis both at home and abroad, and the House of Representatives has had to meet it just as did the President and the Senate. The international crisis threatened imminent thermonuclear cataclysm. At the same time, an unparalleled domestic dilemma found a dynamic but sometimes disordered economy trying to keep pace with the basic needs and expanding desires of an ever-expanding population. The complexity of modern life was enough to perplex the wisest of men, and yet, by the very conditions of national politics, the House of Representatives had to share in both the decisions and the responsibility for the decisions made by the United States government. The basic threat to national safety implicit in Russian imperialism scarcely indicated the full measure of international complications—rising nationalism in Africa, the new independence of the peoples of Asia, the ambitions of Latin-American republics, and the ancient jealousies of Europe. At home, the American people faced the paradox of booming prosperity with nagging and disquieting unemployment high enough to suggest recession, an apparently incurable surplus of farm crops that were more a burden than a blessing, and shortages of houses and schools.

The United States government responded massively to meet these problems. The government spent many billions of dollars on defense, atomic weapons, and space exploration, and many billions more to help militarily and economically its foreign allies and hoped-for friends, with an enlightened generosity unknown in previous history. The country's trade policies and tariff structure were reappraised and revamped to meet the rising competition and need for markets of American-bolstered foreign economies. At home, more billions were spent on highways, airports, housing, economic redevelopment of depressed areas, farm crops, and public works of many kinds. The government struggled to find solutions to the school shortages, the deepening problems of America's aging citizens, inflation, civil rights, and the politically explosive struggle between labor and management. In all these varied and complicated decisions of government action, the President of the United States clearly held the initiative. The course of American history, the claims of earlier Presidents for that power, had determined the pattern of procedure. Yet the President could only propose; he could not decide alone. The President had to share the decision-making with the United States Senate and the House of Representatives, his historic rivals for political power.

The structure of the federal government, as laid down in the United States Constitution by the delegates to the Philadelphia Convention of 1787, had made rivalry inevitable among the three great political arms of the government: the President, the

House, and the Senate. Each had been established with distinct powers of its own, each with checks to curb the powers of the other two. Over the eighteen decades of the American Republic, each at one time or another came to dominate the government, and to set the nation's course as it saw fit. Strong Presidents, like Thomas Jefferson, Andrew Jackson, Woodrow Wilson, and Franklin Roosevelt, humbled Congress. The House, led by such powerful Speakers as Henry Clay, Thomas Reed, and Joseph Cannon, mastered the President and the Senate. The Senate, under forceful leaders like Daniel Webster, Charles Sumner, Henry Cabot Lodge, and Lyndon Johnson spoke for the whole nation. The basic question—Who shall set the tone and temper of the existing government?—remains unanswered, and in a real sense the question can never be answered because the determination of national policy depends in large measure on the interplay of the President, the Senate, and the House on each other, in a never-ending stream of negotiation, maneuver, and pressure politics. Agreements can be reached, or accommodations can be made between the three political arms of the government, but each retains the Constitutional power to check the action of the others. On occasion, one or the other of the government's power rivals simply has blocked action by the others, and a stalemate resulted that frustrated and prevented government decisions on critical problems. The House, the Senate, and even the President at various times in American history have been shunted aside by the other two political arms of the government. This was the fate that befell the Senate in the early years of the Republic, the House in the decades before the Civil War, and the President for close to fifty years after the Civil War. Sporadically, two of the power rivals have discovered themselves in an informal alliance against the third. Such an informal alliance existed between the House and the Senate in the latter half of the nineteenth century. In the middle decades of the twentieth century another such alliance tenuously existed between the President and the Senate against the House of Representatives. This did not mean that the President and the Senate did not have bitter quarrels in these years. They did, but on the great questions of the nation's foreign affairs and economic legislation, the President and the Senate in the main stood together against the temperamentally more conservative House of Representatives. The fact of the House's latent hostility to foreign spending and domestic welfare legislation tempered and conditioned the whole of national politics. This was a curious paradox in American politics, because the Founding Fathers in 1787 clearly expected the House of Representatives to be the most extravagant of the political arms of the government they established. The Founding Fathers, indeed, took deliberate steps to curb the House's expected spendthrift ways. Instead, a century and a half later, the House had become the intransigent foe of government extravagance, the seat of political conservatism in the federal government.

Even so popular a President as Dwight Eisenhower, twice elected by landslide proportions, could not overawe the House of Representatives to give him the legislation and appropriations he wanted. The House, like the Senate, largely yielded to President Eisenhower the power to determine the nation's defense posture and the members voted most, and sometimes more, money than he requested for the military. Yet the House refused to let General Eisenhower reorganize the Defense Department in the way he wanted, and, instead, passed legislation which the President himself proclaimed would foment "insubordination" in the ranks. Every year the House of Representatives slashed Eisenhower's foreign-aid requests, once despite a threat from the President that he would summon Congress back into special session if the House did so. Otto Passman of Louisiana, chairman of the House Appropriations subcommittee that recommended the deep cut in the President's program, believed Eisenhower to be bluffing and said so; the House followed Passman's leadership.

In domestic matters, the House as cavalierly rejected a host of Eisenhower proposals. Repeatedly, the Representatives refused Eisenhower's solutions for the farm surpluses, for housing, for school construction, for aiding depressed areas, for building public works. The Senate sometimes agreed with the House on domestic questions against President Eisenhower, but always the Senate was far more generous than the House in spending federal money, so much so that the Senate Appropriations Committee came to be known as the "court of last appeal" from the House's stinginess. In foreign affairs, once the almost exclusive domain of the Senate, no amity at all existed between the House and the Senate. Where once the Senate shared participation with the House on only one major international matter, the setting of United States tariffs, the growing trend of recent years to use federal programs rather than treaties to implement United States foreign policy gave the House an equal voice on such vital programs as foreign military and economic aid, the Import-Export Bank, the Development Loan Fund, and the International Monetary Fund, as well as United States tariffs. Generally, the Senate sided with the President on these programs and fought his battle against the House. In a continuing fight that cut across domestic and foreign questions over the use of debt transactions, the so-called back-door spending, as a means of financing federal programs, the Senate openly joined the President against the House, even though the financing techniques bypassed the Constitutional powers of the Senate as well as those of the House over federal appropriations.

President John F. Kennedy, when he came to office, inherited the informal Presidential alliance with the Senate, a chamber in which he had served eight years. The Senate ratified, almost without substantive amendment, almost all of Kennedy's many legislative proposals. No such approval came from the House. The Representatives challenged Kennedy's domestic and foreign program at just about every point. Reluctantly they approved his minimum-wage bill, his depressed-areas bill, and his housing bill, but they struck down his school-construction bill, his proposal to make long-range economic loan commitments to underdeveloped foreign countries, and his plan to help older citizens pay their medical expenses. They deeply compromised his tax-reform proposals and his farm bills. To win what he did win from the House, Kennedy had to exert the full powers of his office, and all the added influence he could muster from sympathetic lobbyists. Clearly, however, the House was not prepared to yield to the President's judgment, or to that of the Senate either, on the

21

great questions of the time. In so refusing, the House in essence reclaimed its ancient rights to represent the American people, to set itself as a check on the power of the Senate and the President.

These rights of the House were as old as the House. In 1787, the delegates to the Constitutional Convention at Philadelphia, gave the House and the Senate all legislative powers in the federal government then being created. The Congress then received, in the charter of its creation—the United States Constitution—all power to lay and collect taxes, duties, imposts, and excises, to pay the debts of the United States, to borrow money, to regulate commerce with foreign countries and between the states of the United States, to provide for the naturalization of citizens, to establish rules for bankruptcies, to coin money and set the national standards of weights and measures, to punish counterfeiting, to establish post offices and post roads, to promote science and the useful arts, to create the federal judiciary, to declare war, to establish an army and navy and provide their regulations, to create all federal agencies and officers and decide their limits and salaries, to provide, in short, "for the common defense and general welfare of the United States."

Beyond these powers, however, the Philadelphia delegates granted the House additional great powers for its exclusive use. Foremost among these was sole jurisdiction to originate revenue measures, an original jurisdiction that by custom came to include the appropriation of federal funds as well as the imposing of taxes. This was the great power of the purse, the power that had made the British House of Commons the ruler of the British Isles and Empire. Perhaps as important, the House of Representatives also was assigned the sole authority to impeach federal officers. This made the House of Representatives the Grand Inquest of the Nation and gave it the charge over all federal delinquencies. Implicit in every House investigation of the federal domain has been the House's power, here granted, to call to book any federal officer, including the President himself, and to start proceedings to remove him from office.

Another power granted the House by the Constitution, a power unused since 1825, was the power to elect a President of the

United States in the event that none of the candidates received a majority of the votes cast in the Electoral College. Although this power has not been used by the House for more than a century, it has been by no means insignificant. Twice within recent years, in the Presidential elections of 1948 and 1960, dissident political groups tried to block the election of Democratic candidates Harry S Truman and John F. Kennedy with their own independent slates of electors, and thereby throw the choice of President into the House of Representatives.

The delegates at the Philadelphia Constitutional Convention, the fifty-five men whom Jefferson called "an assembly of demigods," established the House of Representatives as a major power center in the new government. The Senate, armed with the power to amend or reject all legislation coming from the House and to initiate its own, was created, so said Alexander Hamilton at the time, to "correct the prejudices, check the intemperate passions, and regulate the fluctuations" [1] of the House of Representatives. James Madison, like Hamilton one of the Philadelphia delegates, described the new Senate to Jefferson as "the great anchor of the government." [2] It would balance the turbulent democracy of the House and curb any monarchial tendencies of Presidents. Jefferson apparently doubted the wisdom of setting up in free America an institution that smacked so much of aristocracy as did the Senate. He took breakfast one day with George Washington, so goes an old tale, and protested the creation of the Senate as a check on the House of Representatives.

"Why did you pour that coffee into your saucer?" Washington asked Jefferson.

"To cool it," Jefferson replied.

"Even so," said Washington, making his point, "we pour legislation into the senatorial saucer to cool it." [3]

Beyond all other powers granted the House, the Philadelphia delegates gave the House the responsibility to represent the American people. "The design of the House of Representatives," said one eighteenth-century defender of the Constitution, "is to represent the people of the United States, and to protect their

23

liberties." [4] Here lay the House's claim to superiority over the President and the Senate, its claim to write the laws of the land. The Philadelphia delegates, anticipating the inevitable rivalries of the three great political branches of the government, put onto the scales of the House—in the flashing phrase of George Nicholas at the Virginia ratifying convention—"the innate weight of the power of the people." [5]

Despite the check of the Senate and the President's Constitutional power to veto bills, the House possessed powers, as one distinguished member of the House later said, for the members to make their chamber a great assembly, if not the directing agency of the federal government. Elected directly and frequently by the people, with their very nearness to the people, their control of the federal purse, and their power to supervise the entire federal establishment, the Representatives had the opportunity to make their House comparable to the immensely powerful British House of Commons, on which it had been modeled.

In the first years of the American Republic, the House of Representatives normally decided American policy. It was a time when the President saw himself as little more than an administrator of the laws Congress chose to enact and the Senate, often meeting in secret, served largely as an executive council for the President. It was in the House of Representatives that Alexander Hamilton's plans to establish the credit of the government were argued and decided. It was in the House that the two great political parties first took shape. In 1796 the House even threatened to encroach on President Washington's powers to negotiate treaties, an encroachment that Washington resisted only with hesitation. Jefferson, as President, temporarily upset the growing influence of the House over the operations of the government. A skilled politician, he directly interfered in the choice of the House's Speaker and arranged for the election of Nathaniel Macon of North Carolina, a man personally loyal to Jefferson. Jefferson even influenced the appointment of House committee chairmen and, by so doing, made the House subservient to him. His party's leaders in the House looked to him for advice and direction.

Not until the election of Henry Clay of Kentucky as Speaker of the House in 1811 did the House disenthrall itself from this control by the President. At a stroke, Clay not only freed the House from the President's influence, but made the President, James Madison, all but subservient to the House. Clay made himself the political leader of the House as well as Speaker. As Speaker, Clay deeply influenced the operations of the whole federal government. He forced the United States into the War of 1812, against Madison's will. He used his great power to enact a broad domestic program—his "American Plan"—of federally financed highways and canals. He enacted a protective tariff, forced the Congress and President to accept his great Missouri Compromise, and all but took over the management of foreign affairs by forcing the President to recognize the newly created republics in South America. As a final touch, he engineered the election of John Quincy Adams as President in 1825 by the House of Representatives.

The choice of Adams as President came fully within the Constitutional prerogatives of the House, but the House paid for its decision at a costly price. Andrew Jackson had received more Presidential electoral votes than Adams, but not a majority of the total vote cast. The popular favorite, Jackson believed that the House had not only stolen the Presidency from him but had done so in clear violation of the wishes of the majority of the American people. "The majority of the House," one contemporary of Jackson wrote, "had overruled the majority of the people." [6] Four years later Jackson did become President, and his partisans boasted that he entered the White House as the representative of the whole people. "It was a proud day for the people," wrote a Jackson partisan of Jackson's inauguration. "General Jackson is *their own* President." [7]

Jackson himself did not hesitate to make the same claim. When the Senate formally censured him for assuming authority "not conferred by the Constitution," Jackson sent the Senate a fiery retort denouncing their "illegal" resolution of censure and repeatedly slurring the Senate for its unrepresentative character and its failure to be "directly amenable to the people." He claimed that he, the President, was the immediate representative of the people, and he denied this quality even to the House of Representatives. On one occasion, in his historic proclamation against the Ordinance of Nullification of South Carolina, Jackson stated his view that he had been elected by *all* the American people, while the members of the House of Representatives had been chosen merely by local majorities in their home states. This was a new doctrine, a new concept of the Presidency, for earlier Presidents accepted unquestioningly the Constitutional precept that they had been elected indirectly, by the Electoral College, not by the people themselves. In institutional terms, Jackson's concept of the Presidency, that the President represented the whole people, made him superior, and not merely a rival, to the House of Representatives. He denied the House's very cause for being, that its members represented the people and reflected their will. It served little purpose to protest as did John Quincy Adams against Jackson's theory. Adams became a member of the House after Jackson defeated him for the Presidency. "On no account," he screamed at Jackson's claim. "We are the Representatives of the people." [8]

Jackson, however, went even further. As another phase of his democratization of the executive branch of the government, he arbitrarily and systematically removed federal officials and replaced them with his own partisans. "To the victors belong the spoils," crowed William Marcy of New York, a Jackson loyalist in the Senate, and the spoils system of federal patronage had begun. It was a system that could not but diminish—indeed, almost obliterate—the political influence of the House of Representatives. The Senate held the Constitutional authority to advise and consent to the Presidential appointments, and, in time, the Senate acquired an enormous influence over those selected for federal office. The Representatives had no such claim to participate in the doling out of federal jobs. The spoils system debauched American politics, because it established a system of federal service under which officials were rewarded not for their merit but for their partisan political loyalty. Most of all the system debauched the House of Representatives, for it took from the members their will to stand as an independent center in the federal government. Representatives soon were catering to the President and members of the Senate in hopes of gaining some patronage crumbs for their friends and allies back home.

Jackson's democratic principle that federal offices should be rotated, if it made the President a patronage broker, gave him an enormously effective means to persuade Congress—through the careful use of that patronage—to adopt the legislation he desired. The President, with patronage, could reward the obedient and punish the recalcitrant members of Congress. It enormously strengthened the President in the continuing struggle with the House and Senate for power over the federal government.

Until this period, the talented men of the country had directed their ambitions to the House. It was in the House that James Madison had won an enduring fame by writing the Bill of Rights, and to the House also had come such men as Albert Gallatin of Pennsylvania, the fiscal wizard, and Josiah Quincy and Fisher Ames, both of Massachusetts and the most eloquent men of their time. South Carolina sent a great triumvirate to the House, Langdon Cheves, William Lowndes, and John C. Calhoun. New Hampshire and then Massachusetts sent Daniel Webster. In the House they had all made great names. Henry Clay gave up a seat in the Senate that he might serve in the House, and the House provided him with the stage from which he made his name and influence felt throughout the nation. The Jackson assault on the House, the new influence of the Senate over patronage, and the growing difficulty of the House in managing itself— its membership had swollen from the original 65 to 242 in 1830 —all went to make the House a less attractive forum, a deeply weakened rival to the Senate and the President. Some men of talent still ran for the House and there made conspicuous careers, men like John Quincy Adams, the only former President ever to serve in the House, and Howell Cobb, Robert Winthrop, and Alexander H. Stephens. Unmistakably, however, the Senate had become the prize for politically ambitious men. Webster, Clay, and Calhoun transferred there from the House, where they ush-

27

ered in the Senate's golden age, and they were followed by Stephen Douglas, Charles Sumner, and William Seward.

Dark years followed for the House, years in which the growing national argument over Negro slavery embittered American politics. Factionalism broke out in the old political parties, splintering Northern and Southern partisans. Violence became common on the floor of Congress. A Southern Representative, Preston Brooks of South Carolina, actually beat Senator Sumner into insensibility with a cane on the Senate floor, and was hailed for his black deed throughout the South as a hero of the South. Radicals on both sides of the slavery question, the abolitionists of the North and the firebrands of the South, tore away the middle ground of political moderation and eventually drove the country to civil war. The deterioration of American politics caused by this bitter factionalism compromised the Presidency, and men of inferior stamp, men like William Henry Harrison, James K. Polk, Zachary Taylor, Franklin Pierce, and James Buchanan, were chosen to fill the office. The political factionalism had a similar effect on the House of Representatives. Partisanship rankled so bitterly that the chamber at times simply became unmanageable. More than once, there appeared grave danger that the House could not even organize itself by choosing a Speaker. Only in the Senate did the members rise to the peril of the hour. Three great champions, from the North, the West, and the South, rose to great heights: Webster, boldly speaking for the Union of States, Calhoun, desperately defending the Southern way of life, and Clay, struggling to effect compromise that would prevent what another Senator called "the irrepressible conflict." The Senate failed to save the country from madness, but it made an eloquent, gallant effort, unmatched and unrivaled by the President or by the House of Representatives.

The Civil War did more than abolish slavery as an institution and preserve the Federal union. It transformed American politics, destroying the worst of the old factionalism that had pervaded North and South. In the postwar years, the two-party system was restored much as it had existed in the early years of the Republic, although the South was to remain for a century a one-party region. The House of Representatives after the Civil War normally had a clear majority, whether Republican or Democratic, and only rarely did a schismatic third party complicate the House's proceedings.

For the House, in institutional terms, the change amounted to revolution. It meant that the House had, or could have, a clear majority will, and that that majority could speak with one voice and not the babble of factionalism. It meant the opportunity for the majority, whether Republican or Democratic, to make the House a legislative juggernaut to execute that majority's will. For the next two generations, the leaders of the House of both parties worked toward that end, and they achieved it with a series of radical changes in the procedures of the House. The ultimate achievement was the "czardom" of Speaker Joe Cannon who ruled the House tyrannically, who dismissed and ignored the Senate, and who challenged even strong-willed President Theodore Roosevelt for control of the United States government.

The House, in the years following the Civil War, so increased in power that it could, with impunity, vote to remove the President of the United States, Andrew Johnson, from office. The House in 1868 formally impeached Johnson for high crimes and misdemeanors, and Johnson escaped conviction by the Senate, under the House's indictment, only by a single vote.

Even earlier the House and Senate had displayed open contempt and distrust of President Johnson. In those years, the Congress normally adjourned sine die on the last day of its existence as a Congress, March 4 of odd-numbered years. The new Congress did not normally convene until the following December. In 1867, the Thirty-ninth Congress passed a law requiring the Fortieth Congress to meet on March 4, 1867, the same day the Thirty-ninth passed out of existence. The Congress did this so that it could constantly supervise President Johnson and counteract any action he might take.

By 1880, the House had so increased its claim to dominance of the federal government that a Supreme Court Justice, in a private letter, stated that "the House is gradually absorbing all the powers of the government." [9] A few years later, Woodrow

Wilson, then a young scholar, wrote in his book *Congressional Government,* that Congress had become the dominant branch of government and that the office of President "has fallen from its first estate of dignity." [10]

The first of the great innovators who started the House back on the road to power, restoring it as a power rival for both the President and the Senate, was James G. Blaine of Maine. Elected Speaker in 1869, Blaine candidly announced his partisan Republican bias and boldly initiated party discipline as a first principle of political morality. He carried to new extremes the manipulation of committee assignments to guarantee favorable action on desired legislation. Speaker John Carlisle of Kentucky, a Democrat, added new power to the majority. He claimed for the Speaker absolute discretion in recognizing members on the floor of the House either to make speeches or to offer motions. By so doing, he dictated to the House what bills could be brought to a vote. Speaker Thomas Reed of Maine, a Republican, perhaps the greatest of Speakers, destroyed the minority party's ability to filibuster and thus obstruct the majority. Reed also brought into effective use for the first time the House Rules Committee as an instrument of party leadership. The powers of the Rules Committee were further increased by Speaker Charles Crisp of Georgia, a Democrat, and the final touch on the Speaker's mastery of the House was brought by Speaker Joseph Cannon of Illinois, a Republican. He built a personal regime of the party leaders that controlled all legislation, all committee assignments, all hopes of Representatives from either party for political advancement or even political survival.

What happened to the Presidency and the Senate in these years? Inevitably they lost both prestige and power. Systematically, the American people elected noncontroversial men to be President, men like Rutherford B. Hayes, James A. Garfield, and Benjamin Harrison, men who were not and could not become dynamic leaders of the nation. Before them Ulysses S. Grant, a great general, all but abdicated the office of President and permitted corrupt politicians to run loose in his administration. Occasionally as in the two terms of Grover Cleveland and those of

Theodore Roosevelt, the President tried to assert leadership over Congress, but Congress, notably the House, declined to be led by the President. The Senate, meanwhile, tarnished its once bright luster. Men of lesser stamp than Webster, Clay, and Calhoun occupied its Hall, and Henry Adams, a contemporary critic, could write sarcastically that Senators of his day passed belief. "At times the whole Senate seemed to catch hysterics of nervous bucking without apparent reason," he wrote. The leaders of the Senate could not be burlesqued. "They were more grotesque than ridicule could make them." [11] In those days of growing American industrialism, and of moral laxity in American politics, the members of the Senate came to be known nationally as mere spokesmen for vested economic interests and as petty political managers. Adams wrote that it would take a reform President to bring the Senate back to decency, but the American people became convinced that more than that was needed—an amendment to the United States Constitution providing for the popular election of the members of the Senate.

Speaker Cannon brought the ultimate triumph of the House over the Senate. The Senate leaders of his day, despite their renowned personal arrogance, had no choice but to consult with the Speaker, all but hats in hand, in the Speaker's office, on legislative matters in which they were interested. The vast strengthening of the Speakership, however, which had brought the House once more to near dominance of the government was not achieved without cost—and the price was higher than the members of the House wanted to pay. With each increase in the Speaker's powers—those brought by Blaine, Carlisle, Reed, Crisp, and Cannon—the significance of the individual Representative, his personal prestige, diminished more and more until, in the days of Cannon, it all but vanished altogether. In 1910, the House itself rebelled against Cannon, struck a series of mighty blows against his office that reduced the Speakership to near impotence. It also greatly reduced the power of the House, for the power of the House under Cannon depended principally on the power of the Speaker himself.

Woodrow Wilson, elected President two years after the revolt against Cannon, struck the weakened House another massive blow, one that was to alter permanently the relationship between Congress and the President. Like a British Prime Minister, Wilson laid out to Congress a fully formulated legislative program and then used the full powers of his office to induce Congress to enact it. He signaled this major political alteration of the President's role in American politics by dramatically going before Congress in person to address the members. It was the first such appearance of a President before Congress since Jefferson gave up the practice in 1801. Wilson's appearance marked a profound revision of national politics, and it meant a new depreciation of the House of Representatives. Wilson towered over the members of the House. He bypassed Speaker Champ Clark and dealt directly with committee chairmen. His success in his first years was so striking that a Republican House leader, Nicholas Longworth of Ohio, later told his colleagues that they had become the "legislative amanuensis" [12] of the President, that they merely copied down the laws Wilson dictated.

Wilson's transformation of the President's legislative role was to be copied by the men who followed him into the White House, although some with far less success. In earlier years, it had been popularly assumed that the President had exhausted his function in the legislative process when he called to the attention of Congress, in his State of the Union address or perhaps by some special message, the existence of need for legislative action. All through American history, however, Presidents had sporadically, and usually secretively, played a somewhat larger role. The Second Bank Act of 1816 and the Walker Tariff of 1847 were early instances of this. In 1832, the House had been convulsed by an angry debate over the propriety of even mentioning in the House the opinions of the President on a pending question. Abraham Lincoln, as President, stated that the President had been assumed to exert "certain indirect influences"—such as patronage peddling—to affect Congressional action, but that he believed, as a rule, "that Congress should originate as well as perfect its measures without external bias." [13] This scrupulous public policy, however, had not prevented Lincoln himself in one instance from promising patronage rewards to three members of the House provided they voted for a critical Lincoln bill.

As late as 1910, two years before Wilson's election, President William Howard Taft formally asked Congress for railroad legislation and had the effrontery to submit a bill drafted by his attorney general to carry out his proposals. The House Democrats reacted indignantly: "We challenge any member of Congress to point to any instance in the past history of our Republic where a bill was submitted to a committee of the Congress, drawn at the instance and aid of the President of the United States and declared to be the President's bill, and should be made a law." [14]

Such protestations were not long to last, as Wilson proved, but even Wilson's spell over Congress was broken by a revitalized Senate. Under the leadership of Henry Cabot Lodge, the Senate reclaimed some of its old power, struck down Wilson's Versailles Treaty and with it Wilson's hopes for American participation in the League of Nations he had created. The House made no similar immediate return to power. Speakers Champ Clark of Missouri and Frederick Gillett of Massachusetts served principally as presiding officers of the House, not as rivals to the President. Not until Nicholas Longworth of Ohio became Speaker in 1925 did the House again begin to regain some of its lost prestige and power. He candidly announced that he would be the political leader of the House, not its moderator, and he instituted a new concept of the Speakership. The Speaker no longer controlled arbitrarily the iron rules of the House as did Cannon, although the Speaker's powers still were potentially enormous. Longworth depended on personal influence over his Republican party members and private accommodations with the minority Democrats. The Senate, however, continued to dominate the national scene under the lackluster Presidencies of Warren Harding and Calvin Coolidge, and during the troubled years of Herbert Hoover's administration. The Senate conducted the sensational Teapot Dome investigation and deeply influenced much of the nation's foreign affairs.

The inauguration of Franklin Roosevelt in 1933 brought a new change in the functional relationships of the three great

33

political arms of the government. Calling Congress into special session, in the depths of the nation's worst depression, Roosevelt presented a sweeping and even revolutionary program to meet the crisis. Scarcely taking time to read the Roosevelt-drafted bills, the overawed House and Senate quickly ratified a vast amount of new federal legislation. Roosevelt simply ran over Congress, and John Nance Garner of Texas, who gave up the House Speakership to be Roosevelt's Vice President, regretted letting him do so. "He needed a Joe Cannon as Speaker," Garner later said. "That would have been a check on him. Theodore Roosevelt had Cannon to check him in all but the first two years of his administration. I would have liked to play that part in Franklin Roosevelt's administration. . . . I would not have tried to tell him what he could do. But there would have been times when I would have told him what he could not do." [15] All the same, it was the House that eventually slowed and then halted the further enactment of Franklin Roosevelt's New Deal measures. It was the House that buried Roosevelt's plan to pack the Supreme Court and, encouraged, then blocked most of his other domestic bills.

Roosevelt, borrowing the techniques of Jefferson, Jackson, and Wilson in dealing with Congress, did not hesitate to appeal from Congressional decisions against him to the people themselves. He went "over the head" of Congress to the voters in his famous "fireside chats" on radio and through his press conferences, a forum he developed as a major tool of Presidential leadership. Roosevelt worked closely with the Congressional leaders; indeed, he was instrumental in the Senate's selection of Alben Barkley as its floor leader and in the House's choice of Sam Rayburn of Texas for the same office in the House. Roosevelt went further; he altered fundamentally the roles of the Congressional leaders. They had always been the formal leaders of the House or Senate, and they were so still, but under Roosevelt, they became also the President's "lieutenants" on Capitol Hill, with formal public acknowledgment of the fact of their subordination. Speaker Reed had refused even to enter the White House to discuss legislative problems with the President, but now, under Roosevelt, the Congressional leaders discarded all such militant independence. At

34

the suggestion of Sam Rayburn, in 1938, the Congressional leaders of the President's party formally began meeting with the President at the White House every week Congress was in session, there to obtain the President's views on the legislative needs of the hour. These meetings, continued under both Democratic and Republican administrations, in institutional terms meant that the President had become his party's acknowledged chief legislator. In terms of power rivalry, they meant an enormous enhancement of the President's influence over the House and Senate. Soon sessions of Congress were publicly graded according to the percentage of the President's program they had adopted.

That the President assumed this new role, a role adopted also by Truman, Eisenhower, and Kennedy, did not mean that the House or the Senate automatically approved whatever the President told them to enact. The Congressional leaders could not enforce the President's will on their members, and the Congress did not hesitate to strike down priority "must" legislation of Roosevelt, Truman, Eisenhower, and Kennedy. As late as 1939, a House leader could play to that chamber's vanity by claiming, not quite candidly, that the bill under consideration had not even been seen by the White House. A few years later, however, in 1947, a Republican Senator publicly denounced President Truman for failing to submit a draft of an anti-inflation bill he requested, and the Speaker of the House, Joseph Martin of Massachusetts, actually construed the President's failure to send Congress a draft of that bill as evidence that the President did not really want Congress to enact it as a law.

Martin gave total loyalty to President Eisenhower even at the price of alienating his own closest allies and friends in the House of Representatives. "I had loyally to follow President Eisenhower," Martin said of his role as Republican leader of the House.[16] "As leader my loyalty was to him." [17] Eisenhower acknowledged his gratitude for that loyalty. "Never once," he wrote Martin, "have you failed to come forward with your entire array of 'horse, foot, and gun' to make sure of implementing the party's program and the Administration's plan." [18] The House and Senate had moved a long way from their original position as originators of the nation's laws.

Still another change, a reflection of world conditions, altered the basic relationship between the President and the two houses of Congress. The outbreak of World War II, and then United States entrance into that war made President Roosevelt, as Wilson before him, a major world figure. This country's continuing participation in world affairs after World War II gave the same rank to the Presidents who followed Roosevelt. President Truman broke the country's long tradition of isolationism; he instituted the Marshall Plan, gave open help to the Turks and the people of Berlin, and took the nation into the Korean War. Eisenhower ordered United States troops into Lebanon to prevent Communist aggression, and Kennedy gave the order for an abortive invasion of Fidel Castro's Cuba. The Senate and the House necessarily took a secondary role in these high matters of state, and both chambers in fact normally approved whatever military funds or changes the President declared were needed for the nation's safety.

The President's world position, however, did not assure him success with his programs on Capitol Hill. The Congress refused to adopt most of Truman's major domestic legislation, his civil rights proposals, and Fair Deal welfare bills, and it passed over his veto a new and controversial labor bill, the Taft-Hartley Act. Presidents Eisenhower and Kennedy had similar problems with Congress, although Kennedy believed he would be more successful than Eisenhower. "Except for foreign aid, President Eisenhower wasn't interested in legislation," President Kennedy said privately. "I am." The Presidents after Franklin Roosevelt took further steps to improve their chances of winning Congressional approval of their bills. Truman assigned two White House aides to act as his informal liaison representatives with Congress in addition to other chores they performed for the President. Eisenhower formalized the office of Congressional liaison by appointing a skillful House staff veteran, Bryce Harlow, to the post and giving him two assistants to help him. Kennedy assigned his veteran campaign organizer, Lawrence

36

O'Brien, as Congressional liaison chief and gave him a staff of four aides. Earlier Presidents had informally designated assistants to act as contact men with Congress. In Woodrow Wilson's cabinet, for example, Postmaster General Albert Sidney Burleson, a former member of the House, had filled this role. By the 1950's, however, this informality had passed away, and the President's liaison man had developed into a major influence on Congressional action. He could command, as the headquarters lieutenant of the President, a far-reaching and often well-disciplined organization of Administration aides, sympathetic lobbyists, and Congressional partisans of the President. Together, they could concentrate a withering fire on reluctant Congressmen to persuade or pressure them to vote for the President's bills. In institutional terms, this innovation meant a basic change in the processes of the House and Senate in passing legislation.

In recent years, the years since the inauguration of Franklin Roosevelt, a subtle change altered the fundamental relationship between the House and the Senate. The Senate, in large measure, continued to claim the nation's attention as the significant and influential half of Congress. Contributing heavily to this view was a long list of sensational Senate investigations covering the full spectrum of American life, among them the "five-percenter" investigation of influence peddlers, the McCarthy investigation of communism, the Kefauver investigation of crime, the Russell investigation of Truman's ouster of General Douglas MacArthur, and the McClellan investigation of labor racketeering. In terms of actual legislative power, however, the Senate's claims were not so obvious.

In 1913, by adoption of the Seventeenth Amendment to the Constitution, members of the Senate began to be elected by the people of their states, not by the state legislatures. In time, this change altered the Senate's traditional conservative coloration for it made Senators, elected by entire states, more subject than Representatives to a twentieth-century phenomenon, the "bullet vote" of the activist political minorities: labor unions, racial groups, and religious-ethnic organizations, particularly. These minorities, usually concentrated in cities, tended to be liberal, and

37

in closely divided states they frequently controlled a margin of the total vote that could defeat or elect the candidate of their choice. Their influence gradually shifted the Senate to a more liberal stance than the House, reversing the intent of the delegates at the Philadelphia Constitutional Convention who created the Senate to restrain the assumed recklessness and liberality of the House of Representatives. This alteration of the Senate's political orientation was what made the Senate, in mid-century, the informal ally of the President, who himself had become subject to the same bullet-vote pressures. No national party, for example, would dare to send its candidate for President into the campaign without a party platform paying due deference to every one of these activist minority groups. The Senate and President found themselves in substantial agreement on both foreign and domestic affairs.

The more conservative House, where the conservative rural and suburban constituencies were strongly represented, had by this slow process been thrust into the position of checking both the President and the Senate. The change was noticeable as early as 1938 when the House vetoed any further New Deal welfare measures, and it became entirely obvious when Kennedy became President and the House clearly let it be known that its members, and its members alone, would decide what of Kennedy's New Frontier legislation would become law. The Senate had in effect surrendered most of its influence over legislation by its agreement, in substance, with what the President requested. In terms of power, the House's latent hostility to the President's program, reflecting the House's gathering commitment to conservative policies, was purely negative. In institutional terms, however, the House had become again a decisive arena for the determination of national policy, drawing on its ancient claim of representing the American people, and that was great power indeed.

CHAPTER THREE

The House Rules

No body of men, attempting to act together, has ever been able to function effectively without some agreed-upon rules. The House of Representatives, therefore, as its first formal act, appointed a special committee to formulate regulations for its future operations. These first rules, adopted in 1789, have been modified, altered, reformed, and enlarged over the years of the House's existence to such an extent that, in the twentieth century, they formed a body of parliamentary precepts so complex and intricate that they required the House to hire a skilled technician merely to interpret and explain them. The rules of the House have been a matter of bitter controversy in the House from the first. Necessarily, they touched the inner life of the House at its core, and they determined in great measure the character of the House as a legislative assembly. The House of Representatives has made its own rules, under the specific authority of the United States Constitution, and, in a real sense, its rules have helped make the House of Representatives what it has become.

That rules were necessary, no member of the House has ever denied. Thomas Jefferson, who in 1800 wrote a parliamentary manual adopted by the House for its use, put succinctly the case for rules and orderly procedure: "It is much more material that there should be a rule to go by than what the rule is," Jefferson wrote, "that there may be uniformity of proceeding in business not subject to the caprice of the Speaker or captiousness of the members. It is very material that order, decency, and regularity be preserved in a dignified public body." [1] Yet the substance of the rules, the type of procedures they provided, the advantages they offered one party or another, have over the years inspired some of the most ferocious of the quarrels in the history of the House of Representatives. And well they might, for the rules of the House have not only determined in large measure the personal prestige of the members of the House, but even more significantly they have deeply affected the strength and standing of the House itself as a legislative body. The rules have, in fact, permeated the very spirit of the laws of the United States.

In the sense in which Jefferson wrote, the rules of the House, and the precedents of procedure built upon them have governed the House's methods of legislating for the American people. They have always provided for strict decorum, perhaps a paradox in a chamber noted for its turbulence, and they have armed the Speaker to enforce it. They have always provided for the careful consideration of each bill adopted through a complex committee system to evaluate and appraise each measure and numerous parliamentary safeguards to assure prudent management of each bill when it reached the floor of the House for approval by the Representatives. In sum, they provided the means of bringing order out of the chaos that could have otherwise resulted in the legislative processes of an assembly as numerous, as diverse, and as divergent as the House of Representatives. They equipped the House to function as a legislative body.

This has long been the best defense for the rules of the House, that they permitted the House to function. In the days of Speaker Thomas Reed's mastery of the House, one of his lieutenants put this very argument for the rules sarcastically to the members of the House then complaining about their stringency. "Gentlemen declaim against the rules of the House," he said, "and they want a sort of town meeting, where every one of [the] members, clamoring for recognition of the Speaker, shall receive recognition at the same time to make his motion or to make his speech. They want pandemonium." [2] And one of the lieutenants of Speaker

Cannon, who like Reed dominated the House, made a similar argument. "It is a fine thing to declaim about, that right of the individual member and the tyranny of the order which keeps him down," he said, "but it would be a trifle inconvenient to the country to permit him to range in his native freedom unfettered by any rule, for, notwithstanding the noble provisions of our Constitution, we might be left without any lawful or orderly government." [3]

The rules of the House, however, have had a significance far beyond merely keeping order in the chamber and providing for the careful consideration of each bill. They have reflected, in part, the House's response to the economic-social revolution that transformed an eighteenth-century agrarian society of four million people into today's extraordinarily complex United States with its population approaching 200 million. The almost casual legislative needs for operating a tiny, isolated government in the wilderness have been replaced by the pressing legislative requirements of managing the vast federal bureaucracy of a government whose economic and military commitments touch every corner of the earth and even the reaches of space beyond.

The rules also reflected, in part, the difficulty of managing the House itself. The very numbers of the House members complicated the problem. The original House of Representatives contained only 65 members, but, inexorably, the membership increased—to 106 in 1790, to 186 in 1810, to 242 in 1830, to 357 in 1890, and finally to 435 in 1910. The increases resulted both from the enormously expanding population of the United States and the inevitable admission of new states into the Federal Union. The larger the membership of the House grew, the smaller became the significance of the individual member of the House and the more difficult the House found its task of functioning effectively.

The press of the burgeoning workload of the House, complicated by the ever-increasing membership, inevitably forced the House to economize its time. The invention of the steamship, the cotton gin, the railroad, and the telegraph revolutionized American society in the nineteenth century, as did the invention of the

41

radio, the automobile, television, and nuclear power in this century. The federal government automatically expanded its operations to meet the new needs, and the House had to keep pace or cease to function as a viable part of that government. Debate had to be limited, and then limited again and again. Traditional procedures had to be abbreviated or repealed. "The House once debated," Woodrow Wilson, a careful student of the House, wrote in 1908. "Now it does not debate. It has not the time. There would be too many debaters, and there are too many subjects to debate. It is a business body and it must get its business done." [4] Mercilessly, every limitation, every abbreviation, every increase in the legislative workload shrank the importance of the individual Representative. He was buried in sheer numbers. Scarcely permitted to join in the severely limited debate, the average member rarely had a chance to call up for a vote a bill of his own. And even if the member had the opportunity to participate more fully in the House's activities, he could not without great study weave his way successfully through the nearly impenetrable maze of parliamentary rules and procedures that long since had been adopted to make the House a legislative mill. Asher C. Hinds, for many years the House's official Parliamentarian, vividly pointed to the stark realities of the declining importance of the average member when, in 1907, he published his five massive volumes of the precedents of the House of Representatives. The volumes listed, in careful detail, a total of 7,346 separate and distinct technicalities of House procedure, almost every one of which was a restriction of the individual member's natural freedom. "The pages of these volumes," Hinds wrote, "show a constant subordination of the individual to the necessities of the whole House as the voice of the national will." [5]

Very early in the history of the House, the Representatives discovered that the rules of the House, and the application of those rules, could temper and modify the decisions of the House. The partisans of Jefferson's liberalism and of Alexander Hamilton's conservatism fought to control the rules of the House, and to alter the rules to their own advantage, for they knew that the rules of the House could deeply influence and sometimes decide the outcome of their legislative battles. They invented parliamentary techniques both to obstruct legislation, and so defeat it, and to prevent the obstruction and thereby pass the legislation under assault. The techniques of obstruction, and they were many, came to be known as "filibustering," a word adopted from *filibustero,* the name for the desperado freebooters then ravaging the Spanish Main. The techniques of preventing filibusters and of speeding bills toward passage, and they, too, were many, were given the common, generic name of "gag rules," so called because they silenced the obstreperous filibusterers. The House rules took on grave significance when the party partisans in the House discovered that the rules themselves frequently determined whether the majority party of the House could enact its legislative program. At times, no majority party could act at all without the tacit consent of the minority, the techniques of filibustering had become so refined and effective. At other times, the majority party simply swept away the rights of the minority, allowing the minority scarcely the right to protest, and boldly rode over all opposition to enact the party legislation. Only in recent years have the rules of the House provided a decent semblance of balance between the responsibilities of the majority party and the rights of the minority. And even today that party with the votes to elect a Speaker and to control the organization of the House gains a profound, if not necessarily decisive advantage in the legislative struggles. The majority party, for example, automatically has controlled the scheduling of House votes. In the great fight over the Rules Committee in 1961 this power gave perhaps a decisive advantage to Speaker Rayburn. When his lieutenants reported to him that the outcome of the vote appeared doubtful, Rayburn simply postponed the vote for four days to allow him and his men that much extra time to persuade wavering members of the House to their cause.

The Speaker, by the nature of his office, has had wide discretion—from the House rules—on deciding the House's action. He and his lieutenants have been able to fit those operations, in many ways, to effect the best advantage for their party's interests. It was for this reason—the political advantage that the House

43

rules could give a political party—that every change in the rules has always been bitterly opposed. The minority party members invariably have cried "gag!" to the changes that diminished their effectiveness in opposing the majority party's legislation. John Rankin of Mississippi, one of the House's most controversial twentieth-century members and also one of its ablest parliamentarians, stated the average member's dilemma precisely in 1947. "The average member of the House does not want to be gagged on a measure he is against," Rankin said, "but he does not mind being gagged on a measure he is for." [6] The reason was simple: application of the "gag rules" immensely improved the chances of passing the bill under consideration. They prevented filibustering; they prevented crippling amendments; they disarmed the opponents of the bill.

Behind every rule of the House, no matter how controversial at the time of its adoption, has been the harsh reality of the needs of the House, the insistent requirement to tame the instinctive tumultuousness of so large an assembly, and the desire to harness its energies into responsible action. The House, as a result of its long-developing rules, became in time a far more constrained and efficient body than it was in the boisterous, riotous years of the nineteenth century. "The House," as Speaker Sam Rayburn often said, "can work its will." Yet this was not always so.

The first rules of the House, drafted by a committee of which James Madison of Virginia was a member, primarily emphasized decorum. No member of the House was permitted to talk, read, nor move about the chamber while another member was addressing the House. These rules adopted an ancient English technique to facilitate the handling of its major legislation, the so-called Committee of the Whole House. In resolving itself into a Committee of the Whole House—actually an artificial form of the House itself, since every member of the House was automatically a member of this committee—the House could simplify and somewhat restrict the less stringent rules of the House itself. In time, for example, the Committee of the Whole House became the principal means of limiting debate and even the amendments to bills. The House, in these first rules, also directed the Speaker

44

to keep order in the chamber. The Speaker was given a Sergeant at Arms, an officer authorized, if necessary, to arrest the members of the House on the Speaker's order. The Sergeant at Arms was provided with a mace, the great badge of his office and the only physical symbol of the authority of the House of Representatives. In the years that followed, more than once did the Sergeant at Arms have to quell riotous outbursts on the floor of the House by striding into the midst of the melee, with the mace held high over head.

These primitive rules of the House quickly proved inadequate. Partisanship and party rivalry soon dominated the deliberations of the House, and then as later, conservatives and liberals fought for any parliamentary advantage that could sway the decisions of the House to their cause. The first techniques of filibustering came into use. With no limit on debate, the opponents of bills found that, if they were persistent, they could talk a bill to death. One of the greatest of these early filibusterers was John Randolph of Virginia, a wildly eloquent, flamboyant orator despite the high-pitched squeal of his voice. Randolph frequently strode onto the House floor, two hounds at his heel, a riding crop still in his hand, and proceeded to tie up the House's proceedings for hours on end with rambling, often discordant speeches that gave doubt to his sanity. Even Randolph, however, had to take second place as a filibusterer to Barent Gardenier of New York, a fiercely partisan Federalist who, on one occasion, spoke continuously to the House for twenty-four hours to block passage of a bill, and at other times strangled the House's procedures for days at a time with his seemingly interminable speeches. The rules offered no way to stop Gardenier from talking. It was his obstreperous behavior on the House floor as well as personal animosity that once led the opposition floor leader, George Campbell of Tennessee, to try to silence him by killing him in a duel. Gardenier's courage, however, was equal to his verbosity. Although Campbell severely wounded him in the duel, fought just outside Washington in 1808, Gardenier recovered and returned to the Hall of the House as full of long-winded speeches as ever.

Three years later, the House took its first major step to cut off debate, and only the gathering war crisis with England forced the change. Under the influence of Henry Clay of Kentucky, the House approved and then strengthened the so-called motion of the Previous Question as a means of blocking filibusters. The rule, as then adopted, cut off debate when approved and brought the House immediately to a vote on the main question then pending. It was not, however, easily applied, as Henry Wise of Virginia, one of the House's great firebrands, recalled in his book, *Seven Decades of the Union,* in an incident in the Hall not otherwise recorded.

The question before the House, Wise reported, was the momentous question of declaring war against Great Britain. It was June, 1812, and the nation and the House were deeply divided on whether such action should be taken. The New England Federalists in the House knew they were outnumbered by those who wanted war, and so they tried to prevent the House from voting on the measure with every parliamentary trick they knew. Their filibuster ran on, said Wise, for weeks, with the House often in continuous session night and day. The Federalist leaders had organized a phalanx of debaters to sustain the filibuster, one Representative following the other, so as never to lose control of the House floor. The Democratic war hawks, however, devised a plan to break the filibuster. Late one night, with the members of the House nodding sleepily to the monotonous drone of an elderly New England Federalist, a band of Democrats suddenly burst into the House chamber from the lobbies outside. They seized the spittoons on the floor of the House and these they banged lustily and threw around the chamber, making a great clatter and clanging. In the ensuing chaos, with members wildly shouting for order, the Federalist making the filibustering speech took fright and sat down. A Democrat promptly moved the Previous Question, a motion that a majority of the House immediately adopted. That halted the filibuster. Speaker Henry Clay then put the main question—a declaration of war against Great Britain. The House approved it, and the United States entered the War of 1812.

The Previous Question, however efficient a method of cutting off debate, did not suffice to halt filibustering. Its opponents agreed with John Randolph when he denounced the rule as a "gag," even though in practice it did something less than silence the minority. "It is nothing more," said Henry Clay, in defense of the Previous Question rule, "than a declaration of the House that it had heard enough and would proceed to decide." [7] Debate, however, was still unlimited and a member of the House once he had been recognized to speak could talk as long as he wanted or could stand. Debate was often protracted and tedious, seemingly at times interminable. Occasionally, the speeches would drag on so long that members of the House would forget what the debate was about. Once, when a motion was made to lay aside the entire subject under debate, a member pathetically asked, "What subject, Mr. Speaker?" One of the most tedious of these orators in the years after the War of 1812 was Alexander Smyth of Virginia, who had served during that war as a brigadier general. In the midst of one long speech, he addressed Speaker Clay directly.

"You, sir," Smyth said, "speak for the present generation, but I speak for posterity."

"Yes," agreed Clay, wearily, "and you seem resolved to speak until the arrival of your audience." [8]

The membership of the House had risen dramatically in these years, and so had the House's legislative workload. The House and its leaders found they had to have better ways to save time and to protect the House's majority from the continuing obstruction of the minority. The result, after a long fight, was adoption of a rule still in effect that limits every member to one hour for each speech. As early as 1820, in response to a long harangue by John Randolph on the famous Missouri Compromise, an attempt was made to limit each member to one hour's debate on each question. Another attempt was made in 1833, but not until 1841 was the rule adopted. The members vented indignation, ridicule, and vituperation at this rule. No man, it was argued, could delineate his views in a mere hour. "No gentleman can acquit himself well in debate," said one Representative, "whether physically or intellectually, while confined in a strait jacket." [9] Others mocked the rule as cutting all members of the House "to the same length." Senator Thomas Hart Benton of Missouri called the rule "an eminent instance of permanent injury done to free institutions" and "the largest limitation upon freedom of debate which any deliberative assembly ever imposed upon itself." [10] The House, however, saw it otherwise. The majority believed they had to expedite the business of the House and protect the public interest. Unlimited debate had already seriously endangered passage of major appropriations bills, without which the federal government could not operate.

Filibustering by "talking a bill to death" was only somewhat curbed by adoption of the One Hour rule, for the facile parliamentary strategists of the House had already devised other equally effective means of obstructing the procedures of the House. One of the most effective of these was to offer and then endlessly discuss innumerable amendents to the bill under consideration. In 1847, the House acted to restrict this practice by adopting still another rule to limit debate and expedite its business. This was the Five Minute rule, so-called because it limited a member of the House to that brief amount of time to explain the provisions and argue the merits of his amendment. Paradoxically, this rule increased rather than decreased filibustering, because it encouraged the offering of scores of amendments. A member could offer an amendment, explain it, and then withdraw it, thus clearing the way for another member to repeat the same tactic. In 1850, to check this growing evil, the House modified the Five Minute rule to deny the right of withdrawing amendments. This change, however, proved only partially successful. In 1854, for example, in attempting to act on the highly controversial Kansas-Nebraska bill, the House spent five months processing an endless stream of amendments before Alexander Stephens of Georgia, a frail, eloquent man of enormous personal courage, devised a clever parliamentary trick to bring the alarming filibuster to a close. Stephens' tactic, a technical use of a motion to strike out the enacting clause of the bill, brought the bill itself to a vote by the House. Not until 1860, however, did the House finally halt the practice of filibustering with amend-

48

ments by ruling that a majority of the House could prohibit all debate on amendments.

In practice, the House over the years has been far more generous to Representatives offering amendments than this strict Five Minute rule would indicate. Any able and respected member of the House, for example, almost automatically has received additional time to explain a technically complicated or significant amendment. Other means also were found to allow additional members to participate in the debate on amendments, the most convenient of which has been to permit pro-forma amendments to strike out the last word or last two words of the proposed amendment.

The presiding officer occasionally has been known not to keep too close track of the time. John McCormack of Massachusetts, according to one report, won early popularity in the House in the 1930's by his kindly habit of sometimes ignoring the five-minute limitation when he presided over the Committee of the Whole House. He would let a member speak for as much as ten minutes beyond the allotted five minutes before gently tapping his gavel on the Speaker's desk and informing the Representative that "the gentleman has only one minute left." Nevertheless, the Five Minute rule, despite the House's reluctance to enforce it strictly, has served to save the House's time and speed the completion of its ever-increasing work.

Yet a more devastating method of filibustering had been developed even before the adoption of the One Hour and Five Minute rules, a technique devised by no less a man than John Quincy Adams of Massachusetts. Two years after he was defeated for re-election as President of the United States, Adams ran for and was elected to the House of Representatives. There he served for seventeen hectic, turbulent years and despite the ferocity of his partisanship and his adamant position on the slavery question he won the affections of his colleagues and the nickname "Old Man Eloquent," a name by which ever since he has been known to the men of the House. In 1832, as a freshman member of the House, although he had been a Senator, Secretary of State, and President, Adams refused as a matter of conscience to vote on a pending bill. The House threatened him with formal censure for this violation of the House rules, but Adams persisted in his refusal, and his refusal set a precedent that was to alter drastically the proceedings of the House for more than half a century.

Under the Constitution, the House could not transact its business without a quorum of its members, and a quorum had long been defined as half the members of the House plus one. The filibustering technique developed from Adams' obstinancy was simple enough: members of the minority party simply refused to vote. In a narrowly divided House, the majority usually discovered that although they had overwhelmingly passed the bill, a majority of the House had not voted. Some of their own members were invariably absent, sick, forgetful, or back home campaigning for re-election. A quorum call was automatically required to summon the "absent" members, and the minority members then answered to their names as called by the House clerk. A quorum promptly reappeared. Then the vote on the bill was repeated, and again the minority members sat in silence. A quorum of the House was not recorded on the vote—it had technically disappeared again. Again and again, this procedure would be followed: a roll-call vote, followed by a quorum call, followed by another roll-call vote, followed by another quorum call. On occasions, the House clerk grew hoarse from constantly calling the members' names. In 1850, on a bill to admit California into the Union, the House polled its members thirty-one times during a single day. In 1854, there were 101 such roll calls in a single, long legislative day. Needless to say, the House made no progress on enacting the bills then under consideration.

For this filibustering technique, the House had no answer. Proposals were made as early as the Civil War to record as present those who did not respond to their names, and thus halt the "quorum-breaking" of the minority. The House, however, refused to adopt so radical a proposal. Even so daring a Speaker as James G. Blaine of Maine shrank from that responsibility. "The moment you clothe your Speaker with power to go behind your roll call," he said, "and assume that there is a quorum in the Hall, why, gentlemen, you stand upon the very brink of a volcano." [11] The quorum-breaking, however, made it almost impossible for the House to act, unless the minority party acquiesced in the action.

It took an extraordinary man, Thomas Reed of Maine, to make the revolutionary ruling that abolished this enormously effective method of filibustering. Reed, as Speaker, also halted the use of other dilatory tactics as a means of blocking passage of bills. A practice had been perfected of offering motions to adjourn or recess, and then demanding roll-call votes on the motion, as a means of stalling indefinitely the House's proceedings. Reed swept both techniques away in the month of January, 1890. Just newly elected Speaker, Reed blandly declined to accept a highly privileged motion to adjourn on January 2, 1890, on the ground that it was a "dilatory" motion. He went further to announce that he would thereafter accept no dilatory motions at all and that he would decide whether a motion was designed merely to obstruct the House's procedures. The decision rocked the House of Representatives, for it deprived the minority Democrats of one of their most effective parliamentary weapons, but this decision was mild compared to Reed's ruling just four weeks later, on January 30. An election dispute had come up for decision, and it was clear that the Republican majority was going to award the contested House seat to the Republican candidate. On the vote, 161 members voted "aye," 2 voted "no," and 165, almost all Democrats, did not vote at all. A quorum of the House had not voted. Reed coolly directed the clerk of the House to record the members on the floor who had not voted. He called off the names of forty-one of them, then announced that a quorum *was* indeed present, and that the resolution had been passed.

Reed's ruling was a radical departure from past proceedings, and the Democratic minority greeted it with one of the most raucous outbursts in the history of the House of Representatives. For three days, they raged about the House floor, wildly denouncing this new "tyranny" of Speaker Reed, damning him as a "scoundrel" and a "czar." "What becomes of the rights of the minority," one member demanded. "The right of the minority," Reed replied mockingly, "is to draw its salaries and its function

51

is to make a quorum." [12] The uproar almost prevented any semblance of discussion. One Kentucky Democrat, with a parliamentary manual in his hand, tried to debate the ruling with Reed.

"I deny your right, Mr. Speaker," he began, "to count me present . . ."

"The Chair is making a statement of fact that the gentleman from Kentucky is present," Reed retorted. "Does he deny it?" [13]

Reed persisted in the ruling, one that sounded the end of filibustering the House of Representatives. The Democrats tried to resist the ruling. They even accused Reed of counting as part of a quorum the members' hats hanging in the cloakroom. They tried to prevent being counted by dashing out of the Hall of the House when a roll call was ordered and before the doors of the House were locked. One Texan, Constantine Kilgore, once kicked down a locked door to make his escape, and he was afterward known as "Kicking-Buck" Kilgore for this escapade. The Democrats, however, finally acquiesced in Reed's ruling, and, in fact, reluctantly adopted the same rule when they next won a majority of the House. The effect was to make the House a far less tumultuous chamber than it had been up to that date. The effect also was to give the majority party, whether Republican or Democratic, enormous facility in ramming its legislative program through the House. The Reed rules destroyed more than the practice of filibustering. They destroyed the minority party's ability to resist the majority effectively, and they greatly enhanced, even dangerously enhanced, the growing power of the Speaker himself, for Reed was a man who intended to be master of the House.

Reed did more than cripple the minority's power to resist. By reconstituting the functions of the House Rules Committee, then an insignificant committee, he armed the Speaker and his majority party with a positive weapon to carry out its program. The House had had a Rules Committee since its very first session, with the responsibility of recommending rules for the House at the beginning of each Congress. The committee, however, had little else to do, and in time fell to such a minor status that the Speaker occasionally did not even bother to appoint members to serve on it. The committee took on some importance in 1860 and again in 1880, when the rules of the House were recodified, but not until Reed saw the possibilities of this committee did it develop into one of the great power centers of the House. Reed made the Rules Committee the steering committee of the majority party, responsible for determining the House's legislative program. He did so by developing a new concept of floor action —the so-called special rule. With Reed as Rules Committee chairman, the committee would write a special rule for the floor management of a given bill, a rule that determined the amount of time to be spent debating the bill and sometimes even limited the amendments that could be offered to the bill. This special rule could be adopted by a majority vote and the Speaker automatically controlled a majority. The technique gave the Speaker almost unlimited control over floor action. Reed, in fact, would decide in advance with William McKinley of Ohio, later to be President, and Joseph Cannon of Illinois, the two other Republican members of the Rules Committee, the details of the special rules they wanted on a bill. Then Reed, in his own sardonic way, would inform the Democratic members of the committee of their decision. "Gentlemen," he would say, "we have decided to perpetrate the following outrage." [14]

Cannon inherited all the Speaker's arbitrary powers when he was chosen, in 1903, to lead the House. Cannon, however, added his own embellishments to the Speaker's power, primarily a party hierarchy loyal to him that simply overawed the House. Cannon controlled the House in its entirety, and he made the House subservient to his will by the ruthless way he used his arbitrary powers. No bill could be passed without his advance permission; the appointment of every member of every House committee was Cannon's sole responsibility. Cannon controlled all avenues for promotion in the House, and the members of the House shrank deeper into obscurity under his domination than ever before.

Cannon, however, went too far, and a deep-rooted reaction against him eventually burst into open rebellion. In his last term as Speaker, 1909-10, the House systematically stripped him of his powers. In a revolt led by George Norris of Nebraska and Champ Clark of Missouri, the House took from the Speaker his absolute power to appoint House committees, his arbitrary authority to decide who should make a speech or a motion, and his tyrannical control over all legislation. The House disqualified the Speaker from membership on the Rules Committee, a massive blow to the Speaker's power, and then instituted a series of reforms to protect all members of the House, and the minority members in particular, from autocratic actions of future Speakers. The members established a Consent Calendar for handling minor bills and thus took them out of the Speaker's immediate control. They provided a method, the Discharge Petition, to bring to the House floor for passage legislation blocked in any House committee. They established "Calendar Wednesday," a requirement that every Wednesday be set aside for a call of the House's committees. Any committee called then could ask for a vote on a bill otherwise blocked. And the House provided that the minority party, by right, have the privilege of making the motion to recommit any bill before the House voted on its passage. That gave the minority party the right to offer, as part of the motion to recommit, any amendment or even an entire substitute bill as an alternative to the bill under consideration.

Cannon, the most powerful of all Speakers, abruptly had been made one of the very weakest. Cannon so interpreted the revolt against his powers as Speaker that he announced he would entertain a motion to declare the Speaker's chair vacant and allow the House to elect a new Speaker, a motion the House rejected. The House, in total effect, had been freed from the tyranny of its Speaker, but it had not been freed from the driving necessities of getting its work done, nor from its need for leadership. For this reason, in the revolt against Cannon, the House did not touch the powers of the Rules Committee, as developed by Reed, nor did the House repeal the many other rules which had been adopted in the course of a century to expedite its business. Debate was still severely limited; so was the right to offer amendments, and the rules preventing filibusters were left intact.

From time to time, since the destruction of the autocratic powers of Speaker Cannon, the House of Representatives has reappraised its rules and fought again, in differing circumstances, the old fights for parliamentary advantage on the House floor. In recent decades, these parliamentary fights have centered on the Rules Committee, which by the very nature of the House's pressing need to economize its time and energy largely controlled most of the major legislation processed by the House each year. The methods of economizing time, developed in the past, have largely been retained, and no recent member of the House seriously has proposed to eliminate them or the Rules Committee, which has been one of the greatest economizers of all. The struggles instead have revolved around the decisions of the Rules Committee and around methods proposed to bypass that Committee when it has obstructed legislation fervently desired by large numbers of Representatives.

The saving of time made possible by the Rules Committee's unique control over legislation removed real argument about the committee's usefulness. In 1824, for example, the House spent almost ten weeks debating and voting on that year's tariff bill. In 1894, seventy years later, the time allowed for debating a similar tariff bill had been cut to three weeks. In 1962, the House again adopted a tariff bill, this time allowing only two days for floor debate and voting. In processing the 1962 bill, the House made full use of the Rules Committee's power to limit debate severely and even to forbid almost all amendments. In the nineteenth century, the tariff question was normally the most important question facing any Congress, and the House could afford it generous time, but in recent years tariff legislation has had to share the House's attention with a score of other equally important measures. The dramatic shrinking of the hours allowed these bills upon the floor of the House marked, in token, the response of the House to the manifold legislative needs of modern America. Without the special rules proposed by the Rules Committee, and adopted by the House, debate on controversial bills could run on indefinitely: every one of the House's 435 members possessed the right otherwise to speak a full hour on each bill and on each amendment to that bill. The House would be paralyzed. This need to utilize special rules to limit debate has become so grave in the modern House that, when the House has rejected a Rules Committee's

55

special rule limiting debate, the rejection has had the effect of killing the bill. The floor leaders normally have immediately withdrawn the bill from further consideration by the House.

The Rules Committee has escaped any deep assaults on its great powers. Frequently, the committee has come under fire from House members deeply annoyed at the arbitrary use of its great powers, but the committee's powers have been preserved. Occasionally, the House has altered, and then altered again, the numbers of members required to discharge a bill from a House committee—usually a backhanded method of trying to bypass the Rules Committee. These assaults have not seriously touched the committee's powers. Since the adoption of the first discharge rule, in the revolt against Speaker Cannon, only two bills have ever been brought to the floor by this method and ended up as United States laws, the minimum-wage bill of 1938 and a bill to increase the pay of federal employees in 1960. Using the Calendar Wednesday method to bypass the Rules Committee proved difficult and awkward, and has almost fallen out of use in recent years. In 1949, a rule was adopted to allow consideration of bills if the Rules Committee did not schedule them for floor action within twenty-one days, but this proved unsatisfactory to the party leaders and was dropped two years later. The House members in these fights fought the decisions of the committee, not the committee's essential power to limit debate and amendments. The House hardly had a choice of attacking its power to economize the House's time. The pressures on Congress from the vast industrialization of American economic life, the proliferation of American society into a thousand fields, steadily increased rather than reduced the House's basic need to save its time. Not only did old laws have to be revised or repealed, but Congress had to enact entirely new systems of law to regulate business and industrial activities undreamed of by the Founding Fathers at Philadelphia.

From the very beginning of the House, one of its most crucial problems was to restrict debate on questions of procedure. Clarence Cannon of Missouri, the House's official Parliamentarian before he began a long career as a Representative, stated that the House often wasted entire days in "profitless, and frequently acrimonious" arguments over points of order.[15] The House lost as much as one-third of its time in such debates, before Asher Hinds published in 1907 his five huge volumes of precedents of the House of Representatives. Before the appearance of Hinds's precedents, the House had to depend on the memory of some senior member of the House or on the skill of other members in rooting out the earlier House precedents from the hundred and more years of the House's voluminous records. Cannon himself carried forward Hinds's work and published in 1936 an additional three volumes of the precedents of the House. Both works, of course, expedited the work of the House, for they all but eliminated the problem of seeking out the earlier House precedents on which to base the current decisions of House procedure.

The old ritualistic ways of the House's parliamentary proceedings slowly gave way under the pressure of its workload and larger membership from the earliest of its days. As early as 1822, the House formalized a technique simply to suspend the House rules and pass needed bills immediately. It was easier to suspend the rules at times then to figure out what rules applied, but the technique later was developed both as a means to save time and to prevent "logrolling" of amendments onto bills. For decades the House had graciously recessed each day for dinner; these dinner recesses were abandoned in the 1900's. For the first eighty years of the House's history, the Clerk of the House, in calling the roll of the House, called out the members' full names. In 1879, the clerk abbreviated this to calling the members by their surnames with the title "Mister." In 1911, for the sake of brevity, the clerk began calling the members by their surnames only. In the early years, Congress met for three to five months a year, but the sessions grew longer and longer, year after year, as the House tried to keep pace with its work. Finally, in 1933, a Constitutional amendment was adopted providing that the Congress meet at the beginning of each year. Thus, the Congress could continue in session, as it did on occasion, for the entire twelve months of each year. In the early years also, a Representative had to receive formal permission to introduce a bill. In 1849, Abraham Lincoln of Illinois formally notified his colleagues in the House that he

57

intended to ask leave of them to introduce a bill to abolish slavery in the District of Columbia. Gradually, this courtly practice fell away until no restriction at all applied to the introduction of legislation. As this formality was abandoned, the number of bills introduced each year multiplied. In the 1860's only about 400 bills were introduced in each Congress. This increased to 4,000 by the 1870's, to 7,000 by the 1880's, to 17,000 by the early 1900's. Few of these had any real chance of enactment into law. Once the members of the House prided themselves on their oratory, but this, too, gave way, at least in part, to the pressures of saving time. The formal oratory was replaced by the practice, more and more frequently used, of merely arranging to have the speeches published bodily, although unspoken, in the *Congressional Record*. Occasionally members even added parenthetical embellishments to their canned speeches to indicate "applause" or "laughter" at appropriate places in the text, a practice Speaker Rayburn in 1945 formally prohibited. This abuse made the *Congressional Record* an unreliable report of the House's actual proceedings, but without doubt it saved enormous amounts of the House's valuable time.

Until 1857, the House met in a stately, semicircular chamber graced with lovely Corinthian marble columns, but the steadily increasing membership forced the House to build a new and vastly larger arena. Until 1913, each Representative had his own desk on the floor of the House, but by that time the House had to provide seats for its 435 members and no longer could accommodate each with a desk. They were removed. The work of each member was multiplying even faster. Where once each member of the House represented but 40,000 American citizens, in mid-twentieth century the average Representative spoke and voted for more than 400,000 Americans. In Abraham Lincoln's days in the House, a member could keep all his business in the inside rim of his stovepipe hat, but that did not last. In 1908, the House built a giant office building for its members and their newly authorized personal staffs. Even that did not prove sufficient, however, and another and larger office building was completed in 1933. In 1963, a third and still larger office building was being constructed. In the nineteenth century, a Representative had no staff and scarcely any need of a staff, but the press of his increased work forced the House to permit each member to hire a staff of up to eight or nine employees.

These were institutional acknowledgments of the growing burdens of the House of Representatives, prompted by the same impetus that forced the House to shape its rules and mold its procedures to make of itself an efficient legislative assembly. The House lost something in the process. It lost very early the leisurely stateliness that in the twentieth century still mark the proceedings of the United States Senate.

The House, however, gained perhaps as much as it lost by its studied efficiency. Primarily, the House could function. Claiming as its members did, that they in totality best represented the American people, the House could act on the great issues of the hour. The rules of the House gave extraordinary powers to the Speaker, to the Speaker's lieutenants, to the Rules Committee, to the legislative committees, but the rules of the House never abrogated the right of the majority of the Representatives to act as they saw fit. No Speaker, not even Thomas Reed or Joseph Cannon could force the House to do what it did not want to do. The members, under the rules, could sweep away the objections of the Speaker or the objections of any of the other great officers of the House. And, if need be, a majority of the members could enforce its ultimate power to repeal or reform the rules, and, by so doing, review and recast the authority that they had granted to the men they chose as leaders. Altering the rules of the House never has been a thing easily done, for any such process always altered the balance of power between the majority and the minority, but the authority to do so has always rested in the majority of the House. A minority, in the twentieth century, could delay but it could not frustrate indefinitely the majority's right to act. The men who led the House's majority, the Speakers of the House, long have regarded the rules and precedents of the House with profound respect. They perhaps best knew the limits and the reaches of those rules. A former Speaker of the House told Lord Bryce, in the 1880's, that "he thought the rules, taken all in all,

59

as near perfection as any rules could be." [16] Nicholas Longworth of Ohio, Speaker in the 1920's, echoed the same thought. "Long experience has satisfied me," he said, "that, in their essentials, the rules of the House of Representatives cannot be improved upon. We can, and do, transact business there, when necessary, with celerity and dispatch. We have majority rule at all times." [17] Lewis Deschler, the House's Parliamentarian from Speaker Longworth's day to that of John McCormack, said that, in his judgment, the House's rules "are perhaps the most finely adjusted, scientifically balanced, and highly technical rules of any parliamentary body in the world. Under them a majority may work its will at all times in the face of the most determined and vigorous opposition of a minority." [18] Speaker Sam Rayburn agreed. To Rayburn, the rules of the House were "pretty nearly perfect." [19] They allowed the majority of the Representatives of the people to act. It was this quality of the rules that justified their stringency, their crimping of the individual Representative's natural freedoms, for under the rules, as Speaker Rayburn often proudly said, "the House can work its will."

CHAPTER FOUR

Mr. Speaker

W HOEVER at any time, whether for purposes of censure or rebuke or any other motive," declared Thomas Reed, one of the House's great Speakers, "attempts to lower the prestige of that office, by just so much lowers the prestige of the House itself, whose servant and exponent the Speaker is. No attack, whether open or covert, can be made upon that office without leaving to the future a legacy of disorder and of bad government. This is not because the Speaker is himself a sacred creation. It is because he is the embodiment of the House, its power and dignity." [1]

The Speaker, as Reed stated, has always been the great officer of the House of Representatives and one of the great officers of the United States federal government. In power and prestige, the Speaker can be compared only with the President and the Chief Justice of the United States, the heads of the executive and judicial branches of the government. The Speaker's dignity and prestige have rested partly on the method of his election, partly on his duties and responsibilities, and partly on his role as chief of one of the principal branches of the federal government. The Speaker has always been elected, like the President and Vice President, on a national basis, for he is chosen by the Representatives of the whole people. He has been the elect of the elect. No law can be enacted without his signature, and in the event of the death or disability of the President and Vice President, present law has provided that the Speaker succeed them both as President.

The Speaker's power primarily has sprung from the political nature of his office: it has been he who has applied the rules and established the precedents that have controlled and guided the House of Representatives. These rules and precedents have always allowed the Speaker wide discretion in setting the course of the House. Supported by a majority of the Representatives and armed with the great prerogatives of his office, the Speaker has inevitably influenced, for good or ill, the decisions of the House of Representatives, and thus the whole fabric of American law. Because of the fundamental nature of his office, the Speaker necessarily has imposed on the House of Representatives a part of himself, his temperament, and his will. His personality, whether strong or weak, has permeated the inner life of the House of Representatives and quickened or impaired the use of its vast Constitutional powers as a legislative assembly. A weak, vacillating Speaker has meant a weak, vacillating House, shorn of its powers simply because they were not used. Speakers of infirm or hesitant spirit have left the House rudderless and prey to the encroachment of the President or the Senate. Forceful Speakers, men of courage and purpose, have by like token made the House a powerful branch of the government, and, at times, even the dominant political arm of the United States government. The Speaker normally has set the tone of the House of Representatives and, in large measure, determined the dignity, the effectiveness, and the power of the House itself.

A Speaker like Henry Clay, or Thomas Reed, or Sam Rayburn, could lift the House of Representatives, by the force of his character, to a commanding role in the determination of American international and domestic policy. Such leaders of the House have written their judgments across the pages of American history. Clay and Rayburn, each in his time and almost alone, determined the American tariff structure and immeasurably influenced American commerce with the world. Other Speakers, men of less decisive stamp, men like Andrew Stevenson or David Henderson, merely presided over the chamber and permitted the root powers of the House to be dispersed and diluted by the President and

Senate. The House's choice of a Speaker, from the election of Frederick Muhlenberg of Pennsylvania in 1789 to that of his forty-fourth successor, John McCormack of Massachusetts, in 1962, has tempered and modified the very nature of the House. It has been for this reason that the election of a Speaker of the House has had an importance far beyond the mere pageantry of the ceremony, the traditional graciousness of the losers toward the winners, and the solemn swearing of the oath of office. The House has risked much in the choice, and has had much to gain.

The House's election of a Speaker has not only deeply influenced its own inner life, but it has affected as well the House's decisions in carrying out its responsibilities in enacting United States law and setting government policy. The importance of the House's choice of its Speaker has been such as to give grave concern to the President, members of the Senate, and all those interested in the legislation and appropriations coming before the House of Representatives. Presidents since Thomas Jefferson, members of their cabinets, Senators and lobbyists, all have used their influence from time to time in these House elections to help into the Speaker's chair the men they believed most friendly to their own views. Their interference in the House's election of its Speaker, coupled with the ambitions of the men seeking the office, have frequently made these decisions by the House questions of the deepest bitterness and of the highest matters of state.

The House itself has always given special deference to the Speaker. He has always, for example, received higher pay— normally double the pay—than the average Representative or Senator. In 1963, the Speaker received a salary of $35,000 a year plus a $10,000 expense account, just twice the remuneration of the average congressman. In the early years, when rooms in Washington boarding houses were scarce, Representatives and Senators had to double up in those rooms available, but the Speaker was allowed a room of his own. The House also has provided the Speaker with elegant formal headquarters in the Capitol, along with a private hideaway and a private dining room. He also has a chauffeured Cadillac limousine for his daily use.

The Speakers themselves over the years have insisted on their prerogatives to social status in official Washington. Speaker Nathaniel Macon, in President Jefferson's first administration, refused a trivial position assigned him at a public ceremony and took his place next to the President. The Speaker, he insisted, was "the elect of the elect of all the people" [2] and, therefore, entitled to such status. Speaker Robert Winthrop, on taking office in 1847, asked John Quincy Adams, a former President and then a member of the House, for advice on his social duties. "The Speaker of the House of Representatives, as representative of the people's representatives," said Adams, "is next to the President and Vice President. Call upon no one else." [3] Winthrop received further advice from Senator Thomas Hart Benton. "Be as modest as you please," Benton told him, "but don't compromise the House of Representatives." [4] Speaker Reed, who would not call at the White House to discuss legislation with the President because he believed this would denigrate the office he held, declared that the Speaker had "but one superior and no peer" [5] in the American government. The superior was the President. Speaker Joseph Cannon, personally a modest, amiable man, refused to dine at the White House with President Theodore Roosevelt when he was assigned a seat at the table below the attorney general. Roosevelt thereupon responded by holding a White House dinner for Speaker Cannon, a social pleasantry continued ever since by Presidents for the Speakers. Speaker Rayburn shared the same feeling toward his office as did his predecessors, and privately voiced contempt for the pretensions of Senators.

The Speaker has in modern times held great power in the House, in large measure derived from the many rules and precedents of the House that have been developed over the decades. From Henry Clay, the twentieth-century Speaker inherited the first great limitation on debate, the Previous Question. Ready at hand also have been the other milestone rules—the One Hour rule, the Five Minute rule, and the special rules of the now powerful Rules Committee. There were precedents, too, that have enhanced and enlarged the power of the Speaker—his arbitrary power over recognition, derived from Speaker Carlisle; the right to declare motions "dilatory," and thus unacceptable, stemming from Speaker Thomas Reed's revolutionary decision of 1890; and all the lesser precedents and rulings that limited debate and amendments, and destroyed the minority's ability to filibuster. These precedents helped make the House an efficient legislative unit and helped make the Speaker its commanding officer. From the beginning, the Speaker has possessed the authority to keep order and to enforce order even, if necessary, with the power to arrest and punish rambunctious members. All these rules and precedents have armed the modern Speaker with vast power to persuade and lead the House to enact the legislation and appropriate the money the Speaker has favored. Limitations have been placed on the Speaker's arbitrary use of this great power, but the limitations have not denied the Speaker his central role as leader of the House.

One of the greatest powers of the Speaker long has been his right to interpret and apply the rules of the House. The Speaker's rulings have carried with them no writ of positive law, but for all practical purposes they have been almost as definitive as law. The House has always held the power to overturn the Speaker's ruling, but the House has long been reluctant to do so. Only rarely has a Speaker's ruling been appealed successfully, partly because the House has instinctively shrunk from taking such a step, but principally because the Speaker normally has had the backing of the majority party in the House. "I have been fifteen years in Congress," Speaker Reed told a colleague in 1892, "and I never saw a Speaker's decision overruled and you will never live to see it either." [6]

In Champ Clark's eight years as Speaker, only once was one of his decisions overruled. Speaker Longworth twice had rulings overturned in his six years as Speaker, but the effect of the second overruling was to reinstate the first Longworth decision that had been overturned. In the thirty years after Longworth, during the Speakerships of John Nance Garner, Henry Rainey, Joseph Byrns, William Bankhead, Sam Rayburn, and Joseph Martin, the House overruled not a single decision of the Speaker. The over-all effect has been to give the Speaker, who must abide by the ameni-

65

ties of fairness, an otherwise unchallengeable power to guide the affairs of the House as he has seen fit.

The modern Speaker has had at hand the best of authorities to support his decisions. On the one hand he has had the eight massive volumes of the House's precedents compiled by Asher Hinds and Clarence Cannon. On the other, he has had a skilled official parliamentarian at his elbow at all times to assist him in citing these previous precedents and to advise him on establishing new precedents. For a full generation, from Speaker Longworth through Speaker McCormack, the House's Parliamentarian has been Lewis Deschler, who has spent his life in the closest study of the House's rules, precedents, and procedures. Deschler has been more than a mere House official; he has been an intimate and a trusted counselor of these eight Speakers. The modern Speaker has thus been able quickly to cite the previous precedents of the House to support his decisions.

It was not so in earlier years. One Speaker, William Pennington of New Jersey, was reported so ignorant of parliamentary procedure that he had to consult a House page before making his rulings. Samuel Cox, who represented Ohio and later New York in the House, said that Pennington was perhaps "the most thoroughly unaccomplished man in parliamentary law who ever wielded a gavel." [7] He was necessarily an ineffective and weak Speaker. Early Speakers disliked to explain why they made decisions, doubtlessly because the previous precedents of the House were then not readily available. Henry Clay, a masterful Speaker, candidly advised a later Speaker, Robert Winthrop of Massachusetts, never to explain his rulings. "The House," he told Winthrop in the 1840's, "will sustain your decisions, but there will always be men to cavil and quarrel over your reasons." [8] Champ Clark of Missouri had a different argument for not offering explanations. As a youth, he said, he had known a highly successful judge who told him that he rarely gave reasons for a ruling, because he might make the right ruling and give the wrong reasons.[9]

Even beyond the legal powers conferred on the Speaker by the formal rules and precedents, he long has held extralegal powers that in the twentieth century have helped make him the great officer of the House. Despite the enormous growth of the President as a legislative leader, the Speakers adamantly have insisted on their formal independence and even have claimed a Constitutional equality with the President. "I would not be a clerk for any man," said Speaker Champ Clark at the suggestion he could serve under President Woodrow Wilson.[10] Sam Rayburn, who served in the House during the administrations of eight Presidents and who was Speaker during four of their administrations, with equal force denied ever serving "under" a President. "No," snapped Rayburn, "I haven't served under anybody. I have served *with* eight Presidents." [11]

This was not always the view of the Speakers of the House. Nathaniel Macon of North Carolina, elected Speaker in 1801, for example, was merely subservient to President Jefferson. "No man in history has left a better name than Macon," wrote John Quincy Adams acidly in his diary, "but the name was all he left." Andrew Stevenson of Virginia, elected Speaker in 1827, held a similar servile role to President Jackson. Even then, however, there were, in the House, views of the Speakership different from these. Almost from the beginning the House has conceived its Speaker as a great officer of the government. This concept of the Speaker as a political leader of the first rank long ago had worked its way subtly into the mind of the House, its traditions, its attitudes. The Speakers in mid-twentieth century, as a result, have permeated the House with their influence, shaded and colored the actions of the House, and held the prime responsibility for the standing of the House as a legislative assembly.

The concept of the Speaker as leader of the House was first brought forth by Henry Clay, Speaker sporadically from 1811 to 1825. Clay, a bold, immensely self-confident man of great tact and eloquence, charmed his fascinated House colleagues into making the decisions he wanted made. He was the first Speaker who saw intuitively that a strict enforcement of even the primitive House rules then existing could give him command of the House. His never failing geniality, his urbanity, prevented offense from members of the House even while he fearlessly rammed through his far-reaching measures. He saw himself as the leader of the House and not just an umpire of the squabbles between these Representatives of the people. Once, so goes an ancient report, he was questioned, on leaving a convivial party at sunrise, how he could expect to preside that day over the House. "Come up," he said, "and you shall see how I will throw the reins over their necks." [12] His personal magnetism, that made him a perennial candidate for President, thwarted any indignation that might otherwise have arisen among his fellow members of the House. His charm over the House was awesome. He was elected Speaker on his first day as a member of the House. Twice he resigned his membership in the House, and the Speakership, and twice returning to the House, he was promptly re-elected Speaker.

Clay did more than charm the House. He was the first Speaker to insist that he did not lose his essential rights as a member of the House by his elevation to the Speaker's chair. He claimed and freely used his right to debate in the House and his right to vote at any time a vote was put to the House. By so insisting, he differentiated the United States Speaker forever from the Speaker of the British House of Commons, who is both impartial and powerless, and also from the United States Vice President. The United States Constitution provided that the Vice President preside over the Senate, and vote in cases of a tie, but the Vice President has not been a member of the Senate and he has carried no real influence in its decisions. The United States Constitution imposed no qualifications at all for the Speaker; it merely authorized the House to elect its Speaker and left the House free to choose whom the members wished, whether one of themselves or anyone else. The House, however, has always chosen one of its own for the high office, and Henry Clay's concept of the Speakership—that the Speaker was essentially a political leader—settled the nature of the Speakership. His insistence on this concept, and his insistence on his right to speak and vote in the councils of the House, made the United States Speaker in time the most powerful and influential political leader of any free legislature. The United States Vice President, without such a claim, without membership in the chamber over which he presided, has remained among the weakest of presiding officers.

The personal character of the Speaker has profoundly influenced his control of the House, his standing in the House, and his ability to lead the House. Clay, by his force of will, freed the House from the undue influence of the President, and Reed, an equally dynamic man, freed the House's majority from the threat of filibuster by the minority. The rules of the House have offered the Speaker the opportunity to assert himself greatly in the formulation of American law, but the rules had to be applied, as Rayburn once phrased it, by "a man with iron in his backbone and brains in his head." Otherwise the House would founder in the confusion of an undisciplined multitude—or the leadership of the House would be seized by other hands.

By his election as Speaker, no Speaker has automatically become the leader of the House. That has rather depended on how the Speaker has acted in his role. During the Civil War years, and the years immediately following it, Schuyler Colfax of Indiana was Speaker, but Thaddeus Stevens of Pennsylvania seized the actual leadership of the House. Colfax, a Speaker so personally popular that he reportedly had more babies named for him than any public figure since Clay, had Clay's charm but lacked Clay's iron will. Stevens, a fiery, vengeful hater of the Southern slaveholders, took control of the House from his double position as chairman of the Appropriations Committee and as Republican floor leader. He ruled the House so completely that he brought about the only impeachment of a President in United States history.

Other floor leaders likewise have been the real political leaders of the House. After the House stripped Speaker Cannon of his great powers, the Speakers immediately following Cannon tended to be moderators of the House rather than forceful political leaders. Oscar Underwood of Alabama and later Claude Kitchen of North Carolina, both chairmen of the Ways and Means Committee and Democratic floor leaders under Speaker Clark, largely controlled their party's decisions in the House. Kitchen, indeed, had the audacity to resist the early war policies of no less a man

69

than President Woodrow Wilson. Later, under Speaker Gillett, Franklin Mondell of Wyoming controlled the Republican party on the House floor, and he passed control of the party to Nicholas Longworth of Ohio while Gillett continued to preside over the House. Longworth effected a counterrevolution in 1925 when he became Speaker. He baldly announced the return of the political Speaker as he assumed the office. "I believe it to be the duty of the Speaker," Longworth told the House, "standing squarely on the platform of his party, to assist in so far as he properly can the enactment of legislation in accordance with the declared principles of his party. . . ." Longworth explained privately what he meant: "I was able to take the majority leadership from the floor to the Chair." [13]

A dozen years after Longworth's election, another floor leader, Sam Rayburn of Texas, took over political control of his majority party in the House. He did so in large measure because the then Speaker, William Bankhead of Alabama, was ill. Years later, Rayburn advised a close House associate that the real power of the House did not necessarily belong to the Speaker. "You can run the House," he said, "from the Chair or from the floor." [14]

A Speaker demonstrating personal weakness always has left himself open to loss of power to men of strength on the House floor, and in extreme cases, the House has quietly shunted the weak Speaker out of office. Speaker Joseph W. Keifer of Ohio hazarded wide public contempt by arbitrarily handing out choice jobs to his close relatives. He appointed a nephew as clerk to the Speaker, another nephew as clerk to the Speaker's table, and his son as his personal secretary, all at handsome salaries. He was punished, however, by his own party members: they removed him as their leader in the next organization of the House. Ben Perley Poore, nineteenth-century raconteur of Congressional affairs, reported that an early Speaker, John White of Kentucky, delivered an eloquent address to the House at the end of one session only to have it discovered that he had plagiarized the speech from one delivered by Aaron Burr thirty-eight years before. "He was mercilessly ridiculed," Poore said of White, "and committed suicide." [15]

It was Clay's dynamic and revolutionary notion of the Speakership that opened the path for the Speakers who followed him to lead the House and fully exploit the political possibilities of the office. Built on Clay's concept of the Speakership were the careers of James G. Blaine, Thomas Reed, Joseph Cannon, Nicholas Longworth, and Sam Rayburn. Speaker Colfax of Indiana even went to the extreme of leaving the Speaker's chair momentarily to make a motion from the floor to expel a member of the House on the charge of treason. Colfax, Speaker during the Civil War, claimed the precedent set by Clay as his justification for his extraordinary action.

Some Speakers have been reluctant to take the floor, for they feared the loss of their personal prestige in the House. Speaker Clark, however, never so hesitated. In his eight years as Speaker, he made a total of sixty-three speeches from the floor of the House, debating the various measures that came up for action. Later Speakers have done much the same. Speaker Rayburn addressed the House from the floor from time to time, and when he did, even at times of great controversy, the members of the House listened to him in hushed and respectful silence. Speaker Martin and Speaker McCormack did likewise, and both always received the close attention of their colleagues.

Clay was his party's leader in the House, but not until James G. Blaine became Speaker in 1869 were the intricacies of party leadership, and discipline in party ranks, given careful scrutiny. Blaine took command of a House in which Republicans held a two-to-one preponderance over the Democrats. A dignified and courteous Speaker with a consuming ambition to be President, Blaine boldly stated his "political" view of the office. "Chosen by the party representing the political majority in this House," Blaine addressed his colleagues, "the Speaker owes a faithful allegiance to the principles and policy of that party." [16] He did not hesitate to carry out that implicit pledge to partisanship. From very early in the history of the House, the Speaker had had the power to appoint the members of the House's standing committees. Clay had used this power to give prominence to his able young friends in the House, but Blaine did more than this. He carefully calculated the legislation he wanted, and then deliberately appointed to the appropriate committees members of the House who he knew were favorable to that legislation. It was a new ingredient of influence for the Speaker, a technique continued and improved by Speakers Randall, Carlisle, Reed, Crisp, and Cannon. Cannon, in the great revolt against him in 1910, lost this power to appoint committee members. That power was transferred to the House itself, but each party soon set up a special "Committee on Committees" to nominate their candidates for the various committees, nominations the House has always automatically confirmed. In time, the Speaker gained a pervasive influence over his party's Committee on Committees and, in so doing, regained much of his old power of appointing the House's committees. Joseph Martin of Massachusetts, Speaker for two terms after World War II, for example, candidly acknowledged his own influence over the committees of the House—and the control it gave him over his party members hopeful of advancement. "In the four years that I served as Speaker," Martin wrote in his autobiography, "no Republican went on an important committee without my approval." [17] Speaker Rayburn likewise influenced Democratic appointments to committees all during his seventeen years as Speaker. He would not permit a Democrat who opposed the reciprocal-trade program to be elected to the prestigious Ways and Means Committee, which handled that legislation. An Oklahoma Democrat, for example, once telephoned Rayburn to ask for an assignment to the Ways and Means Committee. Rayburn flatly turned him down. "He's got some oil wells in his district that have him worried," Rayburn explained to a friend.[18] Rayburn feared the owners of those oil wells, meeting foreign competition, just might persuade the Representative to vote against the low tariffs the reciprocal-trade program provided.

Blaine's concept of partisan party leadership from the Speaker's chair changed in substance the nature of the Speakership. Prior to Blaine, the Speakers almost without exception had no such view of their office. In the years before the Civil War, the House had reflected the deepening division of the country over slavery. The bitter national debate over slavery fractionalized American

72

politics and broke up the old two-party structure into a disorderly array of splinter groups—the Barnburners, the Locofocos, the Know-Nothings, the Bucktails, the anti-Nebraska party, the Free-Soilers, as well as the Whigs, Democrats, and Republicans. Four major parties offered candidates for the Presidency in 1860. The effect of this fractionalization of American politics on the House of Representatives was normally to prevent majority party rule, for the simple reason that often there was no party that held a clear majority. Four times before the Civil War, in 1839, 1849, 1855, and 1859, the House almost could not choose a Speaker, so seriously were the parties splintered. And in two of those years, the House had to agree to elect a Speaker who could not command the loyalty or the votes of a clear majority of the members. The Speakers chosen in these years were mostly men of mediocre caliber, compromise men chosen because they were not the real leaders of their party in the House, and because they frequently had taken no stand on the major political issue of the time. Blaine, with his commanding Republican majority, ended this dispersion. Under him, the party caucus came into new use for two significant purposes. The first was to force advance agreement on the party's candidate for Speaker; the second was to bind the members of the party to vote for the legislation recommended by the party caucus. Party discipline became a first principle of political morality.

This development of party discipline, through the instrumentality of the party caucus, did almost abolish, for half a century, the hazards of disruptive and discordant elements within the major political parties. The Speaker, who through the caucus frequently could command every member of his majority party in the House, rose to new heights of political power. He began to resemble a British Prime Minister with a program of legislation on his formal agenda and a voting majority at his back. The party caucus in time was to tarnish the reputation of the Republican party, and the Republican party in the twentieth century as a result even stopped calling their party sessions by that name, but in its day, the caucus was an extraordinary instrument of power for the Speaker. In one notable instance, the Republican party caucus, after a furious fight, approved a bitterly controversial bill by a margin of a single vote in the caucus. The party had been severely divided on the issue. Joseph Cannon of Illinois, then a rising party leader, had led the opposition against the bill. Once the party had resolved in favor of the bill, however, Cannon reversed his position and led the advocates of the bill on the House floor. His now united and disciplined Republican party, the majority party, voted almost unanimously for the bill and passed it over the howling protests of the Democrats.

In the twentieth century, after the revolt against Speaker Cannon, the political parties in the House depended less and less on their party caucuses to set policy. The caucus, in practice, became binding on members of the party on only one vote: the vote by which the party chose its candidate for Speaker. Times had changed, and so had the national sense of politics. It now appeared improper for a Representative to permit himself to be forced to vote for a bill on the House floor that he really opposed. Besides, major political divisions troubled the councils of both major parties. These divisions often made difficult unified party action. The conservative Republicans, even in the days of the binding caucus, had been harassed by a progressive, liberal wing that wanted to take the party down a route different from that chosen by Speakers like Reed and Cannon. Speaker Cannon, in fact, lost most of the arbitrary powers of the Speakership when a band of these progressive Republicans, led by George Norris of Nebraska, joined the Democratic minority and stripped him of power. Republican Speakers Frederick Gillett and Nicholas Longworth, in the 1920's, were faced with similar threats from militant Western Republicans.

With the Democrats, the party caucus had never been as effective a tool of the Speaker as it had been with the Republicans. The Democratic party, ever since the Civil War, and even long before, had been deeply split, and it has remained so into mid-twentieth century. The Democrats of the rural South have tended to deep conservatism, with a shading of liberal populist thought ranging some areas, while the Democrats of the North reflected more commonly the traditional liberalism of the party's city

74

strongholds. And the Democratic party long has been embarrassed about civil rights legislation. When Will Rogers said, "I belong to no organized political party—I am a Democrat," he spoke only the simple truth. The binding caucus, or even the nonbinding party caucus, rarely could do anything but acerbate the already deeply divided Democratic party, and the Democratic party caucus fell in time almost entirely out of use. The modern Speakers have not had the power to force their party members to vote against their private views or their own best political interests, but these Speakers have had an influence, by virtue of their office, to persuade wavering members of the House to accept their views. Rayburn, whose influence permeated both major wings of the Democratic party, often claimed he had never asked a Democrat to vote against his conscience, although on occasion—in moments of great national need—he asked them to vote his way even if it meant their political suicide. He did so, when, in August, 1941, he asked his colleagues to vote to extend the unpopular military draft. It was four months before Pearl Harbor and the bill passed by the margin of only one vote, 203 to 202. Rayburn, however, made no effort to hide his annoyance at the Democrat who never supported his party's positions. "If you want to get along in the House," Rayburn frequently counseled Democratic Representatives, "go along."

Speaker Rayburn perhaps best described the nature of the Speaker's modern role in influencing legislation. "The old day of pounding the desk and giving people hell is gone," he once said. "We're all grown up now. A man's got to lead by persuasion and kindness and the best reason—that's the only way he can lead people." [19] Another time, Rayburn put it this way: "My experience with the Speakership has been that you can't lead people by driving them. Persuasion and reason are the only ways to lead them. In that way, the Speaker has influence and power in the House." [20] And, on still another occasion, Rayburn used these words to describe the way a Speaker leads the House: "You can't really say how you lead. You feel your way, receptive to those rolling waves of sentiment. And if a man can't see and hear and feel, why then, of course, he's lost." [21]

From John Carlisle of Kentucky, Speaker in the 1880's, all modern Speakers derived their great power over recognizing members to make motions or to address the House. The earliest House rules merely stated that the Speaker should decide who should be recognized to speak, and it had long been assumed that this meant no more than that he would decide who should speak first. Carlisle, instead, boldly asserted that the Speaker had unlimited discretion as to whom he recognized, and that he could arbitrarily refuse recognition to any Representative he chose not to recognize. The ruling created a major precedent in the House, enormously enhancing the Speaker's authority, for he could then control perfectly all floor operations. He could accept those motions that he choose to accept, and refuse those distasteful to him. Carlisle, a suave, debonair Speaker and a profound scholar of parliamentary procedures, devised a simple question by which he, and all the Speakers who have succeeded him, have been able to avoid recognizing inadvertently a Representative who might offer an unwanted motion. "For what purpose does the gentleman rise?" Carlisle blandly would ask the Representative who stood and requested recognition. The member then had to explain his purpose, and, if the Speaker did not choose to entertain his motion or hear his speech, he simply refused recognition. The Representative was silenced.

In the revolt against Speaker Cannon, this power of the Speaker was somewhat modified. The Speaker, for example, could not avoid recognizing the chairmen of committees, in order, on Calendar Wednesday. The Speaker also had to recognize a designated member of the minority party to offer a motion to recommit to its original committee any bill coming up for a House vote. Yet the basic power over recognition remained in the Speaker's hands, tempered and softened only by the waning furies of earlier party warfare. The Speaker still had major control over who could address the House, who could offer motions, even privileged motions, and who could call up for action bills made privileged by such special House procedures as Suspension of the Rules. Speaker Rayburn, just four months before his death in 1961, spoke his own view on recognizing members of the

House, a view that contrasted sharply with the fiercer partisanship of earlier Speakers. "Every man or woman who is elected to the House of Representatives," said Rayburn, "is the only voice that district's got and they have a right to speak that voice and vote that sentiment, and I give them an opportunity to do it. I recognize everybody there because the district—maybe it has made a mistake, but that isn't my business. Maybe they will cure that mistake. Maybe that fellow will get better, but, anyhow, he has a right to voice the sentiments of his district." [22]

Speaker Rayburn here spoke only his formal views of the Speaker's role in allowing members of the House to speak and vote their constituents' views. He did not mean, however, that he did not attempt to persuade members of the House to change their views, whether in making speeches or voting on legislation. One of Rayburn's great friends in the House, Representative Eugene Cox of Georgia, then the leader of the Southern conservative bloc, presented an example of this. Cox had been angered by President Truman's liberal legislative program, which included sweeping civil rights proposals. "He was all right," said Rayburn of Cox, "if I could keep my hand on his shoulder, but I couldn't keep my hand on his shoulder all the time." One afternoon, Cox took a seat in the front row of the House, obviously intending to ask recognition to make a fiery speech. Rayburn motioned for him to come up to the Speaker's Chair. "Gene," he whispered to his old friend, "you look all swelled up like a tick with a speech against President Truman. Harry Truman is your friend and you are his friend. Now, don't you do it." [23] Cox, an irascible man, protested, but under Rayburn's request, he left the Hall of the House. He did not make the speech against Truman. Rayburn had power to refuse to recognize Cox to make the speech, but with the more kindly methods, he achieved the same result.

These great powers of the Speaker—the power of recognition, of influencing committee assignments, of preventing filibusters by the minority party, of controlling the House with his majority and of applying the rules—have long made the Speaker the preeminent member of the House. He was never given total dictatorial control of the House, however, not even in the years of Speakers Reed and Cannon. Always the House has asserted some limitations on its Speakers, at times almost imperceptibly, and no Speaker ever could so overawe the House as to deprive it utterly of its own sense of itself. The House, for example, three times ignored Speaker Reed on measures of enormous consequence to the nation at the very time Reed was at the peak of his personal power in the House. Reed opposed war with Spain, he opposed annexation of Hawaii, and he opposed the purchase of the Philippine Islands. Despite his severe opposition, the House adopted measures to accomplish all three purposes. Cannon's career as Speaker likewise ended in defeat, a defeat so great that most observers at the time thought the Speakership had been destroyed forever as a political force. Both Reed and Cannon, on occasion, acted with the utmost arbitrariness in handling the House. Once, when a Democratic floor leader was seeking recognition to offer a motion to recognize Cuban belligerency against Spain, Reed calmly ignored him. With no one else seeking recognition, Reed blandly announced that a motion to adjourn had been offered by Nelson Dingley of Maine, then in the Hall of the House but engrossed in studying tariff statistics and not paying any attention to Reed. Reed then put the motion to a vote, announced that the "ayes" were a majority and that the House stood adjourned. On another occasion, when Cannon was Speaker, the Democrats discovered that most of the Republicans had left the House floor. They called up for a vote a bill they wanted passed. After the traditional two callings of the House roll of members, Cannon quietly asked the clerk to call the roll once more, a specific violation of House procedures. The Democrats angrily objected and demanded Cannon's justification for so unprecedented an act. "The Chair will inform the gentlemen," Cannon calmly answered. "The Chair is hoping a few more Republicans will come in." [24] The Democrats burst into laughter at Cannon's candor, and let his lieutenants have the extra time to round up enough Republican votes to defeat their bill.

The modern Speaker occasionally has acted arbitrarily. Speaker Joe Martin, for example, with the help of his then floor leader, Charles Halleck of Indiana, simply bypassed the chairman of the Ways and Means Committee, Daniel Reed of New York, in 1953, to force his committee to send to the floor legislation extending the excess profits tax. The modification of the Speaker's powers and of the American political climate, however, have made such peremptory actions by the Speaker a rare occurrence. The political divisions within the two major parties, already suggested, have also made authoritarian decisions by the Speakers far less acceptable to the House than in the past. There were other reasons, too, of even greater importance.

In the halcyon years of Speaker Cannon, there appeared to be no limit to the Speaker's autocratic power. "An able man and a clever politician in the Chair owns the House of Representatives body, soul and conscience," wrote one contemporary observer of Cannon's House.[25] When a constituent asked his Representative for a copy of the House's rules and regulations, the member sent him a picture of Speaker Cannon. Another time, a woman, attending the opening of a House session with Cannon in the Chair, was shocked to see Cannon stand and bow his head with the other members as the House chaplain entoned the opening prayer. "Thar's old Joe Cannon," she whispered loudly to a friend. "And him a-prayin'. The old hypocrite!" [26] Cannon personally was a modest and kindly man, well liked by his colleagues, despite the public image as the "Czar" of the House that he had won for his tyrannical methods. Modern Speakers have had a far less hostile national image. Partly this has resulted from the limits placed on the Speakers since Cannon, and partly this has come from a change in the attitude of the Speakers themselves. The later Speakers of the House have operated largely with a desire to cooperate as much as possible with the opposition minority party. The minority and majority leaders of the House no longer have seen themselves as blood enemies the way they often did in the past. The closest friend in the House of Republican Speaker Longworth was John Nance Garner of Texas, the Democratic floor leader who succeeded Longworth as Speaker. Speaker Rayburn, a Democrat, and Speaker Martin, a Republican, long boasted of their personal friendship, and it was not an idle boast. Rayburn was once asked to campaign in Massachusetts against Martin. "Speak against Martin?" Rayburn snapped. "Hell, if I lived up there, I'd vote for him." [27]

The revolt against "Cannonism," against the Speaker's autocratic power, altered permanently the Speaker's personal control over the House, but it did not destroy totally, as was at first believed, the Speaker's influence over the decisions of the House. Henry Clay had mastered the House without the benefit of the rules available to Cannon, and Speakers who followed Cannon could learn from Clay's example. Besides, in striking at Cannon's power, the House had not touched the central powers of the Rules Committee, and had carefully left intact the basic rules of the House, its limitations on debate and amendments, on filibustering, and dilatory tactics. The House deprived Cannon of his membership on the Rules Committee, of his authority to appoint House standing committees, and of his power to ignore the rights of the minority and the will of the majority. The House, in effect, took action to force future Speakers to be fair to all members—or risk the consequences. The House did not specifically deny to the Speaker either power or influence.

Curiously, Speaker Cannon himself partially developed the beginnings of what was to become the Speaker's new avenue to power in the House. Speaker Reed, a glacially cold man, had ruled the House alone. Cannon, a convivial prairie-circuit lawyer before his election to the House, loved the fellowship of his colleagues. A poker player of great enthusiasm, Cannon immensely enjoyed a high-stakes game after the sessions of the House. There, in the camaraderie of a poker game and good whiskey, Cannon spent pleasant evenings and, inevitably, he decided much of the business of the House at these private sessions. One of the young members of the House who got his first start up the House promotion ladder at these poker sessions was John Nance Garner. Garner, who it was said began building his personal fortune at the poker table, was Cannon's kind of man. John L. Lewis, president of the United Mine Workers, once called Garner a "labor-baiting, poker-playing, whiskey-drinking, evil old man." [28]

The men with whom Cannon played poker quite naturally

were or became his intimates in the House. They were men, like Garner, marked for power of their own. Cannon did more, however, than play poker with them. He ruled the House through these intimates; he established an oligarchy of powerful men to replace the single rule of Thomas Reed. High on his list of personal favorites were Sereno Payne of New York, chairman of the Ways and Means Committee; John Dalzell of Pennsylvania and James R. Mann of Illinois, two master Republican parliamentarians; and young Nicholas Longworth, son-in-law of President Theodore Roosevelt. These intimates of the Speaker became his trusted lieutenants, and together with the Speaker they controlled every aspect of the House's operations.

Longworth, who became Speaker in 1925, used similar techniques to restore to the Speaker the great influence he once had over the House's operations. Longworth established a similar "commission" of personal lieutenants—John Q. Tilson of Connecticut, his floor leader; Bertrand Snell of New York, chairman of the Rules Committee; and James Begg of Ohio, a personal friend of long standing. The group was called the "Big Four," and they re-established much of the former influence of the Speaker in the House.

Longworth also established, with his friend John Nance Garner, an informal institution that for a generation was to play an enormous but indistinct role in the operations of the House of Representatives. This was the "Board of Education." Originally, Longworth and Garner met for drinks, during World War I days, in a hideaway in the Capitol catacombs called the "Daniel Webster room," a room that Webster reputedly used for similar reasons nearly a century earlier. Later, Garner and Longworth had another room, the "cabinet room," an office on the third floor of the old House Office Building. There they invited colleagues for a drink—Garner always called it "striking a blow for liberty"—and talked over the business coming before the House. Still later, when Longworth became Speaker, they moved to another room, under the Capitol dome, and this was the first "Board of Education." It was so named, not so much because Longworth and Garner were educating young members there in parliamentary strategy and practice as because they used it to learn what was going on in the House. "Well," explained Garner, "you get a couple of drinks in a young Congressman and then you know what he knows and what he can do. We pay the tuition by supplying the liquor." [29]

At these sessions, Longworth and Garner frequently reached agreements on the legislation coming before the House. They were leaders of opposing political parties, and they opposed each other on controversial bills, but even on the controversial measures there were areas where accommodations were possible. The basic aim of the sessions was to expedite the business of the House and to make manageable the large and unwieldy membership. Garner and Longworth provided each other and each other's party with accommodations on the great mass of the House's routine business, all reached by informal gentlemen's agreements. Of course, the sessions were far more than business meetings, and over the legally prohibited whiskey, Longworth and Garner and their intimates, Snell and Tilson, Sam Rayburn of Texas, and John McDuffie of Alabama, regaled each other with the best of stories and political hijinks drawn from their varied careers and pasts. Out of these sessions blossomed great friendships, none stronger than that between Longworth and Garner. The two, utterly different in so many ways, an elegant Cincinnati dilettante with a gift for music and the small talk of elite salons and a Texas wrangler known as "Cactus Jack," were almost inseparable. Late every afternoon Longworth and Garner met to "strike a blow for liberty." Every evening, Longworth took Garner to his hotel residence in the Speaker's official limousine, which they both called "our car," and the next morning Longworth stopped by the hotel again to pick up his old adversary and friend to take him to the Capitol.

Garner continued the "Board of Education" after he became Speaker, and Rayburn kept up the tradition as long as he was Speaker. Rayburn moved the "Board of Education" to a small room on the first floor of the Capitol, behind the members' private dining room, and there he and his intimates swapped stories over drinks and settled the affairs of the House for two decades.

Rayburn never liked the name "Board of Education" and preferred to call his room noncommittally "downstairs." He used the sessions, however, for much the same purpose as did Longworth and Garner before him. There he learned all the gossip of the House and there he planned much of the House's operations. Gathered there were such stalwart friends as Frank Ikard and Homer Thornberry of Texas, Richard Bolling of Missouri, John McCormack of Massachusetts, and Lewis Deschler, the House's Parliamentarian and a veteran of the "Board of Education" since Longworth's years. Others would drop in. Charles Halleck of Indiana, the Republican leader, came by frequently, although he had a nearby hideaway of this own, called "The Clinic," where he dispensed drinks and advice to his fellow Republicans. (Joseph Martin of Massachusetts, a teetotaler and Halleck's rival for Republican leadership, unkindly called Halleck's hideaway "Charlie's drinking room.") Senators also stopped by, Lyndon Johnson most frequently of them all. It was in Rayburn's "Board of Education" that Vice President Harry Truman was found on April 12, 1945, when he was summoned peremptorily to the White House to be told that Franklin Roosevelt was dead and that he was now President.

These private sessions were one of the most useful tools of the Speaker's leadership of the House. They enormously helped the Speakers—Longworth, Garner, and Rayburn—to re-establish the old prestige of their office. In Rayburn's years, John McCormack reported at these sessions on a host of problems familiar to him as floor leader. Ikard kept Rayburn informed on the key Ways and Means Committee, and Bolling and Thornberry did the same for the Rules Committee of which they were members. Deschler helped in mapping strategy, as did the others, with his intimate knowledge of House rules and precedents. Other influential men of the House were invited to these sessions, particularly when their expert knowledge of specific problems was needed, and they, too, would participate in developing the Speaker's strategy. They often left the sessions carrying the Speaker's orders. These meetings gave the Speaker the means of bringing to bear his influence on just about every aspect of the House's business. They helped restore the Speaker to his old role as the master spirit of the House.

These sessions also helped break down any personal animosity between the leaders of the opposing parties in the House, following the example of Longworth and Garner. They eased the problem of reaching agreement about much of the House's operation —the scheduling of legislation, the settlement of party divisions on standing committees, the split of House patronage, and the handling of many other items on the House's complicated agenda. There were accommodations worked out to suit both sides, gentlemen's agreements that helped keep the House in orderly operation. Rayburn once explained why a modern Speaker could not act tyrannically toward the members of the House. "A Speaker has to be fair," he said. "Otherwise they'll tear him to pieces. That's because so much of the House's business is done by 'unanimous consent' of the members, and all it takes is one fellow who thinks he has been done wrong to stand up and say, 'I object.' " [30] A single annoyed Representative had the power, by objecting, to spoil all the carefully arranged gentlemen's agreements.

The power of the modern Speaker had other limits, too, beside the possibilities of counterattack from the floor and the refusal of individual members to go along with the accommodations and program worked out by the leaders of the House. The three great formal limits in the rules against an arbitrary Speaker, all originated in the revolt against Speaker Cannon in 1909 and 1910, were the technicalities involved with Calendar Wednesday, the Discharge Petition, and the motion to recommit—and thus amend or kill—a pending bill. In reality, these limits on the Speaker's power, although potentially powerful, have only rarely been effectively used. The Discharge Petition and Calendar Wednesday, particularly, have proved difficult to execute, and so ineffective that in the first fifty years of its use the Discharge Petition, as already mentioned, has resulted in the enactment of only two laws.

These limits, however, as they have been applied, have been mere formalities in preventing any undue arbitrariness in the modern Speakers, for they have been men intensely aware of the

84

necessity to restrain severely their own partisan feelings. However, they did not prevent the restoration of the Speaker to great power. "The Speaker is the hub of the whole Congress—not just the House," said Carl Albert of Oklahoma, Democratic floor leader under Speaker McCormack. "It's hard to beat him on anything." [31] The mid-twentieth century Speakers had altered the nature of the Speakership from Speaker Cannon's day, and by so doing had reclaimed their great role in the legislative process. "Gentlemen," Cannon bluntly told the House, "I propose to be just as fair and impartial in the performance of my duties here as the exigencies of politics will permit." [32] The Speakers following Cannon have not so qualified their concept of fairness. "In order to maintain his effectiveness," Speaker Martin explained, "a Speaker has to be fair." [33] He added no qualifications. Otherwise, the Speaker would not have a chance of persuading the House to enact the bills he wanted.

John McCormack, for two decades one of the House's most ferocious partisans as Democratic floor leader, knew perfectly well that he lost the right to such partisanship when he was elected Speaker in 1962. "The itch and the urge," he fondly called the old impulse to joust in debate with Charles Halleck of Indiana and Halleck's Republicans, but McCormack knew he could no longer give way to the old partisan urge. He had to be fair; he had to respect the rights of all members of the House. It was not merely the threat of being rebuked by the House that restrained McCormack, or that restrained Sam Rayburn and the other Speakers. It was also a changed view of the office, a feeling of greater tolerance, not dissimilar to the change in the sense of political morality that made it impossible to use the party caucus as a method to force Representatives to vote for bills against their will. It was a feeling of affection for the House as an institution.

In all the years of the House's existence, the members have never failed, at the end of each session, to thank the Speaker by formal resolution for his service as Speaker and for his fairness. In the passionate politics of the nineteenth century, the resolution frequently became a question of partisan party acrimony.

The Speaker's purported "impartiality" was treated as an insult to the minority. In one instance, the majority leader even had to invoke the Previous Question to halt a filibuster against the motion to adopt the resolution of thanks. On others, the minority members insisted on roll-call votes and then voted "no." In recent years, however, no such bitterness has spoiled the gesture. On the contrary, the minority leaders have on these occasions momentarily taken over technical control of the House of Representatives to add to the sense of generosity and benevolence of the ceremony. In 1958, for example, Les Arends of Illinois, the Republican minority whip, took over the Chair as the House's presiding officer. Joseph Martin of Massachusetts, then Republican minority floor leader, made the motion to thank Speaker Rayburn for his fairness and impartiality. The motion was adopted unanimously. Rayburn resumed the Chair and, with emotion, thanked the Representatives, all the Representatives, for their kindness and their courtesy to him.

"I love the House of Representatives," Rayburn said tenderly. "It has been most of my life."

CHAPTER FIVE

The Priesthood of the House

THE Speaker, if he has always held the great seat of power, has never run the House of Representatives without help. The House has been from the beginning such a sprawling, discordant mass of men that the Speaker has had to depend on lieutenants to guide and oversee its multiple operations in its committees and on the floor, and to assure the orderly flow of responsible legislation. Indeed, over the years, a hierarchy of leaders has been constructed in the House to support the Speaker, and opposing this hierarchy has been another, created by the minority party and led by the "shadow" Speaker, the leader of the opposition party. With the hierarchy also has been built a vast array of political and party organizations to assist the Speaker and his lieutenants in the complicated task of making the House a viable, responsible legislative body.

The principal aide of the Speaker long has been the majority floor leader, and he in turn has been helped by the party whip and assistant whips, and, often, by the chairmen of the influential House committees. The Speaker frequently has had other lieutenants, picked from among the ablest men of the House and the members of powerful committees. These lieutenants normally have chaired the political and party organizations in the House— the party caucus, oldest of all; the Rules Committee, long the great "arm" of the Speaker, although in recent years tending to

87

operate independently of the party leadership; the Steering Committee, a group used to regulate the flow of legislation; the Policy Committee, whose function has been to help set party positions; the Committee on Committees, which has allocated committee assignments to party members; the Patronage Committee, which has dispensed Capitol jobs to the party faithful; and the Campaign Committee, whose purpose has been to help members win re-election. Each organization has proved useful to create party harmony and unity, the source of party power.

These lieutenants and the party organizations, none of which were provided for by the Constitution nor even now recognized by the House rules as political agents of the Speaker, could help the Speaker, but none could take over his principal function of leading the House, determining its legislative course, and guiding its response to the demands and needs of the American people.

On the Speaker's judgment, the House's record each session has been largely written, and his techniques and tactics frequently have decided the outcome of his strategy on how best to meet the House's legislative responsibilities of the time. The Speaker's judgment, however, has been one formed with the help of his lieutenants, often in such informal meetings as those of the "Board of Education," and with the help of what Sam Rayburn called the "rolling waves of sentiment" among his colleagues on the House floor. The Speaker has had to judge the mood of the House, the temper of its members, and judge it accurately or risk a disastrous loss of his own prestige and standing as the great officer, the embodiment, of the House.

In the twentieth century, the President has assumed most of the initiative in sponsoring legislation, and the House and Senate have served chiefly to temper or modify, adopt or reject, what legislation the President has requested. Congress, however, has not abdicated entirely its responsibilities in initiating legislation and appropriating money. In the years, particularly, when the White House and the Congress have been controlled by different parties—the Republican Eightieth Congress and Harry Truman, the Democratic Eighty-fourth, Eighty-fifth, and Eighty-sixth Congresses and Dwight Eisenhower—the Congress has reclaimed much of its old legislative initiative. The Eightieth House boldly overrode Truman's veto of the Taft-Hartley Labor Act and his veto of legislation cutting individual income taxes. The three Democratic Houses, the Eighty-fourth, Eighty-fifth, and Eighty-sixth, constantly pressured Eisenhower to alter his housing, farm, and school policies although they overrode his veto of only two less important bills. Whether the President has shared party allegiance with the majority of the House and Senate, however, has not altered the Speaker's responsibility to guide the House in its response to Presidential requests. This responsibility the modern Speaker has shared at least in part with his lieutenants, the men whom one Speaker called "my cabinet."

Different Speakers have utilized their floor leaders and other lieutenants in different ways. David Henderson of Iowa, Speaker from 1899 to 1903, never let a bill go to a vote in the House without carefully reading it himself and then having it thoroughly examined again by one of his lieutenants. "I determined when I became Speaker," he said, "that no legislation should be enacted by the House which was not for the public good, if its enactment could be prevented by the exercise of care on my part." [1] John Nance Garner, Nicholas Longworth, and Sam Rayburn had no interest in the details of a bill. Longworth, an elegant dandy, affected a positive distaste for details, and his friend Garner shared the same feeling. "Hell," Garner said, "don't tell me what the bill says. Tell me what it does." [2] Rayburn had a similar reaction. "I never bother with the details," he said. "First, I don't know them—I'm not smart enough. Second, if the chairman of a committee has a problem, he'll come in and spell it out to me." [3]

Some Speakers have held tightly the reins of control over the House. Others have relaxed their control and freely delegated authority to their lieutenants to act for them. Joseph Cannon ran roughshod over the House and kept strict control of the House through only three lieutenants, who were his floor leader, chairman of Ways and Means, and colleagues on the Rules Committee. "The four rulers of the House of Representatives," reported a contemporary political writer of Cannon and his lieutenants, "are a law unto themselves." [4] Rayburn, a generation after Cannon, had no hesitation in delegating major tasks to his protégés in the House. In the House struggle over the Reciprocal Trade Bill in 1958, he assigned Frank Ikard of Texas, one of the ablest members of the Ways and Means Committee, to negotiate a compromise between the oil lobby and Administration officials on a critical clause that threatened passage of the bill. Frequently Rayburn gave Richard Bolling of Missouri, one of the ablest members of the Rules Committee, responsibility to act for him on major bills coming before the House. Rayburn did not lose power by so delegating authority. Once, at a session of the "Board of Education," Charles Halleck of Indiana, the Republican floor leader, stiffly argued for adjournment of the House for the year without acting on a half-dozen major bills. Bolling argued with Halleck, insisting the House had to act on the bills before adjournment. Halleck was annoyed at having to argue with a lieutenant. "Well," he snapped, "if this guy is going to make the decisions around here, we're not going to get very far." An awkward silence fell on the room, one of embarrassment. Rayburn broke the silence. "I make the decisions around here," he said softly.[5]

Every Speaker has had to make the basic decisions, however much he may have depended on lieutenants for help and advice. Rayburn encouraged his lieutenants to make recommendations, to argue for a line of procedure. Wilbur Mills of Arkansas, chairman of the Ways and Means Committee, frequently presented recommendations to Rayburn in the enormously important fields of taxation, foreign trade, and social security, but Rayburn did not always accept them. Mills, as a party man and Rayburn protégé, normally acquiesced to Rayburn's decision. John McCormack of Massachusetts, Rayburn's floor leader before he became Speaker, sometimes differed with Rayburn on strategy. He argued heatedly for his own plan, but would often yield to Rayburn's judgment when he could not persuade the Speaker. In these cases, the question at hand was a party policy decision, and the Speaker made it. When McCormack became Speaker, he got similar loyalty from his lieutenants.

Rayburn frequently met in caucus with the members of the Ways and Means Committee, there to try to work out any critical pending question before the committee. Garner had done much the same. On one occasion, when the Great Depression was bankrupting millions of American families, Garner called in all the chairmen of the Appropriations subcommittees. He wrung from them a pledge that not a single dollar would be added to President Herbert Hoover's budget and that they would cut every dollar possible from every appropriation bill. Longworth acted similarly. On crucial questions, he called together his informal "board of strategy" to consult with him on how best to proceed. On occasion, the Speaker has called in the minority leader to share in a major decision. In the midst of World War II, Rayburn took just such action with Joseph Martin, the Republican leader. When Martin arrived at Rayburn's office, he found McCormack with the Speaker along with Secretary of War Henry L. Stimson and Army Chief of Staff George C. Marshall. Stimson and Marshall explained to the three House leaders that the government was then engaged in a crash program to build an atomic bomb, then the most secret of projects, and they needed $1,600,000,000 to make the bomb. They asked that the three leaders arrange for the money to be appropriated without a single shred of evidence of what it was for. "No more extraordinary request was ever made to leaders of the House of Representatives, the trustees of the people's money," said Martin years later.[6] Rayburn asked Appropriations Committee Chairman Clarence Cannon of Missouri to approve the money without any questions. Martin made a similar request to John Taber of New York, the ranking Republican member on the Appropriations Committee. Both Cannon and Taber agreed, and the money was appropriated to build the bomb that ended the war.

"I never asked anything from Joe Martin that wasn't fair," Rayburn once said. "He never asked me for anything that wasn't fair." [7]

The first lieutenant of the Speaker, the man on whom he has

normally depended most, long has been the majority party floor leader, a technically unofficial officer of the House, for he has been selected by either the Speaker or the party caucus and not been elected by the House. The floor leader has had over-all management of the majority party on the floor, and has had command of the House's formal agenda. He has been his party's principal spokesman on the floor; it has been he who normally has responded to the minority floor leader; it has been he who, by both word and deed, has had the responsibility of rallying his own party members to his party's cause. On him also has fallen the responsibility of keeping the House busily at work. He has had to make plans to call up legislation for action in a systematic way, so as to avoid unnecessarily jamming the final days of each session. To do so, he has had to consult frequently with all committee chairmen, to learn from them when they expected to report their major bills to the House, and to urge them to keep their bills on schedule so that the House itself could proceed under an orderly timetable. On the majority leader also has rested the responsibility of keeping both his own party members and the minority fully informed of the coming legislative program, normally announcing this program a week in advance. To do so effectively, the majority leader normally has held private consultations with the minority leaders, and to fail to do so would have risked antagonizing the whole membership of the House. Traditionally the floor leader has scrupulously accommodated members of both parties in scheduling bills and votes on the floor. The majority leader, for example, has carefully avoided roll-call votes for days on which any state has held a primary—Representatives from that state quite naturally have wanted to be free of House responsibilities on such a day so that they could return to their Congressional districts and vote in the primary.

As his party's floor leader, John McCormack frequently used the House restaurant as a rendezvous for his friends and allies in the House. Every morning McCormack used to stop off at a table where the Massachusetts Representatives gathered for coffee. On hand normally were Thomas "Tip" O'Neill, William Bates, Edward Boland; normally Joseph Martin, the Republican leader, was there, too. McCormack would settle much of the House's routine business over the morning coffee with Martin. With O'Neill and James Delaney of New York, who also stopped by for coffee, McCormack was kept up to date on the operations of the Rules Committee of which both were members. Boland served on the Appropriations Committee, one equally important. At lunch, McCormack normally ate in the members' private dining room at a large table reserved for the liberal Democrats. There he picked up much of the gossip of the House, the problems and the complaints of the members, and he set forth his own views on pending questions. He used the lunch table as a communications center, somewhat as Sam Rayburn used the "Board of Education."

The floor leader, according to Champ Clark of Missouri, who served as his party's floor leader before he became Speaker, "must possess tact, patience, firmness, ability, courage, quickness of thought, and knowledge of the rules and practices of the House" [8] if he was to succeed as a leader. The modern House leader has had but little power to enforce his will on his fellow members and he has had to depend on his wits and his power of persuasion to woo followers to his cause. "I have never asked a member to vote against his conscience," said John McCormack. "If he mentions his conscience—that's all. I don't press him any further." [9] Joseph Martin had much the same philosophy of leadership. "I didn't give the Democrats hell enough," he said, just after the House Republicans removed him as their leader in 1959 and replaced him with Charles Halleck. "Well, I had a program to get through and you don't give a fellow a crack on the jaw to make him agree with you. I believe in persuasion and conciliation." [10] Martin cited an instance when undue partisanship by Halleck had cost the Republicans a bill. Martin, as his party's floor leader, had worked out an arrangement with the Democrats not to fight a bill President Eisenhower wanted. Halleck made a fiery floor speech against the Democrats, and the Democrats responded by voting down the bill. "Joe," said McCormack to Martin after the vote, "we were going to give you that bill—until Halleck damned us all." [11] Halleck has privately acknowledged that on occasion he has pressured his colleagues too severely. "Some guys say I drive too hard," said Halleck, "that I push too hard. You can't push them too hard. You've got to know when to let up. You can go too far, however, and I have a few times." [12]

Halleck, who has styled himself as a "gut-fighter," has at times become deeply involved emotionally in a pending vote. Once he so harangued a Republican colleague on the House floor that the colleague had to be physically restrained from striking Halleck. Halleck, however, knew the limitations of a leader. "You get pressure from guys who have come along with you on a tough vote about the fellows who went off the reservation," Halleck once said. "Some of them want to read these guys out of the party. But, hell, there may be a vote next week when you need a fellow who has strayed real bad and you can catch him on the rebound." [13] Carl Albert of Oklahoma, Halleck's opponent on the House floor, had much the same view that rough tactics by the floor leader could cost him more votes than such tactics could gain. "If you can't win them by persuasion, you can't win them at all," Albert said. "If you whip them into line every time, by the time you reach the third vote you're through." [14] There have been, in recent years, minor ways of disciplining party members —by denying them choice committee assignments, patronage jobs in the Capitol to hand out to friends, or perhaps more luxurious offices—but these punishments have given the party leaders but little help in controlling their party members. "I can't fire another member of the House," said Halleck. "They're all elected just like me by about the same number of people and they all draw the same pay." [15]

Martin followed a much gentler course than Halleck. "For my own part, I was never dictatorial," he wrote in his autobiography. "I worked by persuasion and drew heavily on long-established personal friendships. Unless it was absolutely necessary I never asked a man to side with me if his vote would hurt him in his district. Whenever I could spare a man this kind of embarrassment I did so and saved him for another time when I might need him more urgently." [16] Carl Albert had a similar view, but acknowledged that the leaders resented Representatives who resisted all unpopular positions. "If a fellow keeps begging off," said Albert, "we tell him that it's his turn to take the heat the next time." [17]

For many decades of the history of the House, the position of party floor leader had no formal standing. Normally, the Speaker merely designated a favorite who acted for him on the floor, and normally this favorite the Speaker also appointed as chairman of the Ways and Means Committee. On occasion, however, the Speaker assigned the post to his principal rival for the Speakership. Until 1865, the Ways and Means Committee had jurisdiction over all taxation, all appropriations, all banking and monetary matters, and the major political issue of the time: the tariff. The chairman of this committee naturally inherited the informal role of floor leader, because the legislation from his committee not only was the most important to come before the House each year, but also took most of the House's time. Even after the House divided the committee's power to create both the Appropriations and the Banking and Currency Committees, the Ways and Means Committee remained the most important legislative committee of the House, and its chairman usually served also as floor leader. Occasionally, however, the role of floor leader was given —or taken—by the chairman of the Appropriations Committee. It was as chairman of the Appropriations Committee that Thaddeus Stevens dominated the House and engineered the impeachment of President Andrew Johnson. It was as Appropriations chairman and Republican floor leader that James Garfield of Ohio first caught the national attention that was to elect him President. He was the only President ever elected directly from the House, and at the time he was elected he was serving as his party's floor leader. Three other Presidents won their first national honors as party floor leaders in the House: James K. Polk of Tennessee, Millard Fillmore of New York, and William McKinley of Ohio. Each served as chairman of Ways and Means at the same time he served as his party's spokesman on the floor.

In the first years of the House, James Madison of Virginia, later President, and Albert Gallatin of Pennsylvania, later a

95

brilliant Secretary of the Treasury, rose to the rank of leaders of the House floor, but they were not so designated. The first officially appointed floor leader was Robert Goodloe Harper of South Carolina, named to the new post in 1797 by Speaker Jonathan Dayton of New Jersey. Harper charmed the House with his eloquence and skillful arguments. In the years that followed, the floor leaders ranked among the ablest men of their time, and, sometimes, the most picturesque. John W. Eppes of Virginia, President Jefferson's son-in-law, was as widely loved, as John Randolph of Virginia, audacious, reckless, and sarcastic, was hated. Among the others were William Lowndes of South Carolina, known in his day as a legislative genius; Samuel "Sunset" Cox of New York, noted for his wit; Thomas Reed of Maine, Samuel Randall of Pennsylvania, and Joseph Cannon of Illinois, all later noted Speakers of the House; William D. "Pig-Iron" Kelley of Pennsylvania, the great advocate of tariff protection; Nelson Dingley of Maine, of whom Reed said that "he'd rather have a pad and pencil on his knee than a pretty girl," [18] and William Springer of Illinois, a favorite target for Reed's caustic wit. Springer once told the House, using Henry Clay's classic expression, that he would "rather be right than President."

Reed promptly retorted, "The gentleman from Illinois will never be either." [19]

After the House revolt against Speaker Cannon, the power to name the majority floor leader was taken from the Speaker and given to the party caucus, and the floor leaders for a dozen years —Oscar Underwood, Claude Kitchen, Franklin Mondell, and Nicholas Longworth—in turn held the real political leadership of the House. The complexity of the legislative requirements of the House during World War I multiplied the responsibilities of the floor leader to the extent that by the early 1920's each party freed its floor leaders from all committee responsibilities. Underwood and Kitchen had been chairmen of Ways and Means, but Mondell and Longworth had no committee assignments. They devoted their entire time to managing the floor business of the House. In institutional terms, this divorce of the party leader from personal participation in committee work and from personal responsibility for writing legislation amounted to revolutionary change. It reflected the House's response to the rapid increase in its own work and it reflected also the House's sense that the federal government and federal legislation had taken a new and critical significance in national life. The elevation of the party floor leader to an independent rank, second only to the Speaker himself, had a profound influence on the attitude of the House toward the man chosen for the post. Earlier floor leaders had occasionally been elected Speaker of the House when vacancies in the House's great office occurred. Since 1919, the year the floor leader first was given unfettered charge of the House's floor operation, the House has elected not a single Speaker who first had not been the party floor leader. From Longworth through McCormack, every one of the eight Speakers chosen had first led his party on the floor of the House.

Even before World War I, another institutional change in party leadership had been under way. This was the creation of the office of party whip, an official chosen originally to keep track of his party members and make sure they came to the Hall of the House for important votes. In time, the responsibilities of the whip were enlarged to the extent that by the 1960's he had become an important party official and, in fact, served as assistant floor leader. The creation and enlargement of the function of the party whip reflected, as did the elevation of the floor leader to independent status, the House's intuitive response to its burgeoning legislative responsibilities.

The first Representative formally designated as his party's whip was James Watson of Indiana, chosen in 1899 by the Republican caucus. Watson was an eloquent debater with a gracious manner who easily made friends—a great asset in persuading his colleagues. The function of whip, if not the formal party position, had existed from the earliest years of the House. In 1811, John Eppes of Virginia, then chairman of the Foreign Affairs Committee, acted as whip in rounding up votes to approve the Previous Question rule, the first great limit on House debate. John W. Taylor of New York, in the years after Eppes, voluntarily took on the chore of sounding out the sentiments of his

97

colleagues and keeping track of those absent, so that he and the other House leaders would know how to calculate House votes. In periods when any political party had an overwhelming majority of the House members, there was little need or use for party whips, but when the House stood in tenuous balance between two parties, every vote became important and the unofficial whips reappeared. Thomas Reed of Maine, in his early years in the House, took on this voluntary assignment. So did Champ Clark of Missouri, like Reed later a Speaker of the House. Clark, in his autobiography, explained why the whips were necessary: always some members of the House "play hooky like a lot of schoolboys" and on some votes they could "decide the fate of important measures." [20]

"The whips are the right hands of the two [floor] leaders," Clark wrote. "To be efficient they must know the membership by sight; be on as friendly a footing with them as possible; know where they reside, both in Washington and at home; know their habits, their recreations, their loafing-places, the condition of their health, and that of their families; the numbers of their telephones; when they are out of the city; when they will return; how they would probably vote on a pending measure; what churches they attend; what theaters they frequent—in short, all about them." [21]

In Clark's years, John Dwight of New York served as Republican whip and developed some of the modern techniques of an effective whip. He could be seen daily, with his whip's book in hand, noting the whereabouts of all members. He could tell the Speaker promptly how many party members were within immediate call and how many could be brought to the House floor in either twelve or twenty-four hours. He would notify members when they could expect the House to reach a vote on a given bill, and if the debate appeared to be closing sooner than his estimate, Dwight encouraged his party's members to keep talking until the hour he had set for their absent colleagues to arrive for the vote. In the great fight to strip Speaker Cannon of his arbitrary powers, a fight touched off by an unexpected motion from George Norris of Nebraska, Cannon kept the House in continuous session for two days while his whips telegraphed absent members around the country to hurry them back to the House floor. In another fight with Cannon, Champ Clark went to extra trouble to bring one of his Democratic members to the House floor to vote. The member complained that he was lame and could not walk to the Hall of the House. Clark gave a porter two dollars to roll the member onto the House floor in a wheel chair. Then, to Clark's chagrin, the member voted against Clark. "How he returned to his hotel," said Clark, "I know not. One thing cocksure—he did not travel at my expense!" [22]

In more recent years, the whip has taken on greater and more delicate duties than merely keeping track of the members and urging them to report to the floor for important votes. He has become a party strategist in his own right and has even substituted for the floor leader as the party's floor spokesman. The whip in recent years has continued to be responsible for rounding up the members of his party for votes, and the system has been perfected to take advantage of modern technology. An hour before an important vote, the whip normally has put out a "whip's call" to all his party's members. This has been handled by telephone, using the Capitol's switchboard operators. Another whip's call has been issued a half hour before the vote, and then a final whip's call just ten minutes before the vote. Technically, the whip's call, although delivered by a switchboard operator, has meant that the party whip had requested the member called to show up for the vote. On matters of great urgency, the party whip has issued, at the direction of the Speaker, a "Speaker's call," which has been delivered in the same way. That call meant that the Speaker himself had requested the member to turn out for the vote, and no ordinary member receiving such a call would dare to ignore it.

The modern whip has also taken over much of the function of sounding out, for the Speaker and floor leader, the feelings of the party members on important legislation coming before the House. The whip's findings have been, at times, of great importance to the leaders. An easy informal relationship has usually existed between the Democratic and Republican whips in recent years, between Democratic whip Carl Albert and Republican whip Leslie Arends of Illinois, for example. On some whip counts, or "nose" counts as they have been called, the rival party whips have even exchanged intelligence: each has told the other how his party members would divide on a given bill. Between them, they have sometimes been able to forecast a House vote almost to the man as much as a week in advance. Armed with such intelligence, the majority and minority party leaders have mapped their strategy on floor action. If the whip's nose count has showed that the House would vote down a bill as it stood, the leaders have agreed to alter the bill with an amendment or two to woo at least some of the bill's opponents into favoring it.

Perhaps the most effective tool of the House leaders, in modern times, has been the Rules Committee. For the first century of the House's existence, the Rules Committee existed only as a relatively unimportant group of men who had the responsibility of drafting the House's rules. Unless the rules were to be altered, the committee had scarcely any real function, and existed only as one of the House's most insignificant committees. This was not to continue, however. As early as 1841, the same year the House adopted the One Hour rule limiting floor debate, the Speaker, then John White of Kentucky, ruled that only a simple majority vote of the House was needed to approve a special resolution from the Rules Committee to change the rules of the House. Normally, the rules of the House could be suspended or changed only with a two-thirds majority. This was the earliest precedent for the later development of the great power of the Rules Committee, but it was a precedent then unappreciated for its possibilities. Not until the 1880's was this precedent used to establish the Rules Committee as the governing body for limiting debate farther than any member of the House had previously dreamed possible. The technique was simple: the committee drafted a special rule to apply to a specific bill that, when adopted by a simple majority of the House, limited debate and even restricted amendments on that bill. Originally, the technique was used to prevent filibustering, but it soon proved the most efficient method of processing the House's crowded agenda of legislation. Where once the House spent five months on a controversial bill, the House in modern years—by adopting special rules from the Rules Committee—has limited debate on such bills to as little as a few hours of a single afternoon. Scarcely any major bills in recent years have been passed by the House under any other method. Asher Hinds, once the House's official Parliamentarian, described this technique of adopting special rules for specific bills as imposing "a form of martial law" on the House.[23] It was scarcely less than that, and it proved greatly useful to House leaders. Controlling a majority of the House, the majority leader could thus act with swiftness and dispatch in ramming through the House the major bills on his party's legislative schedule. This power assumed that the majority of the members of the Rules Committee were responsive to the wishes of the majority party and its leaders, the Speaker and his floor leader. The committee became, under Speakers Reed and Cannon and later under Clark, Longworth, and Garner, the strong arm of the Speaker by which he effectively regulated the flow of legislation through the House. The committee acted as a steering committee and a policy committee of the majority party. The committee was, as one Speaker called it, "the political and policy vehicle" of the House's majority party. "The Committee on Rules is a piece of machinery necessary to assist the majority of the House of Representatives in working its will," said Speaker Cannon.[24] Speaker Clark phrased the same concept differently: "Its chief function is to expedite desirable or necessary legislation." [25]

The committee developed its power, over the years, to an extraordinary degree. First used only to expedite desired legislation, it soon came to have the power to veto undesired legislation. The committee also found that it could, through the special rules it issued, restrict and even prohibit the offering of amendments to bills called up for House action. Those special rules, the ones prohibiting amendments, have always been called "gag" rules, for they effectively silence Representatives desiring to offer amendments. They have been justified, on such legislation as tax bills and tariff bills, on the grounds that the subject matter was too technical to permit floor amendments, that only through careful committee study could the ramifications of amendments on such bills be thoroughly understood.

The Rules Committee had a positive function besides saving the House's time and expediting its legislative business, and that was the power to pigeonhole, and so kill, bills that the committee found for one reason or another undesirable. Unless the committee voted a special rule for a major bill, by which floor debate could be limited on it, there was no practical or easy way for the House to consider the bill. The House could not afford enough time to act on the bill under the regular rules of the House. This power, of course, enormously enhanced the standing of the Rules Committee, and the committee's members long have taken great pride in this aspect of their operations. They were a group carefully selected from both major political parties with the courage to kill bills, like costly bonus bills for veterans, that the other members of the House, fearful of alienating politically active home-district groups, would not dare to resist. The House members then could escape censure from these groups by blaming the Rules Committee. The Rules Committee majority, however, did not always use this power just to kill bills the House floor leaders wanted pigeonholed. The committee, in fact, moved away from Speaker Reed's original concept that it should be an arm of the Speaker and floor leaders, and it took on in the late 1930's independent rank of its own. "My people," said Rules Committee Chairman Howard Smith of Virginia, explaining this new attitude, "did not elect me to Congress to be a traffic cop." [26]

The great powers of this committee quite naturally gave great power to its chairman, and on occasion the chairmen have so used their power that they obstructed entire sessions of Congress. The first of these arbitrary chairmen was Philip Campbell of Kansas, who sported a Napoleonic curl in the center of his forehead. In the 1920's, he devised a technique, actually a personal pocket veto of special rules, that prevented the House from acting on bills that he opposed. "You can go to hell," he once roared at outraged members of the House. "It makes no difference what a majority of you decide. If it meets with my disapproval, it shall not be done. I am the committee. In me reposes absolute obstructive powers." [27] In time, Campbell lost his pocket veto, and his seat in the House, but the chairman still had enormous power. In 1931, a member of the House formally complained that Rules Committee Chairman Bertrand Snell of New York had more power than even the President of the United States. "He can choke to death any piece of legislation," the House member said of Snell.[28]

Occasionally a Rules Committee chairman outmaneuvered even a majority of his own committee if he had the wit or the nerve to push his powers as chairman. Adolph Sabath of Illinois, chairman from 1940 to 1952, outfoxed no less a tactician than Eugene Cox of Georgia in one extraordinary instance, although he had to fake a heart attack to succeed. Cox, second ranking Democrat on the committee, wanted to vote on a resolution to change the committee's rules so that any committee member could call up bills for votes even if the chairman objected. Sabath, then in his eighties, begged Cox not to insist on the resolution. Sabath, his voice breaking, pleaded that he had a weak heart. "Mr. Cox, this will kill me, if you pass this resolution. The humiliation! It will kill me." Cox, leader of the Southern Democrats in the House, was adamant. "I don't care," he said. "You have delayed this too long." Sabath abruptly lurched forward, pitched out of his committee chair and fell sprawling onto the carpeted floor at Cox's feet. He lay motionless. Cox leaped up. "My God," he exclaimed, "I've killed him!" Committee members rushed to Sabath's aid; four of them carried him into the chairman's adjoining office, and laid him out on a large leather couch. All of the committee members, except Clarence Brown of Ohio, dashed off to get medical help. Brown, still puffing from the exertion of carrying Sabath to the couch, stood watch over the prostrate chairman. As Brown watched, Sabath opened one of his eyes, and stole a look around the room. "Why you old rascal," roared Brown, "there's nothing wrong with you."

"Well," said Sabath, smiling, "Mr. Cox didn't get his resolution, did he?" [29]

In less dramatic fashion, Howard Smith of Virginia, who first became chairman in 1955, once blocked passage of a half-dozen important bills, including a housing bill anxiously desired by many city governments. A delegation of mayors from almost every major American city called on Speaker Rayburn to ask for House action on the housing bill, and Rayburn promptly sent them to see Smith, whose committee had to adopt a special rule if the bill were to be enacted. When the mayors tried to find Smith, they discovered he was not in the Capitol. He had, in fact, left town, and he did not return to Washington until it was too late to pass the housing bill. Without him, there was no practical way to call the committee into session that late in the year. Smith expressed mock surprise that he had been missed from Capitol Hill. He had only gone down to his farm, he explained blithely, to check on the damage that an untimely rain storm had done to his crop of hay.

In 1937, the Rules Committee bolted from the control of the majority party leaders, then Speaker William Bankhead of Alabama and his floor leader Sam Rayburn of Texas. The committee still had members sympathetic and responsive to the party leaders and to President Franklin Roosevelt's program that these leaders tried to enact, but a majority of the committee, led by Chairman John O'Connor of New York, established the committee as a power bloc independent of the formal party leaders. For almost a quarter of a century, until the epic struggle between Speaker Rayburn and Rules Committee Chairman Howard Smith in 1961, the committee preserved its independence of the Democratic leaders. Only in the two terms of Speaker Martin in the Eightieth and Eighty-third Congresses, did the committee respond favorably to the Speaker's wishes. In these many years, the Rules Committee established itself as a censor of House legislation. Repeatedly, the committee required the sponsors of bills to alter the provisions of those bills to suit the views of the conservative majority of the committee. Although the Rules Committee had no jurisdiction over the substance of legislation—its function historically had been political rather than legislative—the committee in these years did not hesitate to force a legislative committee to amend bills that committee wanted cleared for floor action. To refuse the terms of the Rules Committee was to tempt the Rules Committee to refuse to send the bill to the House floor with a special rule. More frequently the Rules Committee simply pigeonholed the bill. It did so with the Wage and Hour bill of 1937, the bill that prompted the first cohesion of the bipartisan conservative coalition that was to harass the leadership of Sam Rayburn until the last of his seventeen years as Speaker. The Republicans and Southern Democrats on the committee cooperated to block floor action on that bill—it was later passed by the House under a Discharge Petition—and from then for twenty-four years they controlled the committee and voted together against the economic welfare bills sent to Congress by Presidents Roosevelt, Truman, Eisenhower, and Kennedy. Charles Halleck, a member of the Rules Committee before he became his party's floor leader, defined the committee's function far differently than did those who believed it should be responsive to the majority party leaders: the committee, he said, was a "roadblock to unwise, ill-timed, spendthrift, socialistic measures." [30] In short, the committee had a broader function than merely expediting legislation; it had the responsibility to make a judgment, independently, on whether a bill should be passed by the House. This view, shared by the Democratic and Republican conservatives on the committee, made the committee, a great center of power, independent of the Democratic Speaker.

This independence, however, broke down even in the days of the committee's deepest hostility to the program desired by Speaker Rayburn. In his four years as Speaker, Joseph Martin had no difficulty with the Rules Committee, as he himself acknowledged. He had been a member of the committee and he shared the conservative views of the committee's majority. For Rayburn, however, dealing with the Rules Committee was one of his most difficult problems. Rayburn supported the liberal programs of Roosevelt and Truman and Eisenhower, and, if they were to be enacted, he had to find ways of persuading the Rules Committee to permit these bills to go to the floor. The House of Representatives had become so dependent on the Rules Committee, on the need to use its powers to limit debate and amendments, that no other course was satisfactory. The Rules Committee could be bypassed. It could not resist a Discharge Petition that, if signed by a majority of the House, freed the bill from the Rules Committee and brought it to the House floor for a vote. The Rules Committee also could not prevent the use of Calendar Wednesday to bring legislation it blocked to the House floor. These procedures, however, were cumbersome and difficult to execute.

Rayburn cracked the Rules Committee's reluctance to report out bills the conservatives opposed by persuading his personal friends among the committee's conservatives to help him. He depended most, from 1937 to 1953, on his close personal friend Eugene Cox of Georgia. Later Rayburn depended on his close friend Joseph Martin, the Republican leader, to help persuade one of two of the conservative Republicans to vote for the bills Rayburn felt he needed. Cox, long a member of the Rules Committee and long the leader of the Southern conservative bloc in the House, held great influence in the committee although he never achieved the rank of chairman. He frequently called on Rayburn in the Speaker's office to discuss legislation. Rayburn, when he needed help in getting a bill through the Rules Committee, simply asked Cox for that help, even though Cox himself opposed the bill. "Do you really need this?" Cox asked Rayburn, on bill after bill. When Rayburn said he did, Cox, if he could, arranged for the bill to be cleared by the Rules Committee for a vote on the House floor. Why did Cox do it? Rayburn was his friend. "He was an ornery fellow," said Rayburn of him, and he was devoted to Rayburn. Cox once knocked down a newspaperman who wrote a disparaging story about Rayburn. "He loved me," Rayburn said.[31]

Frequently, however, Rayburn could do nothing with the Rules Committee and its conservative majority. In 1956, for example, the committee struck down a massive housing bill sponsored by Albert Rains of Alabama and supported by the Speaker. "The bill represents eighteen months of hard work," Rains said at the time, "and they killed it in eight minutes—without even reading it."[32] Year after year, similar bills were defeated by the Rules Committee, often by the votes of as few as six of its members.

Despite the massive Democratic majority swept into the House by President Roosevelt's landslide victory in 1936 (the Democrats won 333 of the House's 435 seats), the Rules Committee effectively blocked the President's New Deal programs. The House adopted Roosevelt's Wage and Hour bill in 1938, only by bypassing the Rules Committee, but the passage of that bill marked the end of the New Deal. Thereafter, the House and its Rules Committee stood in the way of Roosevelt's welfare legislation, and the roadblocks it created in 1937 and 1938 were still working in 1961 when President Kennedy entered the White House. Roosevelt vented his fury at the Rules Committee in 1938 by placing the committee chairman, Democrat John O'Connor of New York, on his famous "purge" list of that year. O'Connor, by happenstance, was the only member of Congress on that list who was defeated that year for re-election. In the years after, the committee blocked many bills, bills to liberalize the minimum wage, to admit Hawaii and Alaska as states, to build schools, and to aid depressed areas among them. By 1961 Rayburn reluctantly agreed to take steps to seize political control of the committee. Cox had died. Martin had been replaced by Charles Halleck as the Republican leader. Rayburn saw no other way to move President Kennedy's welfare bills through the House than by altering the political balance of the committee. This he did, in one of the most bitter fights the House had ever experienced.

Rayburn disliked to move against the Rules Committee, for essentially he was a political leader who preferred to work directly with individuals, with friends like Eugene Cox or Joseph Martin. He eschewed the institutional forms of party leadership, like the party caucus and steering committee, as means to set party stances and to enlist party support. He worked instead with the able men of the House, a group that came to be known as Rayburn's protégés. They included such men as Francis Walter of Pennsylvania, one of the House's ablest parliamentarians; Wilbur Mills of Arkansas, who rose to be chairman of the Ways and Means Committee; and many of his fellow Texans in the House. Rayburn's Democratic party had long suffered major divisive splits on both economic and racial beliefs, and Rayburn concentrated on minimizing this divisiveness of his party. "He is the glue that holds the Democrats together," one House colleague said of him.[33] "The avoidance of open controversy," said another, "is his genius." [34]

In modern times, both major political parties in the House have operated party steering committees, even though, technically, this has been the role of the Rules Committee. Under Speaker Gillett, in the early 1920's, a Republican steering committee was formed to shape party action in the House. Gillett, who made no effort to guide the House's direction on legislation, acquiesced to the steering committee's decisions. His floor leader, Nicholas Longworth, however, soon had himself made a member, and then *de facto* chairman, of the group. When Longworth became Speaker, he gradually swallowed the steering committee's functions, for he took over the direction of the party's action himself. The Democrats, under Speaker Henry Rainey, in 1933, also created a steering committee, and it existed into the 1940's when Rayburn first became Speaker. Rayburn, however, soon obliterated the steering commitee's role by depending on his own friends in the House, rather than an institutional group, for guidance and help in setting the course of the House. Longworth, like Rayburn, preferred to operate informally with men he trusted and liked, and it was not an accident that Rayburn continued the "Board of Education" that Longworth had begun as his almost casual political headquarters. Speaker McCormack, for many years a member of Rayburn's inner circle, knew the value of the "Board of Education" and he continued it as a functional part of his leadership after he succeeded Rayburn as Speaker. A strong Speaker, such as Longworth and Rayburn, disliked the existence of formal groups like the steering committees. John Nance Garner as Speaker opposed a steering committee as an "undesirable" limitation on his powers. Rainey, in giving his reasons for supporting a steering committee, in effect gave Garner's exact reason for opposing it: "It takes from the Speaker power he has arbitrarily exercised and gives it back to the House." [35]

Rayburn had a slightly different reason, the same reason he objected to using the party caucus as the means of establishing party positions. "I think caucuses are a waste of time." Rayburn said. "You lose more votes than you gain." [36] Rayburn's objection to the party caucus applied primarily to his own Democratic party, for, divided as it was, the Democratic party caucus called to set party positions on legislation could only end in further irritating the party's factions. The Republicans in the House, not divided so sharply on such basic political issues as the Democrats, have not been confronted with the same problem. Indeed, the Republicans in recent years have frequently called party conferences—actually a party caucus called by another name—to discuss pending legislative questions. They have hesitated, however, to try to bind their party members to vote unanimously on one side of a bill, as Speaker Cannon once did. They have also operated a party policy committee, a representative group established to discuss and plan legislative and party policies. Under Speaker Martin, this policy group scarcely functioned, for Martin, like Rayburn and Longworth, preferred to deal directly and informally with the members of his party and to avoid such formal groups. When Halleck overthrew Martin as party leader, he reinstated the Republican Policy Committee as a major piece of party apparatus, under the chairmanship of John Byrnes of Wisconsin, one of Halleck's ablest lieutenants. The committee took upon itself the task of rebuilding the confidence and self-assurance of Representatives in the Republican ranks, dispirited from repeated election losses by their party. The group served not only to articulate party policy, but to present its members' views to President Eisenhower. The House Democrats could scarcely afford such a committee, for the divided nature of their party inevitably would have led to bitter party dissension. The split personality of the Democratic party has existed for many years in the House. "Nobody," said Democratic leader Charles Crisp of Georgia in the 1890's, "can lead this wrangling, quarrelsome, factionalized Democratic minority." [37] In recent years, almost every House vote has shown the depth of the party split, with large numbers of Democrats on each side of the question. The split has made party leadership and party discipline difficult to impose.

The House leaders have had but little power to discipline their party members. Party patronage has had only small effect on House discipline, primarily because there has been so little of it available for the party leaders to dispense. When a House leader's party also has controlled the executive branch of government, the leader has been able, at times, to dangle inducements in front of some of his party members to encourage them to vote the party position. House members traditionally have controlled appointments of United States postmasters and United States attorneys in their Congressional districts, and, of course, the Postmaster General and other cabinet officers frequently have held the power to decide where to build post offices and other federal buildings.

The House itself has employed several hundred men and boys every year as pages, elevator operators, Capitol police, and doorkeepers. These minor positions have been the major patronage available to party members on Capitol Hill, but few members of the House have taken more than cursory interest in those who have received these jobs. Francis Walter of Pennsylvania, for ten years chairman of the Democratic Patronage Committee under Speaker Rayburn, knew of only one instance in which the dispensing of House jobs altered a vote on a pending bill. Rayburn came to Walter one day and asked him to assign two House patronage jobs to Usher Burdick of North Dakota, a Republican. "If we give Burdick a couple of jobs," said Rayburn, "I think he'll vote with us on this bill." [38]

A more substantive method for the House leaders to influence the voting and behavior of their rank and file has been through the leader's power over committee assignments and legislation. Every House member has always wanted assignment to a choice committee post, to a committee with prestige and power. Although these assignments have been formally alloted by the party's Committee on Committees, the party leaders have always played a central role in the disbursement of the best assignments. In 1959, Charles Porter of Oregon, a Democrat, went to Speaker Rayburn to solicit his help to win a seat on the Foreign Affairs Committee. Rayburn bluntly turned him down. Porter, by his behavior inside and outside the House, had offended both the

Speaker and his fellow Democrats, and Rayburn had no mind to reward him with such a prize. In recent years, both parties have been reluctant to penalize their party members for party irregularity by denying them committee assignments or removing them from choice committees to which they had earlier been assigned. Speaker Cannon, in 1909, did not hesitate to so punish fourteen insurgent Republicans, and in 1925 Speaker Longworth acted in precisely the same way, removing thirteen progressive Republicans from major House committees. Among those Longworth punished was James Frear of Wisconsin, who was denied his seat on the prestigious Ways and Means Committee. In 1961, Speaker Rayburn briefly considered removing William Colmer of Mississippi from the Rules Committee, but then Rayburn decided instead to take personal control of the committee by adding three extra members to it. For refusing to vote for that change, Representative John Flynt of Georgia publicly charged that he was denied assignment to the Appropriations Committee. Rayburn and other recent House leaders, however, generally preferred to use little more than personal appeals to persuade their party's members to stick with the leaders on a given vote. "I hope you can come along with us on this vote," or some such appeal as "We can use your help on this one, if you can see your way clear," normally has been the type of appeal that a House leader has made in recent years. Rayburn never liked House Democrats making their independence of his leadership a chronic habit, but he rarely did more than show the recalcitrant member his annoyance.

The Speaker and floor leader, however, have had many ways of showing their friendship and approval of men of talent and party loyalty. One of the most obvious has been for the Speaker to call a promising young Representative to the rostrum and let him preside over the House in the late afternoon hours while his colleagues make speeches. A more marked token of the Speaker's respect has been for him to ask a member to serve as chairman of the Committee of the Whole House, an assignment to preside over the House when the House has been both debating and amending major legislation. Such assignments, denoting the

Speaker's approval of a member, have always been carefully watched by members of the House. The men receiving them have acquired immediately, in the inner life of the House, recognition by their fellows as friends of the Speaker with the added influence and prestige that such friendship has always meant. These assignments have denoted that the men receiving them have become members, if only minor members at times, of the Speaker's trusted inner circle. Men called frequently to the chair by the Speaker have even acquired the reputation of being likely successors to the Speaker. Other lesser forms of rewards have also been available to the House leaders. Every year, for example, a freshman member of the majority party has been selected to read to the House, on George Washington's birthday, Washington's Farewell Address. The assignment has not been given to obstreperous, recalcitrant party members.

As effective as any help the House leaders have been able to offer their party members has been financial and personal assistance in the members' campaign for re-election. "They somehow always seem to have a few thousand dollars at their disposal in a campaign," one Representative said.[39] Both major political parties in the House have long operated their own campaign committees, designed to help party members win re-election. The Republican committee, by far the more influential of the two, was started in 1866, when the House Republicans revolted against the man nominally their party's President, Andrew Johnson, and established their own campaign committee. In recent years, these committees have been able to help party members financially and also by sending prominent party spokesmen, including the House leaders, into their districts during the campaign. In the 1960 campaign, House Republican Campaign Chairman William Miller of New York, who later became National Republican Chairman, allotted as much as $10,000 to individual Republicans seeking election or re-election to the House. The Democratic Campaign Committee has had to operate on far less funds. Such political contributions immensely eased the recipient's major problem of financing his campaign. Republican leaders of the House have in recent years occasionally threatened to cut off these campaign contributions to party members unduly independent of their leadership. Such threats, however, have had relatively small influence, because no party leader could reasonably be expected to go to the extreme of helping to defeat a party member and thereby helping to elect an opposition party member.

The House Democrats, however, have had a method of dealing with some few of their party members that amounted to near tyranny over them on critical party votes. The technique has been limited to party stalwarts from those cities where the party organization has been unusually strong, so strong that it controlled the nominations of those put up for election. Tammany Hall, in recent years an ineffective force in the House of Representatives, once could direct its members how to vote on bills coming before the House. Rayburn once privately described how this was done by John Carew, Tammany's boss of the New York City delegation in the House during the 1920's. Carew, said Rayburn, bunched his New York Democrats in the front row of the House. Then he shook his fist in their faces and said: "God damn it, you'll vote for this thing, or you won't come back here. I'll see that you don't get renominated." [40] Rayburn recalled another Tammany leader who insisted that his men in the House improve their poor record of attendance on the floor of the House. He told them that if they did not want to attend the sessions of the House, there were others back home who did. The Tammany men took alarm, Rayburn said, and thereafter took prominent front seats in the House for each session. This strict party discipline over the Tammany men in the House broke down in the 1930's, but it was imitated by similar discipline in the ranks of the Chicago Democrats. Thomas O'Brien, onetime sheriff of Cook county, has been the boss of the Chicago Democrats in the House in recent years. He did not brook independence among his men on important votes. He used to call on Rayburn in the Speaker's office. "Mr. Speaker," he would ask, "how do you want the boys to vote?" Rayburn then would tell him. "That's the way they'd vote," Rayburn said. "If Tom O'Brien doesn't want those fellows to come back to the House, they don't come back." [41] William Green of Pennsylvania, political boss of Philadelphia, has denied he has used any similar threats of disciplinary action in keeping his colleagues from Philadelphia in harmony with party policy, but the Philadelphians in the House normally have voted together. "On party matters," Green said, "we are usually agreed ninety-eight or ninety-nine per cent of the time. We usually talk it over before the vote." [42]

Such militant control of individual delegations has provided the House leaders with only limited and specific power over a few House delegations. In the main, the leaders have had to depend on their own persuasion and the instinct of every party member to vote with his party. In a larger sense, however, the House leaders have held power beyond the mere political control of their colleagues, and that power has stemmed from their command of the House's legislative agenda. On them has rested the initiative of the House of Representatives in deciding what bills should be processed each session. They have borne the major responsibility both for the House's action and inaction on legislation. A bill opposed by the House leaders has had little chance of enactment, but a bill endorsed by the leaders has not had automatic approval by the House. "When the work of the session is done," said John Tilson of Connecticut, Republican floor leader in the 1920's, "it will probably be said with truth that the most important work I have done during the session has been in the direction of preventing the passage of bad or unnecessary laws." [43] The decisions of the leaders, the Speaker and his lieutenants, have largely written the record of the House each session, and every member of the House has had to justify himself to his voters back home on the basis of that record. How well the House leaders have made their judgments has often determined how well the individual members of the House have been able to make that justification. In a broader reality, however, the judgments of the leaders, of the men who run the House, have determined how well the House of Representatives itself has met the needs of the United States and the American people.

CHAPTER SIX

The Rank and File

No matter the skill of the House's leaders, no matter their eloquence or powers of persuasion, the decisions of the House of Representatives have rested, ultimately, on the rank and file of the members. The leaders of the House have been able to guide and even, at times, to overawe the House, but they have never held—not even the imperious Speakers of the past—the power to force the members of the House to go where they did not want to go. "Czar" Reed tried and failed; so did "Czar" Cannon, and in the modern House of Representatives the most effective leaders have been those who best read the mood and sentiments of the members of the House. The effective leader of the House, judging aright the mind of the House on a great question of state, could influence and modify the House's ultimate decision, but no leader has been able alone, or with his lieutenants, to force arbitrarily the House's action on any important issue. For example, the 1959 session showed a major and awkward misreading of the House's temper by its leaders. The previous Congressional election, held in the gloom of a major economic recession, had returned a massive Democratic majority to the House. The leaders of the House assumed, as did the nation's press, that the new House had a mandate from the people to spend the country's way out of the recession. This House, however, had an entirely different temper when it assembled in January, 1959. The fiscal budget of the Eisenhower administration was running the government heavily in debt, eventually $12 billion that year. A majority of the House members feared a further watering of the value of the dollar and the inflation that would bring. Almost immediately, the leaders of the House began to pull back their early plans to enact costly federal programs. By the Easter recess they had scrapped several and slashed all of their bills to build airports, highways, and other federal projects. The retrenchment had been forced by the sentiments of the rank-and-file members of the House, who were reflecting national concern about the fiscal stability of the federal government.

The shaping of the consensus of the House has been of great significance in national politics, for the members of the House must give their consent to every law by which the American people are governed. The leaders of the House have played a major role in shaping that consensus, and so, frequently, have members of the rank and file. Sam Rayburn and John McCormack persuaded the House to adopt, by the margin of one vote, a critical extension of the draft in 1941 just before Pearl Harbor. Members from the ranks have at times triggered House decisions just as effectively, if not as frequently. The mood of the House can be changed abruptly, but more frequently the House's mood, the consensus of its members on a given issue, has grown gradually, sometimes over long periods of time, in an enormously complex interplay of the individual Representatives among themselves and with their constituents, their party leaders, and the private groups interested in the question.

Every Representative, like every Congressional district, has been a complex product of the pulling and pushing of myriad individual, economic, social, and political pressures. The rank-and-file members of the House have scarcely had any other common denominators among themselves than their equal pay and the responsibility, technically, of representing a like proportion of the American people. The members of the House have been as different as the districts from which they have come, as different as a Texas range and a Brooklyn slum. In the Hall of the House have echoed all the diverse accents of the American people, and the members themselves have come to the House from as varied personal backgrounds as found in American life: lawyers, farmers, artists, economists, ranchers, truck drivers, journalists, military heroes, labor leaders, merchants, veterinarians, bankers, salesmen, coal miners, auctioneers, physicians, football players, aristocrats, teachers, and industrialists. Officially associated with a political party, every member of the House has had a presumed commitment to a party platform, but the voting records of almost every modern member have shown wide discrepancies and contradictions with his party's formal stance. With only minimal requirements to qualify—they need be only twenty-five years old, citizens of the United States for seven years, and residents of the state they represent—members have been elected to the House with educational standings ranging from illiteracy to graduate scholarship, with social standings ranging from first-generation immigrants to first-family gentry, with financial standings ranging from paupers to millionaires. Yet out of this conglomerate assembly of often conflicting and contradictory elements have come every year the decisions by which American law has been written.

The personal background of the individual member has had no necessary relationship to his effectiveness as a Representative. In mid-twentieth century a bricklayer could become, as John Fogarty of Rhode Island did, the House's foremost authority on medical research. A physician, Walter Judd of Minnesota, became the House's leading specialist on United States policy in Asia. A lawyer, Paul Kilday of Texas, who never served a day in uniform, became the House's most respected scholar on military regulations. The House of Representatives all through its history has had in its ranks men of great ability, ability often unsuspected when their districts first elected them to the House. And the members of the House have often been influenced by these men. Fred Marshall of Minnesota, for example, possessed a reputation for sound political balance. "If Fred Marshall can vote for this," one Representative said to another in 1960, "I guess I can, too." [1] These men, men like Marshall, Kilday, Judd, and Fogarty were

117

trusted by the House, and they helped shape the mood and temper, the mind of the House.

If the House has always displayed confidence in its men of capacity and judgment, the House's record through the years has been marked by the malfeasance and venality of some few of its other members. Perhaps the ugliest incident of all involved the Crédit Mobilier in the 1870's. A member of the House, Oakes Ames of Massachusetts, conspired to influence legislation by giving to the most influential men of the House shares of the Crédit Mobilier, a holding company for the Southern Pacific Railroad. Ames confessed that he allocated the stock "where it will produce the most good." The list of men to whom he gave the shares read like a roster of the House's leadership: Speaker Schuyler Colfax of Indiana, James G. Blaine of Maine and James A. Garfield of Ohio, Republican leaders, and James Brooks of New York, the Democratic floor leader, among them. The unsavory transaction wrecked the career of Colfax and cast a dark shadow across the careers of Garfield, who later became President, and of Blaine, who became Speaker.

As Peter Dunne's Mr. Dooley once said, no member of Congress ever corrupted himself, and the House had instances of corruption of its members both before and after the Crédit Mobilier scandal. In the 1850's a member, Orsamus Matteson of New York, resigned to escape expulsion on charges that he conspired to pass legislation by bribing his fellow members. Ben Perley Poore reported that in the 1830's the Bank of the United States, then a major political issue, had to discount the worthless bank notes of several members of Congress whose support for the bank was won by so doing. In 1870, a Representative from South Carolina, Benjamin Whittemore, resigned to avoid expulsion from the House for selling appointments to West Point and Annapolis. George Hoar of Massachusetts, in his autobiography, said at least three other Representatives were guilty of the same charge.

In modern times, criminal charges have been brought against several members of the House. James Michael Curley of Massachusetts was convicted and sent to jail in 1947 for mail fraud. In

1914 a House committee investigated the activities of James Mc-Dermott of Illinois who, a witness testified, privately boasted that he had received $7,500 from pawnbrokers in the District of Columbia to help defeat a bill. McDermott resigned from the House. More recently, in 1956, Thomas Lane of Massachusetts, was convicted of tax evasion and spent four months in jail while continuing as a member of the House.

From time to time, members of the House have become involved improperly with women. In the 1960's, for example, several such instances were the common gossip of the Speaker's lobby. One Representative's staff resigned because of the alleged indecent proposals he made to his secretary and stenographers. Another had the need for and hired an abortionist. Still another was threatened with formal charges for seducing a young matron. Such activities were not new to the House. One of the oldest and closest-held secrets of the House's inner life was the cause for the unexpected and startling retirement of one of the House's best-known members in the early years of the twentieth century, Speaker David Henderson of Iowa; a United States Senator threatened to kill him, unless he promptly left Washington. The Senator had discovered, according to one of the House's most respected members decades later, that Henderson had had an improper relationship with the Senator's daughter. In the 1880's, a newspaper reporter saw plain evidence in the Hall of the House of some members' relationships with local prostitutes. "I have spotted them in the private galleries reserved for the members' families," wrote Frank Carpenter, "where a member of Congress must have furnished the ticket for their admission." [2] In 1848, Abraham Lincoln of Illinois, then a member of the House, saw a House colleague escorting a whore. "He went home with her," Lincoln wrote, "and if I were to guess, I would say, he went away a somewhat altered man—most likely in his pockets, and in some other particular. The fellow looked conscious of guilt." [3]

The House has also contained, from time to time, men of great personal flamboyance and men of exceptional ignorance. Alexis de Tocqueville recorded, on his visit to the House in 1831, that there were members of the House who could not read or write. In the 1880's, a member from Illinois could scarcely spell; he thought the smallest state in the Union was "rode iland." In the 1840's, a famous violinist gave a concert in Washington and was interrupted in one delicate passage by a roar from Felix Grundy McConnell of Alabama. "None of your high-falutin'," McConnell bellowed, "but give us 'Hail Columbia,' and bear hard on the treble!" [4] An Arkansas Representative, of more recent times, complained to the House in 1937 that the bureaucrats in the Civil Service Commission were making job applicants answer a lot of "psychological questions" that "ordinary people" and "old timers" could not understand. As already noted, the House occasionally has held men like "Sockless" Jerry Simpson of Kansas and David Crockett of Tennessee, the renowned Davy Crockett of the old frontier, as picturesque as any man to serve in the House. Elected in 1827, Crockett served three terms and then rode off to Texas and died in the Alamo. Some of the early Tammany men from New York were equally bizarre. John Morrissey, heavyweight champion of the world in 1858, a gambler, and a ballot-box stuffer, held a seat in the House for two terms and it was said he controlled a percentage in the leading faro game in Washington. Timothy "Big Tim" Sullivan, Tammany's strong-arm boss of the Bowery, after two terms quit the House. "There's nothing in this Congressman business," he laughed. "They know 'em in Washington. The people down there use 'em as hitchin'-posts. Every time they see a Congressman on the streets, they tie their horses to him." [5] Timothy "Tim" Campbell, another of Tammany's Representatives, once asked President Cleveland to sign a pension bill that Cleveland believed unconstitutional. Campbell threw an arm familiarly around the President's shoulders. "What's the Constitution between friends?" he asked. [6]

John Quincy Adams' career in the House stood in marked contrast to those of his lesser colleagues. Entering the House as a freshman member in 1831, two years after leaving the Presidency, Adams won there what Speaker Blaine called a fame as "enduring as the Republic whose history he adorned." [7] Adams took upon himself the task of repealing a rule of the House, adopted at the insistence of Southern firebrands, that forbade the acceptance of petitions on Negro slavery. Day after day, year in year out, Adams argued for the repeal of the rule. "The House has no right," he said in 1836, "to take away or abridge the Constitutional right of petition." [8] Adams won this fight in 1844, when the House finally rescinded the rule and restored fully the right of the people to petition their government. Despite his fierce encounters on the floor, Adams won the deep respect of the whole House. In 1848, Adams collapsed on the floor of the House. He was carried to the Speaker's private room and there he died, after an astonishing career as United States Senator, negotiator of the Treaty of Ghent, United States minister to Russia and England, Secretary of State, President, and finally, for seventeen years, a member of the House.

Adams' career in the House was unique, but there have been many others who graced the Hall with their eloquence, personal character, and upright morality. Many of these rose to the formal leadership of the House, some to the Speakership, but others merely served in the ranks of the House and in the ranks won the respect and confidence of their fellows. In Adams' day, Joshua Giddings of Ohio and Alexander Stephens of Georgia were known as men of intrepid courage. In Clay's House, among the men deeply respected were Langdon Cheves of South Carolina and Richard Johnson of Kentucky, Daniel Webster of New Hampshire, and Philip Barbour of Virginia. Even earlier, there had been Roger Griswold and Uriah Tracy of Connecticut, and Theodore Sedgwick of Massachusetts. In later years, those after the Civil War, the House was graced with George Hoar of Massachusetts and Lucius Quintus Cincinnatus Lamar of Mississippi, the luster of whose personal probity and honor brightened the dark time in which they served.

Over the years, the House has nicknamed many of its members. Henry Clay was known nationwide as the "Mill Boy of the Slashes," and the House followed the practice of applying even more colorful titles to later members. One member, Joseph Walker of Massachusetts, was called the "Gray Eagle of Quinsigamond." Tristam Burgess of Rhode Island, snowy haired with a Roman nose, was known as the "Bald Eagle of the House."

Another Representative, James Belford of Colorado, was honorably called the "Redheaded Rooster of the Rockies," and the nation at large knew Richard Parks Bland of Missouri, persistent advocate of the free coining of silver, as "Silver Dick."

The members of the House were not always kind in the nicknames they gave their fellows. Luman Weller of Iowa, for example, was known as "Calamity" Weller, and Samuel Beardsley of New York was known as "Perish Credit" Beardsley. He had once shouted at his colleagues: "Perish credit! Perish commerce! Perish trade!" Walter Butler of Iowa sponsored a bill to make the pansy the national flower, and he paid the consequences by being labeled "Pansy" Butler. In the House of the 1830's, sat Samuel "Previous Question" Cushman of New Hampshire, so named because of his demands to cut off debate by invoking the Previous Question. Speaker Joseph Cannon was known, affectionately, as "Uncle Joe." The modern House of Representatives has also nicknamed many of its members. John Nance Garner of Texas was widely known as "Cactus Jack," in token of his tough fiber. William Bankhead of Alabama, Speaker from 1937 to 1940, was affectionately known as "Mr. Will," much as Sam Rayburn was called "Mr. Sam." Carl Vinson of Georgia, chairman of the Armed Services Committee, collected a variety of names: "Uncle Carl," the "Admiral," and the "Old Swamp Fox." Clarence Cannon of Missouri, the pinched-faced chairman of the Appropriations Committee, was called the "Mole." Once, when Cannon was accused of being two faced, he snapped: "If I had another face, don't you think I'd use it?" [9] Another member was Frank "Everything Is Made for Love" Boykin of Alabama, a name taken from his campaign slogan, and another from Indiana became known as Randall "Front-Porch" Harmon after it was discovered that he had charged the government to rent the front porch of his home in Indiana.

The nicknames sometimes connoted affection, sometimes scorn, sometimes respect for the individuals named. They did not necessarily suggest the effectiveness of these individuals, but there could be little doubt of the meaning of the nickname the members of the House gave John Quincy Adams. They called him "Old Man Eloquent."

In Adams' day, the House gave only the slightest attention to a member's seniority. The theory and practice of the seniority system has been a political development, actually a political phenomenon, of the twentieth century. In the twentieth-century House, the most effective men of the House have usually been those with the greatest seniority, and, therefore, usually the older men. Under the seniority rules that developed—they were actually precedents rather than rules, for they have never been formally adopted—a Representative grew greater and greater in personal power the longer he remained in the House. This personal power was frequently an ephemeral thing difficult to dissect. It could be seen best, perhaps, in the effect these men had on their colleagues, for it was given to them, in many instances to influence the House's major decisions, to help form that consensus of the members that decided the House's response to the pressing problems of the nation.

In the nineteenth century, a Representative's seniority counted for very little. Henry Clay was elected Speaker of the House on his first day as a member. The Speakers all through the nineteenth century tended to be young men, short on seniority. Clay was only thirty-four when he was chosen Speaker. Robert Hunter of Virginia was elected Speaker when he was thirty. Robert Winthrop of Massachusetts was thirty-eight, and Nathaniel Banks, also of Massachusetts was thirty-nine.

The turnover of the House of Representatives in these years was enormous. Frequently more than half the members of a newly assembled House were taking the oath of office for the first time. The average term of members in mid-nineteenth century was only four years, and only one, "Pig-Iron" Kelley, served continuously through the twenty years between 1861 and 1881. During this period every newly assembled House—ten in all— contained a majority of members serving their first terms. A dramatic transformation took place by 1961. In that House, the Eighty-seventh, fifty-one Representatives had served twenty years or more, nineteen had served more than twenty-five years, ten had served thirty years, three had just been elected to their twentieth two-year term, and two others, Sam Rayburn and Carl Vinson, had been elected to the House for the twenty-fifth consecutive time. In 1961 the average service for members of the House was almost ten years. In institutional meaning, the increase in the average tenure of the Representatives brought a marked change in the House. Rayburn himself noted the difference over the nearly fifty years he served in the House. The Representatives of 1961, he said, were smarter, better equipped, and better educated than those he first met in the House of 1913.

In the last century, many Congressional districts deliberately rotated their Representatives in the House. They did so partially because the voters regarded the seats in the House as something of a good thing, two years in Washington, that ought to be passed around to as many men as possible. The voters also believed, with Andrew Jackson, that a true democracy required the constant changing of public officers, that otherwise a sort of official oligarchy would be established in the United States. Abraham Lincoln was elected in 1846 from such a Congressional district in Illinois. He wanted to run for re-election to the House in 1848. "If nobody else wishes to be elected," Lincoln wrote a friend, "I could not refuse the people the right of sending me again." [10] Someone else did want the job, however, and Lincoln kept his advance commitment to serve only one term. Gradually, in the late years of the previous century, this rotation of House seats began to give way, as it became increasingly obvious that the longer a Representative served, the better he could perform. The state of Maine conclusively proved the case against rotation. At one time, in 1895, the Maine delegation in the House numbered only four men, and they all but totally controlled the House of Representatives. Thomas Reed was Speaker and chairman of the Rules Committee, Nelson Dingley was chairman of the Ways and Means Committee and majority floor leader as well, Charles Boutelle was chairman of the Naval Affairs Committee, and Seth Milliken was chairman of the Public Buildings Committee. Each had long service in the House. No states learned the lesson that Maine taught better than those in the South, and the South's modern claim to an abnormally large share of committee chairmanships has sprung from the tendency of these states to keep sending the same men to the House year after year.

Not only have the members of the House tended to serve for longer periods, but the House itself decisively altered its views on seniority from those of the nineteenth century. Until the House revolt against Speaker Cannon in 1910, the Speaker had an almost free hand in assigning men to committees—and the career of an individual Representative could be made or broken by the committee assignments he received. Every two years, the Speaker assigned whom he pleased to whatever committee he pleased, and he designated as well the chairman. In 1827, for example, the Speaker named Churchill Cambreleng of New York chairman of the Interstate Commerce Committee, and in 1835 switched him to chairman of Ways and Means. In 1867, Civil War hero James Garfield of Ohio was made chairman of the Military Affairs Committee, and in 1871 the Speaker appointed him chairman of the Appropriations Committee. This power of the Speaker to name whom he chose to the House's committees gave him, of course, great power to discipline members of the House. At times, the Speaker even refused to name any members to any committees until the House approved an important bill he wanted passed.

In the latter part of the nineteenth century, a shift took place in the House's attitude toward committee assignments. The House came to feel, institutionally, that the longer a man familiarized himself with a given subject, the more he could know about that subject and the better he could deal with it. It was the beginning of individual specialization in the House, a concept that has grown stronger ever since. It was the beginning also of the seniority concept, of granting the individual Representative a formal "right" to the committee assignment he held, a right that carried over year after year, so long as he continued to be elected to the House. Out of this grew the right of the most senior majority party member of a committee automatically to become its chairman.

The House had a token of respect for seniority long before the seniority system had been developed as the House's now inviolable method of appointing committee chairmen. This was the House's kindly custom, reaching far back into its history, of naming its most senior member the "Father of the House." It was a title without portfolio, merely a token of affection for the member who had served longest. The office carried but one responsibility, and that solely a personal honor: the dean of the House normally administered the oath of office to each newly elected Speaker of the House. A dramatic change has taken place over the years, however, with the men who have held the title. In the early nineteenth century, the "Fathers of the House" tended to be relatively young men and they did not necessarily hold great influence in the House. Dixon Lewis of Alabama became "Father of the House" in 1843 when he was only forty-one years old. John Phelps of Missouri assumed the honorary title in 1859 when he was forty-five. Later in the century, the men so honored were older, usually in their sixties, and frequently their seniority was reflected in the power they held in the House. William "Pig-Iron" Kelley of Pennsylvania, who became dean of the House in 1875, was chairman of the Ways and Means Committee. In more recent years, the change was even more marked. Adolph Sabath of Illinois, chairman of the Rules Committee, was "Father of the House" when he died in 1952 at the age of eighty-six. He was succeeded as dean of the House by Sam Rayburn of Texas, long the House's Speaker. When Rayburn died in 1961 at age seventy-nine, he was succeeded as "Father of the House" by Carl Vinson of Georgia, seventy-eight years old and chairman of the powerful Armed Services Committee.

In the House that Henry Clay first entered in 1811, the centers of power were controlled by young men. Clay, at thirty-four, led an assembly in which many of the most powerful members were as young as he. Langdon Cheves of South Carolina, Clay's floor leader and chairman of Ways and Means, was thirty-five years old. Thomas Newton of Virginia, chairman of the Interstate Commerce Committee, was forty-three. Charles Ingersoll was thirty-one years old when he first became chairman of the Judiciary Committee. A century and a half later, the chairman of the Judiciary Committee was Emanuel Celler of New York, seventy-three years old and a veteran of thirty-eight years service in the House. Howard Smith of Virginia, chairman of the Rules Committee, was seventy-eight; Clarence Cannon of Missouri, chairman of the Appropriations Committee, was eighty-two, and Brent Spence of Kentucky, chairman of the Banking and Currency Committee, was eighty-seven. Together, Smith, Cannon, and Spence had then served a total of ninety-eight years in the House. The House had become, obviously a citadel of power for the men of seniority, men tested and proven over long years of partisan battling in the House committees and on the House floor. And the change altered the nature of the men who most influenced the House's decisions.

Curiously, however, the House has remained an institution for young men of ambition and talent. It long has been a school for men anxious to make names for themselves in national politics and it is so still. The Senate of 1961 had 43 out of its 100 members who had first won their spurs in the House. The Senate Democratic leader, Mike Mansfield of Montana, and the Senate's Republican leader, Everett Dirksen of Illinois, both were veterans of the House, as was the Senate's presiding officer, Vice President Lyndon Johnson of Texas. In the 1960 Presidential race, both major candidates, John Kennedy of Massachusetts and Richard Nixon of California, had made their political starts in the House of Representatives. Many of the House's ablest men moved on to the Senate or to state governorships in the twentieth century, much as they had done in the previous century, but many of the House's ablest men spent their political lives in the House of Representatives. Rayburn, Vinson, Smith, Celler, Cannon, and Spence were obvious examples, but there were many others, too. John McCormack of Massachusetts, Francis Walter of Pennsylvania, Joseph Martin of Massachusetts, John Taber of New York, Wright Patman of Texas, Leslie Arends of Illinois, George Mahon of Texas, Clare Hoffman of Michigan, and Charles Halleck of Indiana were among them. There were younger men, too, following their example and already rising in the House's hierarchy. Among these were Carl Albert of Oklahoma, Gerald Ford of Michigan, Wilbur Mills and Oren Harris of Arkansas, John Byrnes of Wisconsin, Hale Boggs of Louisiana, John Moss of California, and Albert Rains of Alabama. They shared a common dedication to the House as an institution of democratic government, and they shared also a common ingredient in their House careers: every one of them had first entered the House as a young man, before he was forty years old. Their careers offered additional evidence for a political phenomenon about the House first noticed by James G. Blaine in the 1880's. Almost without exception, Blaine wrote in his *Twenty Years of Congress,* the successful men in the House, the men who effectively influenced the House, first entered the House while they were still in their thirties or even younger. Sam Rayburn of Texas, first elected to the House at age thirty-one, in 1960 confirmed Blaine's observation of almost a century before. Rayburn in his forty-eight years in the House had noticed the same thing and he had an explanation for it. A man past forty, Rayburn said, normally had already developed his mental attitudes and habits: he must be younger, more flexible, and more facile and resilient intellectually to master the intricacies of the House's complicated procedures and methods. Starting young, they could expect, in time, to win a larger share than the freshman's lot in influencing the House.

Only a rare Representative has ever made a national reputation in his first term in the House. Henry Clay did so in 1811, and so did John C. Calhoun of South Carolina the following year. Calhoun, then only thirty, sponsored the Foreign Affairs Committee's recommendation of war with England and thereby won national notice immediately. J. William Fulbright of Arkansas, a freshman in the House in 1943, won a similar national celebrity that year when the House adopted his resolution calling for United States participation in what was to be the United Nations. The Fulbright resolution was a historic break with traditional American isolationism and made the thirty-eight-year-old Arkansan better known nationally than many leaders of the House. Occasionally, other freshmen members have caught the country's attention, but almost without exception, the new Representatives must submit to the inconspicuousness and anonymity that has been the lot of newcomers everywhere. "A freshman Congress-man is a lost soul," said Emanuel Celler of New York of his first year in the House in the 1920's. "He cannot find his way. . . . He doesn't know the rules and nobody bothers explaining them." [11] Woodrow Wilson noticed the same dismissal of the freshmen in the 1880's. "Possibly the members from his own state know him and receive him into full fellowship," Wilson wrote, "but no one else knows him, except as an adherent of this or that party, or as a newcomer from this or that state. He finds his station insignificant, and his identity indistinct." [12] In the modern House, the freshmen have still suffered the indignity of anonymity with hardly more to perform than the mortifying re-sponsibility of providing the House with a quorum. The leaders of the House, however, have expended more effort in recent years to help the new men, often offering helpful advice, which, when followed, has led to swifter promotion than mere seniority pro-vided. "Don't try to go too fast," Speaker Rayburn used to tell the freshmen. "Learn your job. Don't ever talk until you know what you're talking about. . . . If you want to get along, go along." [13] In 1959, some of the older members tried to help orientate the new men of that year. They held a series of private, bipartisan seminars for the freshmen at which they outlined the various aspects of the House's operations and suggested ways for the new men to become effective members of the House. Their advice did not differ in substance from that of Champ Clark, forty years before: the new man had to learn his job. "A man must learn to be a Representative or Senator," Champ Clark said, "just as he must learn to be a farmer, carpenter, blacksmith, merchant, engineer, lawyer, doctor, preacher, teacher or anything else. . . . The best plan for a constituency to pursue is to select a man of good sense, good habits, and perfect integrity, young enough to learn, and re-elect him so long as he retains his facul-ties and is faithful to his trust. Such a man grows into power and high position as surely as the sparks fly upward." [14]

The swiftest avenue to influence in the House, for the new member, has long been to specialize in some area of legislation. Champ Clark of Missouri, as a young man, asked Nelson Dingley of Maine, then at the height of his power in the House, for advice. "In order to make a great name for himself in Congress a man must be a specialist," said Dingley, himself a specialist in tariff legislation. "I have been in Congress for many years and I have watched and studied men as they have come and gone. . . . If a man be a specialist on a subject, if he knows more than the ordinary congressman knows or can hope to learn by mere dabbling, then he can compel Congress to listen to him, and he rises to be a power. That is the secret of success here." [15]

Garner had similar advice for the freshmen, a generation later. "You can't know everything well," he said to one freshman in 1925. "Learn one subject thoroughly. . . . Your colleagues here want information and will listen to a man who has knowledge of his subject." [16] The House of the 1960's contained a corps of skilled specialists, men and women who had followed the often-repeated advice of Dingley, Clark, Garner, and their successors on the best method for the new member to take a larger part in shaping the mind of the House on major questions. Each had built a reputation in his field, and when the House touched those fields, the specialists automatically came to the front. Their colleagues listened to them.

Over the decades, the House has had members who have specialized not on major areas, but on one specific idea, a personal "hobby." The Representative, year after year, would try to persuade the House to adopt his pet idea—and usually failed. In the contemporary House, there have been many hobbyists: Frank Bow of Ohio, anxious to repeal the Presidential "status of forces" agreements with foreign countries for the control of United States troops stationed in those countries; Thomas Pelly of Washington, the enemy of so-called back-door spending, an indirect method by which federal agencies financed their operations with loans from the Treasury; and Frank Chelf of Kentucky, whose personal crusade was to increase the House membership. Such hobbyists have long occupied the Hall of the House. William Robinson of New York, for example, harassed the House in the 1880's with his demand that the government buy Ireland and annex it to the United States. He won for himself the nickname the "Twister of the Tail of the British Lion." James Pearce of Maryland made the Congressional Library his hobby in the 1830's and 1840's and personally chose its books, refusing to allow any controversial books on the slavery question into the national library. William Craine of Texas earnestly pressed his idea that the President of the United States be inaugurated on the first Monday in April—even if it was April Fool's Day.

No subject for a personal hobby by a Representative has received more attention, over the years, than the plight of American Negroes. In recent years, Adam Clayton Powell of New York won national attention as the author of the so-called Powell amendment, a proposal to cut off federal funds in varying ways to states practicing racial segregation. The origins of the Powell amendment went back as far as 1819. In that year another New York Representative, James Tallmadge, offered an amendment to the Missouri bill that would have gradually abolished slavery in that new state. In 1846, David Wilmot of Pennsylvania offered a similar proposal, the so-called Wilmot Proviso, that would have forbidden Negro slavery in any of the territory then being taken from Mexico. The proposal touched off a national furor and made Wilmot nationally famous. Wilmot's Proviso, although never enacted into law, led to the Constitutional amendment outlawing slavery. This amendment increased the representation of the Southern states in the House, for it forced the counting of all Negroes in the census figures allocating House seats to the various states. This, in turn, led to another hobby by Northern Representatives: proposals to deny those extra House seats to any Southern state that prohibited Negroes from voting.

The hobbyists as a general rule rarely influenced the House's decisions, although Powell's antisegregation amendment frequently was blamed for defeating bills to which it was added. Adding the Powell amendment to a housing bill, or a school bill, simply prevented any Southerner from voting for that bill.

A more effective group of specialists in the House's history, however, have been the few individuals who assigned themselves the duty of guarding the House floor from legislative raids on the United States Treasury. Their targets normally have been pensions allotted too carelessly and federal projects in the home districts of Representatives. The weapons of these specialists have been a sound understanding of the House's rules and precedents, a sharp eye for detail, and the willingness and nerve to risk offending their fellow members. "He doesn't care what people think of him," said Speaker Rayburn of one of these modern specialists. Frequently a mere objection by a single Representative, or a point of order raised against the item, had the effect of preventing its passage by the House. The House, very early in its history, gave to these spoilers of special projects the informal title of "Watchdogs of the Treasury," or the "Great Objectors." They were titles awarded more out of respect than affection for the individual. The "Great Objector," by the very nature of his preoccupation, had to make himself unpopular with the members whose bills he blocked. Elisha Whittlesey of Ohio, in the 1830's, first won the title of "Watchdog of the Treasury," and he was succeeded in this role, in the 1860's by Elihu Washburne of Illinois. William Holman of Indiana took on the chore after Washburne, and one Speaker credited him with saving the government hundreds of millions of dollars by merely repeating, on bill after bill, year after year, the words: "I object." Holman did more than this, however, to earn his reputation. He devised a special rule of the House, ever after known as the "Holman Rule," that allowed certain legislative amendments to appropriations bills provided they reduced the amount of money in the bill. Holman was succeeded as the "Watchdog of the Treasury" by Constantine "Kicking-Buck" Kilgore of Texas. In the 1890's, the House normally set aside Friday nights for processing private bills, and the evening was popularly called "pension night" because of the type of bills normally considered. Kilgore usually stood in his place every Friday night and killed pension bills by the dozens. Speaker Reed, who admired Kilgore for his courage, once cleverly tricked him. Just as the House was about to start considering private bills, Reed directed Kilgore to take the Speaker's Chair and preside over the House. Acting as the House's presiding officer, Kilgore could not object to the bills that night.

In the twentieth-century House, other men have continued the role of the "Great Objector." In the 1930's, Robert Rich of Pennsylvania, a conservative who objected to most of the New Deal measures, made a career out of one oft-repeated question: "Where are you going to get the money?" A closer counterpart to Whittlesey, Washburne, Kilgore, and Holman, however, came into the House in 1949, H. R. Gross of Iowa. By special arrangement, Gross for years sponsored a bill numbered H. R. 144—one of the rarest of parliamentary phenomena, a legislative pun on the numbering of a bill. H. R. 144, like its sponsor H. R. Gross, proposed a reduction in federal spending. Gross concentrated his activities on the floor of the House. He faithfully attended every session, constantly demanding explanations of bills, constantly making points of order against amendments, and constantly objecting to bills requiring unanimous consent to pass. Gross over the years took a heavy toll of the pet projects of his colleagues and prevented the spending of many millions of dollars. Serving on only minor House committees and with no status as a House leader, Gross proved that a single Representative could have great influence in the House.

To become effective in the House of Representatives, an essential ingredient in the twentieth century was for the member to be repeatedly re-elected. For many members, those from marginal Congressional districts that tended to vote Republican one year and Democratic the next, this was a serious handicap. For many others, however, this was no problem, and the turnover in the House has sharply fallen in this century. In the nineteenth century, the House suffered an attrition of as many as two out of every three members in some elections. In recent years this attrition rate has dropped to only one out of every five or six. The House in the 1950's and 1960's had only about 100 of its 435 Congressional districts that could be considered marginal; that is, there were that few districts so closely divided politically as to make it doubtful whether they would return the same Representative to the House every two years. The Representatives from the other Congressional districts—more than three out of every four members of the House—had reasonable assurances that they could, if they wished, remain in the House for as long as they wanted. In the 1960 election, 349 successful candidates for the House won by margins of at least fifty-five per cent of the total vote in their Congressional districts. The margin of their victories gave most of these members, quite naturally, a greater confidence in their political safety than those who barely squeaked into office. This was a matter of profound importance to the House as an institution, for it gave the House a solidity in its rank and file that was not easily shaken. Most of the House's members, with firm support from their constituents, could not readily be pressured to alter their political views on pending legislation. At the same time, those Representatives from the marginal, doubtful districts often became the decisive members of the House. Their votes frequently could determine the outcome of the House's basic decisions on the major political and economic controversies of the time. It was on these marginal Representatives, the ones in doubt of re-election, that the lobbyists and the President himself concentrated their attention and their pressures in times of legislative controversy, for the direction in which these members swayed often decided the issue at hand.

Every two years, every member of the House has had to face his constituents for a renewal of his franchise to represent them in the House. The Founding Fathers deliberately required frequent elections to assure that the men elected to the House had an "immediate dependence" and "intimate sympathy," with the people for whom they spoke and acted. "Frequent election," wrote the authors of the *Federalist Papers* in 1788, "are unquestionably the only policy by which this dependence and sympathy can be effectually secured." [17] Even in the politically "safe" seats, those districts in the Democratic South and Democratic Northern cities, and the Republican rural strongholds of the Middle West, the Representatives have been challenged and defeated—normally in a primary—when they have neglected or ignored the views and wishes of their constituents. No Representative has ever done so without risking retribution from the voters.

In the early years of the Republic, electioneering for the House often was exuberant and flamboyant. Davy Crockett's exploits as a bear hunter were a major issue of his campaigns. Crockett claimed he had once shot 109 bears in a single year—and his opponent replied that Crockett's claim was an obvious lie because Crockett could not count that high. When another opponent accused Crockett of drunkenness, he refuted the charge by declaring that whiskey had not yet been distilled strong enough to make him drunk. A keg of whiskey or a barrel of beer was a certain way to round up a crowd, and a fiddler lent gaiety to the occasion. Frequently, the opposing candidates toured the district together, riding from meeting place to meeting place where they staged joint debates on the issues of the hour. Stephen Douglas of Illinois, in the 1840's, in one campaign canvassed his district for forty consecutive days with an opponent, debating every day except Sunday. In the twentieth century, closely divided districts have been as furiously contested, and the candidates have had at their disposal all the modern wonders of communication, radio and television as well as newspapers, to advertise their talents to the voters. With the explosion of suburban developments has come the campaign tactic of organizing local "kaffeeklatsches" to meet the candidate informally. More often in modern years the opponents have fallen to denouncing each other for failing to debate the issues then staging the old-fashioned stump debates of the nineteenth century. Personal charges against each other have remained popular, however. In a recent campaign, for example, one candidate charged that his opponent had evaded military service in war and the accused promptly countercharged that his accuser had shown no greater interest in public affairs than sponsoring a bill in the state legislature to solve the problem of stray cats. In time, many Representatives win automatic re-election to the House. Such a Representative was Charles Wolverton of New Jersey, who became ill in the midst of one of his sixteen successful campaigns for the House. "I hope he doesn't die," his opponent reportedly said, "because I would hate to lose to a dead man."

In the years of the House's most furious partisanship—from the outbreak of the slavery question in the 1830's to the revolt against Speaker Cannon in 1910—one of the individual Representative's additional hazards was to be deprived of his seat in the House after he had fairly won it in an election. It became common practice, in close elections, for the loser to challenge the right of his victorious opponent to take his seat in the House. And it became equally common practice for the majority party in the House to award the election to its candidate, no matter the merits of his opponent's claim to the seat. One House member, George Robinson of Massachusetts, quipped in the 1880's that the only politically partisan questions he knew in the House were "election cases." In the 1890's, Speaker Reed, who had ruthlessly thrown Democrats out of their House seats to increase his narrow Republican majority, said baldly that there probably had never been an instance of the majority party allowing a minority party member to keep a contested seat. Thaddeus Stevens of Pennsylvania, Republican floor leader in the 1860's, once asked the point at issue in a contested election case. "There is not much point to it," a colleague replied. "They are both damned scoundrels."

"Well," Stevens asked, "which is the Republican damned scoundrel? I want to go for the Republican damned scoundrel." [18]

The number of these contested elections, with the injudicious manner of their settlement on open invitation for the losers to challenge, multiplied rapidly in the post-Civil War years. By 1895, so many elections were challenged—thirty-one in that year—that the House had to create two extra committees to handle the investigations made necessary. As late as 1904, a distinguished leader of the House, Samuel McCall of Massachusetts, conceded that only in rare instances had a contested election case been decided fairly. The flagrant abuses of the people's right to choose their Representatives—there was no appeal from the House's majority decision—had created a long-standing public scandal. The House gradually responded to the weight of this public opinion, however, as it did in abolishing the binding effect of party caucus decisions. By 1920, it was possible to say that the House itself had grown weary of the scandals involved in the partisan handling of election cases and had begun to insist that reasonable grounds be made by the man declared the winner. Partisanship fell away rapidly, and by the 1950's and 1960's contested elections were rare. A tinge of the old violence remained, however, and one House leader as late as 1960 echoed

Thaddeus Stevens' theme. "I know he's an s.o.b.," he said, explaining his support of his party's candidate in a challenged election. "But he's our s.o.b." [19]

Another hazard to individual Representatives has been the periodic reapportionment of House seats among the several states every ten years. The American people have always been mobile, and the movement of population has required altering the distribution of House seats after almost every national census. The 1950 census, for example, required nine states to give up fourteen of their seats to seven other states. The 1960 census forced sixteen states to give up seats to nine other states. Such shifts have caused convulsions in the House. In 1961 and 1962, for example, the required changes altered the representation of twenty-five states whose House delegations contained 325 Representatives. For each, the redistricting could mean the hazard of his re-election. Until 1910, the House usually tried to soften the losses to state delegations by the simple expedient of increasing the total membership of the House. Thus Massachusetts, with fourteen Representatives in 1790, still had fourteen Representatives in 1960. Maryland had eight House seats in 1790 and seven in 1960. However, after "freezing" the House membership to 435 in 1912, the House found it increasingly difficult to resist pressures from inside the House to enlarge its membership. Primarily, members of the House did not want their own state delegations reduced in size. That not only cost the state's delegation prestige and power in the House, it also risked every member's seat in the delegation. Spurred by this inducement, in 1961, nearly a score of bills were introduced to add from four to thirty-four extra seats to the House's stationary 435 membership.[20] The following year, the House's leaders somewhat reluctantly tried to add three additional seats, and failed. The major objection was, as it long had been, that the House already was too large.

Losses to a state's delegation in the House has troubled members of the House from the earliest years. New Englanders, particularly, resented and resisted the growing importance and representation of the growing Western states. In 1832, John Quincy Adams spent "an entirely sleepless night," as he recorded, worrying about the losses to be suffered by New England in its representation in the House. "I was all night meditating in search of some device, if it were possible, to avert the heavy blow from Massachusetts and from New England," he wrote.[21] He found none.

An even more dangerous risk for the individual Representative was the possibility that a hostile state legislature at home might redraw the boundaries of his district so as to make it difficult or even impossible for him to be re-elected. There were ways to set the limits of a district so that the district would almost automatically send to the House the party man desired by the state legislature. This technique was first formalized and named in Massachusetts in 1812. The state legislature there so drew the boundaries for the seats in the state senate that the Federalist party in the following election won only eleven of the forty seats, even though a majority of the people voted for its candidates. The trick was performed by concentrating all the Federalists in a few districts. Gilbert Stuart, the noted portrait painter, sketched one of these specially designed districts to make it look like a monstrous dragon. "There," he said "that will do for a Salamander." "Salamander!" exclaimed the editor of the local newspaper. "Call it Gerrymander!" [22] Thus was the name of Elbridge Gerry, then governor of Massachusetts, made a part of the American language.

Gerrymandering became the word for all such finagling by state legislatures. Many were the techniques later devised, and the physical shapes of some of the districts thus formed were sometimes even comic. There was the famous "shoestring" district in Mississippi, 500 miles long and 40 miles wide, that was copied in principle later in Missouri, New York, and Illinois. There were the "bacon-strip" districts of North Carolina, designed to weaken Republican voting strength west of the Blue Ridge Mountains. There was the "belt-line" district that ringed Chicago, and the "submarine" district in upper New York State. Many districts were so shaped that they were called "dumb-bell" districts or "saddle-bag" districts. The Congress ostensibly outlawed such physical absurdities and directed as early as 1842 that the Congressional districts be composed of contiguous and compact territory, each district to have roughly the same number of inhabitants. The House, however, had no practical or acceptable means of enforcing this injunction, and gerrymandering has remained popular with all major political parties. Gerrymandering proved so successful that in many states, there were created Congressional districts so safe politically for one party that they could be compared with England's "rotten" boroughs.

As late as 1961, Emanuel Celler of New York, chairman of the Judiciary Committee, tried to push through the House a bill to prevent the gerrymandering of districts. He conceded privately, however, that neither of the major political parties was interested in his bill, for neither wanted to give up the ancient practice of gerrymandering. The bill was not passed. Even while Celler argued for his bill, the Republican-controlled legislature in New York gerrymandered that state's districts to try to prevent the election of at least four House Democrats. The Democratic-controlled legislature in California similarly had so drawn its new Congressional districts that it deprived Republicans of any real chance of winning perhaps eight House seats. One of the California districts, the twenty-sixth, looked like a lobster, and the Republicans protested that the Democrats with their gerrymandering were trying to destroy the two-party system in California. The Democrats replied that they were merely squaring accounts for a Republican gerrymandering spree in California ten years before.

One of the common results of gerrymandering, often complicated by rapidly shifting populations, has been the wide discrepancy between the numbers of people in different Congressional districts. In Texas, for example, Sam Rayburn represented a district of only 216,371 in 1960, while the nearby Dallas district, represented by Bruce Alger, had 951,527. The most populated Congressional district in the nation, California's twentieth district, had 1,014,460. The least populated was Michigan's twelfth with only 177,431. Adolph Sabath's district in Chicago, according to one census, contained only 112,116 persons, and the Chicago *Tribune* promptly labeled him "half a congressman."

139

When only 40,000 votes were cast in his district in the 1942 election, compared to 358,000 in a nearby Chicago district, the *Tribune* revised its designation of Sabath to "only a third of a congressman."

Gerrymandering in the state legislatures at times has been deliberately engineered by the men involved to acquire a seat for themselves in the House of Representatives, and at other times designed deliberately to deprive a prominent member of the House of his seat. John Nance Garner, as chairman of the Texas Assembly's reapportionment committee, after the 1900 Census, deliberately shaped a new Congressional district for himself. He candidly told his fellow Texans that he did so because he planned to go to Washington as a member of the House. The Democrats of Tennessee, embarrassed by Davy Crockett's ardent Whiggism, in the 1830's, tried to gerrymander him out of his House seat and failed by only 202 votes. The Democrats of Pennsylvania, in 1862, however, successfully gerrymandered Galusha Grow, then Speaker of the House, out of his seat—the only instance of a Speaker of the House being defeated for re-election. Perhaps, the most notable instance of gerrymandering, was the 1890 Ohio redistricting that defeated William McKinley. The state legislature so drew McKinley's new Congressional district that he retained only one Republican county, his home county, from his old district. All the other counties were Democratic. McKinley, then chairman of the Ways and Means Committee and the Republican floor leader, was one of the most prominent politicians of his time. He had sponsored the tariff bill of that year, a controversial protectionist bill, and the tariff bill became the major issue of the national campaign. It was a costly mistake for the Ohio Democrats. The people of Ohio resented McKinley's ouster and promptly elected him governor. His overwhelming victory in the gubernatorial race led to his nomination and election as President in 1896.

Over the many years of the House's history, the rank-and-file members developed a vast array of tactics, schemes, and stratagems to ingratiate themselves with their constituents back home and thus make it more certain that they would be re-elected. The simplest method, developed as early as the first years of the nineteenth century, was to answer, faithfully, every letter sent by every constituent. As early as 1808, some of the Representatives had developed the habit of answering every letter they received, frequently writing their letters during desultory House debates. Even the Speaker, while presiding over the House, sometimes took the liberty to scribble off a letter or two. John Randolph of Virginia once spied an early Speaker doing just that. Randolph, a garrulous orator, interrupted his speech. He stood silent on the floor of the House, facing the Speaker. The Speaker finally looked up from his letter and asked Randolph if he had completed his speech. "Mr. Speaker," said Randolph, "I was waiting until you had finished that letter!" [23] Down through the years, members with an eye for re-election have persisted in this habit. Churchill Cambreleng of New York in the 1820's had the reputation of answering every letter, and so did John Lumpkin of Georgia in the 1840's. Prior to 1933 mail from constituents was relatively light, but then, as Joseph Martin reported, with the advent of the New Deal letters came in "a blizzard." Most Representatives have continued to answer all letters, often several hundred a day, and to do so they have had to employ special staffs to keep pace with the incoming flood of mail. Some Representatives ignored abusive letters from constituents, but Wayne Hays of Ohio had a standard letter of reply to such mail. Hays's response was this: "Dear Sir: Today I received a letter from some crackpot who signed your name to it. I thought you ought to know about this before it went any further." [24]

Representatives, however, have refined the technique of letter-writing from a defensive to an offensive tactic. Many of them have subscribed to their home district newspapers, and they have sent off batches of letters in response to what they find in these newspapers. Elderly couples celebrating their fiftieth wedding anniversary have been pleased to receive congratulations from their Representative. Newly married couples have found in their first mail copies of a government pamphlet on food recipes, a gift from their Representative. Couples with newborn children frequently have received a similar pamphlet on infant care from the same source. These gifts to constituents were the modern substitute for the bags of garden and flower seeds that the Agriculture Department used to supply House members to distribute to the people back home. The Representatives have developed other techniques as well to reach their voters. Many Representatives send weekly or monthly newsletters to large numbers of their constituents; the mimeographed newsletters normally explained current legislation in the House and included "homey" touches to show that the Representative was working at his job in Washington. Other Representatives solicit their voters' political views by polling them by mail. These polls served a double purpose: they not only showed the voters that their Representative was interested in their personal views, but they helped the Representative judge the sentiment of his people back home on major issues. Some members use the techniques of modern communication—radio and television—to make periodic reports to the folks at home. The House in the 1960's had a well-equipped studio set up to permit the Representatives ready means to cut both radio and television tapes for use on home-district stations.

No greater tool for the Representative's self-gratulation has existed, however, than the friendly pages of the *Congressional Record*. This has given the individual Representative an opportunity to show his constituents that he has been on the job working in their interest, even if he has been neglecting them. It was this impulse that prompted the speech of the Representative from Buncombe in 1820, and the impulse has remained through the years. Few persons besides members of Congress ever even glance at the *Congressional Record,* but the Congress has long had an arrangement with the Government Printing Office to reproduce, at minimal cost, thousands upon thousands of copies of these individual speeches. These reprints the Representatives and Senators have mailed to their districts at no cost, utilizing both their free stationery and their right to mail their letters postage free, under their franking privileges. The House has also allowed its members complete discretion to remove, rewrite, or extend their remarks made on the floor as they have appeared in the *Congressional Record*. More than this, the House has also permitted its members to insert in the *Congressional Record,* technically the official reporting of the House's debates and actions, speeches that were never even made. Normally, on passage of an important bill, the House has adopted a motion that gave every Representative five additional days to prepare appropriate remarks to be included in the record of the day's action. In earlier periods, many members of the House followed the practice of freely editing their own remarks, even on speeches not made. The practice of rewriting speeches for the *Record* was begun even before the House career of John Quincy Adams, who on occasion rewrote entire speeches. The practice of removing remarks from the *Record* has also been in use for generations. Joseph Martin, in his autobiography, recorded an instance of this by John Nance Garner. "Every time those damn Yankees get a hambone," Garner said in debate, according to Martin, "I'm going to get a hog." [25] The candid remark did not appear in the *Congressional Record.*

Federal projects for the home district have also long been an object of solicitude by members of the House, and a Representative's ability to persuade the House or its Appropriations Committee to include funds for the project in his district has affected his success or failure at the polls. James Frear of Wisconsin recorded that two members of the House in his time—the 1910's— Henderson Jacoway of Arkansas and Oscar Gray of Alabama, lost their seats in the House for their failure to win federal funds to be spent in their districts. The bills that have normally carried these funds, the rivers and harbors bills and the military construction bills, have long been called "grab bags" or "pork-barrel" bills, even though the main thrust of these measures normally has been to further the national interest. In the 1950's, Kenneth Gray of Illinois appealed openly to the House to approve funds for a project in his district on the grounds that he could not be reelected otherwise. In 1960, D. R. "Billy" Matthews of Florida made much the same plea. Their House colleagues, amused by their candor and sympathizing with their plight accepted the amendments they offered. In 1959, Jeffrey Cohelan of California appealed to Chairman Carl Vinson of the Armed Services Committee to include funds in the military construction bill to improve San Francisco Bay, in Cohelan's district. Vinson agreed to add the funds and forthwith directed a staff aide to draft an appropriate amendment. "Mr. Cohelan," Vinson said, "we're going to re-elect you." [26] Such care for local district concerns have been a consideration for almost every member of the House from the beginning. The director of the Bureau of the Budget testified that in one three-month period, he received 200 requests from members of Congress advocating projects for their districts. Like answering letters, sending out child care pamphlets, and stuffing the *Congressional Record,* the winning of federal funds for local projects has been regarded as one of the most effective ways of making re-election more certain.

The House, in outward appearance at least, has never discriminated between the Representatives dedicated to their work as legislators and those interested only in holding the title of a member of Congress. The House has had private ways of showing respect and esteem for its able men and contempt and contumely for those who deserved it, but not even the party floor leaders have received higher pay than the run-of-the-mill members with the poorest attendance records. Instead, all the members of the House, at times, have had to bear national rebuke for increasing their salaries and emoluments of office. In the 1960's members of the House received salaries of $22,500 a year, a far cry from the $6 a day they received in the first years of the House. (The Speaker then received $12 a day.) They also received "mileage" —20 cents a mile for one round trip a year from their home to Washington. From time to time, over the years, they have voted themselves retirement pensions and various allowances for stationery, clerk hire, long-distance and Washington telephoning, telegraph service, and special mail. Traditionally, each additional allowance added to their perquisites has been quietly approved normally without even debate or a roll-call vote. There has been reason for this near secrecy in adding to their benefits of office. Twice in the history of the House, the members have been excoriated nationwide for "salary grabs." In the first instance, in 1816, they voted themselves salaries of $1,500 a year and made the pay raise retroactive to the beginning of the session. The furious outcry across the land caused the defeat of many Representatives. All the members from Ohio, Delaware, and Vermont were defeated, and so were most of the members from Georgia, Maryland, and South Carolina. The House repealed the pay increase the next year, setting the member's salary at a more modest $8 a day. Again in 1873, the House voted another "salary grab"—this time raising members' pay to $7,500 a year. Again the cry was taken up across the land—"thief!" This bill, passed on the last day of the session, again was retroactive. Many of the Representatives who voted for it tried to placate public indignation by refusing the money, others turned the money back to the Treasury, but the protests did not cease until this pay increase also was repealed. The Representatives from the very beginning have been accused of earning more as members of Congress than they could ever earn privately, an accusation never finally refuted. One member of Congress, a Senator, tried to answer it in 1873, in the midst of the "salary grab" furor. "If the people of a state choose to send a man to Congress whose best services are worthless to himself and everybody else, that is their fault," he said. "The question is: What is a fair compensation for the services of a man who is fit to be a member of Congress?" [27]

In a real sense, there has been no way to evaluate in dollars and cents, or by any other criterion, the services of the men and women whose assembled judgments have shaped the national consensus that they have translated into American law. That some of the Representatives were scapegraces and charlatans, the long history of the House provided more than adequate evidence. There has been an argument, however, in defense of even their presence in the House of Representatives. Without such men, how could the House truly claim to be representative of the whole American people? After all, not all American citizens have met the high standards of the national ideal. Indeed, George Mason, the distinguished Virginian constitutionalist, argued at the Constitutional Convention at Philadelphia in 1787 that the House of Representatives then being fashioned should draw its members from all the American people. "It should be so much so," Mason said, "that even the diseases of the people should be represented. If not, how are they to be cured?" There were even, he suggested, hazards in not electing such men. In that same debate, Elbridge Gerry of Massachusetts had argued that the popular election of Representatives inevitably would mean that the "worst men" would be chosen, as even then they were being elected to the Massachusetts legislature. Mason did not deny Gerry's assertion; he acknowledged instead that much could be said against the risk of electing some "men of indigence, ignorance, and baseness"— in Gerry's phrase—that a free choice by the people inevitably would produce. Mason pointed out, however, that "no government was free from imperfections and evils" and the hazards of democratic elections were not to be compared with either the ills of nondemocratic government or the benefits of a government based on "the rights of the people." [28] Clearly, to Mason, the danger of electing some pernicious men was the price of free elections and the price of freedom itself.

The House of Representatives, in its inner life, has always made its own evaluation of its members, a judgment based on the House's intuitional sense of its own dignity and responsibilities. In the furies of political partisanship in the House, there has been a certain toleration of the opponent's position, a live-and-let-live attitude between even the Representatives most bitterly in disagreement. After all, both were merely reflecting the views of their constituents back home. Perhaps no better example of this toleration was the curious friendship between John Rankin of Mississippi, one of the House's most vehement racists, and Vito Marcantonio of New York, who represented Harlem. The two frequently taunted each other in House debate, Rankin denouncing Negroes and Marcantonio with equal intensity defending them. Both men were able parliamentarians and they both admired each other. They often left the chamber together after these verbal encounters, which made equally good reading in Mississippi and Harlem. Their friendship, one of many similar friendships in the ranks of the House between ostensibly bitter political enemies, reflected the toleration of the House itself toward honorable men. There was no such toleration for the liar and the cheat, the fatuous and the pretentious. Sam Rayburn of Texas simply would not deal with a Representative who had lied to him, and he cared not who knew it. Rayburn, in this, reflected the House's inner view of the "mistakes" some Congressional districts had made in selecting their Representatives. They were denied access to the House's fundamental powers. Rayburn's door was always open, however, to the dedicated Representatives of both political parties who strove with energy and devotion to represent their people conscientiously in the federal government. Often these members of the rank and file of the House never received even a token of national recognition. For them, there could be no adequate reward, except perhaps to let them continue their service in the House.

CHAPTER SEVEN

The Oligarchy of Committees

FOR every member of the House of Representatives, his assignment to a formal committee of the House has been the crucial factor in his legislative career. If he won assignment to a ranking committee, one suited to his abilities and talents, he had at least the opportunity to perform effective and influential service in the House of Representatives. Otherwise, he almost certainly had to content himself with what amusements he might find in Washington. He would have little share in the House's legislative business. Even the rules of the House conspired to favor the members of the House committees, as did the instilled prejudice of the House itself against the nonspecialist. "The career of a member of [the] House . . . is determined, except in rare cases, by his assignment to committees," George Hoar of Massachusetts wrote of his years in the House in the 1870's,[1] and the same could be said of the Representatives in the 1960's. Assignment to a minor committee, a committee with jurisdiction over relatively insignificant legislative matters, normally limited the individual Representative to only minor influence in the House. The best he could hope for was to become an authority on the committee's trivia. Assignment, however, to one of the House's major committees, to Appropriations or Ways and Means, for example, opened the way for the individual to become an influential member of the House. As a member of a ranking House committee, the individual Representative automatically won prestige among his colleagues. To gain such an assignment normally implied the approval of his party's leaders. To become the chairman of a ranking House committee, to succeed to the power that such a post carried, meant the almost certain emergence of the fortunate Representative as one of the House's real leaders. From his strategic position, the chairman could guide the House's decisions on all the questions over which his committee had jurisdiction.

The importance of the individual member's committee assignment, like the importance of the committees themselves, went to the heart of the House's inner life as a legislative institution. The very size of the House's membership and the multiplicity of its legislative concerns shaped the establishment of the committee system from the very beginning. From the first weeks of the first session in 1789, the House has depended on special committees of its own members to manage the infinite details of its vast Constitutional powers. A division of labor, a dividing of the work, was clearly required. On any morning of any legislative day in the 1960's, as many as twenty House committees and subcommittees could be found hard at work conducting public hearings or secret sessions on as many varied subjects of contemporary life, from farm fertilizers and public housing to Army modernization and Latin American policy. To its committees, the House delegated the responsibility of examining and weighing all the proposed legislation and appropriations on which it had to act. As long ago as the 1890's, Speaker Thomas Reed called the typical House committee "the eye, the ear, the hand, and very often the brain of the House" on the legislation under its jurisdiction.[2] "Freed from the very great inconvenience of numbers," he said, "it can study a question, obtain full information, and put the proposed legislation into shape for final action." Long before Reed spoke, the House had found that no other method of procedure was practical. Not even in its earliest years did the House have the time to permit a full examination and exploration of even every major question by every member of the House. There were too many questions and too many members. Besides, the House had an institutional sense—inherited from the Constitutional Convention of 1787, the Continental Congress, and the early state legislatures—that the most orderly and efficient method of legislating required a careful examination of every legislative proposal by an elite group of the assembly's most talented members. These men, preferably specialists in the specific field of concern, could best recommend a course of action for the House. It was part of the House's institutional sense of itself that made it an attractive forum for the legislative specialist. The specialists were the men to whom the House listened, and they were the men whom the House followed.

In time, the committees of the House assumed much of the actual authority of the House itself, although they never possessed the legal or even the *de facto* power of the House. To show contempt for a House committee, in effect, was translated to contempt for the House, indeed, to contempt of Congress—and was punished as such. The committees, however, were only the agents of the House, created by the House and acting under the authority and subject to the discipline of the House and the House's leaders. At first, the House appointed only select committees and limited each committee's responsibility to a single bill or resolution. In the Third Congress, 1793-94, 350 such committees existed. Each of these committees ceased to function as soon as its work was done. Shortly afterward, however, it became obvious that certain areas of legislation—taxation, appropriations, interstate commerce, among them—were permanent concerns of the House. The House then began to create permanent, standing committees. Out of these first standing committees evolved the House's complex committee structure of its later years.

The House created new comittees as it confronted new problems. Their development, like the development of the House's rules, paralleled the economic and social growth of the United States. In 1800, the House had but four standing committees. In 1820, it had nine. The burgeoning industrialization of the United States in the post-Civil War years brought the wholesale creation of new House committees. By 1885, there were forty-seven; by 1905, there were sixty-one. The Louisiana Purchase in 1803 prompted the establishment of the Committee on Public Lands. The acquisition of Cuba, Puerto Rico, and the Philippines after the Spanish-American War brought the Committee on Insular Affairs. Some of the committees outlived their usefulness and yet lived on as formal committees of the House. "Many of these committees," wrote one critic in 1906, "never hold a session, never did hold one and never will hold one, to the end of time." [3] The House had a reason for keeping them in existence. Prior to the construction of the first House Office Building in 1908, the members of the House had no private offices. Each committee chairman, however, was entitled to an office in the Capitol, and they were naturally reluctant to give them up. Significantly, in 1909, with the allotment of offices to all House members, the House cut its committee total to fifty-five, dropping such committees as the Committees on Ventilation and Acoustics (before the introduction of air conditioning and loud-speakers, both were problems), Militia, and Private Land Claims. It was the beginning of a major retrenchment of the House's committee structure. In 1927, the House dropped thirteen more committees, and in 1946, under a major reorganization, it reduced the total to nineteen. Since then, the new field of space exploration persuaded the House to create the Committee on Science and Astronautics.

The primary function of the committees of the House has been to examine in detail every aspect of every bill to be considered by the House itself. The committees have held the responsibility to inspect carefully every bill sent to the House floor to guarantee that the House has had full knowledge of its every ramification. On the spending of federal money, an additional safeguard has been imposed: no appropriation can be approved unless the Congress previously has specifically authorized it by a separate act of law. Thus, all federal appropriations have been twice examined at the committee level, first by the legislative committee with formal jurisdiction and then by the Appropriations Committee, and twice by the House itself. Even then, the money need not be spent, for the House and Senate have no way to force the President to use it if he decides against doing so.

A committee's formal processing of a bill, an intensive screening procedure, has normally begun with public hearings at which both government officials and interested private citizens have been called to testify. The committee then has held its own *executive,* or secret, sessions on the bill. In this phase of the bill's legislative career, the committee members have decided not only whether the bill should be recommended to the House for approval but also precisely what should be included in the bill. The over-all operations of the House's committees have been staggeringly complex, with the number of bills processed only suggesting the difficulties of bringing order out of the chaos that would otherwise result. For example, in the Eighty-fifth House, 1957-58, the House's committees received 15,660 bills and resolutions of which they recommended passage of 2,450. In the Eighty-sixth House, 1959-60, they received 15,506 and recommended approval of 2,182. In the Eighty-seventh House, 1961-62, they received 15,751 and recommended approval of 2,301. In 1961 alone, the House's legislative committees held 1,680 meetings. In 1962, its Appropriations Committee held many months of hearings on sixteen separate money bills and recommended the spending of $91,199,482,870.

The delegation of authority to these House committees has given them and the members serving on them, from the beginning, an unusual and even abnormal influence on the legislation they considered. In the very early years, the House formally instructed its committees on the legislation it wanted drafted and reported by the committees. This system gave way, however, to the multiplying concerns of the House, and in the 1820's it became Speaker Henry Clay's normal practice to refer all bills introduced automatically to an appropriate standing committee. That gave the committees vast new power, for it left them free to ignore what bills the committee members chose to ignore and recommend passage of the bills they wanted passed. By 1885, young Woodrow Wilson, in his *Congressional Government,* wrote pathetically and poetically of the fate of the ordinary House bill. "As a rule," he said, "a bill committed is a bill doomed. When it goes from the clerk's desk to a committee room it crosses a parliamentary bridge of sighs to dim dungeons of silence whence it will never return. The means and time of its death are unknown, but its friends never see it again." [4] No other fate was possible for most bills. The Judiciary Committee killed so many bills that it was nicknamed the "Morgue" by the members of the House. In the early years, a Representative had to receive special permission to introduce a bill, but when that requirement was dropped the clerk's desk was soon covered every day with new bills. As many as 25,000 have been introduced by the members in the term of a single House. The House has had scarcely time even to count them, no less to study and act on them. The multiplication of the bills, along with the growing legislative concerns of the federal government, both increased the necessity of utilizing committees for the detailed work and also the importance of those committees. By the same token, this committee power gave opportunity to the members of committees to become men of real influence in the House. "It is as a committeeman that a member does his real work," Lord Bryce observed of the House in the 1880's.[5] Woodrow Wilson, then not yet thirty, boldly asserted that the committees in fact were "miniature legislatures" that performed the real work of the House. "The House sits, not for serious discussion, but to sanction the conclusions of its committees as rapidly as possible," he continued.[6] Wilson's statement, as he himself elsewhere acknowledged, went too far. Wilson conceded that the House never accepted the decisions of the Ways and Means Committee or the Appropriations Committee, in the 1880's, without "due deliberation" and discussion. These two committees controlled the bulk of the House's major legislation in those years, and the House itself has never abdicated its fundamental power to make the decisions on the great questions coming before it. Indeed, a fundamental consideration for the major House committees, and their chairmen, on major issues, has been so to draft the appropriate legislation that it met the approval of the majority of all the Representatives in the House. A skillful chairman, with a keen sense of the mood of the House, of the temper and sentiment of the members, has always modified his own views of the pending legislation, and the views of his committee, to meet the demands of the whole House. To do otherwise, to try to force the House to accept what it did not want, risked almost certain defeat of the bill, and a corresponding loss of confidence in the committee and its chairman. The House in modern times has frequently rejected major legislation from its most important committees. It has defeated school-construction bills, farm bills, and statehood bills, and rejected many of its own committees' most careful recommendations for legislation. In an epic struggle in 1959, the House reversed the Education and Labor Committee's decision on a labor bill, even though the committee had tried to placate the mood of the House with the bill it sent to the House floor. Its bill, however, like others, did not suit the temper of the House, and the House did not hesitate to overturn it, as it did other bills. The questions involved in these bills, it must be stressed, affected major policy decisions of the federal government, and the House simply would not automatically abide by the judgment of its committees. In lesser matters, where legislation has had smaller effect, however, the House in Woodrow Wilson's day and throughout its modern history has permitted its committees almost to assume completely the powers of legislating. The Judiciary Committee in modern years has offered a striking example of a committee allowed a free hand in one area while strictly limited in another. This committee has long handled a host of minor bills, the special bills like immigration bills that apply to only a single person or small group of persons. On these bills, the committee has had almost unrestrained authority to make the House's decisions. The House has normally accepted its recommendations perfunctorily. In another area, civil-rights legislation, the committee has long been seriously challenged. The committee repeatedly tried to have civil-rights legislation enacted and failed time after time. In the two civil-rights bills enacted in the twentieth century, in 1957 and 1960, the measures were severely compromised before being approved by the House. Clearly, in cases of insignificant consequences to the nation, the House was willing to accept this committee's recommendations and that of other committees as well. On matters of national policy, however, the House reserved for itself, as it has always done, the final judgment.

In the modern House, again like the House Wilson saw, the Ways and Means Committee and the Appropriations Committee clearly ranked as the most important of all committees involved in the House's basic role as a legislative body. They held prime jurisdiction over the most important of the House's prerogatives: to authorize the raising of taxes and the spending of those revenues. Their members ranked high with the other members of the House and so did their chairmen among other chairmen. Other House committees also held great prestige in the modern House, if not comparable with that of Appropriations and Ways and Means. The rank of a committee has always depended on the importance of the legislation coming before it, and, thus, with many committees, their rank has fluctuated over the years according to the current demand for legislation under their jurisdiction. Before the Civil War, for example, one of the most important and influential committees of the House was the Committee on Territories. It held jurisdiction over the crisis area in American politics: the formation of new states out of the great heartland territory of America; its bills inevitably raised the explosive political question of whether slavery would be allowed or prohibited in these new states. After the Civil War, this Committee sank gradually into insignificance until finally it was abolished, its work taken over by the Committee on Interior and Insular Affairs. After the Civil War, which brought the first great clamor for Congress to grant pensions to veterans, the Committee on Claims took rank rivaling Ways and Means and Appropriations. Eventually, this committee also sank into oblivion, as the nation's concern moved to other matters. The Judiciary Committee, once chaired by Daniel Webster and always a favorite with the many lawyers in the House, has had an erratic career—of great importance, for example, in the years members were pressing for the impeachment of President Johnson, later declining somewhat in prestige, and now, in modern times, with the reopening of the race question, again taking on major significance. The Foreign Affairs Committee, chaired in its past by some of the House's most distinguished members including John Quincy Adams, has not been of vital consequence until recent years. What brought this new significance was the modern importance of the House itself in international affairs. The shift from treaties to legislative programs as the methods of implementing United States foreign policy automatically transferred to the House a large share of the legislative responsibility for American foreign policy once held exclusively by the Senate. The Committee on Coinage, Weights and Measures ranked high in the 1890's, when the country conducted a furious debate over bimetalism and free silver. The committee's significance, however, died with the issue, and in a period of ten years before its dissolution, the committee did nothing more important than recommend that the words "In God We Trust" be placed on American coins. In the modern House, with the new attempts to deal legislatively both with the growing conflict between labor and management and with growing public concern about the school system, the Committee on Education and Labor has moved to prime rank among House committees. The rank of a committee has not necessarily rated the committee's effectiveness, but it normally has indicated the concern of the House leaders to make certain that these committees have been manned by able Representatives.

In assigning members of the House to committees, the House leaders always have acted with considerable discretion. The tested members of the House, those with seniority and experience, consistently have fared better than the new men, the freshmen. And the able hard-working members have received better assignments than those who neglected their duties. After one twentieth-century reshuffling of committee assignments, Speaker Rayburn reported some of the significant changes. He was asked what assignments had been given to the freshmen. "They got what was left," he said crisply. That the freshmen were so treated surprised no one, but this was not a harsh rule against the newcomers that allowed no exceptions. The House leaders have always made exceptions, even Sam Rayburn himself. Rayburn, for example, arranged for Chester Bowles of Connecticut, a former ambassador to India, to serve on the Foreign Affairs

Committee in his first and only term in the House. Rayburn, like other House leaders before him, tried to use the men in his ranks in the positions where they would best serve the House and themselves. There were sound reasons for this: the best use made of a Representative reflected a better, more effective House and, of course, a credit to its Speaker. It was this that prompted Rayburn and other recent House leaders to watch carefully the incoming freshmen during their first term in the House. A Representative who handled himself well, who did his committee chores faithfully, and who conscientiously worked at his job, however minor, could be certain of promotion to a more active role in the House's important business. This was no new thing in the modern House, for the leaders of the House had always so acted in making committee assignments.

In the earliest years of the House, every committee had a member from every state in the Union. By the time seventeen states had joined the Union, in 1803, this system proved too cumbersome and was abandoned, although the House for more than a century normally allowed but one member from each state's delegation on any committee. Besides, partisan political parties were already in full operation, and this required an entirely different accommodation of the members. The House has always seen its committees as representative groups, and shortly after the formation of political parties these committees have contained men of both major parties in the House. Down until the Civil War, in fact, it was not unusual for the Speaker to give political control of some of the less important House committees to the political minority and even appoint minority stalwarts to be chairmen of them. John Quincy Adams, for example, normally chaired a House committee, no matter which party controlled the House. (He once tried to swap a committee chairmanship he did not want for a choice spot on another committee.) In the modern House, however, the minority party members have been relegated automatically to minority status on all House committees, and the bipartisan division of committee seats between them and the majority party members have generally matched the ratio of the two parties in the whole House. Only on the three most important committees of the recent House have the committee seats been finally set by a gentlemen's agreement between the leaders of both parties. Under that agreement, the majority party has held a two-to-one preponderance in the Rules Committee, the principal political committee of the House. At first this agreement gave the majority eight members, the minority four. Later, in 1961, this was changed to a ten-to-five ratio. The Appropriations Committee, with fifty members, had thirty seats for majority party members and twenty for the minority. The Appropriations Committee was the largest committee in the House, a necessity to man its fourteen subcommittees, each of which held primary jurisdiction for financing a major area of federal activities. The Ways and Means Committee, using the same ratio, had fifteen majority members and ten from the minority.

In allocating seats on the House committees, the Speakers in recent times have had nearly as much control as did the Speakers of the last century who held sole responsibility for appointing committee members. Each political party in the modern House, however, has had its own Committee on Committees to make the designations, but there was no doubt in the parties' ranks of the influence of the party leaders in choosing committee members. Charles Halleck of Indiana, the Republican floor leader, chaired his party's Committee on Committees. The Democratic Committee on Committees was composed of the Democratic members of the House Ways and Means Committee, the Republican committee of a representative from each state sending Republican Representatives to the House. The principal difference in the change was that the Speaker used to consult his party's leaders before making his choices, and the members of the Committees on Committees in modern times consulted the Speaker or the "shadow" Speaker, the minority leader, before making theirs. Ever since the revolt against Speaker Cannon in 1910, the House itself has technically "elected" the members of all standing committees, but this has been a parliamentary fiction. In reality, however, the two major political parties have operated under an acknowledged "gentlemen's agreement" that allowed each party to assign their party members to such committees as they saw fit. The development of the seniority system, under which a committee member could not be removed from his committee without his permission, made the system less flexible than in the nineteenth century and therefore less controllable by the party leaders. Even so, however, Speaker Rayburn in 1949 arbitrarily removed John Rankin of Mississippi and Edward Hébert of Louisiana from the Un-American Activities Committee. Both had displeased Rayburn by their antics on this committee. In 1959, Rayburn persuaded Overton Brooks of Louisiana to give up his post on the Armed Services Committee. Brooks then ranked second to Chairman Carl Vinson of Georgia, then seventy-five years old, and as such Brooks automatically would have succeeded to Vinson's chairmanship in the event of Vinson's death or retirement. Rayburn wanted a man of greater ability in this post than Brooks and so, aided by floor leader John McCormack and Wilbur Mills, chairman of the Democratic Committee on Committees, he persuaded Brooks to resign from the Armed Services Committee in return for being made chairman of the Science and Astronautics Committee, a brand-new and much less important committee. The maneuver put Paul Kilday of Texas, one of the ablest members of the House, in line of succession to Vinson as chairman of the Armed Services Committee.

Occasionally, the modern leadership has decided to switch the entire political orientation of a House committee. This was the reason for the epic struggle in 1961 to enlarge the Rules Committee. The committee had a decided conservative bias, and Rayburn wanted to change it to a liberal bias. The change was accomplished by adding two liberals to the Committee. This was a revolutionary change, executed by the Speaker. There were cases of evolutionary change as well. In 1947, for example, the Committee on Education and Labor had a pronounced conservative tilt. The National Association of Manufacturers reported that year that the committee had but five of its twenty-five members friendly to labor, with all the rest friendly to management. This committee, to which both freshman Richard Nixon of California and freshman John F. Kennedy of Massachusetts had been assigned, played a central role in enacting the Taft-Hartley labor law, which labor leaders denounced as hostile to workingmen. Rayburn decided to alter this committee's conservative orientation and he did so over a period of years by making sure that the new members appointed to it favored liberal policies. Appointed to the committee, under Rayburn's direction, were such liberals as Carl Elliott of Alabama, Lee Metcalf of Montana, James Roosevelt of California, Frank Thompson of New Jersey, Stewart Udall of Arizona, John Brademas of Indiana, James O'Hara of Michigan, and Robert Giaimo of Connecticut. By 1955, Rayburn had succeeded in making the committee marginally liberal. By 1961, the liberals controlled the committee by a clear eighteen-to-thirteen margin. The political orientation of a committee was of obvious importance, because it gave one group or another added influence on the legislation under that committee's jurisdiction.

Rayburn and the Republican leaders as well had less success in their attempts to strengthen the Foreign Affairs Committee. Prior to World War II, this committee had but little work or significance. John Nance Garner of Texas was appointed to it by Speaker Cannon, but he left it as soon as he could, refusing its chairmanship in preference to being the most junior man on the Ways and Means Committee. In the 1920's the committee spent a full week debating whether to authorize $20,000 for an international poultry show in Tulsa, Texas, and in 1933-34 it had little more to do than to authorize projects costing only $102,000. The emergence of the United States as a world leader, however, brought the House and its Foreign Affairs Committee vast new importance. In 1951-52, for example, the committee authorized the spending of $14,121,758,750 to meet American commitments around the globe. The House leaders tried to "pack" the Committee with some of the House's ablest men, but they had difficulty keeping them there once appointed. J. William Fulbright of Arkansas, Mike Mansfield of Montana, George Smathers of Florida, Karl Mundt of South Dakota, Jacob Javits of New York, and Thomas Hennings of Missouri all were assigned to the committee, but soon transferred to the Senate.

Christian Herter of Massachusetts gave up a seat on the Rules Committee to serve on the Foreign Affairs Committee, but then quit to become governor of Massachusetts and later Secretary of State. James Richards of South Carolina, the ablest of the committee's modern chairmen, retired from the House in 1956, and John Vorys of Ohio, an equally able member of the committee, followed his example two years later. Brooks Hays of Arkansas was defeated for re-election, and so was A. S. J. Carnahan of Missouri. Chester Merrow of New Hampshire quit to run for the Senate. Marguerite Stitt Church of Illinois also retired, and Walter Judd of Minnesota was defeated when his Congressional district was gerrymandered in 1962. That left Frances Bolton of Ohio and Peter Frelinghuysen of New Jersey, as the only members of the committee with national reputations. The seniority system has worked poorly on this committee in recent years, bringing Thomas Gordon of Illinois and Robert Chipperfield, also of Illinois, to the chairmanship. Gordon was simply incompetent to handle or even understand international relations. He had to turn over the management of committee bills on the House floor to abler committee members such as Carnahan, and Frank Coffin of Maine. Chipperfield was uninterested in foreign affairs, and it was partially because his seniority on the committee blocked John Vorys' advancement that Vorys finally retired from the House.

On other committees, the House leaders have tried to reach other goals through the men they have assigned to these committees. On the Agriculture Committee, for example, every committee member normally has "represented" a major farm crop. He has been the "ambassador," so to speak, of corn, cattle, rice, hogs, tobacco, wheat, dairy products, cotton, peanuts, soybeans, or feed grains. Only rarely has a member been assigned to the committee from a purely urban, consumer district. As spokesmen for the various great farm crops, these committee members formed the nucleus of the House's powerful farm bloc, a group that for almost thirty years could dictate United States farm policies. Using the committee as headquarters, the various crop "representatives" negotiated their terms for government help to their constituent farmers in one of the last and most effective of the logrolling operations in Congress. Frequently the committee members formed a united front, with each member's home crop adequately provided for, and, thus strengthened, the committee members carried their farm bills through the House to enactment. Not until Ezra Benson, President Eisenhower's Secretary of Agriculture, split the old alliances between the "representatives" of the Southern crops and the "representatives" of the Midwestern crops, did the farm bloc begin to suffer major defeats on the House floor.

Perhaps the most significant distribution of committee assignments, however, has been that of the Democrats on the Ways and Means Committee. These men, because they must represent a national view, have been chosen on a national basis. New England automatically has had a representative. So has Texas, New York, Pennsylvania, Illinois, the border states, the Far West, the Great Plains states, the Southwest, the Middle West, and the Gulf states; the Southern states have had five or six representatives. These committeemen not only had to set party policy on the great questions of taxation, foreign trade, and social security —all in the purview of the committee—but they also assigned their fellow Democrats to committees. It was no wonder that in recent years this committee had in its ranks some of the most personally powerful men in the House: Thomas O'Brien, boss of the Chicago delegation in the House, William Green, boss of the Philadelphia machine, and Eugene Keogh, high-ranking leader of the New York City Democrats. They gravitated to the Ways and Means Committee as natural allies in power. The Republicans had on the committee scarcely less powerful men: Daniel Reed, dean of the New York delegation; Richard Simpson of Pennsylvania, chairman of the powerful Republican Campaign Committee, and John Byrnes of Wisconsin, chairman of the Republican Policy Committee. The Ways and Means Committee was a natural place for power, for it always had been. Indeed, Albert Gallatin of Pennsylvania, Thomas Jefferson's friend and ally, had originally arranged the strengthening of this committee in 1796 to create a power center to resist the encroachments on the House by Treasury Secretary Alexander Hamilton. The committee then handled appropriations as well as taxation and its chairman automatically assumed the position of floor leader of his party. Down through the many years of the House, the roster of this committee has listed many of the House's outstanding men, among them four who later became Presidents of the United States.

To win assignment to this committee marked the Representative as a member trusted and respected by House leaders, as did assignment to either the Rules Committee or the Appropriations Committee. The House careers of John Nance Garner of Texas and Cordell Hull of Tennessee were made by appointment to Ways and Means, and as members of that committee they fought a bitter fight to settle permanently whether the federal government should impose a graduated income tax. Garner, a more skillful cloakroom operator, won and permanently altered the government's methods of imposing taxes. John McCormack of Massachusetts, elected to this committee as a mere sophomore member of the House, leaped into party prominence that was to make him his party's floor leader for two decades and then Speaker. The committee, from its earliest days, was a natural forum for an able man to win abiding influence over the House and the laws enacted by the House.

So was the Appropriations Committee. Created in 1865 to relieve the Ways and Means Committee of a share of its then overwhelming workload, the Appropriations Committee from the start formed a power center in its own right. With the responsibility of appropriating all funds to keep the federal government functioning, this committee quite naturally assumed a commanding posture over the entire federal bureaucracy. On the whim or the fancy of these committeemen depended, in large measure, the scope and functioning of almost every federal agency, and this power made the committeemen among the most solicitously courted men in Washington. Not only did the heads of executive agencies, and the Chief Executive himself, pay court to these men, but so did their fellow colleagues in the House of Representatives. John Kennedy, on the eve of establishing his administration in late December, 1960, cordially entertained John Rooney of New York, chairman of the Appropriations subcommittee on State and Justice, in his Palm Beach vacation headquarters in the hope of persuading Rooney to be more lenient with funds for United States diplomatic missions abroad. Kennedy discovered, on becoming President, that he had only been partially successful, for Rooney remained what he had always been: the scourge of "extravagance" and "waste" in the State Department. For a member of the House to fight this committee, even in the cause of the President, was to risk dreadful consequences to his own political well-being, for this committee had power over all the federal spending in every Representative's home district. Thus was the power of these committeemen enhanced and made almost invulnerable. And to make certain that there was no misunderstanding of the committee's power to retaliate on the individual Representative who might become obstreperous, the committee chairman normally scheduled the Public Works Appropriations Bill—the traditional "pork-barrel" bill—as one of the very last bills to be enacted each year. That left the Representatives concerned about projects in their home districts at the mercy of the Appropriations Committee—and every Representative had such federal projects in his Congressional district, if they were only the post offices.

This power over the political lives of the other Representatives gave the committee almost unlimited influence over government spending. Rarely were the committee's bills ever seriously challenged by the House itself. By the 1960's, it was not deemed remarkable that the House adopted appropriations of as much as $40 billion without a single amendment being offered on the House floor or a single voiced dissent. The committee traditionally has had a severely conservative tendency with a group instinct hostile to governmental spending. The committee long has been a bastion of conservative power in the House of Representatives. On the fifty-man committee in 1961-62, for example, sat thirty-two conservatives, most of them with great seniority, including the chairman, Clarence Cannon of Missouri, and the ranking Republican, John Taber of New York, who had been chairman twice when his party controlled the House of Representatives. Taber, indeed, had been so noted for his conservative ways, that his name had been used as the root of a new word: to "taberize" an appropriations bill meant to slash severely the President's request for money. President Harry Truman, describing Taber's rough handling of appropriations bills, called it the "Taber Dance." Frequently, over the course of the committee's history, the chairman of this committee had been known as the "watchdog of the Treasury" in token of his reluctance and that of his committee to spend the taxpayers' money.

In actuality, the modern House Appropriations Committee has not been a single, monolithic committee. Rather it has been a group of subcommittees, each specializing in a broad area of government. These subcommittees, numbering as few as five members on the appropriations for some of the less important government departments to as many as fourteen on the defense budget, conducted extensive and detailed examinations of each Administration's specific requests for money each year. Each subcommittee then made its own decisions on how much money should be voted for the cited purpose; and these subcommittee recommendations almost always were quickly ratified by the full fifty-man committee, giving them the stamp of approval of one of the House's most prestigious committees. With such backing, these subcommittee recommendations normally have swept to swift passage by the House itself. Only a daredevil Representative risked antagonizing these committee members on whose good will he himself had to depend for the essential ingredient to create his home-district projects: money. Occasionally, committee members themselves led a fight against the committee's recommendations—as did Gerald Ford of Michigan against a deep cut in the foreign-aid bill in 1961. In such contests, other members of the House felt freer to vote against the divided committee than in those more common cases when the committee members themselves were united.

Inevitably, the subcommittees and their chairmen assumed great power in the House and in the whole government. A skillful subcommittee chairman like Otto Passman of Louisiana could carry the whole House against even so popular and politically feared a President as Eisenhower. Eisenhower in fact once tried to persuade Passman into taking a more kindly attitude toward the President's requests for foreign-aid funds. He invited Passman to the White House for a private conference in his study with the Secretary of State and the Chairman of the Joint Chiefs of Staff standing by to support the President's argument. "Mr. President," Passman blurted out to Eisenhower, "you haven't been given the facts." Passman then proceeded to tell Eisenhower what was wrong with the foreign-aid program, giving the President and his chief lieutenants scarcely a chance to defend the program. "Remind me," said President Eisenhower after the session, "never to invite that fellow down here again." [7] Passman that year, 1957, decided to cut Eisenhower's foreign-aid request by twenty-five per cent and the House, as was usual, followed his leadership— despite a threat by the President that he would call a special session of Congress to force Congress to vote the full amount. President Kennedy felt a similar wariness of Passman as did Eisenhower. Kennedy was uncertain as to what course he would take with Passman. "What," the President once asked, "am I going to do about Otto Passman?" [8] There was not much the President could do. Passman had mastered his specialty, foreign aid, and he could carry the House with him. When Kennedy asked for $4,900,000,000 for foreign aid for 1963, Passman had but one comment on the request: "Preposterous!" The President knew immediately that this program was in deep trouble again.

In other Appropriations subcommittees, the chairman became as influential—if not so bold—as Passman. George Mahon of Texas, chairman of the defense-appropriations subcommittee, counted as one of the most important men in the civilian command of the armed forces of the United States. His judgment helped decide whether the air force should develop a proposed new weapons system, whether the navy should build another $100 million aircraft carrier—for he held the respect of his colleagues on the subcommittee, and the subcommittee members held the confidence of the House. "We are the laymen looking over the shoulders of the military," he once explained. "While we don't hold ourselves out as experts, we have the experience to evaluate the validity of what they propose. We can't be military strategists, but we can make judgments on the basis of their presentations." [9] The judgments of Mahon's subcommittee, whose members included Gerald Ford of Michigan, Melvin Laird of Wisconsin, and Robert Sikes of Florida, normally have received the unanimous endorsements of the House.

Like judgments from the Health, Education and Welfare subcommittee led by John Fogarty of Rhode Island, the independent offices subcommittee led by Albert Thomas of Texas, the Interior subcommittee led by Michael Kirwan of Ohio, and the Treasury subcommittee led by Vaughn Gary of Virginia received similar treatment by the House. These subcommittee chairmen could not rival the committee's chairman, Clarence Cannon, in power. Cannon, an arbitrary man, once stripped Thomas of almost all his powers for failing to slash appropriations requests deeply enough—but they filled the definition Woodrow Wilson gave all House committee chairmen in the 1880's.

"The leaders of the House," wrote Wilson, "are the chairmen of the principal Standing Committees. Indeed, to be exactly accurate, the House has as many leaders as there are subjects of legislation; for there are as many Standing Committees as there are leading classes of legislation, and in the consideration of every topic of business the House is guided by a special leader in the person of the chairman of the Standing Committee, charged with the superintendence of measures of the particular class to which that topic belongs." [10]

Wilson described the House at a time when it had forty-seven standing committees, as compared to the twenty committees of the 1960's, and it was a House that had not yet developed in full the hierarchy of leaders that has functioned in the modern House of Representatives. The Speaker had not yet been strengthened with his over-all command of the House, nor had the majority leader or the majority whip been institutionalized as power centers in their own right. The Rules Committee, in Wilson's day, served a minor and technical function only and had not yet been brought forward as a great arm of the House's formal leaders.

With these qualifications, however, the strength Wilson attributed to the committee chairmen and the specialists in leading areas of legislation has remained what it was when he wrote. There have been exceptions, of course, to Wilson's general rule, especially in those instances in which the seniority system has brought to the chairmanship of a great House committee an incompetent or fatuous leader. No better example of the failure of a committee chairman to command his area of jurisdiction has there been in the contemporary House than Thomas Gordon of Illinois, who came to the chairmanship of the Foreign Affairs Committee in 1957 after fourteen years of service in the House. Gordon, so unfitted to the chairmanship that he publicly conceded he could not intelligently discuss foreign affairs, was an example of the failure of the seniority system in the House.

Gordon, a kindly, unpretentious man, could not even speak correct English, no less manage the niceties of the diplomatic dialect. Another instance of the seniority system's failure was the elevation of Fred Hartley of New Jersey as chairman of the Education and Labor Committee in 1947. Mary Norton of New Jersey, who had been chairman of the committee for ten years prior to Hartley's elevation, angrily resigned from the committee rather than serve under Hartley's chairmanship. She said that Hartley had so badly neglected his responsibilities as a committee member that he had attended only six meetings of the committee in the previous ten years.

Under the seniority system as perfected in the twentieth century, a Representative assigned to a House committee automatically rose in his standing on the committee until, at last, he succeeded to its chairmanship. Two major qualifications had to be met for him to become chairman; his political party had to command the House, and all members of his party more senior to him on the committee had to leave the committee, by death, resignation, retirement, or election defeat. The seniority system admittedly was not an ideal method of choosing committee chairmen, but its advocates had two fundamental arguments for its merit. The first, basically negative, was that no other system was better. To allow the Speaker to select the chairmen, as had been done for more than a century, had given the Speaker inordinate personal power. To permit the committee members to choose their own chairmen inevitably would lead to disruptive and destructive politicking among the members for the post: it was better to have an automatic route to the chairmanship. The second argument for the seniority system, basically a positive argument, was that it almost certainly insured the elevation of men tutored and trained in the specific areas of legislation under the committee's jurisdiction. This went to the heart of the House's inner sense of confiding its powers to its specialists. No better example of the effectiveness of this existed in the modern House than the elevation of James P. Richards of South Carolina to the chairmanship of Foreign Affairs in 1955. Richards, who was succeeded two years later by Thomas Gordon, was a skilled legislative tactician, a master of cloakroom maneuver, and a man of judgment who held the confidence of his colleagues. Shortly after he became chairman, he made it plain that he intended to insist on the House's new prerogatives in foreign relations. The State Department failed to keep him and his committee members properly briefed on pending actions. When the department's officials neglected to inform him of a shipment of military tanks to Saudi Arabia, Richards denounced the department publicly for its attitude that the House was a "weak-minded illegitimate son." [11] He then brought the department's officials to heel by broadly hinting that he might indefinitely stall approval of the foreign-aid bill, a critical item in President Eisenhower's foreign policy. Later, after holding extended hearings on the foreign-aid bill, Richards and his committee members slashed more than $1 billion from the proposed program. The cut sent a chill through the Administration and brought a massive attempt to reverse the action on the floor of the House. Working to restore at least part of the money were President Eisenhower, Secretary of State John Foster Dulles, the Joint Chiefs of Staff, Speaker Rayburn, Joseph Martin, the minority leader, and John McCormack, the majority leader, an unprecedented coalition of powerful and influential leaders united to contradict the finding of a single committee chairman and one without a national reputation. The

President himself said publicly—and he was supported by the others—that the cut would endanger the United States' safety. Richards denied the President's claim and quietly argued with his colleagues in the House cloakroom the correctness of his own view. When the question came to a vote in the House, Richards formally presented his case and the House supported his judgment, 192 to 112, an astonishing mark of the House's confidence in him. A year later Richards' judgment was fully vindicated, this time by the Eisenhower administration, for the Administration's officials had to concede that they had not been able to allocate or spend even the money Richards had approved for foreign aid.

Other committee chairmen had comparable personal power to that of James Richards. Carl Vinson of Georgia, chairman of the Armed Services Committee in the 1950's and 1960's, became on the death of Speaker Rayburn in 1961 perhaps the most powerful member of the House. Long an advocate of the Navy's causes, the "Admiral," as he was sometimes called, struck terror into the hearts of his adversaries. When Vinson sympathetically agreed to support President Kennedy's legislative program in 1961, the President's supporters sighed with relief, for Vinson's support made possible passage of at least some of the controversial Kennedy legislation. The fact that he voted for a bill persuaded other conservative Southerners to vote for it, too. Once invited to be Secretary of Defense, Vinson mildly replied that "I'd rather run the Pentagon from up here." [12] His control of military installations, through his committee's power over their expansion, retraction, or even abolition, gave him awesome power among his colleagues, for almost every Congressional district contained at least one politically significant military post. Even the chairman of the Joint Chiefs of Staff did not hesitate to scurry after Vinson when Vinson summoned him. Periodically Vinson publicly displayed his power. In 1958, when President Eisenhower, a former five-star general, proposed a reorganization of the Defense Department, Vinson announced it was unsatisfactory to him. He drafted, with the help of the Pentagon, his own reorganization plan, one that Eisenhower publicly

170

stated would cause "insubordination" in the military ranks. The House, however, followed Vinson—Vinson showed that the language to which Eisenhower objected already was written into law, placed there by Eisenhower's 1953 reorganization of the armed forces. The House approved Vinson's bill, and Eisenhower in effect acknowledged later that he had been wrong and approved it, too.

The House has always given great power to its committee chairmen, and the able chairmen have been able to use it to aid the causes they wished to support. On Appropriations, chairmen like Thaddeus Stevens, James Garfield, and Joseph Cannon won national reputations, but there were others, too, who shaped national policy and the great decisions of the House. James Tawney of Minnesota, chairman under Speaker Cannon, was one of the most skillful of the House's strategists in cloakroom maneuver. Once, on a sugar bill, Tawney rebelled against the seemingly all-powerful Speaker Cannon and utterly defeated him in the ensuing floor fight. John Fitzgerald of New York, who succeeded Tawney as Appropriations chairman, literally forced his way into the House's leadership by his enormous parliamentary skill. Speaker Gillett said Fitzgerald, who had devised two of the House's great parliamentary reforms—Calendar Wednesday and the Unanimous Consent Calendar—"showed such knowledge of the subjects he discussed, such assurance of his parliamentary rights, and such determination to assert and defend them, that before long he convinced the leaders that it was much better to have him inside . . . defending than outside attacking." [13]

The roster of the chairmen of the Ways and Means Committee reads like a list of the great men of the House—and well it might, for on them largely has depended the government's ability to raise the revenues to keep the government alive. John Randolph and John Eppes of Virginia were among the first, and they were followed through the decades by such men as Langdon Cheves and Georgie McDuffie of South Carolina, James K. Polk of Tennessee, Churchill Cambreleng and Millard Fillmore of New York, Samuel Vinton and John Sherman of Ohio, Justin Morrill of Vermont, William "Pig-Iron" Kelley of Pennsylvania, Roger Q. Mills of Texas, William McKinley of Ohio, William Wilson of West Virginia, Sereno Payne of New York, Oscar Underwood of Alabama, and Claude Kitchen of North Carolina, each a powerful man in the House in his day. Many of them won national reputations by their sponsorship of new tariff bills— Morrill, Mills, McKinley, Nelson Dingley of Maine, Wilson, and Underwood. In 1890, the Republican party campaigned on the slogan "Bill McKinley and the McKinley Bill," a tariff bill named for the then chairman of Ways and Means.

Other chairmen of other committees have held like influence in the House. In the 1900's, Theodore Burton of Ohio, chairman of the Rivers and Harbors Committee, terrorized other members of the House. His committee had jurisdiction over the Rivers and Harbors Bill, the traditional "pork-barrel" bill for congressmen for it contained federal funds for their home districts. "The House has come to realize," wrote a contemporary, "that Mr. Burton is the greatest expert on river and harbor legislation Congress has ever known." Burton, a studious man, simply would not allow passage of projects that could not be thoroughly justified. He had such mastery of this field that he could not be successfully challenged in his committee or on the House floor. The Pennsylvania delegation caucused in 1904 to decide on what legislation they should support to improve the Delaware River. The meeting was brought to an abrupt halt by the somber remarks of one of the Pennsylvanians. "What does Mr. Burton say?" questioned Representative Thomas Butler. "There is no use wasting time talking about anything else. What Mr. Burton says will be law for the House of Representatives." [14]

In the House of mid-twentieth century, committee chairmen held equal sway over matters under their committees' jurisdiction. Graham Barden of North Carolina, for example, ruled the House Education and Labor Committee with an arbitrariness that approached tyranny. Barden, a conservative whose committee members often saw the country's legislative needs differently from him, at times simply blocked passage of all legislation under his jurisdiction by refusing to call any sessions of his committee.

With the committee unable to act, the legislation referred to the committee died a-borning. Barden, a rough-and-tumble veteran of many a parliamentary war, lost his arbitrary powers, however, when his operations came under assault from a first-term freshman on the committee, Stewart Udall of Arizona. Udall, a scholar-in-politics known to his friends as "The Navaho," quietly canvassed other members of the committee and won from them pledges to support his plan to reform the committee's rules and practices. With pledges from a majority of the committee members, Udall presented his demands to Barden. Barden, a realist, saw that he was beaten and agreed to Udall's reforms: regular scheduled meetings of the committee and the establishment of subcommittees that operated independently of the chairman's control. Barden's one-man rule of the committee was thus brought to an end. Udall went on to become one of the most effective members of the committee, a leader in labor legislation in Congress. He also became the only member of Congress selected by President Kennedy for his Cabinet.

Udall's success in stripping Barden of his arbitrary powers ran against the normal current of House proceedings, which have always given the senior members of the House a decided edge in the inner struggle for power. Udall's success, in a real sense, was possible only because Barden had pressed his powers too far and because Udall in his own right possessed unique skills as a parliamentary tactician and strategist. Barden did not lose all his powers, for he did not hesitate arbitrarily to deny a subcommittee chairmanship to Adam Clayton Powell of New York, who had clear seniority rights to the very first subcommittee formed. Barden, a North Carolinian, disliked Powell personally and passed him by when he allocated the subcommittee chairmanships. Powell furiously tried to upset Barden's ruling but found he was helpless to do more than protest. Barden, by the nature of his post, retained his essential powers, the powers that made all competent chairmen leaders in the House.

The greatest power of a committee chairman in the House has been his ability to impede or hasten any given bill to House passage. The chairman largely has controlled the timing of legislation to be taken up for consideration—and timing alone can determine a bill's fate. With perhaps 1,000 bills referred to his committee each year the chairman's selection of the order in which they should be considered has made a basic difference in their chances to become law. Necessarily most of the bills could not be considered at all. A bill delayed frequently has been a bill denied in the House's legislative process, for correct timing has always been an intrinsic necessity to parliamentary and political success. Starting belatedly on its parliamentary course, even a bill with wide public appeal and support could be as effectively killed in the parliamentary jam of each session as if it had been suppressed from the start. This power over the consideration of the bills under their jurisdiction has been the root power of the committee chairmen. It has given them the means to intimidate ordinary members of the House and even to force the Speaker himself to cater to their whims and idiosyncrasies. The chairmen have been able to help or hurt the individual Representative's chances of re-election by endorsing or repudiating specific bills. They have been able also, more importantly, to influence and even determine the nature of American law; for they have held the decisive role in the vast screening process through which all legislation has had to pass in the House. The House of Representatives, from its first weeks of existence, has found itself dependent on committees as the only way to cope with the infinite detail of its task of legislating for the American people. This dependence has necessarily required a delegation of the House's great powers to both the committees and the committees' leaders, the chairmen. The alternative, one from which the House has always shrunk, has been chaos.

CHAPTER EIGHT

Grand Inquest of the Nation

THE committees of the House of Representatives have served still another function beyond that of preparing legislation for the House's consideration. By the House's Constitutional responsibilities and prerogatives over the raising and spending of taxes, its power to initiate impeachment proceedings against all federal officials and officers, the House has held vast authority to oversee the entire government establishment. In this capacity, the House has acted as the "Grand Inquest of the Nation," a formal title adopted by the House from the British House of Commons, which has had similar jurisdiction over the British governmental establishment. In this capacity, the House of Representatives has acted with the authority of a grand jury, the jurisdiction of an auditor, and the command of a comptroller of the Treasury. For practical convenience, the House has delegated these powers to its committees, subject to control by the House itself.

From the investigation in 1792 of General Arthur St. Clair's disastrous defeat at the hands of Indian tribesmen to the 1962 investigation of the peculations of Billie Sol Estes, House committees have claimed the right to examine in detail all the vicissitudes of American life. These investigating committees, acting for the House of Representatives, not only held specific grants of power derived from the Constitution, they also exercised the almost unlimited powers implicit and inherent in the House's responsibility to legislate. There seemed no phase of American society not needing exploration by the Representatives. Under examination in the modern House have been the sophisticated new weapons systems of the military, labor racketeering, the structure of the tax code, the motion picture industry, farm surpluses, school facilities, space exploration, the European Common Market, and almost every other imaginable concern of a varied and complex people. In 1961 alone, the House of Representatives authorized its committees to spend $5,469,000 on these investigations.

These committees often were armed with the power to subpoena witnesses and documents, and they were further armed—subject to routine approval by the House itself—with the power to cite contumacious or reluctant witnesses with contempt of Congress, a criminal offense carrying the penalty of jail on conviction.

Only rarely were the House's committees seeking out criminal negligence or offense by federal officials and even more rarely with a view to impeaching them for high crimes and misdemeanors. Most of the House committees, on the contrary, were devoting their time and energies to far less histrionic activities, to the often tedious and humdrum business of examining fully the great mass of legislative proposals constantly and endlessly coming before the House. The House has long prided itself on the care its legislative committees took with the legislation under their jurisdiction. The members of the United States Senate long have scorned the pretensions of the House as a legislative body and the Representatives themselves as insignificant participants in the great business of the government. The members of the House, however, have known in their hearts that they were the legislative specialists of Congress, that in their ranks were the Congressional experts on all phases of the government, and that the Senate, by comparison, was notoriously slipshod in its legislative practices. This was no new thing. In the 1880's, Woodrow Wilson noted that the "painstaking" work of the House of Representatives on legislation, was often made "worthless" [1] by the free-wheeling, careless Senate.

Most fastidious of all the House committees in their consideration of bills have been the Ways and Means Committee and the
Appropriations Committee. They exercised the House's great
prerogatives over tax measures and appropriations, the basic
power of the nation's purse. Records of the hearings of the Ways
and Means committee, collected over its many years of operation,
have formed a vast library of essential information on the fiscal
and financial concerns of the United States and its government.
The Appropriations Committee has been no less scrupulous in
requiring full information on the spending of the taxpayers' every
dollar. Every year, through the Appropriations Committee's
rooms in the Capitol, have trooped a parade of all the government's principal civil and military officers, save the President
alone, to explain not only the operations of their agencies but
the justification of their costs. In the course of many years of
such close examination of the government's affairs, the members
of these committees have often become genuine authorities. It
was because such Representatives as Clarence Cannon of Missouri, Wilbur Mills of Arkansas, John Rooney of New York,
Albert Thomas of Texas, Gerald Ford of Michigan, John Byrnes
of Wisconsin, Otto Passman of Louisiana, and John Fogarty of
Rhode Island paid close attention to their committee work that
they became men of influence in the modern House of Representatives.

In 1955, for example, the Ways and Means Committee spent
more than three full weeks in public hearings on extending the
Trade Agreements Act, legislation already well known to most
of the committee members. The committee members listened to
and questioned Secretary of State John Foster Dulles, Treasury
Secretary George Humphrey, Agriculture Secretary Ezra Benson,
Labor Secretary James P. Mitchell, Commerce Secretary Sinclair Weeks, and 248 other witnesses, most of whom were spokesmen for interested groups. Besides these witnesses, the committee
received 224 further statements and explanations on the bill. The
hearings were published in two volumes totaling 2,601 pages of
detailed testimony and materials. Three years later, on another
extension of the Trade Agreements Act, the process was repeated

and the two volumes of the 1958 published hearings required 2,935 pages. The Appropriations Committee has been no less diligent. In 1962, the foreign operations appropriations subcommittee spent seventy days—averaging more than ten hours a day—listening to a host of witnesses on the President's foreign-aid program. The hearings were published in three volumes, of 3,189 pages, and the subcommittee chairman, Otto Passman of Louisiana, formally asked his House colleagues to support the subcommittee's recommendations on the grounds that its members had given every phase of the program a meticulous examination. That same year, the public-works appropriations subcommittee held two full months of hearings on the public-works appropriations bill. The subcommittee members heard 868 witnesses in that time, and their testimony filled 5,633 pages published in six separate volumes, an astonishing total for a single bill.

The Ways and Means Committee and the Appropriations Committee, by virtue of their fundamental jurisdictions, have always been the elite committees of the House, but there have been others that carried great weight in operating the national government. Principal among these have been the Committees on Agriculture, Armed Services, Banking and Currency, Education and Labor, Foreign Affairs, Government Operations, Interior and Insular Affairs, Interstate and Foreign Commerce, Judiciary, and Public Works. Like Ways and Means and Appropriations, these committees also have spent long weeks examining the major legislative measures coming under their jurisdiction. Occasionally one of these committees carried the most important legislation of the House. The Interstate and Foreign Commerce Committee, under the chairmanship of Sam Rayburn of Texas, in the early 1930's wrote an extraordinary record of legislative achievement, enacting an entirely new concept of government regulation of the stock market and security exchanges to protect American investors. On one measure alone, the Public Utilities Holding Company bill, Rayburn held two months of hearings and took enough testimony to fill 2,320 pages of published material. In more recent years, the Education and Labor Committee has had the double function of enacting legislation to resolve critical labor-management problems and the nation's educational needs. Its members have held extensive hearings on both subjects.

The fundamental right of the House to explore the inner workings of every government agency has stemmed from the Constitution's explicit provision that the House of Representatives "shall have the sole power of impeachment." That power was restricted merely to presenting an indictment, for the Constitution gave to the Senate the responsibility for trying those accused by the House of high crimes, bribery, or misdemeanors. Over the decades, the House has used this great power but sparingly. Indeed, the very processes of impeachment have all but fallen completely into disuse. In the seventeen decades of the history of the House of Representatives, the House has so charged only twelve men. Of these, only four were actually convicted by vote of the United States Senate on the House's indictment. By the very nature of the federal government, impeachment has been almost entirely used against judges on the federal bench. James Wilson, a signer of the United States Constitution, a great legal scholar, and a member of the Supreme Court, found the origin of the impeachment processes in the British House of Commons during the reign of King Edward III, in the fourteenth century. Wilson said that the House of Commons used the procedures "against offenders who were thought to be out of the reach of the ordinary power of the law." [2] In the American federal system, only the President, Vice President, and members of the federal judiciary so qualify, for they cannot be removed from office except by impeachment. The President and Vice President have been elected by the whole people to their posts for specific terms. The members of the judiciary have received appointments for life. Every other member of the executive branch could be removed from office by the President. Members of the House and Senate could be expelled by a vote of their colleagues.

Despite this limited use of formal impeachment proceedings— no impeachment has been voted since 1936—the power to impeach has been implicit in the House's right to investigate the whole of the federal bureaucracy. These rights were claimed for the first time by the House in 1792, when the Representatives ordered an investigation of General St. Clair's humiliating defeat by a band of Miami, Delaware, and Shawnee Indians in the Northwest Territory. On March 27, 1792, the House took up the affair under a resolution that proposed that President Washington be "requested" to investigate the disaster. Members of the House protested, however, that such an investigation was more properly the business of the House of Representatives as the Grand Inquest of the Nation. The House formally rejected, 21 to 35, the resolution to ask Washington to order the investigation, and instead adopted by a vote of 44 to 10 another resolution to create a select committee of the House to conduct the investigation. The committee was formally authorized to subpoena such witnesses and records as might be needed. Thus was born the first Congressional investigation.

Nine days after this momentous decision to conduct its own investigation, the House, by resolution, formally requested President Washington to send to the House the pertinent papers held by the Administration pertaining to General St. Clair's expedition. Washington, a stickler for proper precedents in the government, promptly summoned his Cabinet and asked those officers for their advice. The members of his Cabinet believed the request by the House of such great consequence that they declined to make an immediate answer to the President; they asked time to study properly so grave a matter. The Cabinet, which included both Thomas Jefferson and Alexander Hamilton, in due course reported unanimously to the President that the House, as the Grand Inquest of the Nation, had a right to the papers requested. Acting on this recommendation, Washington directed his Secretary of War, Henry Knox, to deliver the appropriate records to the House of Representatives. The select House committee, after investigating, completely exonerated General St. Clair but sharply criticized Knox's War Department for the "mismanagements" responsible for St. Clair's defeat.

The decision by Washington's Cabinet and George Washington himself to submit to the House the papers requested was also, of course, a historic precedent. It was a precedent, however, carefully limited, for the Cabinet in its recommendation to the President specified that, in the St. Clair investigation, "there was not a paper which might not properly be produced." Obviously, from this language, the Cabinet foresaw the distinct possibility that there could come instances when it would be improper for the President to acquiesce to such a request. Just such a request came to President Washington from the House only four years later. In 1796, the House, by resolution, asked the President for all the Administration's papers and records that bore on the negotiations with Great Britain that led to the Jay Treaty. Washington refused to deliver them. This was a different matter, Washington made plain, and for the President to permit the House to examine all the confidential papers involved in negotiating a treaty, an area outside the House's proper jurisdiction, would set a dangerous precedent. "It is essential," Washington replied to the House, "to the due administration of Government, that the boundaries fixed by the Constitution between the different departments should be preserved. . . ." [3] That was the first instance of a President acting to protect his own Constitutional prerogatives from intrusions by the Congress. In the decades to follow, there were many similar instances, for the House and the President were not always agreed on an identical definition of the Congress's right to know and the President's right to withhold information.

President Jefferson, in 1807, refused a request by the House of Representatives for papers in his possession concerning Aaron Burr's alleged treason. Jefferson replied to the House that the papers he held were "such a mixture of rumors, conjectures, and suspicions as renders it difficult to sift out the real facts." Besides, Jefferson added, many of the papers were given to him on the terms of "private confidence" [4] and he was not free to betray those confidences. This was a significant claim, for Jefferson thus laid down the doctrine that the President's confidential information and advice was his alone and not subject to Congressional scrutiny. President John Tyler made much the same claim in 1843 when the House requested a confidential army report. Tyler asserted that the President had personal discretion in withholding

181

such confidential files. Presidents ever since have been using this same argument in refusing to disclose to Congress the recommendations and reports of their advisers and subordinates.

This, however, was not the only ground that Presidents have used to refuse to grant the House's requests for information from the executive branch of the government. Indeed, more than one President used the House's Constitutional power to impeach as the specific reason for declining to supply the House with requested information. In 1837, President Jackson categorically refused to grant such a request on the ground that the House seemed intent to use the information requested to impeach him and his Cabinet officers. "In open violation of the Constitution and that well-established maxim that 'all men are presumed to be innocent until proven guilty,'" Jackson replied to the House, "you request myself and heads of departments to become our own accusers and to furnish the evidence to convict ourselves." [5] In effect, Jackson relied on the protections of the Constitution's Fifth Amendment. Jackson said he would resist that attempted "invasion" of the principles of justice "as I would the establishment of a Spanish inquisition." In 1860, President Buchanan made much the same reply on a similar request for information from the House. Buchanan told the House that since its power to investigate rested on its power to impeach, the charges suggested—which he said amounted to high crimes and misdemeanors—should be specified and considered first by the House's Judiciary Committee, the regular method of impeachment.

President Grant also was harassed by a request from the House to submit information obviously intended to embarrass him. He had followed the practice of taking extended vacations outside Washington, and the House asked him to list all the Presidential acts he had "performed at a distance from the seat of government" with explanations of why he was absent from the capital city. Grant already had become familiar with House investigations. In 1867, when he was still a general, he had been called to testify on the parole he had granted General Robert E. Lee and Lee's army at Appomattox. "I will state here," said Grant, in response to the hostile questions, "that I am not quite certain whether I am being tried, or who is being tried, by the questions asked." [6] In response to the demand for information he received as President, Grant replied that the request indicated the intent to impeach him. If this was so, he said, it violated the Fifth Amendment, "a Constitutional guarantee which protects every citizen, the President as well as the humblest in the land, from being made a witness against himself."

What Presidents Jackson, Buchanan, and Grant confronted, as did other Presidents as well, was not so much a calculated attempt by the House to inveigle them to reveal such high crimes as would justify their impeachment and removal from office as the simple political purpose of embarrassing them. The House of Representatives, by its very numbers, has long been a legislative assembly more conducive to party spirit than the United States Senate. The House, by the nature of its leadership, has also been a legislative chamber in which the members have been more responsive to party control and influence than the Senate. In the House, strong majority control has been able to discourage and even suppress investigations of administrations under Presidents of the same party. When, however, the House has been controlled by a political party opposing the President's party, the tendency has been for the House to indulge freely in such investigations. Democratic President Buchanan was harassed by a Republican-controlled House in 1860, and Republican President Grant was similarly harassed by a Democratic-controlled House in 1876. Long before these years the House had discovered the political possibilities of attacking the credits of the opposition party's President. The creation of House "fishing committees," or "smelling committees," [7] as Woodrow Wilson once called them, had been practiced for many years, even then.

Ben Perley Poore, a noted nineteenth-century journalist whose personal reminiscences stretched back to the inauguration of John Quincy Adams in 1825, recorded that it was during Adams' administration that "Congressional investigating committees became a part of the political machinery of the day." [8] Their efforts were bent on giving political advantage to the majority party in the House in the coming elections. Poore said that in these years the House "paraded before the public" a long series of political investigations intended to humiliate the prominent politicians by the revelation of personal "scandals." [9] Among them were investigations of the bills for refurnishing the White House, the "bargain" between Adams and Henry Clay that allegedly gave Adams the White House in return for appointing Clay Secretary of State, and General Jackson's marriage to a woman still not divorced from her legal husband. The House "fishing" expeditions before the Civil War were but mild in comparison with those in the years immediately after that war. In 1868, a Democrat recorded with outrage and shock the extremes to which the Republicans carried the House in making such investigations. These investigations, he wrote, had "become a very important branch of business" of the House of Representatives. "If a riot occurs in New Orleans or Memphis, if generals are supposed to have erred or blundered, a collector at New York cheated or been cheated . . . or a murder has been committed and accomplices are unknown, or a printer gets too good a contract or none at all, or it is hoped that the Executive has done or said something wrong, a committee is at once appointed." These excuses were used, he also reported, for early examples of Congressional junkets, trips to far off places at the public expense. "No legislation, but much electioneering, grows out of these expeditions," he said. "Sometimes they sit in Washington, and at others go to the Rocky Mountains, and at others about the country generally. . . . These fishing trips seem to serve the purpose of Congressional holidays, the government paying the expenses of the frolic." [10] Yet another contemporary found that when the Democrats won control of the House in 1875, they used investigating committees for even more partisan political purposes. He reported that more than 100 investigations were ordered by the House to expose the alleged graft, nepotism, and corruption in the Administration. "Every scandal-monger, every one who had anything to tell which would reflect on the honor or character of any Republican official, however humble, was made welcome at the Democratic House," he said. "Dragnets were thrown out in every direction." [11] This reporter, Theron Crawford, said that perhaps one particular

184

investigation best revealed how far the Democratic members of the House went in their partisanship. A Washington grocer was called to testify before the House Judiciary Committee. He said that President Grant had seduced his sister and later forced him into exile in England. The committee "took up the charge gravely and allowed the scandalous story to be published before they had taken the trouble to examine into the character or standing of the man making so infamous a charge against the President of the United States." The committee then recalled the grocer and asked him how Grant had paid his first visit to his sister. The witness testified that Grant had arrived at two o'clock in the morning and floated into his house on a cloud. Only then did the committee members realize that the witness was insane.

Only once has the partisan politics of the House become so violent that the Representatives actually impeached a President of the United States. That happened in 1868, when the radical Republicans in the House, lead by Thaddeus Stevens of Pennsylvania, formally indicted President Andrew Johnson of high crimes and misdemeanors. Stevens' contemporaries agreed that he ruled the House by the sheer force of his imperious will. George Boutwell spoke of Stevens as "a tyrant" in the House, "at once able, bold and unscrupulous." [12] John Sherman of Ohio said he was a sarcastic, cynical, merciless "old bachelor with a deformed foot and with a bitter tongue" [13] who yet was always kind and charitable to the poor. His will was indomitable, his mind was fearless, and he was capable of ironic humor. So feeble in 1866 that he had to be carried by two stalwart servants up the Capitol steps, Stevens asked them one day: "Who will carry me when you are dead, boys?" [14] He swept the House behind him to the impeachment of President Johnson for "malversation in office"—ostensibly for his violation of the Tenure in Office Act, an act Johnson believed unconstitutional. In reality Stevens wanted Johnson, a Democrat, impeached for his refusal to agree to punish the Southern states for the Civil War as Stevens, and his Republicans, wanted the Confederates punished. This was the ultimate appeal the House of Representatives could make against a President—to act to remove him from office, for that was the penalty if the Senate convicted him of the House's charges. Stevens relentlessly pursued Johnson. Despite Stevens' extreme physical debility, he became one of the House managers who presented the House's indictment to the Senate against the President. Too weak to stand, he received permission from the Senate to be seated while he read his own indictment of Johnson. Then, even too feeble to speak, he passed his speech to another of the House managers to read for him.

Party partisanship has waned in the modern House of Representatives from its ferocity of the nineteenth century. In the first half of the twentieth century, only rarely has the House of Representatives been controlled by a political party hostile to the President and the Administration. President Taft had one such hostile House of Representatives, and Presidents Wilson, Hoover, Truman, and Eisenhower also faced a House controlled by the opposition. In each case, the House and the President clashed, often bitterly. President Truman's epic fight with the Eightieth Congress gave him his main national issue in the Presidential election of 1948. These divided governments, however, covered only eight of the first fifty-five years of the century. During all the other years, the House and the Presidency were controlled by men of the same party. Perhaps the most controversial of twentieth-century Presidents, Franklin Roosevelt, enjoyed the luxury of Democratic Houses throughout his twelve years in the White House. The party leaders of the House, throughout these years of the twentieth century, constrained whatever tendencies there were in the House to investigate the administrations for the sake of partisan political advantage. Occasionally, a member of the House, on his own, has demanded the impeachment of a President, but he normally has found himself with but little support in the House.

President Eisenhower served eight years in the White House and for six of those years the House of Representatives was controlled by the opposition Democratic party. No President ever had to deal so long with an opposition party in control of the House. Eisenhower, however, was so politically popular throughout the country that few Democrats in the House dared to attack him openly. One Democrat, Cleveland Bailey of West Virginia, in 1957 did accuse Eisenhower of being a "lousy liar," [15] but when the White House indicated displeasure at Bailey's language, he quickly took refuge by denying that he had ever spoken the words. The Democrats in the House, in these years, normally concentrated their political fire on the men around Eisenhower, notably his Secretary of Agriculture, Ezra Benson. Even here, however, they were hesitant to seek political advantage through the House's powers of investigation. Once House investigators did come close to striking President Eisenhower, when they examined the compromising relationship between Boston textile manufacturer Bernard Goldfine and Eisenhower's White House chief of staff, Sherman Adams. Even then, the House investigating subcommittee treated Adams, a former member of the House, with utmost caution.

The investigation that disclosed Adams' relationship with Goldfine—Goldfine had paid $3,000 worth of hotel bills for Adams—actually stumbled on Goldfine's operations only by accident. The investigating group, the Commerce Committee's subcommittee on legislative oversight, had been commissioned by the House, at Speaker Rayburn's suggestion, to determine whether the government's regulatory agencies were discharging their responsibilities in accordance with Congressional intent. The investigating subcommittee, headed by Morgan Moulder of Missouri, quickly ran wild under its special counsel, Bernard Schwartz. Schwartz issued a series of charges against many members of the regulatory agencies, and even accused members of the subcommittee of trying to "whitewash" the commissioners' alleged offenses. At this point, Oren Harris of Arkansas, chairman of the parent Commerce Committee, removed Moulder as chairman of the subcommittee and fired Schwartz. Meanwhile, however, investigators for the subcommittee had been canvassing Boston on a television-channel application case and there they heard charges that Goldfine had presented many gifts to Adams in return for Adams' help in settling his difficulties with the regulatory agencies. In due course, Goldfine was summoned to testify. So was Adams. Adams denied influencing any federal agency to be lenient with Goldfine, but he admitted financial relations with Goldfine so compromising that President Eisenhower eventually had to ask him to resign. For Goldfine, a different punishment was dealt. He refused to answer some of the subcommittee's questions. The subcommittee thereupon submitted a resolution to the House citing Goldfine for contempt. This resolution the House adopted by a vote of 369 to 8. Goldfine, after formal trial, was sent to jail.

All through the House's history, the power of the House to punish witnesses for contempt has been a major weapon of its investigating committees. Indeed, the House has acted so often to punish contempt that a large body of legal precedents has been constructed on the formal procedures and powers. These have refined and narrowed the discretion of the witnesses to refuse to answer questions; they have also refined and narrowed the House's power to punish recalcitrant witnesses. To hazard contempt of the House, in modern times, has been to risk a court trial and a penalty of $1,000 fine and a year in jail for every count of contempt on which the witness has been convicted.

In the early years of the House, the Representatives did not depend on the federal judiciary to try anyone they believed to be in contempt of the House. The Representatives did so themselves. They claimed the power to do so under common law. In 1795, the House formally directed its Sergeant at Arms to arrest two men, Robert Randall and Charles Whitney, on charges made by members of the House that they had tried to bribe them. Both men were brought before the House, questioned by the Speaker, and imprisoned briefly by a formal vote of the House. In 1818, John Anderson was tried by the House for a similar offense. Anderson sued the Sergeant at Arms for false imprisonment, but the Supreme Court ruled that the House had the legal power to punish Anderson for the contempt he had implicitly shown the House by trying to corrupt one of its members with a gift of $500. In 1857, the House and the Senate approved a law providing that witnesses who defied Congressional investigating committees be cited for contempt and tried, under indictment, in federal court. The penalty for this misdemeanor was fixed at no more than a $1,000 fine and one year in "a common jail." Earlier that same year, the House had been frustrated by a *New York Times*'s reporter who refused to testify before a House committee investigating charges he had made that certain members of the House had offered to sell their votes on legislation. The House debated on what to do with the reporter, James Simonton, if he persisted in his refusal to testify. Howell Cobb of Georgia proposed that he be confined in the city jail for six months. This, however, raised a Constitutional question, whether the House, under common law, could continue the imprisonment of the defiant witness after the House itself had ceased to exist. The House then was but six weeks from its own automatic dissolution on March 4. This limitation led to the adoption of the law on contempt. Theretofore, in confining witnesses or others for contempt, the House had done so for periods not beyond its own annual adjournment. By adoption of the law giving the power of punishment to the federal courts, a recalcitrant witness could be sent to jail for a full year. In giving this power to the federal courts, the House and the Senate retained their own powers, under the common law, to imprison and fine anyone found in contempt. Indeed, in one case, brought against John Walcott, a recalcitrant witness in a bribery investigation, the House not only imprisoned him in 1858 but also turned him over to a federal court under the new law. The court found him guilty and sentenced him to pay a $1,000 fine. This was a unique case, for Walcott was punished twice for the same offense, despite the Constitution's prohibition against double jeopardy.

All through the 1850's, 1860's, and 1870's, the House used its common-law powers to punish contempts, largely ignoring the law permitting the federal courts to adjudicate these questions. In 1876, in one of these cases, the House ordered the imprisonment of Hallet Kilbourn, a witness who refused to answer a House committee's questions. Kilbourn was locked up in the city jail for forty-five days and won his release only by obtaining a writ of habeus corpus from a federal court. He thereupon sued the House's Sergeant at Arms, the Speaker, and members of the committee for false arrest. The case reached the Supreme Court

189

in 1880, and the Court then laid down a far-reaching decision on the House's power to investigate and to punish for contempt. The decision exonerated Kilbourn and awarded him a judgment against the Sergeant at Arms, John Thompson. More than that, however, the Supreme Court ruled that the House had no right to investigate the private affairs of citizens unless there was a demonstrable need for the information desired to help the House enact new law.

Not until 1916 did the House again imprison anyone for contempt. In this instance, the House ordered the arrest of Snowden Marshall, a United States attorney then under investigation for impeachment. Marshall's arrest was prompted by a defamatory and insulting letter he wrote to the chairman of the House Judiciary Committee. Marshall won release by obtaining a writ of habeus corpus from the Supreme Court. The Supreme Court ruled that the House had no authority to punish anyone for criticizing the House. A full twenty years passed, before the House again acted to punish a witness for contempt. This time, in 1936, the person charged was Francis Townsend, author of the Townsend Plan to help the aged. He walked out of a committee session rather than answer any more hostile questions. He was tried and convicted in federal court for contempt, and received a pardon from President Franklin Roosevelt.

The House of Representatives had been severely restricted by the 1880 ruling of the Supreme Court, a decision that left in doubt the House's exact rights to investigate. Where the House had considered forty-nine cases of contempt or alleged contempt in the thirty years before the Supreme Court ruling on the Kilbourn case, the House considered only six such cases—and took action in only four of these—in the sixty years after that Supreme Court ruling. In large measure, the Senate had taken over much of the Congressional activity in conducting investigations, and not until the House of Representatives took an active interest in communism and Communist infiltration did the House again assert its ancient power to investigate and to cite contumacious witnesses under the law of 1857.

As early as 1930, the House of Representatives had shown an

interest in communism and "un-American" activities. In May of that year, the House authorized a special committee, headed by Hamilton Fish of New York, to "investigate Communist propaganda in the United States." Four years later, in 1934, the House authorized another similar investigation, this time by a select committee chaired by John McCormack of Massachusetts. The investigation was noteworthy for its careful and dignified hearings, its proposal that resulted in the enactment of a law requiring the registration of the agents of foreign governments, and the candor of the testimony by American Communists. Earl Browder, for example, freely gave the McCormack Committee full details on the American Communist party's relationship to and dependence on international communism originating in Moscow. Not until the 1940's did Communists claim the protection of the Fifth Amendment against giving any testimony at all to Congressional committees.

In 1938, still another select committee was created by the House of Representatives, this one at the suggestion of Martin Dies of Texas, to investigate various "un-American" activities including communism. Dies, in asking for the committee, said he expected it could complete its work in seven months; it was still going strong a quarter of a century later as a permanent standing committee of the House of Representatives. Dies operated the first Un-American Activities Committee largely on his own; he was bitterly criticized for attacking labor unions, the administration of President Roosevelt, minority groups, and individuals. President Roosevelt in 1939 accused Dies's committee of being "sordid, flagrantly unfair, and un-American," [16] to which Dies replied that he knew there were thousands of Communists in the federal government. Walter Lippman described the committee members as vigilantes, "often lawless in spirit and disorderly in their methods." The Congress of Industrial Organizations formally resolved that Dies, as chairman, had been "sordid and reprehensible" in his conduct. Emanuel Celler of New York, later to be chairman of the House Judiciary Committee, denounced the Un-American Activities Committee for disseminating "irresponsible slanders against honest public

191

servants and private individuals . . . on testimony consisting of surmise, conjecture, unfounded opinion, unsupported conclusions and unwarranted deductions, without any attempt at verification or confirmation." [17]

This was but the beginning of a furious and embittered quarrel between the advocates and the opponents of the House Un-American Activities Committee, a quarrel that made that committee the most controversial in the history of Congress. The committee's enemies equated its operations with the denial of the fundamental American rights of personal freedom. The committee's friends equated its operations with the very defense of the nation itself. The entrance of the United States into World War II and the resulting alliance with Russia briefly quieted the operations of the Un-American Activities Committee. By 1944, the committee had almost ceased to exist, holding that year only a single one-day hearing, and Dies himself retired from the House. The postwar resumption of domestic politics and international rivalry with Russia, however, brought the Un-American Activities Committee to an even greater notoriety than in the years Dies had been chairman. In 1947, the committee engaged in a widely publicized investigation of communism in Hollywood. Summoned before the committee were such motion-picture stars as Adolph Menjou, Ginger Rogers, and Robert Taylor. The committee hearings often took on the atmosphere of comic opera. A committee aide suggested that Shirley Temple, a child actress, had Communist leanings. A committee member, Joe Starnes of Alabama, seriously asked whether Christopher Marlowe, the sixteenth-century playwright, was a Marxist Communist. Another committee member, John McDowell of Pennsylvania, frequently enlivened the hearings with his pompous and confused imagery. He once complimented a witness for walking "through the valley of the shadow of publicity"; another time he accused a witness of conspiring "to drive us down an alley of blind ownership of a car." Committee Chairman J. Parnell Thomas of New Jersey brazenly sought the limelight with coarse humor and political jibes; he described Frank Sinatra, the popular singer, as "sort of a Mrs. Roosevelt in pants." [18] Thomas later was convicted of accepting "kick backs" from employees on his Congressional staff and sent to jail. In an official report to the House, Thomas asserted that "some of the most flagrant Communist propaganda films are produced as a result of White House pressure." [19] Thomas and other committee members frequently grabbed for headlines by leaking to the press almost daily "sensations" that often proved groundless. They talked of "surprise" hearings, "mystery" witnesses, and "shocking" new disclosures to come. McDowell kept alive for many days an unsubstantiated story that Benito Mussolini's mistress had illegally entered the United States and was, even then, under the surveillance of the committee's agents. The committee staff created scare headlines by leaking to the press the purported escapades of "Scientist X," a mystery witness supposedly engaged in atomic espionage. So irresponsible did the official committee leaks to the press become that the three national news services, the Associated Press, United Press, and International News Service, finally adopted an informal "gentlemen's agreement" not to report any committee activities except formal hearings and reports.

In 1948, the committee embarked on a new round of spectacular hearings, based on the testimony of former Communist agents Elizabeth Bentley and Whittaker Chambers. Chambers accused Alger Hiss, once a trusted official in the State Department, of serving Russia's cause by giving him transcripts of secret government documents for transmission to Moscow. The revelations of Miss Bentley and Chambers rocked Washington and the nation, for they gave intimate details of Communist cells, at work for Russia, inside the most sensitive United States agencies. The Truman administration was severely embarrassed politically; the President himself called the investigation "a red herring" brought to notoriety for political purposes. The Administration was even more embarrassed when Hiss was formally convicted and sent to jail on a charge of perjury for denying he had betrayed his country. The investigations by the committee tore away the middle ground of moderation in American politics; opponents of the Democratic administration freely spoke of treason and disloyalty in high places, not exempting the President himself.

That the committee had stumbled into stunning disclosures of disloyalty and espionage by officials of the government no one could deny who accredited the formal judicial proceedings of the United States Government. Hiss was convicted; so was William Remington; and President Truman himself installed a loyalty-security system to patrol the federal government. And Americans at large slowly became aware of the invidiousness of the Russian conspiracy to penetrate the United States Government with their own hidden agents. That the committee also had brought contumely on the Congress by its methods of procedure no dispassionate observer could dispute. Legal scholars charged that the committee's operations threatened the very fabric of American law. The committee's exaggerations and the antics of its members made many Americans question angrily whether there was in truth any such thing as subversion in America, despite unimpeachable evidence to the contrary. Speaker Sam Rayburn took cognizance of the embarrassment the committee was bringing on the House of Representatives by two deliberate actions. In 1949, he forced the removal from the committee of two of its most active Democratic members, John Rankin of Mississippi and Edward Hébert of Louisiana; and he replaced them with Democrats who he believed would prove more judicial. Among these was Francis Walter of Pennsylvania, a Rayburn "protégé" and one of the House's ablest parliamentarians. Rayburn also ruled that hereafter no photographs could be taken of any House committee while that committee was formally in session. Years before, Will Rogers had joked that "Congressional investigations are for the benefit of the photographers." Rayburn hoped to induce a more decorous atmosphere at committee sessions by this ruling.

Despite the attempts to temper the committee's notoriety, periodically, in the years that followed, its activities created new angry controversies. In 1953, Committee Chairman Harold Velde of Illinois launched an investigation of some of the country's most revered universities. Without even consulting his fellow committee members he boldly issued a subpoena for former President Harry Truman, a subpoena Truman ignored. In 1957, a subpoenaed witness, William Sherwood, committed suicide just before he was to appear before the committee at a hearing in San Francisco. Sherwood left a note stating that he could not go through the ordeal of the planned televised hearing. Rayburn promptly extended his ruling against photography of any kind to hearings outside Washington as well as those in the capital. Three years later, on May 13, 1960, another committee session in San Francisco erupted into a wild riot by critics of the committee. Local police drove the rioters from San Francisco's City Hall with fire hoses, and twelve persons were injured, eight of them policemen. The committee later issued a film—"Operation Abolition"—that created a new controversy. The committee's critics claimed the film had been "doctored" to throw the events into a false light; the committee itself argued that the film proved that the riot had been conducted by American Communists.

The committee had become the most active investigating committee of the House. In the period from 1945 through 1957, it held more than 230 series of public hearings at which more than 3,000 witnesses testified. In 1953 and 1954, alone, the committee held 178 days of hearings and heard from 650 witnesses. The committee had an erratic popularity with members of the House. In 1947, there was keen competition among the members to win assignment to it, but two years later the openings on the committee went begging. Sam Rayburn, it was reported, received 101 letters from Democrats making requests for committee assignments and not one asked for the Un-American Activities Committee. By 1953 membership on the committee had again become popular, and Representatives were competing to get on it. The committee, over its hectic life, cited more persons for contempt than all the other committees of Congress since the beginning of the United States government in 1789. The first contempts voted came just before United States entry into World War II, when the committee brought charges against five witnesses, three of whom later were convicted and fined. In the twelve years, from 1945 to 1957, 135 other witnesses were cited for contempt. The protests of these witnesses followed an observable pattern. Through 1947 they all argued against the power of the committee to question them about their beliefs; and they claimed the protection of the Constitution's First Amendment—which protects freedom of speech—as their defense against answering the committee's questions. Almost without exception, the thirty-five persons who made this claim were convicted of contempt. In later years, hostile witnesses claimed the protection of the Constitution's Fifth Amendment—which protects the individual from being forced to testify against himself—and the federal courts then began to acquit those charged by the committee with contempt. The federal courts, in short, credited the right of the committee to conduct the investigations, but excused those witnesses who stated that their answers might tend to incriminate them. Richard Nixon of California, a member of the committee for four years, explained years later one reason why the committee's activities in the years immediately after World War II received such bitter criticism. In this period, the witnesses claimed that the right of free speech was endangered. Nixon said that the committee's critics were, with few exceptions, not motivated by sympathy with communism. "It was, rather, because such investigations seemed in that period to involve an attack on the free expression of ideas." [20] The shift of the witnesses from the protection of the First Amendment to that of the Fifth gradually made plain that these witnesses were more deeply involved in the conspiracies under investigation than had been generally believed.

Nixon, ironically, first made his name known in national politics as a member of the Un-American Activities Committee at the time, 1947-48, when the committee was most severely under nationwide criticism for its objectionable behavior. The committee then was under the chairmanship of J. Parnell Thomas of New Jersey, and Nixon, thirty-five years old, was but a freshman member of the House. In 1948, the committee heard Whittaker Chambers testify against Alger Hiss and then heard Hiss categorically deny the truth of Chambers' testimony. Public opinion clearly sided with Hiss, but Nixon was suspicious. By studious preparations and dogged questioning of both Chambers and Hiss, Nixon laid the groundwork for Hiss's spectacular conviction for perjury. Although only a freshman, Nixon became the dominant member of the committee during the Chambers-Hiss hearings and leaped into national prominence. His success as a member of the Un-American Activities Committee gave Nixon the personal credits to become one of the most important political leaders of mid-century. Two years after the Chambers-Hiss hearings began, Nixon was elected to the United States Senate, and two years after that he was elected Vice President of the United States. From that post, in 1960, Nixon was chosen as the nominee for President of the Republican party.

In the long history of the House, no unknown freshman had ever made so rapid an advance in national politics, although periodically over the decades an investigation has hurtled an unknown member of the House into national prominence. Such was the case in 1875 with Joseph Blackburn of Kentucky, then a freshman Representative. As a member of the Committee on Expenditures in the War Department, Blackburn discovered the peculations of the Secretary of War, William Belknap, and brought his improprieties to public knowledge. As a result, the House of Representatives formally impeached Belknap, who promptly resigned from President Grant's Cabinet. Blackburn's political future was made; he missed winning the Speakership of the House by only two votes and then went on to serve eighteen years in the United States Senate.

The abuse of witnesses by members of House committees also was not a modern phenomenon, although rarely has any investigative body gone to the extreme that a House committee did in 1837 with a terrified witness. The witness, Reuben Whitney, was arraigned before the House on a charge of contempt, but he was excused when the facts of his case became known. He had declined to answer the questions put to him by members of a House committee investigating the Treasury Department. One of the committee members, Balie Peyton of Tennessee, believed that Whitney's replies would be offensive to him. "Mr. Chairman," Peyton said, "I wish you would inform this witness that he is not to insult me in his answers. If he does, I will take his life on the spot." Whitney promptly asked protection from the committee.

"You shan't speak," Peyton shouted at him. "You shan't say one word while you are in this room. If you do I will put you to death." The committee chairman, Henry Wise of Virginia, agreed completely with Peyton. "Yes," said Wise, "this insolence is insufferable." The witness was denied even the right to look at Peyton, and Chairman Wise, who was armed, was equally ready to kill him. "I watched the motion of that right arm," Wise said later of Whitney, "the elbow of which could be seen by me, and had it moved one inch he had died on the spot. This was my determination." [21] It was scarcely any wonder that the House of Representatives formally found it "inexpedient" to prosecute Whitney for contempt.

A modern phenomenon of the House's investigatory powers has been the growing practice of Representatives to travel about the United States and the world at public cost, ostensibly as part of their duties as legislators. Any such trip has come to be known as a "junket," a word that originally meant a banquet or any delicate food but that came to be used in the United States for any outing at the taxpayer's expense. In the years prior to the entrance of the United States into world politics, Congressional junkets were confined within the United States or to United States possessions like the Canal Zone, Puerto Rico, or the Philippines. In the nineteenth century, American railroads were more than generous in giving members of the House and Senate passes that permitted them to ride free anywhere the railroads ran. That the Congress had jurisdiction over legislation affecting the railroads troubled at least some of the Representatives, who declined to accept them. No less a Representative, however, than Schuyler Colfax of Indiana, as Speaker of the House in House debate formally defended the practice of accepting and using these free passes. He stated that he never returned the railroad passes sent to him and hoped his colleagues would do likewise. "I am perfectly willing to receive as many as the companies see fit to send," he said, "and have never supposed that my independent action would be controlled by receiving them." [22] He saw no impropriety in accepting such gifts, and not until the public at large protested were the free railroad passes discontinued. Even then, however, a more attractive benefit had been offered Representatives and Senators—free transportation on American steamships, whose owners long have been subsidized by the federal government. The members of the House and Senate not only made use of these free accommodations, but they often took their wives and families along with them. Not until 1960 was this questionable practice finally prohibited by Congressional action. By then, the Representatives had unprecedented opportunity to travel wherever they wanted to go around the world at public cost under the existing usages of the House. The justification for such trips was sound: the Representatives had to acquaint themselves with existing world situations to educate themselves so that they could form valid judgments in enacting federal law. Even so, however, many of the Representatives' trips more closely resembled taxpayer-paid vacations than study missions, and even the most scrupulous of Representatives preferred normally to make such trips quietly, without undue publicity. American voters had been tutored over many decades to suspect that all such trips were little better than legalized pilfering of government funds.

Perhaps the most scandalous of Congressional junkets were the funeral parties that flourished well into the 1930's. Such parties were arranged almost every time a member of the House or Senate died in office. A luxurious train would be hired to convey the body of the dead Congressman back to his home district, and a cortege of Representatives was appointed to accompany the remains of their colleague to his final resting place. In the 1880's, these funeral parties were already a public disgrace. The funeral march, reported one Washington correspondent at the time, more closely resembled a traveling drunken brawl. "Its baggage is largely made up of wines and liquors," he wrote. "Champagne flows like water, and the bills for meals are the heaviest items of the expense account." [23] He found that one lunch cost $122, an enormous amount at that time. By the 1920's, there had been but little improvement in the décor of these mournful obsequies. A Washington correspondent reported in 1927 that the drinking and revelry on these funeral trips were interrupted scarcely long enough for the actual burial of the deceased. These trips were so popular, that correspondent reported, that one freshman member of the House informed the Speaker that he would cheerfully forego all other committee assignments if he could be permanently assigned to travel with all funeral parties.[24]

The entrance of the United States into World War I first opened to Congressional junketeers the possibilities of European travel. Representatives and Senators embarked week after week for Europe to inspect the men at the front or the military buildup behind the lines. Not infrequently the Congressmen also "inspected" the boulevards and night life of Paris. Officially sponsored trips abroad multiplied after that war, with the Congressmen frequently commandeering the services of battleships or army transports to carry them to their destinations. Those on these junkets, however, limited themselves to United States possessions: Alaska, Hawaii, the Panama Canal, the Virgin Islands, Puerto Rico, or the Philippines. There were still domestic trips to be made, however, to such scenic spots as Yellowstone National Park. One such trip to St. Louis, ostensibly to dedicate a memorial to Thomas Jefferson, brought a stinging rebuke from John Nance Garner of Texas for the bills run up by those on that junket. Garner took Thomas Heflin of Alabama, one of the junketeers, to task on the expense. "How does the gentleman account for the fact that it takes $350 for each individual to go to St. Louis, stay one day and return?" Garner asked. "I have no confidence in anybody who figures it will cost $350 for a man to go to St. Louis for a day." [25]

The mid-1930's brought the first of the tours of foreign countries. Thomas McMillan of South Carolina, chairman of the State Department Appropriations subcommittee, in 1936 visited twenty-eight United States diplomatic and consular posts abroad. Until then Representatives traveling abroad normally went as tourists and paid their own way. World War II brought an explosion of junkets to foreign countries, prompted by Congressional interest in all kinds of new concerns, from foreign aid to hoof-and-mouth disease. Members of the House Foreign Affairs Committee in earlier years had largely pre-empted most of the foreign travel by Representatives, but after World War II just about every committee of the House found it had grave concern in the affairs of foreign lands. In 1953 and 1954, the Foreign Affairs Committee officially assigned members of the committee to make surveys in Australia, Belgium, Brazil, Colombia, Denmark, the Dominican Republic, El Salvador, England, France, Germany, Greece, Guatemala, Haiti, India, Indonesia, Iraq, Israel, Italy, Jordan, Lebanon, Malay, Mexico, the Netherlands, Nicaragua, Norway, Pakistan, Panama, Peru, Portugal, Spain, Sweden, Switzerland, Syria, Trieste, Turkey, Uruguay, Venezuela, and Yugoslavia. Other committees of the House were equally active. The Judiciary Committee, for example, in 1960, sent Representatives to Argentina, Brazil, France, Germany, Italy, the Netherlands, Switzerland, Great Britain, Hong Kong, Japan, Korea, the Philippines, Morocco, Spain, Senegal, Denmark, Belgium, Poland, Taiwan, Egypt, Iraq, Jordan, Lebanon, and Sudan. Many of the postwar trips were financed in part by so-called counterpart funds, local currencies owned in the foreign countries by the United States as a by-product of foreign aid. By ordinary usage, the visiting Representatives and Senators had merely to ask United States diplomats in these countries for as much of the counterpart funds as they wanted. There was no supervision over how much they received or how they spent it. In 1957, 117 Representatives made such trips abroad, the great bulk of them going to Europe. In 1958, these House committees authorized trips to foreign lands: Agriculture, Armed Services, Banking and Currency, District of Columbia, Education and Labor, Foreign Affairs, Government Operations, Interstate and Foreign Commerce, Judiciary, Post Office and Civil Service, Public Works, Veterans Affairs, and Ways and Means. In all, they spent $356,493 of the government's counterpart funds in the countries they visited, plus the money for their transportation and expenses not covered by the counterpart funds. International conferences had become a favorite with the Representatives; among the attractions in 1958 were the conference of NATO parliamentarians in Paris, the Interparliamentary Union meeting in Rio de Janeiro, and a conference on atomic energy in Geneva.

201

Transparently some members of the House abused their prerogatives to use government money to pay their expenses abroad, and, periodically, the newspapers exposed the flamboyant excursion of a Representative who was less than discreet on his foreign travels. In 1961, for example, Richard Lankford of Maryland made a thirty-eight-day trip around the world, visiting Honolulu, Tokyo, Saigon, Bangkok, Pakistan, Italy, Vienna, Germany, Paris, London, and Scotland. He turned in an expense account, which was paid, for $6,082.95. He spent four days in Hong Kong and listed $298 as "miscellaneous" expenses. He listed his hotel room in London at $66 a night and the cost of his meals there averaged $27. In all, he listed $1,379 for miscellaneous expenses; he did not itemize these costs and later, when questioned about them, he said he supposed some of that money "went for tips." The following year, 1962, Adam Clayton Powell of New York, chairman of the Education and Labor Committee, set off on a six-week trip to Europe when the House of Representatives was about to consider some of the major bills of President Kennedy's legislative program. Powell, accompanied by two women employees of his staff, traveled to London, Rome, Paris, Vienna, Spain, and Greece, ostensibly to study "job opportunities" of European women. He had requested, in advance of the trip, State Department assistance in getting him and his aides tickets to the Vienna film festival, reservations at various European night clubs, and a six-day cruise of the Aegean Sea.

Occasionally public disclosure of abuses by congressmen have brought restrictions on these activities. Such was the case in 1960 when two reporters published a series of articles detailing misuse of official expense accounts. The reporters, Walter Pincus and Don Oberdorfer, examined 25,329 vouchers paid by the House of Representatives over a period of two years and discovered cases where members had charged off to the government vacations with their wives, night-clubbing, and expensive parties. They found that one Representative had charged the government $25 for yacht club flags and another the cost of framing an oil painting of a "nude lady." The reaction to the disclosure came quickly. Eugene Siler of Kentucky, who had never made a junket, denounced the practice and said that three out of four of these trips were unnecessary. "Free bread and free circuses preceded the downfall of Rome," he said. "Shall free luxury suites and free nightclub entertainment . . . precede the twilight hours of this country?" [26] The House Administration Committee, with jurisdiction over the Representatives' expense accounts, adopted a new regulation that limited each traveling Representative to $25 a day in official expenses. In January, 1963, the House itself acted to restrict the foreign travels of its members. Responding in part to the junkets of Lankford in 1961 and Powell in 1962, the House unanimously forbade such trips in the future without its consent.

Many junkets, of course, have proved of real value to Congress and the country. One of the most remarkable of these was a delegation led by Christian Herter of Massachusetts, just after World War II. The members examined war-blighted Europe, and they saw with their own eyes the desperate conditions of the countries of Europe. Their findings played an important role in the adoption of the Marshall Plan to extend United States aid to these countries. Many less dramatic but useful trips have also been made, in which the Representatives have studied at first hand the far-flung interests of the United States government and the House of Representatives. One such trip examined the educational system of Russia. On this junket were Edith Green of Oregon, John Brademas of Indiana, Robert Giaimo of Connecticut, Neal Smith of Iowa, Albert Quie of Minnesota, Charles Goodell of New York, and Peter Garland of Maine, all members of the Education and Labor Committee and responsible for federal legislation dealing with United States education.

The expansion of House investigations into the world at large has reflected the ever-expanding interests of the nation and the Congress. The formal investigations in Washington and around the United States, the junkets to far-off lands, though subject to abuse, have helped provide the House of Representatives with the information needed to deal with the many-faceted concerns of the American people. The justification of these inquiries has been that, without them, the House itself would be blind to the realities of modern times. At best, an individual Representative could make himself master of scarcely more than a single field, and even to do this he had constantly to keep abreast of the changing conditions in that field, whether it was the nation's defense posture, the advance of medical science, or the problems of juvenile delinquency. The thrust of the United States into a position of world prominence, both militarily and economically, has enormously complicated the problem of the House of Representatives to understand the nuances and intricacies of the kaleidoscope that the United States has become in the middle years of the twentieth century.

In 1791, the year before the House's first investigation, Justice Wilson of the Supreme Court was lecturing in Philadelphia on the new government he had helped to shape as a member of the Constitutional Convention at Philadelphia four years earlier. "The House of Representatives," he explained, "form the grand inquest of the state. They will diligently inquire into grievances, arising both from men and things." [27] An unflagging interest in men and things has been a role of the House of Representatives, part of the responsibilities laid on the Representatives by the Founding Fathers in creating the American government.

CHAPTER NINE

Lions in the Lobby

THE decisions of the House of Representatives, by the very nature of the institution, have never been made in a vacuum. The matters passing in review before the House—great questions of national policy as well as specific items of interest to special groups—have been of too large a concern to permit the Representatives, dispassionately and disinterestedly, to weigh and balance their judgments on the abstract merits of each individual question. The House, in fact, long has been subjected to ferocious pressures and tuggings from a wide assortment of deeply interested persons outside the House itself. Joseph Cannon of Illinois, looking back in 1923 to his half century in the House, lamented the change that had come over the House of Representatives in his time, a change he blamed on the formalizing of the practice of lobbying.

"In the olden days, when public life offered greater attractions and honors, perhaps the men stood for more," Cannon said sadly of his colleagues. "Certainly they stood for greater independence of thought. They were not swayed by propaganda as now. Forty years ago there was no propaganda; certainly no organized agencies and lobbyists. Bills then originated in committees and represented the mature thought of the members. Now they are written and forced through Congress by outside organizations. The Constitution meant what it says. Now it is a thing to be shot at, after the agitators and legislators cannot find any other way of getting what they want. . . . In the old days bills were few. . . . A man had an opportunity to study legislation and could vote intelligently. Now the lobbyist comes to you and says 'We want this,' and generally he gets it. I ask whether legislation of today is anything more than hodgepodge? Forty years ago it represented the mature thought of the members." [1]

Cannon, perhaps forgetting the harsh discipline he himself once enforced on his party's ranks, spoke of a House of Representatives that never was—a House in which the members were unpestered by outside influence. In 1869, four years before Cannon first came to the House, George Hoar of Massachusetts reported that "the corridors of the Capitol and the committee rooms were crowded with lobbyists." [2] And in 1822, one hundred and one years before Cannon voiced his complaint, the lobbyists —although not then called by that name—were actively pressuring the members of Congress. Thomas Hart Benton recorded that "those interested" in an Indian bill "were vigilant and active" on Capitol Hill, "visiting the members who would permit such visits." [3] Not until 1832 were such visitors known as lobbyists in Washington, but the House of Representatives from its beginning has come under the fire of men vitally interested in the outcome of its decisions as a legislative body. In the earliest of its years, the pressures from outside the House came from men who were themselves public officials, men like Alexander Hamilton, President Washington's Secretary of the Treasury, or President Thomas Jefferson. Only later did the private lobbyists appear, but they were a major part of the Washington scene long before Cannon first arrived as a freshman member of the House of Representatives. Indeed, the swarming of the lobbyists into Washington for the opening of each session of Congress had already become one of the political phenomena many years before. Cannon, however, saw accurately that the nature and role of the lobbyist had radically changed during his years in the House. Where once the lobbyists, with but few exceptions, were political idlers desperately trying to grub a living from the greed of individuals seeking to win some minor pelf from the government, by the 1920's lobbying had become the highly skilled, technical profession of influencing the great decisions of the government. The lobbyists were men of rank in the nation's capital, although they still carried as a heritage from their predecessors a somewhat unsavory general reputation. Cannon saw lobbyists who had become specialists in creating, by propaganda and private pressures, the sense of national judgment on national questions. The skills they possessed that distressed Cannon were vastly improved from the tawdry improprieties that the lobbyists had once almost exclusively used, but they were naïve skills compared to what they were to become in the forty years after Cannon voiced his dismay. Where once the lobbyists were men viewed with hardly less respect than that of common criminals, by mid-twentieth century, they could be—as some were—the acknowledged political allies of the President himself with easy access to all the great officials of the government. Where once the lobbyists skulked in the lobbies of the Capitol, from which they took their name, in this century great committees of the Congress hesitated to act on important legislation without formally calling the lobbyists of the groups most vitally concerned to testify on the pending matter. The lobbyists had become not merely spokesmen for special interests, but political strategists of great ability and importance. As a group their interests had broadened to touch every aspect of American life, and no important bill, and scarcely even a minor bill, could proceed through Congress without a host of lobbyists ranged both for and against it.

What brought the lobbyists to Capitol Hill in the first place was the desire to influence legislation. What multiplied their number greatly over the years, until in the 1960's they numbered perhaps 4,000, was the proliferation of the federal government into a thousand fields of activity unknown to it in its earliest years; that, and the ever increasing awareness of economic, ethnic, political groups, themselves fractionalized many times over, that they had best maintain a lobbyist or a group of lobbyists in Washington to represent their personal interests in the decisions of the government. The range of the lobbyists by the 1960's was enormous. There were the great conservative lobbies, many of long standing on Capitol Hill, like the National Association of Manufacturers, the U.S. Chamber of Commerce, and the American Medical Association, perhaps the single most effective lobby in Washington. There were the great liberal lobbies, also long active in Washington, led by the American Federation of Labor-Congress of Industrial Organizations. The railroads, veterans, Negroes, insurance companies, schoolteachers, and hundreds of others, all had their lobbyists, too. Some, like the Teamsters Union, had built handsome and huge buildings nearby the Capitol to house their manifold lobbying activities. Others, like the tiny lobby to protect the wild horses of Wyoming, appeared to operate almost out of the lobbyist's suitcase. All had a profound concern for the political temper and mood of the House of Representatives.

Some of the lobbyists, men like Andrew Biemiller of the AFL-CIO, Cecil Dickson of the AMA, and Clarence Mitchell of the National Association for the Advancement of Colored People, had a refined instinct for the sense of the House. Biemiller was a former member of the House from Wisconsin; Dickson had a long intimacy with Speaker Sam Rayburn; Mitchell, a political intuition bred of long experience. They, and many of like skills, could touch the core of the House's wellspring of power, for they could read the moods of the House. They could sense its drift. Above all, with their lieutenants and allies, they could "count" the House: they could determine, in advance of a vote, the outcome of that vote on the floor of the House. And with that knowledge, they could at times so maneuver their own forces in the parliamentary arena that they could actually alter the vote of the House on legislation in which they were interested. Their parliamentary skills were a far cry from the crudities of their lobbyist predecessors a century before.

Perhaps the most colorful and picturesque of all the early lobbyists was Sam Ward, who flourished in Washington in the years immediately following the Civil War. A short, stout man with the imperial white beard of a French count, Ward was known as the "King of the Lobby." A man of refined education, who sported diamond studs in his shirts and never appeared without a rose in his coat lapel, Ward won his pre-eminence among the lobbyists by the sheer grandeur of his style. He entertained nightly the political leaders of Washington at a table groaning with choice viands and fine wines. Himself a wit and a gentleman of culture, Ward lavished on his guests a plentiful bounty with never so much as an indelicate suggestion of his ulterior motives: he never asked a man for a favor at his table. That came later, and statesmen, diplomats, politicians, and even the President occasionally sat with gusto at his table. "His operations were on a grand scale," wrote a contemporary, "and he dealt only with prominent men. He really had influence, and he did not stoop to petty means to gain his ends." [4] His services were available—for a price—to the railroads and other financial interests then most concerned with federal legislation.

Even before Sam Ward, the capital had seen a lobbyist of almost equal rank and style. This was Edward Pendleton, who operated the "Palace of Fortune," a gambling house on Pennsylvania Avenue. Known better to its customers as the "Hall of the Bleeding Heart," Pendleton's establishment catered to Senators, Representatives, journalists, and lobbyists, not a few of whom went broke at the gambling tables. Pendleton's Palace was a natural rendezvous for politicians in a city that then offered but slight social entertainments. His chefs were the best in town, and his wine cellar was selected with the care of a connoisseur. Pendleton was a member of one of Virginia's first families, and his wife was the daughter of the architect of the Treasury; and, in a gentlemanly way, he did not hesitate to lend money to members of Congress who went broke at his tables. This was the source of his power as a lobbyist, and he proved successful many times in having bills passed for his clients. "A broker in parliamentary notes," wrote a contemporary of Pendleton, "is an inevitable retainer of broker voters." [5]

Pendleton and Ward, whose activities would not have escaped censure a century later, were merely the most prominent members of a wolf pack of lobbyists even then harassing members of the House. The others could not afford such elegance as Pendleton and Ward put on their operations, and the others frequently appealed to even baser instincts in the politicians in power. Frequently, they appealed to the underpaid Congressmen with the offers of bribes; and frequently also, from contemporary accounts, they appealed to lonely Congressmen with the offer of women. The railroads for many years provided Representatives with passes to travel free over their lines, a certain method to ingratiate themselves with the lawmakers. Many corporations, in the years after the Civil War, hired former members of the House as their lobbyists, assuming that they had the proper "contacts" in the House to influence the decisions made there. These ex-Representatives, said one observer, "hover about the Capitol like birds of prey." [6] And some, like the Southern Pacific Railroad, hired sitting members of the House like Oakes Ames of Massachusetts, who passed out valuable stocks to his fellow members "where it would do the most good." [7] Still others, according to contemporaries, hired ill-paid newspapermen "to prostitute their pens" in the interest of their cause.

The use of women as lobbyists was common in the years after the Civil War. "Women make excellent lobbyists," said one contemporary, "as they are more plausible than men, and cannot be shaken off as rudely." [8] Lord Bryce noticed the same thing in the 1880's. "Women are said to be the most active and successful lobbyists at Washington," he wrote primly.[9] Inevitably, these women lobbyists became the subjects of whispered scandal-mongering, with the clear implication that they offered more than merely arguments to sway the susceptible members of the House. Ben Perley Poore, writing of the years just before the Civil War, found that the most active participants in the "disgraceful schemes" to plunder the United States Treasury were these women lobbyists.

> Some of them were the widows of officers of the army or navy, others the daughters of Congressmen, and others had drifted from home localities where they had found themselves the subjects of scandalous comments. The parlors of some of these dames were exquisitely furnished with works of art and bric-a-brac, donated by admirers. Every evening they received, and in the winter their blazing wood fires were surrounded by a

distinguished circle. Some would treat favored guests to a game of euchre, and as midnight approached there was always an adjournment to the dining-room, where a choice supper was served. A cold duck, a venison pie, broiled oysters, or some other exquisitely cooked dish with salads and cheese, generally constituted the repast, with iced champagne or Burgundy at blood-heat. Who could blame the Congressman for leaving the bad cooking of his hotel or boardinghouse, with an absence of all home comforts, to walk into the parlor web which the adroit spider lobbyist had cunningly woven for him.[10]

Edward Winslow Martin, a Washington correspondent of the 1870's, wrote even more revealingly of the improprieties of these "vampires" of the lobby, as he called them. They preyed, he said, primarily among naïve Congressmen and those with loose social habits who were not generally accepted in regular Washington society. And with them, a pretense of propriety was maintained.

Each day in the dining-room the proprieties will grow limper [Martin wrote]. Honorables who eat with their knives and come in with unkempt hair to dinner will be welcomed to the board with the set stage smile, and their greedy eyeballs will leave the perusal of the powdered face to roll coarsely down to and over the snowy shoulders as the swaying body from its chair bends forward to salute the man without a virtue but not without a vote. The meals will be more a revel than a repast. Before the first course is under way, hotel wines, which bloat coarseness, passion, fellowship, and corruption to high tide, are ordered, and the popping of corks makes the jeering jests inaudible, and all but unheard for the time is the hollow laugh of the prandial fools of tonight, who are also the parliamentary knaves of tomorrow and yesterday. Wine begins, accompanies, and closes the eating; and from the table will the party adjourn to the private parlor to more wine, to cards, to flash music, to general chaff, and to such commerce of charms against votes as can be struck between a drunken, conscienceless man and a wily, willing woman.

In any single 'first-class' hotel in Washington, at any time during midsession, at least half a dozen of these lobbyesses are thus at work at once, each one roping in her dozen or ten of wild-cat

Congressmen. The lever of lust is used to pry up more legislators to the sticking point than money itself avails to seduce. Given a 'member,' with his family and all who can or would care to tell on him hundreds of miles away, and present to him all the delights and none of the dangers or expenses of wantonness, and ten to one he falls. The address and cunning with which he can pursue his path rob the vice of half its hesitation in sheering off its grossness. That a public and respectable hotel should or would brothelize itself is not to be supposed. Moreover, unlike the Gospel, this thing is done in a corner; this lobbying is transacted under the guise and guild of social visits—open sesame to a Congressman any and everywhere in Washington.[11]

As early as the 1790's, there were dark rumors that members of the House had sold their votes for bribes. Delaware's very first Representative, John Vining, reportedly accepted a large bribe to cast the deciding vote on Alexander Hamilton's plan to fund the national debt, but Senator William Maclay doubted the report on the acid grounds that Vining's vote could have been bought "for a tenth part of the sum"[12] that it was rumored he was paid. Over the years, similar rumors were gossiped around the Capitol about members of the House and Senate. In the 1850's the House conducted an investigation of the attempted bribery of members by a lobbyist sent to Washington by Massachusetts manufacturers with $58,000 to dispense to gain favorable treatment in a tariff bill. In the same period, the House arrested and detained a correspondent of the *New York Times* for failing to testify on "a corrupt organization of Congressmen and certain lobbyists" that he reported in his newspaper. Still later, the House investigated the activities of a lobbyist for the Pacific Steamship Company, who was the leader of a lobby group that spent $800,000 to win a government subsidy for the company. "The investigating committee could not prove that any member of Congress had received money," a contemporary reported of this operation, "but it will be a cold day at Washington when $800,-000 is spent to influence legislation and some members of Congress do not get a large share of it."[13] The Crédit Mobilier case, in the 1870's, was the most damaging to both the House of Representatives and the lobby. It tarnished the names of Speaker James G. Blaine, former Speaker Schuyler Colfax, and most of the leaders of the House. The passing around of the company's stock at below-value prices to these members simply revealed the extent to which a determined lobbyist would go to win votes and influence in the House. Blaine and later Speaker John Carlisle suffered in personal reputation for their known intimacy with "gentlemen of the lobby."

The lobbyists, however, devised a far more subtle means of passing money to members of Congress than by ugly and obvious bribes. This was the technique of deliberately losing at cards to Congressmen, a technique used as late as the Harding administration in the 1920's. A writer in the 1880's stated that "a true account" of the money thus exchanged "would give a deep insight into the secret history of legislation." How could it be otherwise? "What Representative," asked this writer, "could vote against the claim of a man whose money he had been winning, in small sums, it is true, all winter?" [14]

Few of the lobbyists in the nineteenth century, however, had the personal standing of Pendleton or Sam Ward. The lobbyist for one railroad baron was paid, it was common knowledge, $25,000 a year, an immense sum in the 1880's, and he received comparable respect from members of Congress, who were then paid only one quarter as much. Most of the other lobbyists, however, were regarded by the rank-and-file members of the House as merely "pests," and it was not unusual for a member of the House to tear up, angrily, the card sent into the Hall of the House by the lobbyist to request a conference with the Representative. A Texas Representative likened the lobbyists to so many coyotes. Others had different words of contempt for the lobbyists, among them "leeches" and "genteel loafers." They were, however, called in sum the "third house" of Congress because of their effectiveness at times in influencing and even deciding the fate of legislation. It was not unusual for members of the House to recognize that, for example, it was the pilot's lobby that killed a bill regulating sailing ships in 1888, or that the whiskey syndicate was the true enemy in 1894 of extending taxation on bonded whiskey. Only rarely did the lobbyists try to defeat a recalcitrant member of the House for re-election, although in one notable case the tariff lobbyists spent a small fortune in 1894 to defeat William Wilson of West Virginia, chairman of the Ways and Means Committee and author of the Wilson tariff bill of that year.

The lobbyists themselves were almost completely indifferent to political parties. They played both sides of the political fence with utter impunity. Jay Gould, the multimillionaire owner of the Erie railroad, put the lobbyists' political creed in a nutshell. "In a Republican district," he said, "I was a Republican. In a Democratic district, I was a Democrat. And in a doubtful district I was doubtful—but I was always Erie." [15] Joseph Grundy, a prominent lobbyist in his day, expressed bluntly the strategy of the old-style lobbyist in his approach to the Congress. "In Congress," he said, "from my experience, the fellow that makes the most noise, and the fellow that makes the most demands, that keeps his problems in front of them all the time, he gets service. If he doesn't; if he depends upon somebody else to do it for him, he is going to get what we all get when we don't go after the thing the way we ought to—nothing." [16]

A new day was coming to lobbying, however, a change wrought partially by a series of Congressional investigations into lobbying activities, partially by a growing public awareness and concern for the processes of national legislation, and partially from a realization by the lobbyists themselves that the old and often corrupt ways of the past would neither be tolerated nor, in fact, any longer work. The lobbyists still called on the men on Capitol Hill personally, but the chief function at least of the most effective lobbyists was to temper the whole climate in which legislation was passed. They worked through the press, radio, and television to create a sympathetic public view of their proposed legislation. They organized in combinations with agents around the country to stir up blizzards of letters and telegrams from "the folks" back home. And they sought out the men who were friends and associates of the members of Congress and urged them to pressure the Representatives and Senators to vote their way. The lobbyists, by the skillful use of campaign contributions, held both a promise and a threat to the re-election chances of the Congressmen. This was not to say that all the lobbyists in Washington had reformed and purified their operations. Occasionally, there was evidence that a lobbyist had provided "call girls" for a willing member of the House, or that a bribe had been offered to a Representative. As late as 1959, one lobbyist offered a Representative a bribe of $10,000 on condition that he use his best efforts to remove a phrase from a critically important labor bill. The bribe was refused. The city of Washington had changed, and so had the men in the national government. Washington no longer was a provincial town, with no other accommodations than boarding houses for the members of Congress. Most members of the House bought or rented their own homes in Washington, and lived there quietly with their wives and children. Only rarely did a Representative gain a reputation for squandering his time and energy in Washington's night life, and only a few made the rounds of even the respectable cocktail circuit. Most of the responsible members of the House, when their day's work was done on Capitol Hill, simply went home. For many years, the House has had a group of members, dating back to Joseph Cannon in the 1890's, who met frequently for poker games. In mid-twentieth century, this poker game was scrupulously limited to members and former members of the House. The Representatives played the game for sport among themselves—and they were careful not to permit lobbyists into the game for fear of a seeming impropriety or unpleasantness.

The first thorough investigation of the lobbyists in Washington was prompted by no less a person than President Wilson in 1913, just two months after he entered the White House. Wilson had been shocked at the efforts by lobbyists, notably the National Association of Manufacturers, to defeat the Underwood Tariff then under consideration by the House of Representatives. In a formal statement, Wilson decried the "insidious" lobbyists who were spending money "without limit" to influence the decisions of the House and Senate. A House committee promptly investigated the President's charges, and in the course of the investigation cast new light on the methods and activities of the lobbyists in Washington. "Some petty roguery was exposed," wrote one commentator on the investigation, "the reputations of a few public men were injured, some notorious lobbyists were forced to leave town." [17] The committee, in a carefully drawn report, upheld the right of any individual or association of individuals to appear in person or through agents or attorneys to argue the merits of legislation. "This we think is the true spirit of the right of petition guaranteed by the Constitution to the citizens of the Republic," the committee reported. "To place the Congressman in a cloister to legislate, rendering him immune to extraneous influences, would be impossible, and if possible, it would be exceedingly ridiculous." [18] However, wrote the committee, for the lobbyists under the name of the right of petition to conspire by secret means, by encouraging with rewards or threatening with punishments, to influence the legislator's judgment was to menace the whole fabric of American government and deserved the severest condemnation. The committee made no recommendations on regulating the activities of lobbyists. That did not come until after two more Congressional investigations, the Senate investigation by Hugo Black of Alabama and the joint House-Senate investigation by Mike Monroney of Oklahoma and Robert LaFollette, Jr., of Wisconsin, in 1945. The Black investigation in 1935, prompted largely by lobbying efforts to defeat regulatory legislation on public utilities, revealed an astonishing device used by the lobbyists to create the impression of widespread public indignation at the proposed law. In two days, Representatives Denis Driscoll of Pennsylvania, a freshman, had received 816 telegrams opposing the bill. Driscoll became suspicious and notified the Black investigating committee. The committee discovered that the public utilities were flooding Capitol Hill with telegrams, as many as 4,000 an hour, that were signed with names picked at random and with no authority from the telephone books of the Congressmen's home districts. The revelation helped pass the regulatory bill. Black, later to become a Supreme Court Justice, denounced the lobby activity. "Contrary to tradition, against the public morals, and hostile to good government, the lobby has reached such a position of power that it threatens government itself," he said. "Its size, its power, its capacity for evil; its greed, trickery, deception and fraud condemn it to the death it deserves." [19] It was not to be so condemned, however. Not until 1946 was there even an attempt to curb the lobbies legally One House committee uncovered new and questionable methods being employed by the lobbies. The Committee for Constitutional Government, for example, admitted mailing free from eight to ten million pieces of its literature in four years by using the franking privileges of sympathetic Congressmen. The LaFollette-Monroney Committee recommended, and Congress adopted, a law requiring lobbyists to register formally and report their expenses quarterly, a law never strictly enforced. In the first year, 731 lobbyists registered and by 1962 more than 4,500 had formally acknowledged their interest in influencing legislation.

A full generation before Congress passed the law requiring lobbyists to register, a marked change had come over the activities of lobbyists. Partly this was caused by the revelations of scandal by the "muckrakers" who ranged Washington in the first years of the twentieth century. Partly, this was caused by the growing interest of the nation at large in Washington's affairs and in national legislation. Partly, this was caused by changes in Congressional procedures, particularly in the House of Representatives. In former years, committees normally met in secret when considering legislation—a technique that Woodrow Wilson felt at the time gave a peculiar advantage to corrupt lobbyists to influence the nature of that legislation, for they needed to influence only a majority of a single committee. At the turn of the century, however, the committees began holding open hearings on all important bills, giving both opponents and proponents an equal chance to voice their views publicly on the legislation. This reform tended to encourage the lobbyists to become specialists on the legislation, not merely connivers contriving by surreptitious means to defeat or pass laws. The revolt against Speaker Cannon in 1910, and the rules changes then adopted, broke the old oligarchy of House leaders and gave all the Representatives a larger share in the House's actions. "This was a blow to the old lobby," wrote one historian of the change. "It was patently impossible to attempt to cajole or bribe an entire Congress." [20] The final blow to the old style of lobbying was the 1913 Congressional investigation, the one prompted by President Wilson, which exposed specific cases of corruption—Representative James McDermott of Illinois resigned after testimony that he had been bribed by the N.A.M. "for favors received"—and also revealed the malaise in which legislation was considered.

By the 1920's, an entirely new approach had been adopted by the effective Washington lobbyists, new methods that still gave deep concern to those anxious about the health of American politics. "The old-time lobbyist has gone," said Robert Luce of Massachusetts, a great scholar of parliamentary procedures, "but the new brand, though more respectable, has perhaps a more damaging effect by working on the timidity of lawmakers rather than their cupidity." [21] They no longer tried to bribe members, an easy thing for an honest Representative to reject. Instead, they built massive and systematic networks to indoctrinate the American people with their propaganda and thus sway public opinion in their favor. Where this proved difficult, they devised methods of at least making it seem that the people at large supported their views. The techniques took many forms, some of them highly questionable and all of them designed to convince the lawmakers that the American voters favored the cause the lobbyists advocated. The most influential technique of all on susceptible Representatives was the prompting of "grass roots" sentiment, or the appearance of it, for or against a bill. The lobbyists developed techniques to flood Congress with mail and telegrams from the voters back home. They set up Washington offices, operating all-year round, and hired legislative specialists, lawyers, and public-relations advisers. They issued press releases periodically, sent experts to Capitol Hill to testify on pending bills, and bought newspapers and radio advertising. Nationwide organizations like the American Legion, the American Federation of Labor, and the U. S. Chamber of Commerce alerted their widespread member units of the importance to them of making their own views known to Congress; and they suggested how to write and to whom to write to be most effective. No Representative could be expected to ignore a great outpouring of mail from his home district—although the more intelligent members soon perfected sound ways to differentiate between mail inspired by lobbyists and mail from voters writing on their own. The inspired mail inevitably contained the same telltale phrases suggested by the lobbyist. The lobbyists, in turn, tried to correct this flaw by telling their people to include personal matters in their letters to throw the Representatives off the scent. The lobbyists had no solution, however, for preventing one thousand letters on the same subject sent to the same Representative from sounding remarkably similar in tone and content and suspiciously as if they had been stimulated from the same source.

With the quickening awareness of the people generally of the significance of the national government in their lives, there developed also the realization that individual voters, banded together, could play more pronounced roles in the whole process of legislation from the election of Congressmen to the very votes they cast. Where once the important lobbyists represented mostly the business interests, notably the railroads, and the veterans, in latter years other groups came into active political existence. They discovered quickly that their primary strength was their ability to affect the re-election chances of the members of Congress. These activist political groups, especially labor unions and women's organizations, made up a new force in American politics: the "bullet vote" that threatened extinction to the careers of politicians careless of their interests. The Woman's Suffrage movement that revolutionized American politics in 1920 by gaining the right to vote for women and the Anti-Saloon League that brought the prohibition of alcoholic beverages in the United States in the same year were the envy of other lobbyist groups. They proved above all the value of an open campaign carrying the intimidating threat of retaliation at the polls to those Congressmen who failed to heed the group's demands. "The really effective lobby no longer works through back doors," wrote a newspaperman in 1927. "It no longer wears a mask or waits for darkness to come for an opportunity to strike. . . .The lobby—the intelligent lobby—has changed to conform to new conditions. It has become more scientific, more refined. It is better directed and less suspiciously clothed." [22]

Among the more "scientific" techniques developed in these years was the use of card files to keep track of every Congressman's voting record, friends, clubs, professional associates, church, relatives, and hobbies. "When a lobbyist sets out to convert or to argue with an unfriendly legislator," according to one scholar of the technique in 1929, "the more he knows about him the better armed he is." [23] Kept up to date faithfully, and fully indexed, such a card file could prove immensely useful. Not only did it permit the lobbyist himself to make an effective appeal to the Representative by playing on his sympathies, but it gave the lobbyist the means of enlisting the Representative's friends and associates to help sway the Representative the way the lobbyist desired. Perhaps no organization has made better use of this technique than the American Medical Association, a technique still used effectively by the AMA in the 1960's. The AMA long has operated a Washington office out of which have worked its skilled lobbyists. These lobbyists, limiting themselves to legislation affecting medicine, continuously canvassed Congress and so effectively that they could predict almost exactly the vote in the House or Senate on any medical bill. When they found a Representative hostile to the AMA's views or uncertain on how he would vote, they notified their agents around the country. Having been duly notified of the Representative needing "pressure," an AMA field agent in turn alerted the appropriate state or county medical association. The local group then began pouring mail and telegrams into the Representative's office. More specifically, however, the local medical association notified the Representative's family physician and asked him to argue the AMA's cause with his patient, the Representative. "What we do," explained an AMA official in 1961, "is to find the Congressman's family doctor and get him to work on the Congressmen." [24] What better lobbyist! By definition, the Representative's family doctor is trusted and respected by the Representative, or he would not be the Representative's family doctor. The effectiveness of this AMA technique in lobbying long has won the admiration of other lobbyists.

"I wish I could do the same," said one labor lobbyist of the AMA's general plan. "Sometimes I can reach a fellow that close to a Congressman—and I'll tell you, it works!" [25]

This method of bringing effective pressure on individual Representatives has been widely used by all the major lobbies in Washington. The railroad lobbyists, among the most effective in Washington for more than a century, have made full use of the very same technique, even if they did not pinpoint as specifically as the AMA the individuals to be enlisted in each case. "I have the impression," confided a railroad lobbyist, "that most of the Congressmen, particularly those living in the smaller states and in rural districts, depend for their support upon a comparatively few men in each county in their respective districts. If we could reach the men upon whom a Congressman depends for advice and assistance in his political campaign, we could go far toward having the problem solved." [26] The sophistication of the modern lobbyist and the subtlety of his approach stood in stark contrast with the vulgarities of his predecessors in the time of Sam Ward.

The propaganda efforts of the lobbyists have been equally refined over the years. Even in the 1920's, various lobbying groups were shipping out of Washington and their home-office headquarters literally tons of partisan literature. They published pamphlets by the score and even books for general distribution. They reprinted vast quantities of speeches and articles. They produced and distributed motion pictures to build up public support for their policies. They utilized all forms of advertising to get across their point of view. They financed research projects and published the results, frequently making the materials available to individual Congressmen sometimes to the extent of "ghosting" speeches for them. They persuaded colleges to offer courses on the subjects of their special concern as another way to "sell" their point of view. They sent agents around the country to organize clubs and to give lectures. They provided small country newspapers with propaganda masquerading as news articles ready to be placed on the presses, sparing the editors the cost of editing or even setting the type. And, of course, they made more legitimate "news" by providing expert witnesses to testify before Congressional committees.

In this same period of development of more effective lobbying techniques, the lobbyists hit on the plan of paying the expenses of potentially influential persons from a Representative's home district to come to Washington to visit his Congressman or to testify before an appropriate Congressional committee. This technique has been carried to such an extent that on occasions it has interfered with the Representatives' ability to conduct any other business. During the great labor bill fight of 1959, the halls and corridors surrounding the House chamber were so crowded with labor lobbyists, many brought into town for that single purpose, that it was even difficult for Representatives to squeeze past them to enter the Hall of the House.

Coupled with these new techniques of lobbying came another that perhaps was more important than all the others. Actually, in a way, it was the aim of all the others: the implicit threat to hurt the re-election of those Representatives not responsive to the lobby's wishes and the promise to help those who were. Joseph Cannon credited Sampel Gompers of the American Federation of Labor with introducing the "black list" into lobbying and politics in 1906. Among those "black-listed" that year was Cannon. By 1926, the AFL sent out to all organized labor, under the signature of AFL President William Green, a detailed recital of how every one of the 435 Representatives had voted in the previous House. Green warned all labor unions of the "insidious" campaign then under way to discredit those Representatives friendly to labor, and he urged all workingmen to support them. Other organizations interested in national legislation copied the AFL's strategy. In 1944, the Congress of Industrial Organizations, which later united with the AFL, established its own political action group, the Committee on Political Education (COPE), as a political arm for its activities. By the 1950's and 1960's, many lobbying organizations were publishing the voting records of the members of the House and rating them according to the group's own political criteria. Among the more influential of these, besides the AFL-CIO, were Americans for

Democratic Action, the National Farmers Union, the American Farm Bureau Federation, the Civic Affairs Associates, and Americans for Constitutional Action. The last three were conservative lobbies, the first three liberal. The "grades" they gave the Representatives were, naturally enough, the reverse of each other. In 1962, for example, the ADA rated eighty-six Representatives as voting 100 per cent "liberal" and ninety-one as zero. The ACA graded sixteen Representatives at 100 and seventy-six at zero. The ADA rated Clem Miller of California at 100, while the ACA rated Miller at zero. The ACA, on the other hand, rated John Bell Williams of Mississippi at 100 while the ADA gave Williams zero. The score cards were deliberately designed to guide the followers of the various groups in their voting. The lobbyists, however, went further than this; many actively contributed financially to the Representatives' individual political campaigns. The AFL-CIO, for example, in 1960 contributed to the campaigns of 193 candidates for the House of Representatives. In that same election, James Hoffa of the Teamsters Union announced plans to "purge" fifty-six Representatives who had voted for the Landrum-Griffin labor bill in 1959, and the Teamsters contributed financially to the opponents of forty of the fifty-six. Of these, only one—Francis Dorn of New York—was defeated. The Teamsters proved unsuccessful in their lobbying and their threats to end the careers of those Representatives who opposed the union's views, but other lobbyist organizations have had far better results. The American Legion particularly proved effective with the House in its lobbying, for not one Congressional district existed without active Legionnaire posts whose members were anxious and even desperate for further veterans' bonuses and benefits from the government. In 1935, for example, the Legion forced through Congress an expensive bonus plan to help the depression-harassed veterans. President Roosevelt vetoed it, and, feeling strongly that the legislation was ill considered, addressed a joint session of Congress in the Hall of the House to state his reasons. This was a remarkable act, for it was the only time in American history that a President had read a veto message to Congress. Normally the President has merely sent them by

223

messenger. The House of Representatives, overwhelmingly controlled by the President's party, nevertheless overrode the veto by a vote of 322 to 98. The Senate, however, failed to override it, and the Legion again induced Congress to enact a similar bonus plan the very next year, 1936, an election year. Again President Roosevelt vetoed the bill, this time penning the veto message he sent to the House in his own hand, again an unusual gesture. This time the House overrode the President's veto 326 to 61, a reflection of the veterans' political power. "Legislation is literally made outside the halls of Congress," Legionnaire lobbyist John Thomas Taylor said cynically, "by groups of persons interested in legislation, mainly with economic motives, and the deliberative process within Congress constitutes a sort of formal ratification." [27]

With such power available to them, the lobbyists quite naturally became major influences on the legislation that passed through Congress. In time, they developed working alliances both with the leaders of Congress and even, some of them, with the President himself. As early as the 1920's, the lobbyists of similar views began to pool their resources. At first this was a merely informal, largely social activity. The railroad-labor lobbyists, for example, met from time to time for lunch. They chatted about their affairs, about different members of the House and Senate, and about pending legislation in which they were interested. The opportunity to coordinate their activities and thereby strengthen their chances for success was obvious. They appointed a leader, jointly scouted Capitol Hill, and then reported their findings to each other. If a bill proved crucial to one railroad brotherhood, all the agents joined their efforts to help the cause of the affected union. The lobbyists for industry and management in the 1920's had a similar organization, called the "Monday Lunch Club." These lobbyists, representing such groups as the National Petroleum Association, the American Meat Packers, and the Portland Cement Association, met every Monday for lunch to exchange information of mutual interest. More than sixty separate lobbying organizations were part of this group, and their members could pool a vast reservoir of invaluable intelligence on the House and Senate for the entire business community. The power of these lobbies and of others besides offered facilities for the leaders of the House and the Senate that could prove crucial in passing legislation desired by those Congressional leaders. What was more natural for the conservative lobbies than to team up with the conservative leaders in Congress? Or for the liberal lobbies to join forces with the liberal leaders? The financial resources of some of these lobbies were immense. The American Medical Association, for example, in 1949 assessed each of its members $25 to build a war chest of $1,100,000 to fight a compulsory health-insurance bill advocated by President Truman. The money was allotted this way: $560,000 for newspaper advertising, $300,000 for radio ads, and $250,000 for ads in magazines. That was not all the AMA spent in this fight. It published propaganda pamphlets in batches of 7,500,000 and distributed them to AMA doctors across the country to hand out to their patients. This campaign by the AMA, coupled with skillful coordination with conservative leaders in the House, defeated the President's bill.

Franklin Roosevelt was the first President to rely on lobbies to support and help persuade Congress to enact his legislative program. "He had little choice," wrote one contemporary. "They were the only allies he could trust." [28] Arrayed against Roosevelt's New Deal program were a host of conservative lobbies, representing business and industry. They proved decisive, in that contemporary's view, in finally halting the passage of New Deal legislation, a halt effected by the conservatives in the House of Representatives. President Truman had similar support and opposition from the lobbies as did Roosevelt. The liberal labor lobbies backed his programs; the conservative lobbies of business and industry opposed them. Truman, piqued at the effectiveness of the lobbying of the National Association of Real Estate Boards, publicly denounced the real estate lobby as "the real enemy of the American home." [29] The NAREB had assessed its 44,000 members $5 each to build a war chest to fight Truman's proposed rent controls. When asked about the lobbyists favoring rent controls, President Truman grinned broadly. "Those people weren't lobbyists," he said. "They were advocates of sound government policy." [30] President Eisenhower largely held the support of the conservative lobbies, with the liberal lobbies opposed to his programs. Supporting his position, for example, on the labor bill fight in 1959 were the National Association of Manufacturers, the American Farm Bureau Federation, the U. S. Chamber of Commerce, among others. With their help, and a speech by the President carefully timed to bring a flood of spontaneous mail on the House of Representatives at the critical moment before the vote, the President's view prevailed in the House. When President Kennedy took office, he had ready for his use perhaps the most effective lobby organization that Capitol Hill had ever known.

John Kennedy campaigned for the Presidency on an enormous number of domestic issues, to each of which he pledged the Administration's support if he were elected President. High on his list of priority legislation were bills to increase the minimum wage paid to workers, provide medical benefits to older persons under the social security program, build with federal money schools and classrooms all over America, aid those sections of the country economically depressed, and further help the construction of houses. There were a host of other commitments, too, in civil rights, farming, unemployment, taxation, highways, dependent children, and postal rates. Kennedy found, arrayed in support of his sweeping legislative proposals, a corps of skilled lobbyists working on behalf of a broad group of politically active organizations. Among them were the National Education Association, representing 750,000 teachers; the National Farmers Union, representing 300,000 farm families; the U. S. Conference of Mayors, representing most cities with a population of more than 30,000; the United Mine Workers, representing 200,000 coal miners; the National Rural Electric Cooperative Association, representing 930 cooperatives and public power districts; Americans for Democratic Action with 45,000 members dedicated to liberal causes; the National Association for the Advancement of Colored People with 350,000 members; and the National Housing Conference with 3,000 members. These groups supported a variety of Kennedy-proposed bills, but perhaps more influential than any of them was the AFL-CIO, representing 13,000,000 union workers. The AFL-CIO had endorsed the entire Kennedy program from its minimum-wage proposal to foreign aid. Its lobbyists, led by Andrew Biemiller, spoke for a dozen major unions and formed a nucleus for the President and his leaders in Congress, particularly in the House, to build a viable and coordinated campaign to win passage for the Kennedy bills.

Opposing these lobbies and the Kennedy program, as a major counterforce, were another battery of lobbies, among whom were men equally skilled and seasoned as those supporting the President. Among them were the U. S. Chamber of Commerce, spokesman for 3,800 local and state chambers with a total membership of 2,900,000 businessmen; the National Association of Manufacturers, representing 20,300 business firms; the American Bankers Association, representing 17,000 bankers; the National Retail Merchants Association, representing 11,000 stores; the American Farm Bureau Federation, representing 1,600,000 farm families; the National Association of Home Builders, representing 40,000 home builders; the National Association of Real Estate Boards, representing 60,000 realtors; and the American Medical Association, representing 175,000 doctors. The AMA, interested primarily in blocking Kennedy's plan for medical care for the aged, largely stuck to its own field, but the others tended to unite against the entire Kennedy program. There were dozens of others, on both sides of the legislative argument, perhaps equally important and politically active on Capitol Hill. Many like the American Legion and the insurance companies' lobby concentrated their activities on their own limited field of legislation. Others, however, like the American Municipal Association and the Southern States Industrial Council, could be expected to act on a broader field.

Long before President Kennedy took office, these lobbyists had taken sides in the continuing political war in Washington, between liberals and conservatives, that raged no place more ferociously than on Capitol Hill. They had refined and perfected the techniques of the 1920's. Where once the lobbyists met informally for lunch and to exchange shop talk, by 1961 their meetings more often were business sessions of the gravest significance. They had set up clearing houses to coordinate their efforts on specific bills, and they had developed techniques as sophisticated as those of the party whip to calculate exactly a coming vote on any given bill they believed important. They played with raw power, the power to pass the nation's laws, but they did not offer their services for charitable reasons. "Each lobbyist is in it for his own interest," confided one veteran lobbyist.[31] By joining forces, they knew that they could be more powerful and more effective. The liberal lobbies, those basically committed to President Kennedy's domestic program, long before had formed a working alliance with Sam Rayburn of Texas, the Speaker, and with John Mc-Cormack of Massachusetts, Democratic floor leader under Rayburn before he became Speaker. McCormack, for example, automatically informed the AFL-CIO's Biemiller of the coming legislative program in the House of Representatives, for timing played a key role in the lobbyists' calculations for making their efforts most effective. Biemiller had worked closely with McCormack for years, and their cooperation ranged the whole scale of House operations. "I always consult my good friend Andrew Biemiller on Labor Committee appointments," McCormack once said publicly to mark his esteem for the AFL-CIO lobbyist.[32] Rayburn worked amicably with Biemiller, too, and among Rayburn's close friends were some of the ablest lobbyists, including Robert Oliver, one-time lobbyist for the United Auto Workers and later a free-lance liberal lobbyist. The conservative lobbyists had equally close working arrangements with the conservative leaders of the House, with Charles Halleck of Indiana, the Republican floor leader, and with Howard W. Smith of Virginia, leader of the conservative Southern Democrats. The conservative leaders were as pleased as the liberal leaders to have the help of able lobbyists. Both sides needed all the help they could muster for their cause on critical votes. Not even the President hesitated to deal directly with the lobbyists favoring his legislation; and frequently a White House official, representing the President, sat in on the most secret of the meetings of the lobbyists where they together plotted strategy and tactics on pending legislation. To these meetings also came liaison officers from the

228

executive departments and members of Congress most intimately involved in handling the bill at hand.

The scale of these meetings and the importance of the participants were what had utterly altered the role of the chief lobbyists in the legislative process. That and the sophisticated techniques of the lobbyists were what totally differentiated the modern lobbyists from those of the nineteenth century. In the 1880's, in a notorious case, a man pretending to the skill of a lobbyist was paid a reported $40,000 to help pass a railroad bill. The fellow did no more for his hire than scurry about the Capitol each day shaking the hand of every Congressman directly or even indirectly concerned with the bill and asking him, "How's she going?" In the 1950's and 1960's, a skilled lobbyist could accurately count the House of Representatives by the number of members who would favor or disapprove a given bill. How was this done? Primarily by personal contact with each member of the House. The job, however, was made infinitely easier for the individual lobbyist if he were part of a joint team of lobbyists working on the same bill. And the job, of course, was also made easier by keeping full records of each Representative and how he had voted previously. For a meeting on a major bill, pending before the House, perhaps as many as thirty different lobbyists representing as many organizations normally turned up at the clearing-house meetings. The first order of business quite naturally was to assess the status of the bill in the House. The group normally had already chosen or designated one of themselves as chairman of the team concentrating on this particular bill. Quickly they would run through the roll of the House, alphabetically state by state, and tick off how they could expect the Representatives to vote. "We take the easy ones first, the ones who have made commitments on the bill," said a frequent participant at these meetings. This normally has accounted for most of the total membership of the House. Only a relatively small number of the Representatives have not made previous commitments or cannot be safely assumed to be on one or the other side of every question. "You can boil the House down pretty quickly to about fifty or sixty members who are not committed," said one of these technicians.[33] "They are the 'doubtfuls.' " That has meant that about 375 members of the House normally have already decided their positions on just about every question coming before the House. The conservatives and the liberals could normally both count on strong delegations every year in the House; the biennial elections, however, could give a marginal advantage to either side. In the Eighty-sixth House, 1959-60, the liberals had a marginal advantage, but they lost it to the conservatives in the 1960 election. In the Eighty-seventh Congress, 1961-62, the House John Kennedy first faced as President, Andrew Biemiller and other able lobbyists calculated that the committed Representatives divided just about exactly even— 180 for Kennedy's program and 180 against. That left seventy-odd members of the House in the middle ground. They were the "doubtfuls" who automatically became the targets for the pressures of the lobbyists, the President, and the Congressional leaders themselves. The committed members were not difficult to determine. On the conservative side, the great bulk of the Southerners were solidly committed to conservatism. So were most of the Republicans from the Middle West and the Far West. The Northern and Western Democrats were almost equally committed to liberal causes, and there were a few scattered Southerners and Northeast Republicans who also could be counted in this camp. The "doubtful" Representatives—the target Representatives— were largely political moderates, the bulk of them Republicans from the Northeast and Southerners from somewhat progressive Congressional districts, but a few also among the Democrats of the Northern and border states. At a meeting of skilled lobbyists, they could quickly be identified. Once identified, the lobbyists had to estimate how to swing these crucial members—for on their votes hung the decisions of the House—to the cause of the lobbyists advocated.

"This," said one of them, "is where we win or lose." [34]

President Kennedy inherited this lobbying operation to support his proposed legislation—and to oppose it, too, for both sides used roughly the same techniques. And like Presidents before him, Kennedy used it. Kennedy's school-construction bill, for example, was one of the first of his proposals to receive full-scale lobby support. Attending the lobbyists' strategy meetings on this bill were John Edelman, lobbyist for the Textile Workers Union and dean of Washington's labor lobbyists; John Sheehan, lobbyist for the Steelworkers Union, and representatives of the National Education Association, the National Council of Jewish Women, the National Council of Churches, the American Veterans Committee, and a score of other active lobbies. Also sitting in on the meetings were Representatives Frank Thompson of New Jersey, House sponsor of the Kennedy bill, James O'Hara of Michigan, and John Brademas of Indiana, all influential members of the House Education and Labor Committee. Liaison officers from the Department of Health, Education and Welfare also attended the sessions, as did Henry Hall Wilson, White House liaison man for the House of Representatives, representing Lawrence O'Brien, the President's Congressional liaison chief. The sessions were held in various places around Washington, occasionally in Health, Education and Welfare Secretary Abraham Ribicoff's office, sometimes in a committee room in one of the House office buildings, more frequently in a hotel. The principal aims were to coordinate the activities of the individual lobbyists, the department, and White House liaison officials, and the Representatives favorable to the bill. The primary goal was to muster enough votes to have the bill passed by the House. With the House numbering 435 members, that meant wooing 218 Representatives— plus a few more for safety's sake.

To start with, the clearing-house group knew they had an uphill fight. A similar school-construction bill had passed the House of Representatives a year before by a margin of only seventeen votes. Because an antisegregation amendment had been added to that bill, not a single Southern Democrat had voted for it, although about fifteen Southerners had committed themselves to vote for it without the antisegregation amendment. In that election year, forty-four Republicans had been persuaded to vote for the bill, but now that a Democrat occupied the White House the lobbyists could not figure to hold them all in favor of the bill. Besides that, the Democrats had lost twenty-one members in the 1960 election, all from the ranks of supporters of the

231

bill. Obviously it would be difficult to produce a new majority of the House for the bill. The lobbyists quickly located their target Representatives and then systematically assigned the "doubtfuls," the "negotiables," one by one, among themselves. "Okay, who wants him?" the chairman asked. "Who can talk to him?" [35] One or more of the lobbyists volunteered for each doubtful Representative. They volunteered for the responsibility on their personal ability to woo the particular Representative. "The assignments were given to whoever could take them," said one participant. In the main, most of the lobbyists were assigned to pressure the Republicans. Wilson, the White House man, and the departmental aides took the bulk of the Southern Democratic "doubtfuls," although they were greatly helped by the National Education Association, whose field agents already were heavily pressuring the Georgia and other Southern delegations in the House. Wilson, a native North Carolinian and friend of North Carolina Governor Terry Sanford, had a natural entree to the North Carolina delegation in the House; and his White House credentials gave him leverage in talking to any House Democrat. The lobbyists met periodically, normally every week or so, to report their results and to exchange information they had learned that could be useful to the others. Gradually, the number of votes certain for the Administration's bill grew. John Lumley of the National Education Association reported vast new inroads in the House delegations from the Southern states, particularly Georgia. There, the state teachers had been very active. They had wrung from the Georgia House of Representatives a petition urging the Georgians in the United States House to support the President's bill. The North Carolina delegation showed definite signs of following Wilson's advice. By April, 1961, the lobbyists had commitments from thirty-four Southern Representatives that they would vote for the school-construction bill. The lobbyists were making headway among the House Republicans, too, although not so much as with the Southern Democrats. They calculated that twenty-eight Republicans would vote for the bill. At a session in mid-April, the lobbyist clearing-house group saw the possibility that they could then muster 228 votes in the House on the bill, but that total included about forty Representatives who were only "leaners"; that is, they would probably vote for the bill. That was only a tenuous margin, and it was based on the assumption that the bill would contain in its final form no antisegregation amendment or aid to parochial schools—clauses that would have politically forced the Southerners to vote against the bill. It was also the high-water mark for the lobbyists favoring the bill. Their cause now was struck by a series of heavy blows—the unfortunate leaking of an Administration study paper that made it appear as though the federal government would interfere directly in the curriculum of schools, a tightening of Republican party discipline in the face of continued victories for the Democratic administration in the House, and the effective work of the opposition lobbyists. "That killed us," said one of the lobbyists favoring the school bill.[36] The Republicans in the House pulled away from the bill so fast that soon the lobbyists could only count six Republicans willing to vote for the bill. The advocates of the bill no longer had a chance to win a majority. All through this period, the private meetings of the clearing house continued, "although lately," said one of the members, "the meetings have just been held to exchange gruesome details." [37] They tried to pick up votes by cutting back the size of the school-construction program provided in the bill. Then they reduced it still more. They could not get commitments from a majority of the House. Finally, the clearing-house members found themselves supporting a mere skeleton of the original bill. That skeleton bill was the one offered to the House—and the House summarily rejected it, 242 to 170.

This was the rough outline of a lobbying clearing house dealing with but one bill. Every important bill, coming to a vote in the modern House, has had similar treatment by the lobbyists working closely with the House leaders and often with officials of the White House or government departments. The lobbyist members of these clearing houses, of course, changed from bill to bill, largely in accordance with their support or opposition to the particular bill. The United Mine Workers lobbyists, for example, worked closely with the AFL-CIO lobbyists on some legislation important to labor, but on a tariff bill, they naturally were

233

on opposing sides. Business lobbyists had similar fallings-out and comings-together on all the varied legislation that touched their closest interests. Inevitably, there were strong lobby pressures on both sides of each piece of legislation. A new clearing house would be established for either side, many made up of the most veteran lobbyists in Washington, and the systematic work of counting the House began again, name by name over the full roster of the members. Each lobbyist had his own particular skills, his own particular friends in the House, and his own organization backing him from the field. Assigned but a few members of the House to persuade to a given cause, the individual lobbyist could trigger a massive assault on those members. He had, normally, a complex and influential organization behind him to help, and he had all the techniques developed over the years to impress the Representatives that the people back home wanted him to vote a certain way.

"The Congressmen only go with their constituents," said one of Washington's veteran lobbyists. "We try to let the constituents know the situation. We ask them to write. We create the environment in which Congressmen feel their people are for a certain bill. It's a gradual buildup. The big thing is the people back home. We carry out an over-all educational program. Our guys in the district work for that. This gives the Congressman the support he needs to come in and vote for the bill." [38]

The successful lobbyists in mid-twentieth century were those who could best create those environments of public opinion, or at least give the Representatives the impression that such an environment existed back home. Without that environment, they could not win on any important bill. With it, they could scarcely lose.

CHAPTER TEN

The Chief Legislator

THE President of the United States, by a strict interpretation of the Constitution, could have but little effect on the drafting and enactment of American law. That was a function specifically granted to the House of Representatives and the Senate, in Congress assembled. The Constitution carefully spelled out the separate and independent powers of the three great branches of the federal government—the legislative, the executive, and the judicial—and deliberately divorced each from the others. In theory at least, the President was denied the authority to influence the decisions of the House of Representatives and the Senate. The President was restricted to but few formal contacts with either branch of Congress, and Presidents like George Washington and John Adams were loath to permit even the suggestion that they might encroach on the prerogatives of the House or Senate. Under the Constitution the President was authorized to send "from time to time" such messages and legislative proposals to the Congress as in his judgment seemed fit and proper. He could, in times of national need or emergency, summon the House or Senate, or both, into special session. He could veto, and thereby nullify at least temporarily, any legislation enacted by Congress, but even in asserting this power, it was generally assumed the President would limit its use to those bills he believed violated the spirit of the Constitution. In theory, the House and the Senate were to be scrupulously independent and remote from the President, whose chief function was to execute, or administer, not to determine, the laws that Congress enacted.

In practice, however, the theory broke down, and broke down almost at the very beginning of the American Republic. President Washington did in fact act with severe and strict formality in his official and private dealings with Congress and the members of Congress. His one attempt to deal personally with Congress— an attempt to receive in person the "advice" of the Senate on an Indian treaty—resulted in a preposterous and embittering personal humiliation to him. He visited the Senate, obviously expecting immediate action on the treaty, but the Senate declined to act hastily and postponed giving its approval. A man quick to anger, Washington kept away from both chambers of Congress after that. His chief lieutenants in his first Cabinet, Alexander Hamilton and Thomas Jefferson, had no such sense of the technical proprieties of the independence of the Congress from the executive branch, and they battled as rivals to implant their ideas into the fabric of new law flowing from Congress. As things then stood, the primary legislative struggles were held in the House of Representatives, and it was there that the great debates on public policy took place. Hamilton's influence on the House became so persuasive in fiscal matters that the House, as already noted in this book, created its Ways and Means Committee as an agency to resist it. When Jefferson became President in 1801, he played perhaps an even more persuasive role than Hamilton with the House. He helped formulate the inmost decisions of the House, including the election of its Speaker and the appointment of its committee chairmen. On legislative matters, he discovered private means to temper and modify the House's action. In 1808, for example, he persuaded the House to reduce a proposed increase in the size of the United States Army by what John Quincy Adams called an "extra-official hint." [1]

In the decades that followed, different Presidents acted quite differently in their approach to Congress. President William Henry Harrison, for example, in 1841 publicly and formally denied himself any function at all in the formulation of tax legislation on the grounds that this was solely the concern of Congress. Other Presidents made no secret of their pleasure in being rid of Congress entirely. In 1844, during an early experiment with Samuel Morse's magnetic telegraph, Chief Justice Roger Taney sent a message from Baltimore, extended his compliments to President Tyler at the Capitol and inquired for Tyler's health. "The President," recorded an observer, "returned his compliments immediately, stating that he enjoyed good health, and felt much better, since Congress had finally adjourned." [2] Periodically, a forceful President took office, men like Andrew Jackson and Abraham Lincoln. In such times, the President enlarged his sphere of influence over Congress and the legislation enacted by Congress, and not all the actions by these Presidents could bear too close an examination. Abraham Lincoln, for example, at a critical point literally bribed three members of the House of Representatives with patronage jobs to win their reluctant votes for an important bill. The encroachments by these Presidents, however, on the prerogatives of the House and Senate were sporadic and inconclusive. They left precedents on which later Presidents could draw, but these precedents were not fully utilized until the twentieth century. As late as 1893, a Washington correspondent recorded that the President had scarcely any influence at all on legislation or Congress. "No one has apparently less influence upon Congressional legislation than the President of the United States," said Theron Crawford. "His message is treated always as a perfunctory document, and while it is regularly and respectfully referred to the proper committees for consideration, it is very rare that any suggestion made by the Executive has any practical result." [3]

This, however, was not to last. The President, as a government officer, had accumulated over the years broad powers to initiate legislation, and the lobbyists ranging Capitol Hill had developed a multitude of techniques for persuading the House and Senate. These the President could copy and use for his own purposes. Theodore Roosevelt, not a man to be bounded unduly by the historic limitations of his office, was the first President to offer Congress a formalized *Presidential* program, the "Square Deal."

This was a new idea, that the President submit a legislative program. Previously, such programs had been offered but normally by Speakers of the House. Henry Clay, for example, had sponsored his "American Plan," a diversified program of internal improvements and tariff protection. Washington politicians and newspaper correspondents learned later to examine carefully the lists of committee appointments made by Speakers as a telltale indication of the legislation the *Speaker* intended to sponsor and enact. Theodore Roosevelt's Presidential program met a sharp rebuff from Speaker Cannon, and not until Woodrow Wilson became President in 1913 did the Chief Executive find both the opportunity and the means of enacting a Presidential program. Wilson, as his political writings showed, felt keenly that the United States needed a legislative leader comparable to the British Prime Minister, an official responsible for the formulation and the enactment of a systematic body of legislation. He offered such a program under the formal title of the "New Freedom," and he carried his fight to enact that program right into the committee rooms of Congress. He summoned the House and Senate into joint sessions to hear him argue for his legislation. Wilson broke the rigid formalities of the past and made himself, in effect, the Chief Legislator of the United States.

However dramatic Wilson's action appeared to his contemporaries, his boldness seemed but mild from the vantage point of the 1960's. Wilson did indeed permanently transform the office of the President in legislative matters, but even he hesitated to take steps regarded as commonplace for later Presidents. Franklin Roosevelt, for example, not only thrust at Congress his "New Deal" program and actively lobbied the members of Congress for its passage, but he appealed over the heads of the members of Congress to the American people. His development of the "fireside chat" and the Presidential press conference as a means of influencing public opinion and thereby Congressional decisions brought a vast enhancement of Presidential *legislative* power. His weekly meetings with the leaders of Congress made them, in effect, *his* legislative leaders. Harry S Truman followed Roosevelt with a "Fair Deal" program, although he was far less successful in persuading Congress to enact it. Dwight Eisenhower made broad advances on increasing the President's legislative powers, although he frequently appeared uninterested in the legislative bills he sponsored. Eisenhower not only utilized techniques of television for the President's purposes, much as Roosevelt had done with those of radio, but he also assigned one of his special White House assistants as his chief lobbyist on Capitol Hill. Presidents as early as Woodrow Wilson had designated aides or Cabinet officers to serve informally as liaison men for them with Congress, but none before Eisenhower had appointed an official to his staff who had no other function. John F. Kennedy as President drew on the experience and techniques of his predecessors to pressure Congress for his "New Frontier" program. He combined the presidential press conference with television and utilized both far beyond what even Eisenhower had envisioned. As an intense partisan for his own legislative program, he used the vast influence of the Presidency to forward that program through Congress. As the only twentieth-century President who had served in both the House and Senate, he knew better than any previous President the pressure points of both houses of Congress and how to use them to best advantage. He not only multiplied the number of White House liaison men roving over Capitol Hill, but he promoted his chief liaison officer to first rank among his political lieutenants. Kennedy so enhanced the role of the President in the legislative process that he had become within a year of taking office not merely the Chief Legislator of the United States, as Wilson and Franklin Roosevelt had been, but also, in effect, the Chief Lobbyist for his legislative program.

The office of President had been transformed by the growth and power of the nation that he led. As early as the Presidency of Theodore Roosevelt, the President had been recognized as a world leader in his own right. Roosevelt singlehandedly settled the Russo-Japanese War of 1904 and by so doing won the Nobel Peace Prize. Woodrow Wilson, as President, won the reverence of the world for his high idealism and his attempt to end war as the means of settling disputes among nations. The fact of the President's world stature enormously enhanced his prestige at home and gave him a radically different standing with Congress. In the nineteenth century, it had not been uncommon for Congressional leaders to view the President with mild contempt. By the middle of this century, the office of President had been so altered, the nation's safety had become so dependent on the President's judgment, that even great House leaders like Sam Rayburn treated the holder of that office with a deference amounting to awe. In a world of thermonuclear bombs and intercontinental missiles, the life of the nation in a very real sense rested in the hands of the President.

That fact made natural and obvious the expansion of the President's role in the legislative process. In times of national crisis— and by mid-century the nation appeared to be in perpetual crisis —even the President's most acerbic Congressional critics unflinchingly and unhesitatingly gave him their fullest support in all matters of national defense. Leaders of both parties on Capitol Hill developed a bipartisan approach to United States foreign policy that muted this once volatile topic of national debate. In domestic legislation, the near deification of the President gave him new power to carry his legislative proposals through the House of Representatives and the Senate. That did not mean that either the House of Representatives or the Senate automatically approved all the President's legislative proposals. Far from it. Each legislative bill normally entailed an enormously complicated process of negotiation and compromise before it was finally enacted. The President, however, had marked political advantages now in the ancient rivalry with the Congress for power, and a skillful President could use those advantages to persuade even a hostile Congress to enact at least a major portion of his proposed legislation.

In the 1960's, the President had at hand a variety of tools by which to persuade the House of Representatives to accept his legislative leadership. Some of these devices were inherent to the office of President, as his initiative in proposing legislation and his right to veto such bills as he disapproved. Others had been gradually developed over the years, as the President's power to manipulate the awarding of patronage jobs and so interfere directly with the way individual Representatives cast their votes. Still others were the product of the revolutionary advances in American communications and the change in the nature of the office of President. The Presidential news conference had developed into a major propaganda instrument for the President's use in summoning national sentiment to his cause. Radio and television and the quickening of national interest in national affairs had provided a national audience to which no one could appeal more directly or more effectively than the President. All these tools were available to the President, as well as the artful skills perfected by the professional lobbyists to sway the members of Congress. An activist President like John Kennedy used them all.

The fact that the Constitution required the President to inform Congress periodically of his views of the nation and its government gave the President in effect a prerogative to initiate legislation, although that right was not fully exercised by the President until modern times. From the very beginning, however, the President's annual State of the Union address to Congress became one of the great ceremonials of the government. In the first years, the Congress replied to the President with a formal address of its own, duly delivered by the Vice President and Speaker of the House accompanied by members of both legislative chambers. This, however, proved cumbersome and clumsy, and was soon abandoned. The early Presidents, in their State of the Union addresses, literally reported on the state of the federal government and their management of it. The President normally used this address as an instrument to lay down his own policies rather than to try specifically to direct Congressional action. James Monroe, for example, in 1823 thus set forth his policy—the Monroe Doctrine—of opposing any further interference by European countries in the affairs of the Western Hemisphere. In 1862, in the midst of the Civil War, Abraham Lincoln eloquently suggested that Congress enact legislation to compensate slaveholders for freeing their slaves. He did not press Congress to enact this bill, but instead, under his powers as President and Commander in Chief, he issued the Emancipation Proclamation that declared free all slaves within the lines of the Confederate armies. Lincoln thus sidestepped the legislative jurisdiction of Congress in executing a revolutionary change in American society, although Congress and the states later in effect ratified the action by adopting a Constitutional amendment abolishing slavery. A century after Lincoln, a profound change had been wrought in the President's legislative role. In the 1880's, Woodrow Wilson, then a young scholar of American politics, recorded that the President's function in legislation was purely negative, dependent entirely on "his prerogative of veto." [4] Wilson himself, when he became President in 1913, revolutionized the President's legislative role. Just after the election of 1912, for example, and even before he took the oath of President, Wilson summoned Carter Glass of Virginia, then chairman of the House Banking and Currency Committee, to Trenton, New Jersey. There they began drafting what was to become the Federal Reserve Banking and Currency Act, the basic monetary law of the United States. Wilson, once President, helped Glass push the bill through the House of Representatives, and when the bill's fate was threatened by opposition from the Senate's members of a joint conference committee, Wilson helped again. "Glass," Wilson asked peremptorily, "have you got the votes in the committee to override these gentlemen?" Glass said he did. "Then," said Wilson, "outvote them, damn them, outvote them!" [5]

The Presidents who followed Wilson expanded the President's participation in the entire legislative process. Franklin Roosevelt multiplied many times over their Presidential activity. The response of the House and Senate to Roosevelt's proposed legislation in 1933 not only caused Congress to be branded as a "rubber stamp," but also Roosevelt's success during those now-famous "100 days" of 1933 has stood as a landmark in American history of a President overawing the legislative branch of government. Roosevelt did more. In the years that followed he actually "appointed" special committees of his own, composed of members of his Cabinet, the House, and Senate, to draft the legislation he wanted. He then used these committee members to push the bills through Congress. Newspaper correspondents soon began grading each annual session of the House and Senate, and even the individual Representatives and Senators, on the percentages of their votes favoring or opposing the President's program of bills. More significant, however, was the fact that the initiative in legislation had been transferred from Congress to the President, and in the years that followed Roosevelt's terms as President, only rarely did the House or Senate inspire the enactment of laws of major consequence. That function had been pre-empted by the President. He took the initiative not only in foreign affairs and defense matters but in domestic questions as well. There were exceptions, of course. In the 1930's, Congress initiated the neutrality acts, and later in the 1940's and 1950's, the Congress originated major limitations on United States' dealings with Communist-dominated countries. The labor laws of 1947 and 1959 both had their roots in Congress, as did the efforts to enact a program of medical care for the aged. The mass of modern legislation, however, has first come to significant Congressional attention through the formal endorsement of the President, not from members of Congress.

The President's Constitutional power to veto Congressional legislation long offered a way for the President to temper or defeat Congressional action, but only in relatively recent years has this power proved dramatically effective. In the seventy-two years from George Washington's first inauguration to Lincoln's first, 1789 to 1861, only fifty bills passed by Congress were vetoed. Seven Presidents, among them John Adams, Thomas Jefferson, and Martin Van Buren, vetoed not a single bill. In the next 100 years, however, Presidents vetoed 2,095 Congressional bills. Grover Cleveland alone vetoed 583 and Franklin Roosevelt 633. Most of these were insignificant bills, individual pensions for war veterans or other individual claims against the government, but many were major acts of a Congress defying the President's views. Harry Truman, for example, who vetoed a total of 250 bills, had a Congress, the Eightieth, that ran roughshod over his domestic program and wrote one of its own, enacting over his veto such bills as the Taft-Hartley labor law and legislation to reduce individual income tax payments. Truman faced only one Congress that was controlled by the opposition party; Dwight Eisenhower confronted three, and Eisenhower in time learned to use the threat of a Presidential veto to modify if not actually to control the legislative actions of the House and Senate. No better example of Eisenhower's use of the veto and the threat of the veto occurred than in the first session of the Eighty-sixth Congress. That session opened in January, 1959, with the newly elected Congress massively Democratic and manifestly antagonistic to Eisenhower's growing concern for a balanced federal budget. Democrats controlled the House of Representatives by a margin of 283 to 153 Republicans, and the Senate, 65 to 35. The Democratic Congressional leaders planned to enact a broad domestic program, ranging from construction of airports and highways to new farm and housing legislation. Eisenhower warned them that he would use his veto freely if they so proceeded, and the Congressional Democrats accepted the challenge. They deliberately chose a popular bill affecting the Rural Electrification Administration to test Eisenhower's intentions, and they sent it first to the White House. Back came the bill with a Presidential veto, and their attempt to override the veto—which required a two-thirds margin to carry—failed in the House by a mere four votes. President Eisenhower asked his party's Congressional leaders, Charles Halleck of Indiana in the House and Everett Dirksen of Illinois in the Senate, to support him with "one-third plus one" of the members of the House and Senate, the necessary margin to uphold his vetoes, and he could block the ambitions of this Democratic Congress. Twice the Congress passed liberal housing bills only to have them vetoed; and the Democratic liberals finally had to compromise their housing legislation enough to meet Eisenhower's specific requirements. Eisenhower vetoed the Democrats' "pork-barrel" Civil Functions Appropriations bill, and then vetoed another reduced version of it. This veto, in its only instance of clear success this session, the Democratic Congress overrode. The Democrats on Capitol Hill, however, had even earlier sounded a retreat on much of their program. They cut back drastically the millions of dollars provided in their airports bill, enough to win Eisenhower's approval. They lost a

House floor fight to enact their own labor legislation and had to be content with a version of this legislation that the President endorsed. The session showed the remarkable effect the President could have on Congress when armed with little more than the veto and the threat of the veto. He could not normally persuade the House or the Senate to enact his legislation, notably his bills providing federal aid to school construction and assistance to depressed economic areas of the country. His Republican party ranks on Capitol Hill were too depleted for that. He could, however, effectively block or force into compromise the legislation a clear majority of the House and Senate would otherwise enact into law.

In these years of the growing power of the President over Congressional decisions, through his initiative in proposing legislation, the skillful use of the veto, and his enhanced world stature, one aspect of his potential influence over members of Congress noticeably declined. This was the President's power over federal patronage. In 1829 President Andrew Jackson had formally inaugurated the spoils system as an administration policy. He swept out of federal office those officials he believed hostile to him and replaced them with his friends and followers. The patronage system thus dramatically endorsed was not new; it had existed, if on more modest terms, at least for a score of years even then. As early as 1811, a Representative had offered a Constitutional amendment to limit the right of members of Congress to accept jobs from the President, and another Representative, Josiah Quincy of Massachusetts, had gone even further to suggest that Congressmen's relatives also be disqualified. Quincy, in a speech on the House floor that still rings with passion, suggested that existing patronage practices of the White House were "corrupting" the American Congress. "I never have seen, and I never shall see," he said, "any of these notorious solicitors of office for themselves or their relations, standing on this or the other [Senate] floor, bawling and bullying, or coming down with dead votes in support of executive measures, but I think I see a hackney laboring for hire in a most degrading service. . . ." [6] A half century later, and for another half century after that, the awarding of patronage played a major role in American politics at the federal level. Every President was harassed by hordes of office seekers, among them the members of the House and Senate. Occasionally, the awarding of federal jobs could affect the votes of members of Congress; but the demand for office always far outstripped the supply, and every President had to find his own means of dealing with the job hunters.

Abraham Lincoln devised a disarming technique. He told them stories and then ushered them out of his office unsatisfied. One Representative told in detail his own experience with this Lincolnian maneuver. He had gone to the White House four days in a row, waiting each day patiently for a chance to speak to Lincoln. Finally he was led into the President's office, and he bluntly told Lincoln what he wanted. "Do you know," said Lincoln, "I heard a good thing yesterday about the difference between an Amsterdam Dutchman and any other 'dam' Dutchman." The Representative had no choice; he had to abide the President's storytelling. "He told three," the Representative recounted, "and I didn't listen to a word he said. I was mad enough to knock the old fellow down." At this point, into the President's office walked Secretary of State William Seward and announced that he had to confer immediately with the President in private. Lincoln politely asked the Representative to call again. "Bother his impudence, I say," fumed the enraged Representative. "To keep me listening to his jokes for two hours, and then ask me to call again!" [7]

Lincoln, however, did use patronage to alter votes in the House. In 1864, for example, he decided to press for the adoption of a Constitutional amendment abolishing slavery. He found that he could not be sure that enough states would ratify such an amendment, and so he determined to create an additional state, Nevada. The necessary legislation to do this, however, ran into trouble in the House of Representatives, and passage of the bill was in doubt. Three Representatives appeared willing to bargain away their votes, and Lincoln authorized his assistant Secretary of the Navy, Charles A. Dana, to negotiate with them for their votes. "What do they want?" Dana asked Lincoln.

"I don't know," said the President. "It makes no difference. We must carry this vote or be compelled to raise another million men and fight, no one knows how long. It is a question of three votes or new armies. . . . Whatever promises you make, I will perform." [8]

Dana thereupon met with the three Representatives and promised them "on the authority of the President" the patronage jobs they wanted. Nevada was brought into the Union and did ratify the Thirteenth Amendment abolishing slavery. Ironically, only two of the three Representatives received their patronage jobs. The third was denied his because Lincoln was assassinated and Andrew Johnson, who succeeded Lincoln as President, refused to honor the pledge. "I have observed in the course of my experience," Johnson said, "that such bargains tend to immorality." [9]

The members of the House have never been entirely agreed on either the propriety or even the usefulness to themselves of being allowed to designate the persons to receive federal jobs. The Senate held the Constitutional power to advise and consent to the President's appointments, and out of this power grew the Senate's larger share of the federal patronage. By an early and informal arrangement with the Senators, the members of the House were granted the prerogative of naming those to receive the lesser federal offices available in their Congressional districts, such as postmasters and United States attorneys. The Senators retained the "right" to designate the recipients of the more important offices like federal judgeships. For many Representatives, this was an entirely satisfactory division of the spoils, but many others disliked the responsibility—and the harassment that went with it. Paul Kilday of Texas, speaking of party patronage in 1961, questioned the political advantage of such spoils to the individual Representative. The Texas delegation long before, in 1933, formally notified Postmaster General James Farley, President Roosevelt's patronage dispenser, that the individual Texas Representative would "control" all postmasters and other minor officers in his Congressional district, and Kilday had long been familiar with such matters. He pointed out that a Representative normally had as many as 100 constituents applying for every federal job available. The Representative had to pick one of them. "You make ninety-nine fellows mad at you and get one ingrate," said Kilday.[10] Kilday himself unconsciously echoed one of the most ancient of objections to patronage, that it hurt the patronage dispensers. John Adams, who had been an unhappy President, said much the same thing long before in 1822. "No man who ever held the office of President," said Adams, "would congratulate a friend on obtaining it. He will make one man ungrateful and a hundred men his enemies for every office he can bestow." [11] And even Adams then had merely rephrased an epigram attributed by Voltaire to Louis XIV of France, who died in 1715. "Every time I fill a vacancy," said the King, "I make one hundred men unhappy and one man ungrateful."

In the 1860's, George Hoar of Massachusetts simply refused to have anything to do with the patronage to which he was entitled as a Representative. He wrote to the Secretary of the Treasury disclaiming all his prerogatives over patronage in his Congressional district. He did not want to be bothered with the myriad applicants. James Buffington, also from Massachusetts and a Representative in the 1850's, devised an utterly different plan. He recommended for public office every one of his constituents who applied to him for help in getting a federal job. Privately, however, Buffington arranged with the officials of each federal department to ignore most of his recommendations. He told the appointing officers that if he spelled his name correctly in his letter of recommendation, that meant he really did recommend the applicant for the job. If, however, he spelled his name "Buffinton," dropping the "g," they should not take the letter seriously. It was a neat trick to avoid the enmity of constituents he could not endorse.

Different Presidents made differing uses of the patronage jobs they had to distribute. Ulysses S. Grant in the 1870's, for example, inspired party harmony by surrendering control over federal appointments entirely to the members of Congress. William McKinley, in the 1890's, took an opposite tack. He bluntly threatened retribution on Representatives by refusing to fill but a few critical government posts until Congress enacted a tariff bill he wanted. In 1904, a political writer reported that McKinley's successor, Theodore Roosevelt, had greatly strengthened his influence over Congress by maintaining successfully his own authority in awarding federal jobs. "Members of Congress," this writer said, "are thus made dependent on the Executive, who, in controlling appointments, holds in his hands a weapon whereby he may wrest legislation from a hesitating or unwilling Congress." [12]

The resisting of Congressional pressures for federal jobs has always cost the President at least some personal abuse from members of Congress—and presumably some of their votes. For example, Grover Cleveland in the 1880's tightened his control over his party in Congress by restricting patronage awards. He became so dismayed at the insistence of some Congressmen for jobs for their friends that he refused finally to hold any further personal interviews on the subject. His action embittered more than one of his party's members in the House of Representatives. One Democratic member roundly denounced him. "The fate of the party and the Administration," this Representative said, "lies in the crossroads post offices." [13] This same theme echoed down through the years.

Long before Kennedy became President, the political power of patronage had largely been eroded by the development and growth of the civil service system. This not only put most federal jobs on a career basis but forbade civil service employees from participating in active politics. Even so, President Kennedy found that patronage still carried its old lure for at least some of the Representatives and Senators. Although the broadening of the civil service system had removed most federal jobs from political partisanship and party influence, the new President still had at his disposal an estimated 10,000 federal offices not subject to civil service restrictions. The filling of these posts caused Kennedy continuing difficulty with both Senators and Representatives and even endangered passage of some of his important legislation.

The first Kennedy bill to reach the House floor for a vote in 1961, an emergency bill to relieve feed-grain farmers, met an open threat from some Democrats who were dissatisfied with the President's handling of patronage. The Democrats from New

York, twenty-two votes strong, were particularly angry. They had been caught in the middle of a party quarrel between President Kennedy and the New York Democratic party leaders, Michael Prendergast and Carmine DiSapio, and had been cut off from their normal patronage. Indeed, the Kennedy administration even had indicated the intention of appointing a Connecticut lawyer as the new United States attorney for the Southern District of New York, an offensive suggestion to the New York Democrats. The Italo-Americans in the House, fourteen members from Northeastern states, were equally unhappy. President Kennedy had not appointed a single American of Italian descent to a major Administration office. The President had named two Jews to his Cabinet, and the Italo-Americans in the House believed they were entitled to at least equal "recognition." Alfred Santangelo of New York, a Tammany leader as well as a spokesman for the Italo-Americans, had threatened even earlier to vote against the Administration in a critical fight over the House rules, and to carry two other Italo-Americans with him, if he was denied, as he had been, an interview with Attorney General Robert Kennedy, the President's brother and a major dispenser of Administration patronage. Santangelo had received the interview, but had not been able to persuade Robert Kennedy to act on the Italo-Americans' patronage recommendations. This group, which often functioned like a minor political bloc in the House, then appointed Peter Rodino of New Jersey, a veteran of seven House terms, to act as the Italo-Americans' agent in pressing for the appointment of Americans of Italian descent to federal office. They decided to concentrate their efforts on securing the appointment of Salvatore Bontempo as Administrator of the State Department's Bureau of Security and Consular Affairs, a significant office to this group because of its influence on United States immigration. The hostility of the New York delegation and the Italo-Americans in the House endangered Kennedy's first bill. To be defeated on his very first bill to come before the House, of course, would have greatly embarrassed the new President. His House supporters had little basis to argue the merits of a farm bill to these urban Representatives, and so they merely pleaded for the bill on the grounds that it was Kennedy's. "Let's win this one for Jack, Jackie, and little Caroline," they urged. The New York Democrats and the Italo-Americans, angry as they were, hesitated to deliver so crushing a blow against the President on his first bill. Both groups reluctantly decided to go along with the President on this bill—but to let him know that their opposition could have killed it. "We want to show him," said one of the New Yorkers of the President, just before the House vote, "that we are bigger than he is." With their support the bill was passed by a margin of seven votes, 209 to 202. Either group could have reversed the outcome.

A few weeks later Bontempo was appointed Administrator of the Bureau of Security and Consular Affairs; and the President also named as Bontempo's deputy Michael Cieplinski, a gesture of good will toward the less militant eleven-man Polish-American bloc in the House. In time, also, the New York Democrats in the House began to receive some token patronage that relieved immediately the desire of these hostile Democrats to retaliate against the President with their votes on his bills. With some Representatives, however, there was no way to satisfy their demands for special White House consideration. D. S. Saund of California provided a case in point in Kennedy's first year as President. Saund insisted that the Kennedy administration reopen the Corona Naval Hospital in Saund's Congressional district; it had been closed during the Eisenhower administration on the grounds that its continued operation was fiscally unsound. Saund himself had written a book, *Congressman from India,* in which he revealingly showed himself as a furious scrambler for federal plums for his Congressional district. ("I was successful in my first two years in office in getting nine new post-office buildings in Riverside and Imperial counties," Saund wrote.) The Kennedy administration refused to reverse the Eisenhower administration's decision on closing the naval hospital in Saund's district. On fiscal grounds, the White House could not justify such an action. Saund, a member of the House Foreign Affairs Committee, then threatened that if the Administration did not relent on the hospital, he would attack a key section of the President's foreign-aid bill on the House floor. The President and his White House aides still refused. When the foreign-aid bill did reach the House floor, Saund offered an amendment to kill a key section of the bill; and the House adopted Saund's amendment. Kennedy had his own means of repaying Saund. The following year, in March, 1962, the President flew to California and made a major speech in Saund's Congressional district. Pointedly, he chose not to invite Saund to take part in the ceremony, thus clearly showing Saund's constituents how highly their Representative rated with the President.

Kennedy discovered as President that the political effect of party patronage had been overrated, but that in some instances in the legislative process it could prove useful politically. "It does give us some influence," he said.[14]

Far more effective were the President's personal relations with individual members of Congress and the President's stature as a national and world figure. The ever-increasing importance of the United States government, domestically and internationally, had elevated the President to a position of near majesty, a position of awe. The complications of an industrial society forced a growing dependence by the Congress on the President for legislative leadership. This, inevitably, made necessary closer working relationships between the two great branches of the government. Woodrow Wilson had shown how a President could become almost as much a legislative leader as a British Prime Minister. Dealing directly with members of Congress and committee chairmen, Wilson frequently bypassed the formal leaders of the House and Senate. When Claude Kitchen of North Carolina, Democratic leader of the House, opposed Wilson's war policies and programs, Wilson appealed directly to the Representatives to win support for his bills. Wilson was the first President to devise specific techniques of lobbying the House of Representatives for the legislation he wanted. He appointed, for example, men to act as his liaison with the House. In Wilson's day, these appointments were purely informal and discreetly concealed from the Congress and the public. He chose Albert Burleson of Texas, an eight-term member of the House, to be his Postmaster General; and he assigned Burleson the unofficial chore of acting as his chief Congressional liaison officer. Burleson, as a former member of the House Appropriations Committee and with the disposal of post offices and postmasterships at his command, had a natural influence over the members of the House. At Burleson's suggestion, Wilson also asked John Nance Garner of Texas, then a rising member of the Ways and Means Committee, to serve him as a confidential liaison man inside the House. This relationship, of course, had to be concealed from the formal leaders of the House. Twice a week Garner left Capitol Hill by streetcar, ostensibly on his own business. He got off near the White House, walked into the building through a side door and was ushered into Wilson's private study for his meetings with the President.

This anonymity fell away to a large degree when Franklin Roosevelt became President. Roosevelt used several of his White House aides as liaison men, James Rowe, Benjamin Cohen, and Thomas Corcoran among them. None, however, had the specific assignment of Congressional liaison man for the President; and their official duties ranged far beyond Congressional legislation. They did, however, freely take part in the drafting of New Deal legislation and in the inside struggle to persuade members of Congress to vote for that legislation. Roosevelt's Postmaster General, James A. Farley, was the President's patronage dispenser, and he, occasionally, used these powers to influence decisions in the House. For example, the New York City Democrats once voted against a Roosevelt bill and Farley pointedly remarked— in tones clearly indicating that party patronage was dependent on party loyalty to the President—that "the President has a program that must be adopted." The New York Democrats took heed. President Truman also used his White House aides, Charles Murphy and Clark Clifford, in the role of Congressional liaison, but like Roosevelt, he assigned them other tasks as well. Their liaison work was only a part of their White House jobs.

Wilson, Roosevelt, and Truman, in not publicly designating their liaison men to Congress, kept up a pretense of staying within the traditional strictures of the assumed independence of the President and the Congress. They felt the need for such intimate contact with the members of Congress, but they hesitated to offend the sensibilities of the House and Senate as institutions. It was such a hesitation as would exist in the 1960's for the President to name formally a confidential agent to argue his personal views, privately, with the justices of the Supreme Court. By the time Dwight Eisenhower became President in 1953, there was no longer any reason for not acknowledging publicly the now essential role played by the President's liaison men with Congress. Eisenhower chose a veteran staff lieutenant from the House of Representatives, Bryce Harlow, as his Congressional lobbyist. Harlow knew the House well, for he had spent years on Capitol Hill as a staff official of the House Armed Services Committee. Operating first under the title of "Administrative Assistant to the President," Harlow served eight years as Eisenhower's chief lobbyist on Capitol Hill. His job was no longer anonymous, nor did he have any other assignments at the White House, as did his predecessors. Even so, Harlow felt the need to remain inconspicuous. He normally operated from his White House office, answering and making telephone calls, perhaps as many as 125 a day. Only rarely did he slip up to the House of Representatives and usually even then only to have a private lunch with Charles Halleck of Indiana, one of the Republican leaders, in Halleck's hideaway in the Capitol, "The Clinic." Harlow kept the Republican party's Congressional leaders informed of forthcoming Eisenhower legislative proposals and kept in touch also with the Democratic leaders. Frequently, he escorted Speaker Sam Rayburn and Senate Majority Leader Lyndon Johnson into the White House late in the day for a highball and chat with the President. Harlow ranked far down in the White House hierarchy, beneath Sherman Adams, Wilton Persons, James Hagerty, and perhaps a half-dozen other Presidential lieutenants; and he was handicapped in his dealings with members of Congress by the coldness Adams, Eisenhower's chief of staff, displayed toward Representatives and Senators. Harlow later was promoted to "Deputy Assistant to the President for Congressional Affairs," a frank acknowledgment of his formal duties. He was given a full-time assistant, Jack Z. Anderson, a former Representative from

California, to help out with the liaison work with the House of Representatives.

Harlow appreciated the delicacy of his office. "It is," he said, "an ambulatory bridge across a Constitutional gulf." There was no Constitutional provision for such an office, even by implication, and indeed not even a Constitutional justification. That there was a vital need for such an office was obvious. The President and the executive branch of the government could not function in a vacuum, separated aseptically from Congress. Harlow saw his primary role as keeping in constant touch with the members of Congress and in sensing their drifts and moods. "That's the key to this trade," he said. "You have to know what they're doing." He tried to satisfy the requests of members and tried to persuade them to support the President's programs. "In this game," he said, "it's what you've done lately that counts." [15] Harlow worked closely with "every friendly influence" that he could find, principally the conservative lobbies, to help enact President Eisenhower's program. Harlow tried to avoid the patronage problem of the members. He believed that dispensing patronage could only hurt his efforts to pass the President's bills. "You have to turn down ten men for every one to whom you can say 'yes,'" Harlow said. "You make people unhappy instead of happy." [16] Besides, President Eisenhower had a rough-and-tumble patronage dispenser, Arthur Summerfield, his Postmaster General. Summerfield did not shrink from bluntly threatening to cut party patronage, particularly post offices and postmasterships, from Republican Representatives breaking party ranks. He often borrowed Halleck's office in the Capitol on such occasions and had Republican Representatives summoned into his presence, there to receive from him a tongue-lashing for their suspected insurgency. Harlow himself questioned the effectiveness of such action. Republican Representatives like John Saylor of Pennsylvania, a fiercely independent man who made up his own mind, resented Summerfield's abuse. Saylor did not admire—or fear—Summerfield, and Summerfield's threats hurt rather than helped Eisenhower's cause with such a Representative.

When John Kennedy became President in 1961, he confronted

255

a hostile House of Representatives, as had Franklin Roosevelt, Harry Truman, and Dwight Eisenhower before him. Ostensibly, the House was totally under the control of Kennedy's fellow Democrats, but unmistakably the temper of the House was conservative, much more conservative than the liberal domestic program the new President wanted that House to enact. As far back as 1938, when the House buried the remnants of Roosevelt's New Deal legislation, the House had been the more conservative of the two halves of Congress. President Kennedy, however, had assets as President—many the product of the twentieth-century modernization of the Presidency—that gave him at least the opportunity to sway the House of Representatives to his point of view. He had good reason to use those assets; for, unless he could alter the conservative tilt of the House, almost none of his major legislative proposals could become law. From earlier Presidents, he had inherited the powers of initiating legislation and the dispensing of party patronage for political advantage. Since Roosevelt's second term, the Speaker and the Speaker's lieutenants had been the President's legislative lieutenants in the House. And Kennedy could use precedents going back to Wilson to interfere directly himself, and through his staff, to persuade the members of the House to vote for his bills. Kennedy understood the nature of the House, and in the course of his very first year as President he added new dimensions to the growing intimacy of the President with the House of Representatives.

Even before he took the oath as President, Kennedy began the job of wooing the House of Representatives. He invited to his Palm Beach headquarters, one after another, some of the House's most influential members, some of them almost unknown to the country at large. With them he discussed his forthcoming legislative program, giving them his views, getting theirs in return. It was part of a process of communication with the Representatives that the President showed he would continue as long as he was in office, that he could neglect only at the hazard of his legislative program.

President Kennedy dealt personally with the leaders of the House and with the members of the rank and file, with any member who could help or hurt the legislation he sponsored. He demonstrated conclusively that he was a President intensely interested in legislation and one who intended to write a major legislative record. No better proof of this was his appointment of Lawrence (Larry) F. O'Brien as his Congressional liaison chief. O'Brien long had been a Kennedy intimate, a devoted campaigner who had been one of the inner Kennedy high command for a decade. In designating O'Brien as his "Special Assistant for Congressional Affairs," the President gave O'Brien coequal rank with the highest ranking members of his White House staff, the highest rank ever bestowed on a President's Congressional lobbyist. Kennedy's promotion of the role of Congressional liaison in actuality went much further than mere formal rank; it extended to giving O'Brien the authority to speak and act for him in legislative matters. Kennedy himself insisted that all major legislative questions be cleared through O'Brien, not only those coming from his own Cabinet members but also those coming from Congress. To even the most influential Senators who telephoned Kennedy in the first weeks of his Presidency, the President had a stock reply: "Have you discussed this with Larry O'Brien?" The word spread quickly on Capitol Hill that O'Brien was the man through whom Senators and Representatives could reach the President's ear. More than that, the Congressmen soon discovered that O'Brien also had authority to accept or reject the very substance of legislation. In the negotiating stages of important bills, O'Brien could approve or disapprove proposed compromises, as he did in a critical moment in 1961 when the House leaders had to rewrite important sections of the President's minimum-wage bill.

Initially, O'Brien's most difficult chore was to learn the political tendencies and problems of the 400-odd members of the House. He already knew from the 1960 Presidential campaign some of the House's ablest Democratic members. Richard Bolling of Missouri had been Kennedy's campaign liaison man with the Democratic candidates for the House. Frank Thompson of New Jersey had been chairman of the national Democratic registration drive. William Green of Pennsylvania had been influential in setting up campaign organizations across the country. Edward Boland of Massachusetts, a long-time O'Brien friend, had been Kennedy's coordinator for Ohio. In February, 1961, just a few weeks after Kennedy became President, O'Brien met privately in a suite at the Mayflower Hotel in downtown Washington with Bolling, Thompson, and Carl Elliott of Alabama for a detailed discussion of the House members. With O'Brien were Henry Hall Wilson, a lanky North Carolinian brought to Washington by O'Brien as his lieutenant for liaison with the House, and Richard Donohue, a young Massachusetts lawyer who had long been a Kennedy intimate and now was O'Brien's assistant on patronage matters. Bolling, Thompson, and Elliott had excellent qualifications: they were master counters of the House. Only a few days before, they had helped Speaker Rayburn win one of Rayburn's greatest personal victories in the House: the enlargement of the Rules Committee against the bitter opposition of the powerful conservative coalition in the House. Bolling, Thompson, and Elliott were political liberals in full support of President Kennedy's domestic legislative program. While O'Brien, Wilson, and Donohue took notes, the three Representatives systematically canvassed every member of the House of Representatives. Thompson had compiled a card file on most members of the House that provided significant political information on almost every Representative. Bolling, with his intuitive mind, carried almost as much information in his head. Elliott knew the Southerners. Name by name, they went over the list detailing each Representative's background and the possibilities of gaining his support for the President's program. Bolling had earlier made his own count of the House and he calculated that only one Administration bill, the housing bill, had a real chance of approval by the House. The rest of the program, by Bolling's calculations, could not be passed without major effort by the President, the White House liaison staff, the House leaders, and the sympathetic lobbyists. In the canvass of the House made for O'Brien and his two lieutenants, this glum picture for the President's bills became obvious. Of the 437 members of the House, roughly 180 could be safely counted as favoring the President's domestic legislation.

Another 180 could just as surely be counted as opposed to it. In doubt were the remaining seventy-odd Representatives. They could be persuaded; they were the same group counted by the lobbyists as "negotiable." The Democrats controlled the House by a 263-to-174 margin over the Republicans, but party designations did not accurately indicate the political tendencies of the individual members. The 263 Democrats were split. Most of the ninety-nine Democrats from Southern states were conservatives, although a dozen or so—some from Alabama, a few from Texas, one from Florida—were economic liberals. Almost all the 164 Northern and Western Democrats were committed to the President's program, although a scattered few tended to be conservative. The 174 Republicans, with perhaps a dozen exceptions from Eastern states, tended to be conservative and opposed to the President's bills. The House had a decided conservative tilt, a decided opposition to the liberal legislation advocated by John Kennedy. There were, however, the seventy-odd negotiables. Largely they were Republicans from industrial or urban Congressional districts in the East or Southern Democrats with districts still affected by the old-time populism of William Jennings Bryan. They became for Larry O'Brien the target Representatives, for on their votes would depend the outcome of Kennedy's legislative program.

At the same meeting with O'Brien, the three Representatives spelled out the influence of various important House members on their fellow members. None was more important than Carl Vinson of Georgia, chairman of the House Armed Services Committee, second only to Speaker Rayburn in seniority and second only to Howard Smith of Virginia, chairman of the Rules Committee, in influence with the Southern delegations in the House. "Vinson," said one of the Representatives to O'Brien, "is the absolute key to the whole session of Congress." [17] Vinson already had shown his power in this session of Congress. He had joined Sam Rayburn's cause in the Rules Committee fight and helped pull into Rayburn's camp enough Southerners to let Rayburn win. Vinson, said the Representative, had to be wooed and won by John Kennedy to the Kennedy program. As a young

Representative, Kennedy had had an office near Vinson's in the Old House Office Building, and the two had come to know and respect each other. He was also a Democrat and proud to have a Democrat in the White House.

O'Brien also set out, systematically, to meet the members of the House. He wanted to know them and he wanted them to know him. No longer was the role of Presidential liaison man to be concealed, as a shameful, hidden force. He asked Edward Boland to act as host for a series of cocktail parties, all held in House committee rooms, at which O'Brien could meet the members of the House on a purely social basis. At these parties, O'Brien made plain his obvious interest in being helpful to the individual Representatives. Even Republican Representatives, with scarcely much hope of White House consideration, were impressed. "He's a guy you can talk to," said Republican Ben Jensen of Iowa [18] after attending one of the cocktail parties for O'Brien. O'Brien, in return, reciprocated with invitations to the House members to come to the White House for coffee with the President. They were invited in groups of fifty, and each Representative had a chance for an informal chat with the President. For each House committee chairman, there was an even more gracious O'Brien invitation—a half hour's private audience with the President. The purpose was obvious: to enhance the chances of passing the President's program in the House of Representatives. O'Brien went further. He met at dinner with most of the 100-odd members of the House's Democratic Study Group, members of which were in reality the Democratic liberal bloc in the House and the hard core of the President's House supporters. There O'Brien spelled out for these members the sort of service they could get from the White House, everything from patronage to autographed pictures of President Kennedy. And he told them bluntly that President Kennedy would not be at all reluctant to help them win re-election in their next campaign. "The White House certainly remembers who its friends are," O'Brien said, "and can be counted on to apply significant assistance in the campaign." [19] No words could be more welcome to Representatives from marginal Congressional districts.

O'Brien scarcely rested from his chore of winning friends for the President's program. He normally worked a twelve-hour day, frequently through Saturday, and devoted even part of Sunday to his job. At his Georgetown home, he usually served Sunday brunch to a small group of Representatives, Senators, and members of the Cabinet. While his gracious wife Elva entertained the wives of these officials, O'Brien talked politics and program with such Representatives as Albert Rains of Alabama, George Mahon of Texas, Hale Boggs of Louisiana, and Albert Thomas of Texas, all immensely influential in House affairs.

President Kennedy had others besides O'Brien working for his program. Chief among these were the members of his own Cabinet and the powerful lobbies favorable to his causes. Both groups quickly learned to clear their operations with O'Brien's White House high command. That made for more effective pressure on the House of Representatives. Robert McNamara, the Defense Secretary, made overtures to the members of the Armed Services and Appropriations Committees. To no one was he more solicitous than to Carl Vinson of Georgia, the Representative already designated as the key to success for Kennedy's program in the House. Secretary of State Dean Rusk dealt directly with the members of the House Foreign Affairs Committee, briefing them in secret on the state of the world. Agriculture Secretary Orville Freeman perhaps worked harder than any Cabinet officer to make the President's farm legislation palatable to the House. Treasury Secretary Douglas Dillon kept in almost daily contact with Ways and Means Committee Chairman Wilbur Mills; and Secretary of Health, Education and Welfare Abraham Ribicoff worked as hard as he could to induce the reluctant House to approve Kennedy's school-construction legislation. Each secretary had his own staff of Congressional liaison men, none better qualified than Brooks Hays at State and Joseph Barr at Treasury, both veterans of the House of Representatives. Michael Monroney, the Post Office Department's liaison man, directed that every "action" taken by the department on behalf of a member of Congress be recorded on an appropriate card file to be forwarded to O'Brien. This was a list of "favors" granted to the members of Congress, a list de-

261

signed to be useful in persuading these members to vote for the President's bills. The liaison men from the departments drafted speeches for Representatives to read to the House and even provided special technicians to help answer any hostile mail.

Among the lobbyists, none stood more firmly for the Kennedy program than did Andrew Biemiller, chief agent for the AFL-CIO. He and O'Brien quickly coalesced their lobbying activities. O'Brien did not hesitate to work candidly with Biemiller, a House veteran himself, and with many of the other lobbyists sympathetic to the various Kennedy bills. Henry Wilson, O'Brien's lieutenant for liaison with the House of Representatives, frequently attended the private sessions of the lobbyists as the White House representative when these meetings were called to concentrate the joint fire of the lobbies on House members in behalf of specific Kennedy bills. Like the other lobbyists, Wilson took assignments to make contact with specific Representatives among the "negotiables" to try to persuade them to support the bill in question. Wilson, as a major assignment, had charge primarily of the Southern Democrats, whose natural hostility to the liberal Kennedy bills had to be broken if the bills were to be passed. Wilson later received additional White House support in his dealings with the House Democrats. O'Brien assigned Richard Donohue, once House patronage matters were largely settled, to deal with the "machine" Democrats in the House, those from Chicago, Philadelphia, New York, and Massachusetts. For the other Northern and Western Democrats, O'Brien appointed Charles Daly to act as White House agent. They brought to four the total of White House liaison men working on members of the House, the largest number ever so assigned, and they were aided by the numerous liaison men from every federal agency and department. For the Senate liaison, O'Brien had but one assistant, Mike Manatos. O'Brien had little way to influence Republican members of the House, although he and Republican leader Charles Halleck, both political professionals, soon developed a mutual respect and personal friendship. On the lobbyists, particularly the labor lobbyists, O'Brien had to depend to woo the "negotiable" Republican Representatives, those from industrial Congressional districts, to support the Kennedy bills. In this operation, Biemiller was the key man as the chief lobbyist for the largest and most powerful of the labor organizations. He was in contact with O'Brien personally and by telephone as frequently as some members of the Kennedy Cabinet.

In the delicate area of patronage, O'Brien took Bryce Harlow's advice and largely divorced his liaison work from the business of handing out patronage plums to the friends and allies of House members. That job was given to John Bailey, Chairman of the Democratic National Committee. O'Brien, however, long had worked with Bailey on behalf of Kennedy, and they encountered no difficulty in developing a workable arrangement in their new roles. O'Brien could say honestly, as he did, that he did not dispense the party's patronage. "I can only try to persuade the National Committee," he said. "I can try to persuade the National Committee to carry out the requests of Congressmen. We have a normal discussion of these things, and I'm the advocate of the Senators and Congressmen. I'm really a trouble shooter in patronage, not the dispenser. I will explore a problem and try to be helpful. I can't bring about what the Congressman wants. I can only bring in his views, get across the idea that they ought to be considered." [20] Bailey had the responsibility, but, like O'Brien, he saw his responsibility in terms of the Kennedy legislative program. "The important thing," he said, describing his role, "is to get the program through." [21] Bailey protected O'Brien's operations as lobbyist for Kennedy's bills by taking the blame for refusing patronage jobs. O'Brien and his aides, however, did not divorce themselves entirely from the other side of the question, the granting of favors and patronage. When they could help a Representative, they did, and they let him know it. Sometimes they could do nothing, however. One Representative on the Rules Committee threatened to block the President's school-construction bill with his vote. O'Brien checked hard to find out whether the Representative had asked for anything. "He didn't want a thing," said O'Brien. "I wish he had." [22] That Representative's vote did block the school-construction bill. Frequently, however, O'Brien or his aides could help a Representative. For instance,

Democratic Representatives Victor Anfuso and John Rooney had had their two Congressional districts in Brooklyn lumped together in the 1961 redistricting in New York. The White House helped arrange a municipal judgeship for Anfuso in New York, thus relieving both Representatives of a political crisis. Alfred Santangelo had had his Manhattan district wiped out in the same redistricting. Again the White House helped, this time under the pressure of persuading Santangelo to vote for the President's tax-revision bill. Almost all the New York delegation opposed the bill, and Richard Donohue tried hard to change them. "This is an important bill," said Donohue to Santangelo. "The President needs this one. Can we help you in any way?"

"Talk to Charley Buckley," Santangelo replied.

Buckley was not only a Representative, he was also Democratic boss of the Bronx. Donohue, perfectly familiar with New York local politics, knew immediately what Santangelo meant. "We will," he said to Santangelo, "and we'll talk to Bob Wagner, too." [23] Donohue telephoned Buckley and Mayor Wagner, quickly arranged for both to support Santangelo as Democratic candidate for Representative from the Bronx, across the Harlem river from Santangelo's old Manhattan district. Santangelo voted for the tax-revision bill.

The most powerful weapon of all in O'Brien's arsenal was the President himself. The fact that O'Brien spoke for the President gave O'Brien his influence to affect Congressional action. An even more effective method was for the President to speak for himself. A seasoned politician in his own right, Kennedy had an instinctive grasp of every political situation that rose in the House to threaten his bills, and he frequently engaged personally in the behind-the-scenes lobbying for his own program. On occasion, he invited individual Representatives to the White House for private talks with him. In the 1962 fight over his farm bill, Kennedy invited John Fogarty of Rhode Island to his office. Fogarty, long an enemy of farm subsidies, was a respected member of the House whose vote would influence the way other Representatives voted. Fogarty declined to accede to the President's wishes, and the bill was defeated in the House by the narrow margin of 215 to 205.

In a more successful instance, in 1961, Kennedy won the support of Armistead Selden of Alabama, an influential member of the House Foreign Affairs Committee, for the President's request for authority to make long-term loans to foreign countries. Selden had led a successful fight to kill a similar proposal requested four years before by President Eisenhower. Kennedy met privately with Selden at the White House and persuaded him to reverse his earlier position. The President's request had no difficulty—with Selden's support—in clearing the House committee, although it later was defeated by the House itself. Kennedy frequently telephoned members of the House, sometimes to ask for their support of measures, sometimes to get their views, sometimes merely to chat. Perhaps no member of Congress received more attention than Wilbur Mills of Arkansas. As chairman of the House Ways and Means Committee, Mills had charge, in 1962, of almost all the major Kennedy bills—a major tax-revision bill, a reform of the nation's foreign-trade program, an increase in the federal debt ceiling, and, most controversial of all, a federal program to provide medical care for citizens over sixty-five. The President had to have Mills's support, and where he got it on the tax, trade, and debt-ceiling bills, those bills passed the House. Mills declined to support the President's medical-care bill, and it died that year in Mills's committee.

The direct lobbying by the President with individual Representatives had a profound effect on how they voted. He had next to no influence on Republican Representatives, and he and his White House aides scarcely bothered to try to win their votes. Indeed, after the first few months of his Presidency when he did get substantial Republican support for his bills, Kennedy could hardly count even a single House Republican for any of his bills. In 1962, only one Republican voted for his tax-revision bill; only one Republican voted for his farm bill; only nine voted for his request to increase the legal limit on the national debt, normally a nonpartisan question. With Democrats, however, the President proved extraordinarily effective and most dramatically effective with the Representatives from the Southern states. When he came to office in 1961, most of the Southerners were conservative and hostile to Kennedy's brand of liberal legislation. Not a single Southerner voted for the 1960 version of the school-construction bill, but thirty-two Southerners voted for Kennedy's comparable bill a year later. In even more remarkable fashion, Kennedy cracked the opposition of the Southerners to his legislation dealing with farming, taxes, depressed areas, foreign trade, and minimum wages. By mid-1962, President Kennedy could count on heavy support from the Representatives from the South. Partly this was due to Carl Vinson's adherence to Kennedy's program. Vinson, dean of the House after Sam Rayburn died, voted for every one of Kennedy's major bills and the Georgian's support helped swing other Southern Representatives behind the President's legislative program. He had been won over by Kennedy and O'Brien, with help from Defense Secretary McNamara. Kennedy himself had taken care not to ask for civil-rights legislation, an area certain to stir hostility in the South. More importantly, however, the President and his aides were openly courting the Democrats in the House, from North and South and West. "I'll tell you why I'm supporting this Administration," said Charles Bennett of Florida, normally a conservative. "It's because they're consulting us and listening to our problems." That was the root of the President's effectiveness in the House, the reason he had been able to win support from the Representatives from the South. "You never know," explained a Representative from Alabama, "when you're going to pick up the phone and find Jack Kennedy on the other end of it."

President Kennedy made use of his position to appeal nationally for support of his programs. His news conferences, frequently televised "live" across the country, offered an obvious opportunity to make such appeals. So did his speaking engagements around the country, whether at a convention of the AFL-CIO or at a commencement exercise at Yale University. Kennedy, however, was circumspect in these appeals, never blatantly seeking to go over the head of Congress to the voters back home. "The Congress represents the people," O'Brien explained, "and it's far better for the President and us to deal with the Congress. The last thing we wanted to do was to obliquely threaten the

266

Congress. We had to be patient." O'Brien had learned to respect the House as a legislative body. "With all its weaknesses," he said, "the Congress is as close as you can come to representative government. This House of Representatives is truly representative of the American people. You can't discount an elected official. People somehow have approved him. He represents someone. Members of Congress have been successful in the most difficult of systems. Even in the one-party states, the clawing process goes on, and the candidates have to go through it." [24] That was the principal reason why President Kennedy and O'Brien preferred to work directly with the Representatives. They did not believe that they could successfully appeal beyond Congress to the people and felt that, if they tried, they would more likely stir deeper antagonisms toward Kennedy's program than already existed.

A similar reason prompted O'Brien's approach to lobbying with the Representatives on behalf of Kennedy's bills. He knew, of course, about the rough-and-tumble tactics employed by Arthur Summerfield, President Eisenhower's Postmaster General, but he believed they could not prove effective in the long run. "We use a soft sell of the President's program," O'Brien said, "I don't understand the Summerfield hard sell. I've leaned over backward to avoid any suggestion that we would strong-arm anyone. If for no other reason, it's simply not practical to do that. We're going to be here for several years. We have to think of victory today, yes, and also in the years ahead. I don't understand the techniques of using chains and whipping the boys." O'Brien found, as did President Kennedy, that members of the House were always willing to listen to them and their arguments, even if they were not always willing to go along. "Maybe they can come along," O'Brien said, "maybe they can't. They're always concerned about the effect of their votes back home, and we'd be completely ineffective if we were naïve enough to ask a member to commit political suicide." [25]

That reasonable attitude by O'Brien did not prevent him from struggling as hard as he could to sway the Representatives to back the President's bills. Gone was any real awkwardness about the delicacy, in Constitutional terms, of the assumed separation of the Presidency and the Congress. O'Brien openly lobbied for the President's program. On days when the House was voting on Kennedy's bills, O'Brien and his assistants, Richard Donohue, Henry Wilson, and Charles Daly, normally worked right out of the Speaker's office off the floor and in the corridors around the House. They sent messengers into the House chamber to fetch those Representatives still hesitating about voting for the bill then under consideration, and they argued with them about its merits frequently right up to the moment when the final vote was taken. They took full part in the House's own inner struggle over legislation; they had become, in fact, major operators in those struggles. The White House liaison staff made their own counts of the House on every major bill, assisted by the liaison staff of the executive department involved, by the sympathetic lobbyists, and by the House's own party leaders. They used those counts to locate the President's strength and weakness on every major bill and then turned their efforts to persuading a majority of the House to support the President's position.

Larry O'Brien had but one hesitancy. He would not enter the gallery of the House either to listen to debate or to watch the House vote. He had as much right to enter the gallery as any of the thousands of tourists who streamed through the Capitol: it was a public place. O'Brien felt, however, that because of his position as the President's man on Capitol Hill it would not be proper for him to be seen in the gallery of the House or that of the Senate. He could read the debate and count the vote in the *Congressional Record* the next day. To appear in the gallery, however, might smack of an impropriety; it might seem that he was asserting an undue pressure on the members of Congress. O'Brien's sensitivity here was a trace, a faint trace, of the old Constitutional separatism between the executive and legislative branches of the government. There were scarcely any others left. The rest had been eroded by the imperious demands of modern America. The nature of the American government, altered to meet the ever-increasing complexity of American life, had been profoundly changed—not the Presidency alone, but the Congress and the courts as well. In mid-twentieth century, no major bill could move through the House of Representatives without the active interest and frequently the intervention of the President in the proceedings. The President had become, in terms of the House of Representatives and the Senate, the chief advocate, the chief lobbyist, and the chief legislator of the United States.

CHAPTER ELEVEN

The Inside Struggle

HOWEVER popular the President of the United States might be, however skillful in maneuver and intrigue, he could not, even in the 1960's, force the House of Representatives to act when a majority of its members chose not to act—nor could the most efficient and effective of the Washington lobbyists. The President and his allies could persuade individual members of the House, and they could profoundly influence decisions of the House, including some of its most important decisions; but they could not take control of the House of Representatives. Always they had to accept the basic nature of the House as a legislative assembly, if they were to succeed at all in leading the House in the direction they wished. The President had a far more commanding position than all of the veteran lobbyists, but even the President never could be certain just how far he could persuade the House to go. The House of Representatives in the mid-twentieth century was the sum of its 435 individual members, plus something more. It was a product of its own past, its rules, its precedents, its traditions. The House had a mind of its own, a sense of itself, that defied specific analysis. By a type of osmosis, influenced as it was from myriad outside and inside sources, the House of Representatives frequently made its own decisions in its own way. This was so despite all the modern techniques and tactics devised by the Speaker and the party floor leaders, by the President and the lobbyists. There was more involved to the shaping of a consensus of the House than either the persuasion of the formal House leaders or the pressure of the most powerful outside forces. The modern President and the lobbyists, even the most adroit, have frequently failed to win the assent of the House of Representatives, notwithstanding the perfected pressure devices that made those of their precedessors seem merely primitive and naïve. Franklin Roosevelt, with the party loyalty in 1937 of 333 of the House's 435 members, had failed in perhaps the most dramatic instance of all; but Presidents Truman, Eisenhower, and Kennedy had met with similar defeats. Kennedy, in fact, lost in the Eighty-seventh House his domestic legislation of highest priority, the school-construction bill, even though he placed his own reputation in hazard on its behalf and had allied with him the House's hierarchy, an active and energetic Cabinet officer, a skilled White House liaison corps, and one of the most effective campaigns by the lobby organizations in years. The House, or rather a clear majority of the House, declined to follow this leadership. The members reached their conclusion by other means. Involved here, as has been the case in every major question coming before the House, were fundamental elements of the House's inner life; for the members of the House did more than merely respond to the requests of Presidents, party leaders, and vested interests. Indeed, over its many years, the House had evolved within itself powerful, informal forces of its own. They were coalitions, power blocs, alliances that cut across party affiliations and loyalties, and often set at naught the most powerful of outside forces attempting to control the actions of the House. They engaged, in moments of the House's highest drama, when great questions of public policy hung in the balance, in a massive inside struggle to decide those issues.

The outside pressures playing on the individual Representatives often were obvious. A Representative from a wheat district could not be expected to vote to abolish the government's farm-price-support program, any more than a Representative from West Virginia could be expected to vote to increase imports of pottery and coal. The inside pressures, influencing the Representative's view, were frequently more subtle, and they were at work on the individual Representative at every stage of an important bill's parliamentary course. They started soon after the bill's formal introduction, if not before, and carried through the hearings and recommendations by the legislative committee; through the action by the Rules Committee that gave the bill clearance to the House floor; in the cloakrooms, private offices, and corridors of the House, wherever the member met his colleagues and friends. Not only was the individual Representative moved by an instinct for political survival that prompted a desire to placate influential groups and just plain voters back home. Also affecting his decisions were his feelings of party loyalty, his own bent toward liberalism or conservatism, his sense of camaraderie with his colleagues in the House. He found himself in a web of influence from which he could not escape—colleagues to whom he was indebted for their help, associations with his fellow members in scores of ways. The great inside power blocs, to which he often found himself aligned in support or opposition, were the conservative coalition, a working alliance between Republicans and Southern Democrats; the liberal bloc, masked somewhat under the guise of a disarming name, the "Democratic Study Group"; the farm bloc; and the Southern bloc. There were many others, too, most of whom seemed scarcely more than social groups. There were a variety of informal clubs, the "Buckwheat Club," the "S.O.S. Club," the "Marching and Chowder Club," among them. There were ethnic groups, like the Italo-Americans or the Polish-Americans in the House who acted at times as voting blocs. There was a Catholic "vote," for in the House in recent years roughly one out of five of its members have belonged to the Catholic Church, and occasionally their religious affiliation has played a role in a legislative fight. Some state delegations, like those of New York and Ohio, took on political overtones as voting blocs, for their members tended to seek each other's advice before voting on controversial questions. All of these groups, and more, played a legislative function in the House's inner life; and they helped shape the House's decisions, as did the more formal House power

272

groups—the party leaders, the important House committees, and their chairmen.

In the inside struggle to set the House's stance on a question of public policy, rarely has the decision involved for the individual Representative a moral choice between right and wrong. Involved rather has been a complex and often confusing choice of alternatives, and not necessarily contradictory or conflicting alternatives. The question normally has not been: Shall this bill pass? More frequently, rather has it been: How can this bill be amended so that it will pass? It has been here, in the shaping and molding of legislation, that the blocs inside the House have had great power, for frequently even a relatively small group of Representatives have been able to decide the House's response to major questions. On some issues, such as a federal school-construction program, the House had had to decide whether or not such a program should be instituted, yes or no. On others, like an increase in the minimum wage, the question has been a matter of degree. In both instances, however, votes could be won or lost for the bill by the amendments proposed to woo different groups inside the House. Normally on legislation, there has always been an area of possible compromise, legitimate compromise, and this possibility has caused the bargaining implicit in the formulation of almost all legislation. The adoption of even an amendment of seemingly little or no consequence sometimes has provided the votes needed to pass an entire bill. At other times, major surgery has had to be performed before the house would adopt the measure. At still others, nothing at all could be done to persuade a majority of the House.

Such maneuvering for votes has existed for many decades. As early as 1820, the word "logrolling" was familiar. It meant, bluntly, the wooing of a majority to favor a bill by offering each Representative willing to commit his vote to the bill the inducement of including in the bill an item politically important to him. In 1868, Ransom Gillet of New York looked back at his years in the House in the 1830's and explained candidly the then perfected technique of building a majority in the House for a tariff bill. The sponsors of the bill simply made the bill attractive

273

to the local interests of enough Representatives to assure its passage.

"Interest, and not principle, determines what shall be done," Gillet wrote. "If votes from Louisiana and Texas are needed, sugar will come in for favor. If support is needed from Illinois, Wisconsin, Minnesota, and Michigan, lead, copper, and pine lumber are provided for. If the votes of Pennsylvania are wanted, coal and iron receive full attention. . . .The principle of protection under a tariff never expands beyond the objects necessary to carry a bill." [1]

The commercial interest of the states Gillet cited have changed in the past century, but the cynical technique he described for creating a majority in the House in favor of a bill has not been forgotten. Indeed, roughly the same technique has been used in only recent years to pass other tariff bills. In 1958, for example, Frank Ikard of Texas, at the behest of Speaker Rayburn, worked for weeks to draft an amendment that would nullify the opposition of the oil interests in Texas, Oklahoma, and Louisiana to an extension of the reciprocal-trade program.

The Representatives from agricultural states in the 1920's built the powerful farm bloc in the House on the principle of providing government financial help to a variety of politically important farm crops in the South and Middle West—thus uniting the votes of the Southern Democrats and the Midwestern Republicans. By joining forces, they could almost dictate United States farm policy.

These blocs inside the House frequently crossed party lines, and often brought veteran party stalwarts into complete opposition to their party's formal leaders. This was no new thing in the House, for both major political parties in the House have been fragmented since the modern development of the Republican and Democratic parties after the Civil War. Prior to the revolt against Speaker Cannon in 1910 and the abandonment of the binding party caucus as a means of enforcing party discipline, the Republican party in the House had been able to show the country remarkable unanimity on national questions. That was so largely because two-thirds of the House Republicans could then force any dissident Republicans to toe the party line. The formal Republican unity on votes in the House, however, did not mean even then that all Republicans in the House had a monolithic stand on all national questions, any more than did the Democrats. Indeed, the defection of Republican progressives, led by George Norris of Nebraska, to the cause of "reform," was the essential reason for the success of the House revolt against Republican Speaker Cannon in 1910. These Republican progressives, largely from the Middle West, were to harass the party's regulars in the House for another two decades.

The Democratic party, all through its long history, has shown a natural cleavage that has plagued its leaders in the House of Representatives. In the 1890's, Charles Crisp of Georgia was the leader of the House Democrats and the fragmentation of his party left him so frustrated that he quit the House to run for a seat in the Senate. Democratic leaders in the House after Crisp had much the same experience. One observer in 1906 called the Democrats in the House a "disorganized, undisciplined mob" incapable of unity except on a "pork-barrel" bill. "Chaos is its best word of description," he said of the Democratic party. "A ploughing, snorting herd of Texas steers, suddenly released from all restraint, is its nearest analogue." [2] The Democratic party, like the Republican to a lesser degree, was fundamentally divided on economic issues. The Southern Democrats, who made up most of the party's conservatives in the House, had a further differentiation from their Northern and Western colleagues: they were politically committed to resisting any social, political, or economic advance of the Negro.

The Republicans in the House have had a similar economic cleavage. In the main the Republicans since Lincoln's day have been economic conservatives, dedicated like most Southern Democrats to resisting the enlargement of the federal government. That has not stopped insurgency in the Republican ranks. A Republican progressive movement sprang up in the Middle West in the late nineteenth century and harassed the Republican Old Guard well into the 1930's. Norris and Robert La Follette of Wisconsin were early leaders of these progressives in the House; and, when they moved into the Senate, their places were taken by other equally fiery leaders. Their fierce partisanship deeply annoyed Republican Speaker Nicholas Longworth in the 1920's. "I like stability and responsibility," said Longworth. "I do not like to see legislation as the product of bluster and back-alley trading among groups." [3] Longworth, however, came to terms with the insurgents: for their votes were vital to him. Constantly he had to fight off the legislation pushed by his party insurgents under the leadership of James Frear and John Nelson of Wisconsin and Roy Woodruff of Michigan. Later, in the early 1930's, Fiorello La Guardia of New York, the first of the Eastern Republican progressives, took command of this bloc in the House; and he proved an effective and dangerous opponent to the Old Guard. La Guardia, at his prime, led a progressive band of Republicans perfectly willing to join forces with the House Democrats when that served their cause. John Nance Garner of Texas, the Democratic leader, had profound respect for La Guardia's ability to deliver his bloc on the tough votes. La Guardia led a band of fifteen Republican progressives. "He never made a promise he couldn't keep," said Garner. "He never overestimated the number of votes he could deliver on a roll call. I always knew just how many votes he would bring in." [4]

With the passing of the Midwestern Republican progressives, a new group of Republican liberals appeared, partly as a result of the new political power of labor unions in the 1930's. These were Republicans from Northeastern industrial districts, politicians who like their Northern Democratic counterparts were dependent on labor and urban voters to send them to the House of Representatives. Reflecting their constituents, they favored welfare legislation. From New England west to Ohio, these new Republican progressives appeared, wedded to industry and the city rather than the farmlands of the earlier breed. They scarcely were more numerous than the agrarian progressives of the 1920's; but in a tightly divided House they could provide, as President Kennedy discovered, the votes necessary to pass welfare legislation. In Kennedy's first session of Congress, in 1961, not a single major bill was passed by the House without a substantial number of Republican votes and in all but one instance these major bills would have been defeated without that Republican support.

The Democratic party in the House of Representatives has long had a much deeper cleavage than that of the Republicans. Indeed, a case might be made that the Democrats have had a half-dozen or more fractional parties in the House. The Northern Democrats, although all tending toward political liberalism, have been sharply divided between the "machine" politicians of Boston, New York, Philadelphia, and Chicago and the academic liberals whose political roots have been in university life rather than political ward heeling. The Southerners, although mainly conservative, for many years have had a progressive splinter group in such states as Tennessee, Texas, and Alabama. The border states, Maryland, West Virginia, Kentucky, Missouri, and Oklahoma, have sent a breed of Democrats to the House of Representatives often distinctly different in political response from those from the South or the North. The Democrats from the West have been a breed apart, too. The Democrats from some states, like those from Pennsylvania, Ohio, West Virginia, and Kentucky have their own differentiation for many of them have been dependent on the United Mine Workers or the Steelworkers Union for their political base. And even Representatives from the same areas, with the same conservative or liberal instincts, have had entirely different grounds for their political positions. The Northern liberals have offered such an example. The organization Democrats, often totally responsive to a city political machine, have come to support liberal welfare legislation largely from a practical response to the needs of their constituents, not unlike the old-time machine tactic of delivering Christmas baskets of food to the poor. The academic liberals, voting the same way on the same bills, frequently have found their justification in intellectual terms, in economic theorems or statistical analyses.

In the South, the Democratic conservatives likewise have shown distinctive variations in their political instincts. Many of those from Mississippi, South Carolina, and parts of Georgia have spent their political lives fighting over the segregation question, and even campaigned for election on the single issue of white supremacy. In other Southern states, like Arkansas, Alabama, and Louisiana, at least some of the Representatives, although segregationists, have concentrated their principal attention on national issues and largely ignored the South's often parochial concern over the Negro. Albert Rains of Alabama, for example, for years has been the House's great authority on national housing; Hale Boggs of Louisiana, the House's authority on foreign trade; Wilbur Mills of Arkansas, the House's specialist on taxation; and Otto Passman of Louisiana, the House's expert on foreign aid. This was no modern phenomenon. The same differentiation among Southerners was just as prevalent in the early years of the nineteenth century. "He votes as a Southern man and votes sectionally," said Thomas Benton of Missouri of a Georgia Representative. "I also am a Southern man, but vote nationally on national questions." [5] The differentiations among the Democrats in the House, only suggested here, have caused—like the variations among Republicans—great problems for the House's formal leaders. In modern times, even on votes directly appealing to party loyalties, almost invariably major segments of both parties have switched to the cause of the other party. In the House, there has been scarcely a partisan vote, except for that electing a Speaker, that has not found Republicans supporting the Democratic position and Democrats the Republican position to such an extent that at times party affiliations have appeared useful and desirable almost only for the sake of electing the Speaker and other leaders of the House. These intraparty conflicts have made meaningless any assumption that the political party controlling the House automatically has had the power to enact its party program.

President Kennedy, as we have seen, found a House of Representatives in 1961 in which his Democrats far outnumbered the Republicans, 263 to 174. On the surface, it seemed that the President would have no difficulty at all in persuading such a House to enact his proposed legislation. Not so, however. The actual temper of that House was conservative, in opposition to his liberal legislation. To alter that political bias, Kennedy and his supporters had to make major inroads into the ranks of the

Republicans and the Southern Democrats. That he was partly successful in so doing could be attributed to his own political skills, to the skills of his supporters, and to the fact that there were marginal Representatives in the House who could be persuaded to support the President's cause. The hard-core liberals and the hard-core conservatives in the House of Representatives, the members who know automatically their political position on almost any issue that might arise, have usually regarded the "marginal" Representatives, those who were classed "negotiable," with mild contempt. In the privacy of the House, they have been called "shaky legged" or "weak kneed," for they often remained in doubt on how they would vote until the very last moment. There was justification, however, for the existence of these "negotiables." The House itself was designed as an assembly representative of the American people, and the American people always has contained a segment, as shown repeatedly by professional polls, that was in doubt and could be swayed one way or another on every political question. More than that, many Congressional districts had no firm political commitment to Republicans or Democrats, to conservatism or liberalism, and the Representatives from these marginal districts could be expected, if they adequately represented their districts, to swing back and forth politically and avoid polarization on one side or the other. One California Representative read with dismay the decision of the California legislature in redistricting the state in 1961. A liberal Democrat, he had hoped the Democratic legislature would redraw the lines on his Congressional district in such a way that the liberal voters would clearly and safely outnumber his conservative constituents. Instead, the legislature left his Congressional district just as it was. "I could have been a statesman," this Representative exclaimed privately, "if they had cut off a few of those conservatives. Now I'll have to continue going this way and that way, back and forth. I'm a cracker-ass Congressman— and I could have been a statesman." [6] This Representative, like others from marginally divided Congressional districts, politically had to wind up with a "balanced" voting record at the end of each Congressional session, not too liberal, not too conservative, or face political ruin.

The fact that there were Representatives who wanted balanced records and that others genuinely had doubts how they should vote on a given bill made the House a far more volatile legislative assembly than a wooden recital of the members' party allegiances indicated. These Representatives could be persuaded, or pressured, to take either side of a legislative controversy. Their votes were in doubt, and thus on matters of narrow controversy the way these Representatives voted decided the issue. The lobbyists, the White House liaison men, and the House leaders normally found in the modern House that about fifty to sixty of the seventy-odd negotiable Representatives could be classified as doubtful on any given major issue that drew taut the lines of political controversy. They formed a swing group in the House of Representatives and prompted furious struggles inside the House for their votes. They attracted not only the closest attention of the formal leaders of the House, but they also automatically drew on themselves the concentrated and sometimes withering fire of the interested and competing lobbyists. They were worth courting, for it was they who could ultimately mean victory or defeat for the contending sides.

In the Eighty-seventh House, which first convened in January, 1961, Charles Halleck of Indiana led a Republican minority of 174 members, a far cry from the number needed to control the House of Representatives. Most of Halleck's Republican rank-and-file members were conservatives. Their conservatism ranged, however, from the hard-core primitivism of men like Noah Mason of Illinois and Edgar Hiestand of California to the moderation of such men as William Avery of Kansas, William Ayres of Ohio, and William Bates of Massachusetts. Halleck's ranks contained perhaps a dozen members who could be classed as Republican progressives or liberals, men like Chester Merrow of New Hampshire, John Saylor of Pennsylvania, and John Lindsay of New York. Halleck could hold most of his Republicans in line, primarily because most of them were agreed in advance on a conservative approach, but only rarely could he hold them all. And in rough-

and-tumble scrambling for votes on fundamental economic questions, Halleck often found his House opponents pulling away from his leadership some of the middle-of-the-road Republicans. Halleck, however, was more than the Republican floor leader in the House; he was also co-leader of the powerful conservative coalition, which since 1937 had often dominated the proceedings of the House of Representatives. The other leader of this bloc was Howard Smith of Virginia, chairman of the House Rules Committee and leader, without portfolio, of the Southern conservatives in the House.

Smith had inherited, by the rule of seniority, his chairmanship of the Rules Committee; but he gained his ascendancy over the Southern conservatives by sheer ability. Perhaps the ablest parliamentarian in the House, a master both of the House rules and legislative strategy, Smith had the gracious manner of a Virginia gentleman and the tactical skill of Stonewall Jackson. From his post as chairman of the Rules Committee, he commanded the flow of legislation to the floor of the House. This gave him power not only over the agenda of the House's proceedings but frequently over the substance of the bills to be considered. In the Eighty-seventh House, Smith's Democratic Southern colleagues, those from the eleven Confederate states, numbered ninety-nine, most of whom, like Halleck's Republicans, tended to be conservative. Their conservatism, however, had as wide a range as did that of the Republicans. There were deep conservatives, like William Colmer of Mississippi and William Jennings Bryan Dorn of South Carolina. There were moderate conservatives like Herbert Bonner of North Carolina, Paul Rogers of Florida, and Carl Vinson of Georgia, who as chairman of the Armed Services Committee was second to Smith in influence over the Southerners. Here and there through the Southern delegations there were progressives, men like Jack Brooks of Texas, Ross Bass of Tennessee, and Dante Fascell of Florida, in all perhaps a dozen or fifteen. On an economic question, Smith at best could expect to hold eighty-five of the Southerners to the conservative cause, assuming there were no major defections from his ranks. That was why, as noted in the previous chapter, the allegiance of

Vinson was regarded as so crucial to the bills of President Kennedy. Vinson's defection from the conservative coalition to the President reverberated through the Southern delegations and was a major cause in swinging other Southern Representatives to Kennedy's program. On a question involving civil rights, Smith could hold all the Southerners. With the full cooperation and coordination of Smith's Southerners and Halleck's Republicans, the conservative coalition could command the decisions of the House. They held, at their best, almost two hundred and fifty votes in the House, a clear majority. Their ranks, however, were subject to constant raiding by the progressives and the liberals, the lobbyists, the House Democratic leaders, and the President himself; and it was this raiding that accounted for most of President Kennedy's early legislative success.

The Halleck-Smith alliance was not a new thing in the House. They had come to know each other well when they both served as members of the Rules Committee. Even earlier, however, the founders of the modern conservative coalition had met as members of the same committee. These were Eugene Cox of Georgia, leader of Southerners in the House before Smith, and Joseph Martin of Massachusetts, leader of the Republicans in the House before Halleck. "Cox was the real leader of the Southerners in the House," Martin wrote in his autobiography. "He was a good speaker and wielded considerable influence. He and I came to Congress in the same year [1925], and we became friends while serving together on the Rules Committee. After I was chosen [Republican] leader he and I were the principal points of contact between the Northern Republicans and the Southern Democratic conservatives." [7] In the 1920's, the Southern Democrats were almost the only Democrats in the House. In 1921, for example, 99 of the House's 134 Democrats came from the South. In 1929, the Southern Democrats numbered 101 of the 190 Democrats in the House. Not only did they outnumber the non-Southern Democrats in the House, but they also outranked them in seniority. Of the fourteen most important House committees in 1929, the ranking Democrat on no less than twelve of these came from the South. It gave the Southerners an added influence in the

House then as it still did a full generation later. These Southerners gave Franklin Roosevelt his earliest national support, helped nominate and elect him President in 1932, and voted for his bills in his first years as President. A Representative like John Rankin of Mississippi, later a staunch conservative, would boast as long as he lived of the role he played in pushing through the House such early New Deal measures as the Tennessee Valley Authority. Many of the Southerners, however, soon became disquieted by Roosevelt's domestic policies, his courting of the urban voter of the North, the labor unions, and the minority groups. Roosevelt's attempt to "pack" the Supreme Court in 1937 and his attempted "purge" of Democratic conservatives in Congress the following year completed the Southern disenchantment with the New Deal. Out of this disenchantment was the modern conservative coalition born. Many of the Southern progressives, men like William Bankhead of Alabama and Sam Rayburn of Texas, stayed with Roosevelt; but the rest drifted away into militant opposition. Joseph Martin of Massachusetts, the Republican floor leader, found he had more in common with Eugene Cox of Georgia than he had suspected. Together they created the beginning of the modern conservative coalition.

This coalition did not function on each and every roll-call vote in the House. That was not its purpose. On the great economic questions, however, the coalition was an effective way to mass the House conservatives into a solid phalanx, unaffected by party labels. Martin later described how he used to join forces with Cox and later with Howard Smith, the Southern Democratic leaders, on major questions. It was a somewhat informal, casual team that they made. Martin would find Cox and mention the forthcoming legislation. "Gene," he would ask Cox, "why don't you and John Rankin and some of your men get me some votes on this?" The technique, however, was not all that simple, as Martin further explained. The Republican strategists conferred with the Southern Democratic tacticians, and together they agreed on a joint plan of action. The secret to success was for Martin to permit the Southern Democrats to carry the fight on the House floor. They would make the main speeches, they would make the motions, they would offer the substitutes and the amendments. The design was to encourage Democrats to join the opposition. "We won a number of victories by this device," said Martin, "proving that wavering Democrats would often support a measure offered by one of their own party whereas they would balk if it was sponsored by a Republican." [8] The technique once learned proved a major weapon in the conservative coalition's arsenal. Martin used it against Roosevelt measures and Truman measures, and Charles Halleck used it against Kennedy bills. It was no accident that Phillip Landrum of Georgia, a conservative Democrat, offered the Eisenhower labor bill in 1959 or that James C. Davis of Georgia, even more conservative than Landrum, offered the Eisenhower airport-construction bill. Both had been chosen by Halleck and Smith as the Southerners most likely to encourage other Democrats to join the conservative cause. In 1959, the Republicans wanted to offer a substitute for the liberal housing bill sponsored that year by the Democrats. A bill was carefully drafted under Halleck's over-all supervision and then formally sponsored in the House by Sydney Herlong of Florida, a conservative Democrat. Halleck and his Republican lieutenants passed the word through the Republican ranks that the Herlong bill had their endorsement, and the Republican conservatives voted en bloc for it.

This was a tactic, of course, that both sides could use, and the choice of the formal sponsor of a bill was often as carefully discussed as the substance of the legislation itself. To counteract the effect on Democrats, particularly Southern Democrats, the Democratic leaders frequently picked a progressive Southern Democrat to sponsor their version of a bill. Thus, in 1959, when the conservative coalition joined forces behind the Landrum labor bill, the Democratic leaders under Speaker Rayburn replied in kind. They selected as the sponsor of their bill Carl Elliott of Alabama, one of the most popular and respected of Representatives. Their hope was that Elliott, a Democratic liberal, would nullify with his personal popularity the favorable effect Landrum's sponsorship had on the conservative coalition's bill. In choosing a sponsor in 1955 for a Democratic school-construction bill, a newly proposed federal program opposed by the House conservatives, the Democratic leaders again made a careful choice. The bill, which automatically helped public primary schools, offended the Roman Catholic hierarchy, who felt that such legislation discriminated against their parochial and other private schools. To offset the effect of the Catholic hierarchy on members of the House, the Democratic leaders chose Augustine Kelly of Pennsylvania, a devout Catholic, to sponsor the bill. "Gus Kelly's name on that bill is worth fifty Catholic votes in the House," said one Democratic House strategist.[9] Nevertheless, the bill was defeated. Another such bill, backed by President Kennedy, was formally sponsored in the House by Frank Thompson of New Jersey, also a Catholic. It, too, failed. The plan to have a Catholic sponsor the bill was designed to make it easier for other Catholics in the House—there were eighty-eight Catholics in the Eighty-seventh House—to vote for the bill, despite the formal opposition of their church leaders.

The Southerners in the House long had held great power, and for as long acted as a political bloc. From the earliest years, it appears, the South sent two distinct types of men, the firebrands and the more urbane Southern gentlemen, to the House. To argue with some of the Southern firebrands in the years before the Civil War meant to risk the challenge of a duel. The friends of Josiah Quincy in President Jefferson's day actually believed he was in danger of assassination by Southern members of the House. For a period of years, many Southern Representatives carried pistols on their persons in the Hall of the House. John Sherman of Ohio, writing of his days in the House just before the outbreak of the Civil War, said some of the Southerners—and he named Laurence Keitt of South Carolina, William Barksdale of Mississippi, and Albert Rust and Thomas Hindman of Arkansas —were "offensive in their conduct and their language." [10] There were others, however, men like John C. Calhoun of South Carolina, John Eppes of Virginia, Howell Cobb of Georgia, Lucius Quintus Cincinnatus Lamar of Mississippi, and Alexander Stephens of Georgia who would have graced any assembly in which they sat. The Southerners in the House battled furiously in the

1830's, 1840's, and 1850's against the Northern abolitionists, whose set purpose was to limit and then abolish Negro slavery. A century later, they were still fighting a similar cause, this time to prevent the Northerners from altering the status of the Negro in the South. In both periods, the Southern bloc utilized the caucus as a means of organizing their defense and planning their strategy. The modern House still had the same two types of Representatives, firebrands like John Bell Williams of Mississippi and E. L. Forrester of Georgia, and soft-spoken gentlemen like James Trimble of Arkansas and Porter Hardy and Burr Harrison of Virginia. When in 1956 the Southern Congressmen issued their Southern Manifesto, protesting the Supreme Court's ruling against segregation in public schools, the Southerners were but repeating a political tactic used in 1850. In that year, the Southern members of Congress met in caucus and issued a similar "address" to the public. "All that we ask is, that [every Southern man] shall consider the Constitutional rights of the South, which are involved in the great abolition movement, as paramount to all party and other considerations," the 1850 Manifesto read. "And surely the time has come when all Southern men should unite for purposes of self-defense." Even earlier the Southerners had used the caucus to plot strategy. In 1837, for example, the Southerners met in a caucus to denounce the North in inflammatory words and openly threaten disunion. The caucus approved a resolution, formally sponsored by John Patton of Virginia, that was adopted the next day by the House of Representatives: the "gag" resolution that stifled all petitions to the House that touched slavery. The Southern tactic brought John Quincy Adams to his feet. With the House in wild disorder, "Old Man Eloquent" denounced the resolution. "I hold the resolution," he shouted, "to be a violation of the Constitution of the United States, of the right of petition, and of freedom of speech to myself as a member of this House." [11] More than a century later, the Southerners still met in caucus when they believed it served their purpose. In 1960, at such a caucus, the question at hand was a civil-rights bill. And the old fire still burned in at least some of the Southerners. Up for discussion and action was another resolution, which read: "Resolved, that it is the fixed determination of this group to oppose by every device and argument the passage of a civil-rights bill, and particularly the registration amendment which will be offered. We are utterly weary of the constant efforts of the proponents of this legislation to adopt punitive measures aimed at the Southern States." It was another summons to battle for the cause of the South.

The frustration of these Southerners, those most concerned with civil-rights legislation, could drive some of them to the breaking point. In the floor debate on the 1960 civil-rights bill, Jamie Whitten of Mississippi openly threatened to take at least part of the Southern Democrats out of the party "not merely to prevent another Reconstruction era in the South, but to save the nation from destruction." [12] Claiming the support of thirty-one other Representatives from Southern states, Whitten said they just might refuse to vote to elect Sam Rayburn Speaker at the beginning of the next House. It was an ill-considered outburst, for Whitten's expected supporters vanished. No such revolt developed against Rayburn. Instead, at the time of his tenth election as Speaker, Rayburn had plans to remove Whitten from his influential position on the Appropriations Committee.

The Southerners in the House long have been the most adept at power-bloc politics, and they have from the earliest years of the House held a decisive advantage in the sheer ability of their members. As early as 1820, Edward Dowse of Massachusetts acknowledged formally that the Southern Representatives "have a great preponderancy of talent against us." [13] James G. Blaine of Maine, two full generations later, recognized the same "superiority" of the Southerners in the House of Representatives. He credited this to the tendency of the "best and most talented" [14] men in the South to enter politics while only a small percentage of the best Northern men did so. In the modern House, the Southerners have continued their marked pre-eminence in the Hall of the House. Here and there among the Northern and Western delegations, Representatives of great talent and parliamentary ability have appeared, but the large delegations from New York, Pennsylvania, and Ohio frequently have contained but a handful of really competent and skillful members. The delegations from the South, however, notably those of Alabama, Arkansas, and Texas, have contained a wealth of Representatives gifted in legislative tactics and parliamentary practice. The Southern Representatives not only have operated with great success as an independent bloc, they have also perhaps fared best of any group in their alliances, for specific purposes, with other groups in the House. In their formal political alliance with the Northern and Western Democrats, the Southerners in the House long have gained, under the seniority rule, the major share of committee chairmanships, a basic source of power in the House. In their alliance with the Republican conservatives, for a generation they either dictated or severely tempered the House's legislative action. A side effect of this alliance has been for the South to win some support from rural Republicans in their fights against civil-rights legislation. This frequently has been denied by the Republican leaders, but men in their ranks have not always been discreet. Ben Jensen of Iowa, for example, made no attempt to conceal his willingness to vote against civil-rights legislation, when he asked in 1949 for Southern support of an amendment he offered to an appropriations bill. "May I say," Jensen said, addressing himself to the Southerners on the floor, "that as one member of Congress I have been with you folks from the South right down the line on states' rights issues. Quite a few of us feel that your states should decide the kind of election laws you want without government interference. . . ." [15] There was a latent hostility among the Republicans in the House from rural districts toward the Negro voters, who had switched allegiance from the Republican party to the Democratic in the 1930's. After the 1960 election, in which urban Negroes voted heavily for John Kennedy, a House Republican leader urged his colleagues privately to ignore future civil-rights bills. "When are we going to learn," he asked several of his colleagues in the Republican cloakroom, "that we can't win the nigger vote?" Still another alliance, by which the South has won great advantages for their geographic section of the country, was the farm bloc, a combination of Republicans from the Middle West and Southern Democrats. How skillfully the Southerners maneuvered in this alliance could be seen by the results. Of the six major crops supported by massive federal subsidies, four—cotton, tobacco, peanuts, and rice—were basically Southern crops.

The farm bloc did not come into existence by accident. It was deliberately put together in 1921 by farm-state Senators and Representatives for the calculated purpose of promoting legislation helpful to the farmers. The nation's farmers had enjoyed great prosperity during the First World War, but in 1920 they suffered a major depression. In the House, Lester Dickinson of Iowa took the lead in creating the bipartisan bloc. Dickinson, a Republican, acting with the cooperation of the American Farm Bureau Federation, mustered Midwestern Republicans and Southern Democrats into a powerful legislative bloc. As early as 1842, a Representative, Joshua Giddings of Ohio, had tried to promote legislation beneficial for the farmer, and in the latter part of the nineteenth century the Middle West and South had been ravaged by agrarian unrest. Out of this unrest grew the Granger Movement, the Greenback party, the Farmers' Alliance, and finally the Populist party as political attempts to redress the "wrongs" perpetrated against the American farmer. As the Populist candidate for President in 1892, James Weaver of Iowa, a former member of the House, received more than 1,000,000 votes and carried four states. Higher farm prices calmed the farmers in the early years of the twentieth century and not until the depression of 1920 did they again become fully active in politics. Using the latest devices of up-to-date lobbyists, the farm bloc scored immediate legislative gains. The Farm Bureau boldly defended the bipartisan effort—after all, the farmers' plight was the issue, not party loyalty. The Farm Bureau served as a clearing house for the farm bloc members, and its staff publicized the voting records of congressmen so their constituents would know who were the "friends," who the "enemies," of the American farmer. Ignoring partisan party lines, the farm bloc members successfully passed a series of bills that provided for control of packers and grain exchanges, federal roads, and federal help on farm financing and crop exports. This early success in the 1920's led to further cooperation in the 1930's; and in time the Congressional farm bloc put together a massive and complex structure of law beneficial to the American farmers, not least of which were federal subsidies on surplus production of basic crops. These subsidies, in a period of twenty-five years, cost the government a total of more than $51 billion. There were political strains on the bipartisan effort, however; and under the hammer blows of President Eisenhower's Secretary of Agriculture, Ezra Benson, the farm bloc came apart in the 1950's. Benson dealt administratively with the farmers, crop by crop, and in the course of his eight years in the Cabinet, he put the Representatives of the various basic crops in competition and eventually at war with each other. The House Agriculture Committee, long the seat of the farm bloc's bipartisan power, became a battle ground between rival Republican and Democratic agricultural bills. Urban Democrats had frequently "gone along" with their Southern Democratic colleagues on farm bills. John McCormack of Massachusetts, who represented a district in Boston without a single farm, boasted that in thirty-three years as a member of the House he had never voted against a farm bill. The high cost of the farm subsidies, however, withered the Northern Democratic support at the very time the farm bloc Representatives themselves were dividing on party lines. In 1960, the House debate on a pending farm bill revealed how badly the once powerful farm bloc had been divided. The Democratic farm spokesmen in the House, who were mainly from the South, decided to cut wheat production drastically, restrain corn prices, and drop the subsidies on feed grains. The bill inflamed the resentment of the Republicans from the Middle West, where these crops are grown. Carl Andersen of Minnesota and Ben Jensen of Iowa pleaded with the Southern Democrats to remember the old days and to spare their farmers from the intended blow. They reminded the Southerners that the Midwesterners had always voted to help the Southern farmers.

"I am sure the *Record* will show," Jensen said, "that the gentleman from Minnesota and I have always helped the cotton and tobacco farmers."

"And the peanut farmers," said Anderson.

"And the rice farmers of America," added Jensen.

"All through my twenty-two years," pleaded Andersen, "we have helped you gentlemen from the South to get a fair break for your commodities, but we have no fair break in this bill as far as corn and feed grains are concerned, my friends." [16]

The farm bloc lay broken in the 1960's and its legislative achievements, notably the subsidy program for basic crops, were under severe attack for creating unneeded and costly farm surpluses. This bloc, in a sense, was an adjunct of the conservative coalition, many of whose members came from the rural South or Midwest. The conservative coalition, in a pure test with the House's Northern and Western liberals and progressives, still held a majority of the whole House; but the conservative coalition was under assault, too. As early as 1935 there had been a semblance of a formal liberal bloc in the House, composed entirely of Democrats. The founder and chairman of this group was Maury Maverick of Texas, grandson of the Texas rancher whose refusal to brand his cattle had made the Maverick name a household word for a political or any other kind of stray. As a member of the House, Maury Maverick himself coined a notable word: "gobbledygook" to describe bureaucratic verbosity and officialese. Jerry Voorhis of California, who was to be defeated by Richard Nixon in 1947, was elected secretary of "Maverick's Young Turks," and the group met almost every week in a dingy room over a second-rate Capitol Hill restaurant to discuss legislation and politics. Periodically, the group drafted policy statements that were given to the press, but they never formed a viable political bloc. In fact, they did not always even vote alike. After a few years, Maverick's liberals disbanded as a group. Maverick himself was defeated for re-election in 1938.

In the 1950's a new liberal bloc began to take shape around Eugene McCarthy of Minnesota, an extraordinarily articulate and witty Representative. McCarthy's group, which fittingly was called "McCarthy's Mavericks," at first met casually and informally. By 1956 they had instituted a loose form of organization with "whips" to keep like-minded members alerted to pending questions. McCarthy had become a close student of parliamentary procedures and pressure politics in the House, and under his tutelage an effective group of pragmatic liberals began to take shape. In 1957, taking a cue from the southern bloc, the liberal bloc issued a manifesto of its own outlining the group's legislative goals. The document was signed by twenty-eight Northern and Western Democrats. Among them were Lee Metcalf of Montana, Stewart Udall of Arizona, Henry Reuss of Wisconsin, and Frank Thompson of New Jersey. Richard Bolling of Missouri stayed somewhat aloof from formal identification with the liberal bloc; but he, as an intimate of Sam Rayburn, provided them with close liaison with the Speaker. The liberal bloc members lacked the seniority, the experience, and the parliamentary skill of their colleagues in the conservative coalition; and in 1958 they lost their leader, Eugene McCarthy, who was elected to the Senate. That same year, however, the Democrats won sweeping control of the House. Almost all of the forty-seven new Democrats in the House were liberals and McCarthy took the first steps toward a more formal organization as a bloc. In the two months after the election, members of the informal group quietly contacted most of the Northern and Western Democrats, including those just elected to the House. They asked for their support for a change in the Rules Committee, then the conservative coalition's strongest bastion to fend off liberal legislation. By January, the liberals were able to claim commitments of varying degree—some merely expressed "interest"—from 170 Democrats in the House, and with these in hand, the group plotted its next step. They knew, of course, that they could not alter the Rules Committee or the rules of the House without the approval of Speaker Rayburn. The Rules Committee, under conservative domination, long had harassed Rayburn's operations, but would Rayburn be willing to engineer a change? The liberal group dispatched Chet Holifield of California, then dean of the liberal bloc's members, to find out. Holifield explained the liberals' purpose to Rayburn on the Saturday before the opening of the 1959 session of the House—they wanted to strengthen Rayburn's control over the Rules Committee. Holifield suggested three different ways to work the change: add an extra Democrat to the Rules

Committee, allow as few as 150 members to discharge legislation from the committee, and provide that unless the Rules Committee acted within twenty-one days on a bill duly reported to its jurisdiction the bill could be brought automatically to the House floor for a vote. To each proposal Rayburn said "no"—the first would have violated an agreement he had made with Joseph Martin, the Republican leader, and the other two had been tried in earlier Houses and proved unsatisfactory. Speaker Rayburn disliked tampering with the rules of the House. Besides, he preferred working directly with men, not through institutional reforms. Rayburn, however, assured Holifield that he would see to it that those bills duly considered and recommended by legislative committees would be brought before the House for a vote. He would not permit the Rules Committee to block them.

In the session that followed, the Rules Committee blocked a long series of the liberal bills. Not only that, but the conservative coalition had won the most important political fight of the session, adoption of the Landrum bill to outlaw racketeering in the labor unions. In September, 1959, as the session was coming to a close, the liberal leaders decided that politically they needed a stronger organization in the House. Working to put this together were Metcalf, Holifield, Udall, Thompson, James Roosevelt of California, John Blatnik of Minnesota, and George Rhodes of Pennsylvania. The organization they formed, although named the Democratic Study Group, became the formal liberal bloc of the House. Metcalf was chosen chairman; Roosevelt vice chairman; and a thirty-three-man policy committee was appointed. The group selected formal "whips" with the responsibility to keep DSG members informed of floor activities and to alert them to turn up for important floor votes. Metcalf appointed "task forces" to study problems and to plan the DSG's over-all strategy on the proposed bills. A staff, headed by William Phillips, a legislative technician, was hired. To help pay for the costs of the operation, each of the 100-odd members was charged $25-a-year dues. In January, 1960, the liberal bloc presented a formal seven-point program for the session. Included were recommendations for a federal construction bill, a civil-rights bill, an increase in minimum wages, and medical care for the aged. All had the support of the formal Democratic leaders, Sam Rayburn and John Mc-Cormack, for the liberal bloc avowed no other purpose than to support Rayburn as far as possible against the conservative coalition. Still working closely with the liberal bloc members, although not formally signed up as a member of the DSG, was Richard Bolling of Missouri—Rayburn's confidant and a parliamentary strategist of great skill.

The liberal bloc, the farm bloc, the Southern bloc, and the conservative coalition were the most powerful of the partisan groups that had existed independently of the House's formal party leadership; but there were others, too, some of them scarcely more than social, that operated on a lesser scale to influence the decisions of the House. All played a role in the House's inner struggle to create a national consensus. They took part in the continuing dialogue of politics and legislation that has always been the essence of the House. Some, perhaps, had a greater reputation than they deserved. The AFL-CIO, for example, claimed in 1960 that 200 of the House's members were committed to the views of labor on legislation, but this did not mean that those 200 members belonged to an organization inside the House that performed the normal function of a power bloc. It merely meant that the AFL-CIO officials felt confident of the votes of that many Representatives on labor questions. In actuality, the number of labor-orientated Representatives was far less; and very few saw themselves as special Representatives of labor unions in the House. Some, however, did represent specific labor unions in the House, much the same as some rural Representatives represented specific farm crops. In the delegations from Pennsylvania, West Virginia, Kentucky, Ohio, and Michigan sat Representatives who closely reflected the views of such powerful labor unions as the United Mine Workers, the Steelworkers, and the Autoworkers. Many Representatives, like John Dent and Elmer Holland of Pennsylvania and John Shelley and Jeffery Cohelan of California, had been active members of labor unions before their election to the House. As a general rule, however, they did not function as a partisan bloc in the House, planning strategy and soliciting votes from their colleagues on labor bills. That function normally was performed by the labor lobbyists outside the House—men like Andrew Biemiller of the AFL-CIO.

Of a more informal nature were many private or semi-private groupings of the members of the House. Perhaps the best known in recent years was the "Marching and Chowder Club," founded in 1947 by a group of young Republicans including Richard Nixon. The club, originally limited to sixteen members, normally met late Wednesday afternoons in a member's office and over drinks the club members candidly discussed the issues of the day. The club added new members as old members were defeated, elected to other offices, or retired from the House. Such clubs were a familiar part of the Republicans' operations in the House. Others like the "S.O.S. Club" and the "Acorn Club" have long been familiar on Capitol Hill. Speaker Nicholas Longworth, mimicking his father-in-law, President Theodore Roosevelt, led an informal group on regular two-hours walks through Washington's Rock Creek Park; they were known, jocularly, as the "States-man's Sunday Morning Marching Club." Fiorello La Guardia and John J. Boylan of New York conducted a bipartisan club known as the "La Guardia-Boylan Spaghetti Association" to whose periodic spaghetti dinners came Longworth, John Nance Garner, and other members of the House. One, founded in 1901, had the sole purpose of defending freshmen Republicans in the House. A freshman that year, Robert Nevin of Ohio, had sought to question Eugene Loud of California, chairman of the Post Office Committee, during floor debate on one of Loud's bills. "I assume that the gentleman who asked me this question is a new member," said Loud scathingly, "and that he has asked the question for no other purpose than to get his name in the *Congressional Record*. I do not think I will gratify his ambition." [17] Loud thereupon continued his own speech. Nevin and the other freshmen Republicans were outraged. They promptly organized a club which they called the "Tantalus Club," after the mythical Greek king whose fate for revealing the secrets of the gods prompted the creation of the word "tantalize." Tantalus was forced to stand in water up to his chin, which receded every time he stooped to drink; luscious fruit dangling before him likewise pulled away when he reached for it. "The new member of Congress was very much in the situation of Tantulus," said one of the founders of the club. "Everything that he wanted was just out of his reach." [18] The club members agreed to stand together and support as fully as possible every bill in which any of them had an interest.

Occasionally, some of the informal groupings have been bipartisan. J. William Fulbright of Arkansas, for example, started such a group shortly after he entered the House in 1943. He invited active and intelligent freshmen, among them Mike Mansfield of Montana, Walter Judd of Minnesota, and Christian Herter of Massachusetts, to sessions in his office to discuss foreign affairs—a common interest they all shared. Among the Democrats two groups have taken shape in recent years along ethnic lines among Representatives of Italian extraction and Polish descent; both groups numbered a dozen or more members. The Italo-Americans in the House were far more militant than the Polish-Americans. The Polish group met for lunch every month or so, and at these luncheons Representatives like Thaddeus Machrowicz of Michigan, Frank Kowalski of Connecticut, Clement Zablocki of Wisconsin, and Daniel Rostenkowski of Illinois discussed Polish affairs. Only rarely, as on adding funds to the foreign-aid bill to build a children's hospital in Poland, did the group take joint action in legislation. The Italo-Americans, however, had far greater interest and effect as a pressure group inside the House legislatively. They fought to alter the restrictions in United States immigration law, which discriminated against Southern-European peoples, including the Italians. Alfred Santangelo of New York, a Tammany district leader as well as a leader in the Italo-American bloc in the House, won a formal commitment from President Kennedy to support legislation abolishing the national-origins quota system. Peter Rodino of New Jersey served as the group's spokesman in arguing with the Kennedy administration for the appointment of Italo-Americans to high federal office. Victor Anfuso of New York was the group's spokesman in a running fight with newspaper columnist Walter

Winchell. Winchell reported that President Kennedy had been unable to appoint an Italo-American to high office because all those suggested had backgrounds involving the Mafia, an Italian criminal ring. Anfuso demanded an immediate apology and got Attorney General Robert Kennedy to brand Winchell's statement as "completely false." The Italo-Americans in the House not only did persuade the Kennedy administration to appoint several Italo-Americans to federal office, but forced Winchell to apologize as well.

Still another group of associations, the state delegations, served in much the same role. Many of the larger delegations, like New York, California, Pennsylvania, Missouri, Texas, and Ohio, had natural group instincts. The New Yorkers, for example, had bipartisan leaders duly chosen by all of the forty-odd Representatives from New York. Chairman of the New York delegation was Emanuel Celler in the Eighty-seventh Congress; and the steering committee was composed of such stalwarts as John Taber, James Delaney, and William Miller. The Republicans and Democrats of New York frequently joined forces on state problems, such as the army's proposed deactivation of its Brooklyn Terminal. The Californians had a similar organization under the chairmanship of Gordon McDonough, the state's ranking Republican in the House. Some state delegations had regular meeting dates each week when the Representatives would gather for breakfast or lunch. The natural subjects at these meetings, of course, were politics and legislation. John Nance Garner, dean of the Texans, used to argue with his Texas colleagues that they had best stick together on important votes or risk encouraging an attack from home. Charles Halleck, the Republican leader, frequently appealed for similar help from the Republican deans of House delegations. For example, he frequently asked Ivor Fenton, dean of the Pennsylvania Republicans, to try to persuade his perpetually bolting Pennsylvanians to stick within the party lines.

All these groups played a role in the legislative decisions of the House. They all were part of the dialogue. And when the great decisions came to be made in the House, those that touched

297

basics of national policy, these blocs and clubs and delegations mustered their ranks for the ensuing struggle that almost always accompanied such decisions. Even so casual a group as those attending William Fulbright's foreign-policy sessions could prove important in the affairs of the House; for the men who sat in on those sessions provided a vital bipartisan bloc to help Fulbright persuade the House to adopt his resolution that placed the Congress on record, for the first time, in favor of United States participation in the United Nations. These groups of Representatives, as well as the power blocs, frequently engaged in the behind-the-scenes struggles over the spirit and function of United States law. In the House cloakrooms, the private offices, the caucuses, and the conferences, these conflicts often were settled and determined long before the bill reached the floor of the House. In other instances, the outcome of the almost hidden struggle was unknown until the vote was actually out.

Only rarely did House debate affect the outcome of these fights between conservatives and liberals, between urban and rural forces, between isolationists and internationalists. There were marginal Representatives to be swayed one way or the other on every question. The decisions were made in a seemingly chaotic complex of party pressure, lobbying, and personal argument. Many an outside influence played on the House of Representatives, but in a real sense these outside pressures were almost purposeless unless there were men inside the House capable of translating them into a viable majority. Even the President normally had to deal directly with his party leaders in the House.

The tactical problem of persuading even a single Representative could be exquisitely complicated. Perhaps as many as thirty or forty different individuals, each with a different claim to the Representative's attention, might be called into play. No one could ever be sure precisely who won him to the cause, if in fact he was won. From outside the House, a widely dispersed chorus of voices had pleaded with the Representative—a half-dozen lobbyists, perhaps the party chairman of his home county, the governor of his state, a veterans' leader, his campaign supporters, his doctor, the President, his wife's brother, his law partner, members of the Cabinet, a golfing companion or two. From inside the House, perhaps even greater pressures had been applied. The Speaker personally may have asked him for his vote: "I need you on this one." The other party leaders doubtlessly discussed the matter with him. So perhaps did the dean of his state delegation, and other colleagues from his state, the chairman of his House committee and his fellow committee members, the chairman of his party's campaign or patronage committee, the leaders of the different blocs, the members of his House club or discussion group, and a dozen other Representatives whom he knew as personal friends. The Representative had many strains placed on him. He had group instincts, some of them in conflict now, and he disliked to vote against friends. Many of the House members asking him to vote their way had helped him in the past; he was personally indebted to them for favors, and it was not easy to ignore such an "I.O.U."

Out of this vortex of pressure and pleading, the Representative had to make his decisions. On rare occasions, it became too much for the individual, the pressures were too great, and the Representative simply refused to vote at all. The process had to be repeated, in some form, for almost every member of the House; for the leaders of the House were no more exempt from pressure than the slightest freshman. And out of the sum total of all came the decisions of the House.

CHAPTER TWELVE

Revise and Extend

IN the House of Representatives, for generations, even the members themselves have assumed that their debates played but an insignificant role in the House's proceedings. It has been a commonplace that floor debate in the House was of small consequence in shaping the House's consensus on any major question coming before the Representatives for decision. House debate has been regarded in fact as scarcely more than a necessary annoyance in the formal legislative process. Most of the Representatives have made up their minds on how they would vote before the legislation has come to the floor for formal House action. The extensive preliminary operations, the committee's consideration of the bill, the lobbying from the various groups interested in the bill, the cloakroom struggle for votes, have in advance committed all but a few of the Representatives either for or against the legislation. In such instances, there seemed little function for House debate; and most of the Representatives have showed how little by not even bothering to attend those sessions of the House given over to formal debate. Only when the House has been actually voting on bills has the attendance on the floor of the House normally approached the full membership.

The limitations on debate imposed by the House's stringent rules, the rules required to speed handling of the House's congested calendars of business, served largely to denigrate the quality of debate and its influence on the members. Thomas Hart Benton of Missouri stated, without qualifications, that the House's adoption of the one-hour limitation of speeches in 1841 was a suicidal act that did "permanent injury" to the House itself.[1] The limitations made on debate in the decades since that rule was adopted have restricted the Representative's opportunity to speak even more. In the modern House, it has been almost unknown for a member of the House to be allowed to address the House for even an hour on the grave matters coming before that assembly. The fundamental changes in American society and the enlargement of the federal sphere of the government to watch those changes, in all national questions have forced this economizing on time. The changes have placed the emphasis in the House more on action and less on talk. In the modern House of Representatives, parliamentary tactics have been more important than debate.

In mid-twentieth century, the House rarely has allotted even two afternoons of debate for the most consequential legislation. On lesser questions, the time for debate has been frequently cut to only an hour for the 435 members to debate those questions. If every Representative took the floor in such a debate and shared equally in the allotted time, none could have more than eight seconds to speak. Of course, every member of the House has never wanted to take part in a single debate, and no member of the House could be expected to sit through such an extravaganza of verbiage. In House debates the members who normally have monopolized the time of the House have been those most interested in the legislation under consideration, and these Representatives normally have been the members of the committees that had jurisdiction over the bill in question. The rules and customs of the House have been especially designed to guarantee that the members of the sponsoring committee have the largest share of the time available. Every major bill approved by the House normally has been processed on the floor in the so-called Committee of the Whole House. Under special restrictions on debate the chairman of the legislative committee sponsoring the bill and the ranking minority member of that committee have controlled the time allocations in these formal debates. They have parceled out time to those requesting it at their own discretion; and, by long custom, they have given most of the time to their fellow committee members. By similar rule, the presiding officer of the House has had to recognize a member of the sponsoring committee in preference to any other member of the House seeking to speak on the floor. The House of Representatives, however, has long followed a custom that has made the system less prejudicial than it has outwardly seemed. The House has permitted every Representative to "revise and extend" his remarks as he chose in the *Congressional Record*.

"Mr. Speaker," the Representative would say, "I ask unanimous consent to revise and extend my remarks in the *Record*."

Such consent has always been granted to every Representative requesting it. Technically, the authority to "revise and extend" his words in the *Congressional Record* has only given the individual Representative the right to alter words already spoken. The Representative presumably has addressed the House and granting the request to "revise and extend" his remarks has merely allowed him to edit the remarks he made, straighten out jumbled sentences, and correct any normal errors. That, however, has not been the only way the authority to "revise and extend" has been used. Instead, it has also been used as an open license for the Representative to insert anything he desired into the *Congressional Record*. Every member of the House, before he has begun to address the House, has automatically asked for this authority. Some of the Representatives never have exercised the extraordinary license thus granted, preferring to let their formal remarks stand in the *Congressional Record* as spoken. Most of the members, however, have taken advantage of this opportunity to cram the *Record* with speeches never spoken on the floor. Indeed, some Representatives who have rarely addressed their colleagues in formal debate have appeared in the *Congressional Record* to be the most talkative members of the House. They have been free to use the *Record* for that purpose. The House has even encouraged it. After every major bill has been passed, the chairman of the sponsoring committee by custom has made a general request to allow all members of the House to add to the *Congressional Record* of the debate whatever they wished. "Mr. Speaker," the committee chairman perfunctorily would say, "I ask unanimous consent that all members of the House be granted five legislative days to revise and extend their remarks at this point in the *Record*." That authority, automatically granted, has allowed any member of the House to insert in the *Record* any speech he composed as much as five days after the House has voted; and on most important bills a dozen or more Representatives have taken advantage of the privilege. The practice thus indulged has made the *Congressional Record* a questionable source for the historian, but it has served its primary purpose of economizing the House's time. The practice, by its very pretensions, has tended to minimize even in the minds of the Representatives themselves the value and quality of House debate.

The House of Representatives was established under the Constitution as a parliamentary assembly in which the representatives of the American people were to meet to debate and decide American law. The very meaning of "parliament" is to speak, to debate. The Founding Fathers at Philadelphia in 1787 specifically guaranteed that debate in the American parliament be free, totally free, by granting its members immunity from libel and slander laws. They wrote into the Constitution this proviso on the debates by the members of Congress: "for any speech or debate in either House, they shall not be questioned in any other place." The Representatives were not merely allowed to debate; they were thus formally encouraged to debate freely, without reservation. They could not be questioned, and, therefore, not punished, for anything they said in debate. The Philadelphia delegates provided this freedom of debate to assure that the House, in particular, would obtain from the Representatives of all the American people their candid views by which to determine national law. Here on the floor of the House the Representatives were to foregather, and here on the floor of the House the Representatives of all the contending forces of American life—the farm against the city, liberal against conservative, labor against owners, debtors against creditors—were to argue their various causes.

There on the floor of the House, they have met, all the competing powers of this country's vastly varied life. And there on the floor of the House, the Representatives, often torn with conflicting passions, have pronounced their decisions in the name of the American people. They have argued, it is true, and even engaged at times in what justly could be called great debates; but over the decades the country grew and the federal government grew in ways that could not have been imagined by the men who wrote the Constitution and created the House of Representatives. The forced limitations on debate, the rise of political parties and party loyalties, the swarming of the lobbyists and the refinement of their persuasive skills, all worked to destroy the efficacy of debate on the floor of the House. Most Representatives, as we have seen, have found themselves committed to one or another side of every major question long before that question was formally raised in the House for debate. House debate took on a secondary significance in the House's procedures; and the formal procedures themselves became so complicated that only a master parliamentarian, familiar with the intricacies of the House's rules and precedents and long practiced in their use, could manage them purposefully. Woodrow Wilson wrote in the 1880's, obviously with regret, that the House of Representatives met only to ratify the decisions of its standing committees. In the majority of cases, this was patently so, for party loyalties and discipline gave the Speaker of that time great power to drive such legislation as he wanted through the House. The processes of the House, however, were more subtle than that, even then; for even in those years a skilled parliamentarian could wreck the most efficient of political machines in operation on the House floor. And so, too, could an eloquent orator if he could gain the confidence of his colleagues.

Despite the long demeaning of House debate, a process begun in the very first year of the history of the House, debate there has proved decisive in settling great national questions. Such debates were rare, but they have occurred all through the decades. The House of Representatives in the 1960's had little time or patience to listen to the oratorical enthusiasms of the charlatan or the demagogue, but the House did listen to the Representative who had something worth while to say.

Lord Bryce said in 1890 that the debates of the House of Representatives were scarcely mentioned in the national press and they did little to instruct or influence national opinion, and the same could be said of House debates in the 1960's. In the same year that Bryce had observed the House, Thomas Reed of Maine, then Speaker, made an even more caustic remark on the House's floor proceedings. "The House of Representatives," he said, "is no longer a deliberative body." [2] Reed himself had played a revolutionary role in making the House what it had become, a legislative mill, by crippling the minority party's power to filibuster and by arming the majority with parliamentary weapons to ram its legislation through the House. Reed, more than any man, made tactics and floor maneuver more important than debate. That did not mean that the House no longer had brilliant debaters or that the House ignored them. Reed himself was one of the most brilliant. The members of the House had always been willing to listen to and follow the man of sense. "If you have common sense," Speaker Sam Rayburn often said, "you have all the sense there is." It was what the House normally wanted, common sense, when the members debated a bill, not oratorical flourishes. Indeed, whenever Rayburn stepped into the well of the House to speak, a hush fell over the chamber; and Rayburn was not the only member of the House in the 1960's who could command the attention of his colleagues. Paul Kilday of Texas, John Byrnes of Wisconsin, Wilbur Mills of Arkansas, Hale Boggs of Louisiana, and Howard Smith of Virginia could pull their colleagues from the cloakrooms to hear what they had to say.

The House has always had such men. Cordell Hull of Tennessee, Nicholas Longworth of Ohio, and Champ Clark of Missouri always attracted a crowd on the floor when they spoke. "They had something to say," explained James Frear of Wisconsin, a contemporary of them all. Those Representatives, Frear said, "who talked on any and every subject usually addressed empty seats." [3] The House has had a rich tradition of eloquence and debate. From its earliest years, men have stood on its floor and, by their words, moved other men. Sam Rayburn's moving tribute to his dead friend Alben W. Barkley of Kentucky, in its plain, unadorned language, deeply touched the emotions of his listeners, much as had the words of other men addressing the House in other times. "Out there somewhere, where the mighty spirits are gathered," said Rayburn, his voice choking, "the approach of Alben Barkley was received with open arms, because he was the equal of the mightiest spirits that assemble wherever that land or that clime may be. God bless his memory. God comfort his loved ones. God comfort me." [4]

More often in the history of the House, however, the debate has been rough and tumble, no holds barred, bruising, taunting, raucous, sometimes brutal. The floor of the House has been no place for the timid or the craven. At times, men have spoken on the floor of the House with their very lives at hazard. For most of the nineteenth century, the House's debates were punctuated with fierce physical violence and even the deaths of Representatives. By Constitutional stipulation, the words of a Representative spoken on the floor of the House could be questioned in no other place. But for a half-dozen decades Representatives did not hesitate to tell the House that they were prepared to answer for their words "here and elsewhere." By that they meant simply that they were prepared to back their words with pistols. The list of men from the House who fought duels was long, and was headed by no less a man than Henry Clay himself. The death of one Representative, Jonathan Cilley of Maine, in a duel with another Representative, William Graves of Kentucky, led to the enactment in 1839 of the first antidueling law by Congress. Not all the personal encounters were cloaked in the strict formalities of the *code duello:* even more frequently free-style brawling broke out on the House floor. Once a pistol fell out of a member's pocket onto the floor in front of the Speaker's chair; another time, a Representative, John Dawson of Louisiana, cocked his pistol and prepared to kill a colleague, Joshua Giddings of Ohio, on the floor of the House of Representatives. On still another occasion, during a furiously partisan debate, thirty or more Representatives flourished pistols on the floor of the House. In the 1880's the

Speaker, Warren Keifer of Ohio, so goes one report, actually presided over the House with a pistol stuffed in his pocket to resist, if he had to, a plot to hurl him bodily from the Speaker's chair.

Duels were common before the Civil War, and, according to one contemporary, "a case of dueling pistols was a part of the outfit of the Southern and Western Congressmen." [5] Many of the members favored the weapons produced by the celebrated Philadelphia gunsmith, Henry Deringer, who invented a pistol small enough to fit in a man's trouser pocket. To a Representative like William Yancey of Alabama, most daring of the firebrands in the 1840's, "a duel was only a pleasant morning recreation." [6] The weapons chosen varied widely. The Southern artistocrats preferred stylish dueling pistols inlaid with gold. The duel between Cilley and Graves, in which Cilley lost his life, was fought, incredibly, with rifles at the normal pistol distance of ten paces. Another duel between two Representatives was but narrowly avoided when the challenged man, John Potter of Wisconsin, insisted stubbornly that the weapons be Bowie knives. He was ever afterward known as "Bowie-Knife" Potter.

Many of the quarrels of Representatives came close to mere assault and battery, or plain murder. Matthew Lyon of Vermont, in a fight on the floor of the House with Roger Griswold of Connecticut, not only spit in Griswold's face to reply to Griswold's insult but belabored him as well with the tongs from the House's fireplace. Samuel Houston of Tennessee, later the hero of Texas, assaulted a fellow member of the House, William Stanbery of Ohio, on the street with his hickory cane. Stanbery responded by pulling a pistol, but the weapon misfired, and neither was seriously injured. In 1856, Philemon T. Herbert of California shot and killed a waiter at Willard's Hotel who had not promptly served him. Daniel Sickles of New York, who later lost a leg at Gettysburg, murdered Philip Barton Key, the seducer of his wife, in the streets of Washington in 1859. Preston Brooks of South Carolina in 1856 coldly stalked Senator Charles Sumner of Massachusetts and beat him into insensibility with a cane on the floor of the Senate.

Two years after Brooks's assault on Sumner, the House itself erupted into a wild melee during an angry debate on the admission of Kansas as a state. A fistfight broke out between Galusha Grow of Pennsylvania, later to be Speaker, and Laurence Keitt of South Carolina over words spoken in debate, and Grow knocked Keitt down. Partisans of both hastened to join the battling, and immediately the House floor was the scene of rioting. One member picked up a spittoon to brain his enemies. William Barksdale of Mississippi seized Grow and was wrestling with him, when he himself was assaulted. He swung wildly at Elihu Washburne (who preferred to spell his surname with a final "e") of Illinois, and Washburne's brother, Cadwallader Washburn of Wisconsin, also a member of the House, came to Elihu's aid. "Bowie-Knife" Potter of Wisconsin grabbed Barksdale by the hair, only to discover to his surprise that he had pulled off the Mississippian's wig. "Hooray, boys," Potter shouted above the din. "I've got his scalp!" [7] That broke up the quarrel in a wave of equally riotous laughter.

More frequently than not, particularly after the enactment of the antidueling law, duels were prevented by the interference of friends of both would-be duelists. President Franklin Pierce interposed to prevent a duel between John C. Breckinridge of Kentucky and Francis Cutting of New York, who had gravely offended each other in a House debate. Not all Presidents so acted. It was said that President Andrew Jackson, who himself had killed a man in a duel, looked upon Speaker James K. Polk as a coward because Polk, who also was to become President, declined to challenge a man who had unceremoniously pulled his nose. The language of debate was often highly provocative. Members freely indulged in such epithets as "liar," "scoundrel," "moral traitor," and "puppy," all certain to give offense. As early as 1790, with the House of Representatives not yet a year old, Fisher Ames of Massachusetts complained scathingly of the "low, indecent, and profane" [8] language used in House debate and the violence and cheap wit of his colleagues. The House to William Holman of Indiana "looked more like a Texas barroom than the Congress of the United States." [9] Representatives needed nerve to speak their minds on the floor; some, like Josiah Quincy of

Massachusetts, refused to be silenced by open threats to their personal safety. Quincy, the Federalist leader in the House, resolved at the start of his career in the House in 1805 that he would boldly speak his views and neither be provoked into sending a challenge nor shamed into accepting one. It was not an easy resolve to keep; for his friend and colleague, Barent Gardenier of New York, was shot down, severely wounded, in a duel with George Campbell of Tennessee, Democratic leader of the House, and Quincy more than once believed that Campbell and Henry Clay, too, were trying to lure him into a duel. It was no wonder that the House acquired the name of the "Bear Garden" for its turbulence and furious partisanship.

The very size of the Hall of the House, and the large number of Representatives crowded into it, conspired to produce confusion and chaos. For a century and a half, until the 1930's, the members had to suffer excruciating personal discomfort. The acoustics of the old Hall, now used to exhibit statues, and of the new Hall as well were appalling. So was the ventilation. Unless a Representative had a great voice—of one loud-voiced member, John P. Hale of New Hampshire, it was said that he could stand atop Mount Washington and address his entire native state—he could not be heard beyond the immediate vicinity on the floor from which he spoke. Before the construction of the first office building for Representatives, the members had no other place to transact their business than from their desks on the floor. There they read their local newspapers, answered their constituents' letters, and consulted with their colleagues. The clatter from the slamming desk drawers, the rustling of paper, the hurly-burly of pages scampering about the Hall, and the hum of many voices raised a din through which only an exceptional voice could penetrate. "If ever anything worth while is said," commented a Washington reporter in 1931 on House debate, "few can hear it and still fewer pay any attention." [10] Speaking to the House, said another reporter in 1878, was "like trying to address the people in the Broadway omnibuses from the curbstone in front of the Astor House." [11] Samuel McCall of Massachusetts made this complaint in 1911: "It does not always happen that a powerful mind and a powerful voice are combined in the same individual, and often the member with the real message cannot be heard." [12] Still the debate never seemed to cease, unless stopped by force, and a Washington correspondent in 1839 could say that Samuel "Previous Question" Cushman of New Hampshire deserved "a monument as a public benefactor" for his constant efforts to halt debate by invoking the Previous Question rule.[13]

The loud-speaker system, installed in 1938, relieved the immediate problem of merely being heard, and the air-conditioning of the Hall that same year made a like contribution to the physical comfort of the members. Before that was done, palm-leaf fans and ice water were in constant demand in the House, and the Hall itself was known as the "Oven." The heat in the Hall was often so oppressive that it made one Representative sympathize with a baked oyster. The ventilation was so poor that the foul air took on a perceptible cloudy-blue color. Breathing this poisonous atmosphere contributed at least indirectly, it was believed, to the deaths of two or three Representatives each year. The very foulness of the House's atmosphere encouraged the members to adjourn each year before Washington's summer came on with its sultry, humid weather. The physical discomfort of the Hall normally bred irritation in the members.

In such a chamber, merely to preserve order and some semblance of decorum was a severe test for the presiding officer. Representatives lounged all over the floor. They fell asleep with their feet up on their desks. (Speaker Reed once sent a page to deliver this message to a Representative who had his white-stockinged feet atop his desk: "Haul down those flags of truce!") Smoking was forbidden on the House floor, and members were required to wear coats, but often in the heat of debate and of the room a Representative would fling off his coat that he might assail his opponents with more vehemence. Joseph Cannon of Illinois did so almost every time he took the floor. Tobacco-chewing was a common practice, and the House always has been well supplied with spittoons strategically located about the Hall. Even here the carelessness of the members was notorious, and the House's handsome carpet showed it, for it was stained everywhere by misdirected tobacco juice. "I was surprised to learn," said Charles Dickens, the English novelist, showing his disgust at this unseemly practice in the House of Representatives, "that even steady, old chewers of great experience are not always good marksmen." [14]

The practice of chewing tobacco was largely abandoned in the twentieth century, and modern air-conditioning provided the needed physical comfort in the hall. The loud-speaker system of the House of Representatives in mid-twentieth century allowed even a soft-spoken man to be heard, although some of the members, like Robert Poage of Texas, still shouted into the microphones in the stump-speech style of the prairies whenever they addressed the House. The construction of office buildings relieved the constant congestion on the floor and in the nearby lobbies. Much of the violence passed away from the House's proceedings as the Civil War and its cause faded in memory. No longer did any of the Representatives seriously consider killing any of their colleagues. Modern American society simply would not be as tolerant of the killing of a man, whatever the cause and method, as had been the America of the previous century with its frontier morality. In this century, members of the House periodically exploded in physical hostility toward their fellows, but they used their fists, not pistols and canes. Sol Bloom of New York engaged Thomas Blanton of Texas in a fistfight on the floor in 1927. Blanton, on another occasion, threw an inkwell at Ogden Mills of New York, who later became Secretary of the Treasury; and another member hurled a copy of the Revised Statutes of the United States, a heavy volume, at a colleague. Franklin Mondell, of Wyoming, when Republican floor leader, exchanged a few punches with James Wickersham of Alaska; John Rankin of Mississippi, who had a fiery temper, frequently had fights with his colleagues, once with Frank Hook of Michigan who was twice Rankin's size. Clarence Cannon of Missouri, peppery chairman of the Appropriations Committee, once bloodied the nose of John Taber of New York, and scuffled briefly with John Phillips of California. As recently as 1956, Cleveland Bailey of West Virginia knocked Adam Clayton Powell of New York to the

311

floor; but, obviously, the temper of the House had changed. This was a far cry from killing a colleague in a duel. It was a sobering of the House of Representatives that reflected a similar sobering in the minds of the American people as they moved from a young frontier nation into a state of mature world leadership.

In the early years of the House, when Henry Clay was Speaker, the members occasionally silenced a colleague whom they did not want to hear by raising a clatter of noise to drown out his words. They coughed loudly, scraped their feet, and banged their desk covers until the offending member had to take his seat. This, too, has passed from the modern House, where the members indicated their impatience with a colleague by merely shouting, "Vote, vote, vote!" This did not prevent the members from speaking. Fiorello La Guardia of New York was not disturbed by one such demonstration against him. "Oh," he yelled back at his colleagues, "you can holler 'vote' as much as you like." [15] And he gamely went on with his speech. More frequently in the modern House, however, the Representative has recognized that he could gain nothing by talking and, therefore, cut short his words.

Only rarely, in recent times, has a Representative appeared in the House who could truly be called eloquent. Pure oratory, the set formal speech on a national issue in the great tradition of Webster, Clay, and Calhoun, gave way in the House almost entirely under the severe restrictions on debate, the imposition of the One Hour Rule, and the transfer of the orators to the Senate. A different school of speakers developed in the House over the years, a school in which the practitioners were trained to daring and quick wits, to hurl forceful, compact, and persuasive arguments at the opportune moment into the ranks of the opposition. The history of the House of Representatives abounds with instances of a single member, at the precisely right moment, uttering a flashing phrase that carried the question in dispute. Henry L. Dawes of Massachusetts once destroyed a tariff bill by adroitly advocating a free breakfast table for the country. James A. Garfield of Ohio rescued the necessary appropriations bills to carry on the government by boldly charging that the Southern opposition to these bills came from former enemies of the government who having failed to shoot the government to death now proposed to starve it to death. During World War II, while the House was debating legislation to eradicate Japanese beetles, a member shouted: "Let us fight the Japs and not the beetles"—and that killed the proposal. Yet, even with the House's emphasis on brevity and the telling phrase, orators of the first rank have appeared from time to time on the roster.

In the earliest years, when the House was truly the national forum, men of eloquence were almost commonplace. These men held national reputations, and their words deeply influenced the outcome of the great issues of the day. James Madison of Virginia, from the floor of the House, inaugurated the necessary legislation to write the Bill of Rights into the United States Constitution. Albert Gallatin of Pennsylvania, William Giles of Virginia, and Robert Goodloe Harper of South Carolina led national opinion from the floor of the House. Harper electrified the nation with his heroic cry in 1798: "Millions for defense, but not one cent for tribute!"

Perhaps the most eloquent of them all was Fisher Ames of Massachusetts, earliest leader of the Federalist party in the House. His speech in the great debate of 1796 over the Jay Treaty was one of the most brilliant ever given in the House, remembered ever afterward by those who heard it. The international quarrels of France and England had intruded into American politics, dividing the two major political parties in a bitter contest. The treaty with England negotiated by John Jay was assailed as nearly treasonable by the partisans of Thomas Jefferson. Fisher Ames, pale and weak from incipient disease, stood on the floor to plead with the House not to block the execution of the treaty by refusing to appropriate the necessary funds. He first defended his own Federalist party against the charge that it had an undue attachment for the interests of England. "I detest the man and distain the spirit," Ames said, "that can ever bend to a mean subserviency to the views of any [foreign] nation. It is enough to be an American." Then, as with his dying breath, he begged acceptance of the treaty's intent. "I have perhaps as little personal interest in the event as anyone here," he said. "There is, I believe, no member who will not think his chance to be a witness of the consequences greater than mine. If, however, the vote should pass to reject, and a spirit should rise, as rise it will, with the public disorders to make confusion worse confounded, even I, slender and almost broken as my hold upon life is, may outlive the government and Constitution of my country." [16] This moving appeal proved decisive, and the House voted the appropriations.

In later years, other members of the House held comparable powers of eloquence. Alexander Stephens of Georgia was such a one. A frail, sickly man who never weighed one hundred pounds, he had personal courage unsurpassed in his time. He once prevented his own assassination, having been eighteen times stabbed by his attacker, by grabbing the naked blade in his bare hand. He was so tiny that Senator Matthew Carpenter of Wisconsin wrote this of him: "An empty coach halted at the Treasury Department and Aleck Stephens got out of it." An opponent in House debate, a huge man whom Stephens had angered, once roared that he could swallow Stephens whole. "If you do," snapped Stephens, "you will have more brains in your belly than you ever had in your head." [17] In the great House debate over President Polk's policies in the Mexican War of 1848, Stephens spoke with an eloquence that more than moved his colleague Abraham Lincoln of Illinois. "My old, withered, dry eyes," wrote Lincoln to a friend, "are full of tears yet." [18]

On a rare occasion, a House speech has caught the attention of the entire nation. Such a speech was made on April 28, 1874, by Lucius Quintus Cincinnatus Lamar of Mississippi. Lamar had been a colonel in the Confederate Army. His state was still occupied by federal troops. Senator Charles Sumner of Massachusetts, perhaps the most hated man in the South, had died. It was only eighteen years since Preston Brooks of South Carolina had been hailed in the South for brutally assaulting this Northern abolitionist. No Southern man of prominence had spoken a word to placate the North since the end of the Civil War, nine years before. Despite all these inducements to silence, Lamar rose in his place in the House of Representatives to eulogize the

314

dead Northern leader. "Charles Sumner," he said, "was born with an instinctive love of freedom, and was educated from his earliest infancy to the belief that freedom is the natural and indefeasible right of every intelligent being having the outward form of man. In him, in fact, this creed seems to have been something more than a doctrine imbibed from teachers, or a result of education. To him it was a grand intuitive truth, inscribed in blazing letters upon the tablet of his inner consciousness, to deny which would have been for him to deny that he himself existed. And along with this all-controlling love of freedom he possessed a moral sensibility keenly intense and vivid, a conscientiousness which would never permit him to swerve by the breadth of a hair from what he pictured to himself as the path of duty. Thus were combined in him the characteristics which have in all ages given to religion her martyrs, and to patriotism her self-sacrificing heroes." [19] This graceful and affectionate speech created a national sensation. George Hoar of Massachusetts, astonished at Lamar's daring, said that probably no other man in the South could have uttered those words and escaped political death. The words were not idly spoken; they were meant to close the breach between the North and the South, to offer real peace for the enmity that still existed. Lamar later became a Senator, a member of President Cleveland's Cabinet, and finally a Justice of the Supreme Court; but that single speech in the House of Representatives gave him, as to no other man in the South, the love and confidence of his countrymen. That speech began the healing of the wounds of the Civil War.

Other Representatives won similar reputations, if not with the dramatic impact of Lamar. Bourke Cochran of New York, long a Tammany Hall stalwart, spoke to the House with all the charm and poetry of his native County Sligo in Ireland. One speech of his, on a tariff bill, was called by those who heard it as the most beautiful ever uttered in Congress. Long after he died in 1923, men recalled his eloquence in the House. "One can close his eyes now," said an admirer of Cochran, years after his death, "and hear the echo of his melodious voice in that Hall." [20]

The House did not always respond to its men of eloquence.

William Jennings Bryan of Nebraska, in House debate on December 22, 1894, was almost unnoticed for his speech of that day. The great question of the time was the validity of the gold standard. "I shall not help crucify mankind upon a cross of gold," he said to the House. "I shall not aid in pressing down upon the bleeding brow of labor this crown of thorns." [21] A short nineteen months later he addressed the Democratic National Convention in Chicago and he made much the same speech, although he had polished the words and refined the syntax. "You shall not press down upon the brow of labor this crown of thorns," he said. "You shall not crucify mankind upon a cross of gold." Bryan went to Chicago an unknown man; he left Chicago, solely by virtue of that speech, as the Democratic party's candidate for President.

More familiar to the House than eloquence have been the personal encounters of the House's leaders, the collision of men of nerve and power. Henry Clay of Kentucky, who never served a day in the House except as its Speaker, had such a bitter quarrel with Josiah Quincy of Massachusetts, the Federalist leader. Clay once left the Speaker's chair to take the floor and accuse Quincy of treason. Quincy was a leader of the Essex Junto in his native state, a political group violently opposed to President Jefferson that conspired to have New England secede from the Federal Union. Quincy had moved in the House that Jefferson be impeached for high crimes and misdemeanors. "Sir," said Clay to Quincy, "the gentleman soils the spot he stands upon." [22] Four years later, Clay unleashed on Quincy a speech of impassioned vitriol. "When the gentleman to whom I have been compelled to allude," Clay said of Quincy, "shall have mingled his dust with that of his abused ancestors—when he shall be consigned to oblivion, or, if he lives at all, shall live only in the treasonable annals of a certain junto—the name of Jefferson will be hailed as the second founder of the liberties of this people. . . . I beg the gentleman's pardon; he has secured to himself a more imperishable fame. I think it was about this time four years ago, that the gentleman submitted to the House of Representatives an initiative proposition for an impeachment of Mr. Jefferson. . . . The House decided it in most solemn manner; and . . . the final vote stood

316

one for the proposition and 117 against it! The same historical page that transmitted to posterity the virtues and glories of Henry the Great of France, for their admiration and example, has preserved the infamous name of the fanatic assassin of that excellent monarch. The same sacred pen that portrayed the sufferings and crucification of the Saviour of mankind has recorded, for universal execration, the name of him who was guilty, not of betraying his country, but, a kindred crime, of betraying his God!" [23]

Clay himself was to suffer the malignity of personal abuse from one of its great masters, John Randolph of Virginia. Clay and Randolph had long quarrelled. Randolph, in formal debate, took Clay's parents to task for their son, "this being, so brilliant yet so corrupt, which, like a rotten mackerel by moonlight, shined and stunk." [24] It was no wonder that the two finally met on the dueling grounds.

John Quincy Adams of Massachusetts gave no quarter in debate and he was nicknamed "Old Man Eloquent" for his virtuosity on the House floor. When he came to the House in 1831, he felt so unaccustomed to speech-making that he confessed in his diary after his first House speech that "I was not a little agitated by the sound of my own voice." He quickly lost his self-consciousness in the furious debates of the time and became himself one of the most punishing of debaters. A master of personal invective, he made even the most brazen of the Southern firebrands quail before him on the floor of the House. On one occasion, when he was almost eighty, he stood on the floor of the House for four days, screaming defiance at his enemies, and challenged them to censure him by a formal vote of the House if they dared. His defense on the floor of the House of the right of the people to petition their government, as guaranteed by the Constitution, was one of the epics of parliamentary history, fraught with significance for future generations of Americans. He scathingly described one opponent on the House floor as "a man with his hands and face dripping with the blood of murder, the blotches of which are yet hanging on him." [25] When he died, an enemy wrote of him that the nation did not have a man bold enough or bad enough to take his place. Yet the House loved him for his courage. Just a year before he died, he entered the House after a long illness. The House suspended its debate; and William Moseley of New York and Isaac Holmes of South Carolina, symbolizing the North and the South, each took him by an arm and escorted him to his seat. Representatives from states all over the nation clustered around him to congratulate him on his return to the House. Adams, his voice enfeebled, briefly addressed the House to thank his colleagues for the honor they had paid him. The House then resumed its debate.

Perhaps the most spontaneous and violent burst of invective came from James G. Blaine of Maine, who in a bitter moment castigated his colleague and rival, Roscoe Conkling of New York, so ferociously that they never again spoke to one another. It was 1866 and the two were engaged in a personal quarrel on the House floor in which Blaine had accused Conkling of illegally accepting pay as a judge advocate while serving as a member of the House. Conkling insultingly scorned Blaine's accusation and told the House he was "profoundly indifferent . . . to his opinion on this subject, or on any subject." [26]

Blaine at once responded. "As to the gentleman's cruel sarcasm, I hope he will not be too severe. The contempt of that large-minded gentleman is so wilting, his haughty disdain, his grandiloquent swell, his majestic over-powering turkey-gobbler strut has been so crushing to myself and to all the members of the House, that I know it was an act of the greatest temerity for me to venture upon a controversy with him. But, sir, I know who is responsible for all this. I know that within the last five weeks, as members of the House will recollect, an extra strut has characterized the gentleman's bearing." The blame, said Blaine, belonged to a New York newspaper writer who had satirically suggested that Conkling was the natural successor to Henry Winter Davis of Maryland, a powerful leader in the House. "The gentleman took it seriously, and it has given his strut additional pomposity. The resemblance is great. It is striking. Hyperion to a Satyr, Thersites to Hercules, mud to marble, dunghill to diamond, a singed cat to a Bengal tiger, a whining puppy to a roaring lion. Shade of the mighty Davis, forgive the almost profanation of that jocose satire!" [27] The speech was cruel, for it depicted Conkling's pomposity exactly, and the members of the House laughed with delight at Conkling's humiliation. For Blaine it proved a costly speech, for it could be blamed at least in part for his loss of the Presidency eighteen years later. Conkling had become the Republican leader of New York and still indignant over that attack, he refused to support Blaine as the Republican Presidential candidate. Blaine was also hurt by his failure to repudiate a minister's charge that the Democratic party was the party of "Rum, Romanism, and Rebellion." Blaine lost New York by the narrow margin of 1,200 votes and with New York the election as President.

In the modern House, the House of Representatives since Reed's rules were adopted in 1890, a much greater emphasis has been placed on tactical parliamentary skill. Formal debate had even by Speaker Reed's time fallen in both quality and interest. As early as 1820, the majority of members of the House choked the *Congressional Globe* and its successor, the *Congressional Record,* with "speeches for Buncombe"—bunk for the constituents back home. Patriotism was a favorite theme of the Representatives in these speeches; and so was the American eagle, which more than one member described as the "Bird of Liberty." Indeed, one Representative, Williamson Cobb of Alabama, went so far as to describe the American eagle as a bird of magnificent dimensions: it rested its feet on the Rocky Mountains, drank from the Pacific Ocean, and laid an egg on Cuba! Such speech-making was a common weakness of members of the House; and few did not avail themselves of the forum of the House to utter at least one such effusion a year, to be reprinted and mailed out to their constituents under the members' free franking privileges. As early as Tocqueville's visit to the House in 1831, this was common practice. In the years that followed, it became accepted practice for the members merely to insert their speeches into the *Congressional Record* without bothering to read them. The House, said one commentator in the 1870's, gladly consented to the requests rather than suffer the infliction of listening to such speeches. Champ Clark of Missouri, like many other members, was repelled by the practice—a practice ever afterward continued in the House. "But I finally changed my mind on that subject," he wrote in his autobiography in 1920. "I concluded that it was preferable to let them be printed rather than be compelled to listen to them." [28]

Not all the Representatives in the House have taken this short cut to stuff the *Congressional Record* with speeches unspoken on the House floor. In the 1860's the practice had been adopted to set aside time "for debate only"—periods when the House was kept in session merely to listen to such oratory. A century later, this practice was still heavily used. Members could ask for a "special order" to address the House, at the conclusion of all legislative business on a given day, for up to an hour. The announcement by the Speaker that this time had arrived normally cleared the Hall of the House. "We knew a member," wrote a historian of Congress in 1848, "whose rising with intent to make a speech was the signal at which the benches, in every quarter of the Hall, were precipitately vacated." [29] There was more than one member of the House in mid-twentieth century who prompted the same reaction from his colleagues.

Debate in the House of Representatives never reached the stage of being totally tedious and tiresome. Always the House has had its men of wit, men with a natural flair for humor, who attracted the House's attention almost every time they rose to speak. Usher Burdick of North Dakota and Clare Hoffman of Michigan, in the modern House, scarcely ever took the floor but that they pulled laughter from their colleagues, and they were but the most recent examples of the men of the House with an apt sense of the ridiculous and the comic. Abraham Lincoln of Illinois, in the 1840's when he served a single term in the House, sparkled his speeches on the floor with the humor that was to make him famous. In one notable speech in 1848, Lincoln spent an hour making fun of Lewis Cass, the Democratic candidate for President. Cass's partisans were trying to make him seem to be another Andrew Jackson. "Like a horde of hungry ticks," Lincoln said to the Democrats on the House floor, "you have stuck to the tail of the Hermitage lion to the end of his life; and you are still sticking to it, and drawing a loathsome sustenance from it, after he is dead."

The Democrats had had Jackson, "Old Hickory," and then James K. Polk, "Young Hickory," and now they were calling Cass "of the true Hickory stripe." That reminded Lincoln of a story: "A fellow once advertised that he had made a discovery by which he could make a new man out of an old one, and have enough of the stuff left to make a little yellow dog." Lincoln ridiculed Cass's military record by comparing it with his own. "By the way, Mr. Speaker, did you know that I am a military hero?" Lincoln began. He had served in the Black Hawk Indian War, he said, and if he had not ever actually seen a live Indian, he had heroically charged a patch of wild onions. If he had not been actually wounded by the enemy, he had been severely wounded by mosquito bites.[30]

Samuel Cox of Ohio, who later also represented New York, was for years one of the House's noted wits as well as one of its ablest parliamentary leaders. For one flamboyant speech describing a sunset, he was ever afterward known as "Sunset" Cox. Cox could be withering in satire. He once convulsed the House with a humorous assault on William "Pig-Iron" Kelley of Pennsylvania. Kelley was the House's leading advocate of a protective tariff, and Cox made fun of him by offering a resolution against free sunshine: "Resolved, that all windows, skylights, inside and outside shutters, curtains and blinds shall be permanently closed, as also all openings, holes, chinks, clefts, and fissures through which the light and heat of the sun have been allowed to enter houses to the prejudice and injury of meritorious miners and dealers in gas-coal to protect domestic industry." "The sun," mocked Cox, "is a foreigner. He comes from abroad. . . ."[31] Cox could be equally devastating in replying to an opponent's speech. On one occasion, one of the House's most eloquent members, Julius Caesar Burrows of Michigan, was making an unusually telling speech to the House. It had a familiar ring to Cox, and he sent a page to bring him a copy of the *Columbian Reader* from the library. Sure enough, Cox found that Burrows was plagiarizing another speech. As soon as Burrows completed his speech, Cox stood up and read to the House the same speech from the book the page had brought him, to Burrow's utter embarrassment. Burrows afterward was known, humorously, as the "Columbian Orator."

A deft phrase could equally destroy an eloquent speech. John Bingham of Ohio once deeply moved the House with a speech, and for a moment after Bingham concluded the members sat in rapt silence. Benjamin Butler of Massachusetts broke the spell, and utterly ruined Bingham's effect on the House. "I always did like that speech," said Butler [32] in a voice that could be heard through most of the Hall.

Other wits periodically turned up in the House membership. James Proctor Knott of Kentucky won a national reputation for a comic speech in 1881 about the city of Duluth, Minnesota. He called it the "Zenith City of the Unsalted Seas." No humorist ever got more immediate recognition, however, than John Allen of Mississippi, who won election to the House as "Private" Allen of the Confederate Army against a full colonel. Allen was a freshman member in 1885 when he tried to get the floor to make a speech. The House leaders had a natural dislike of allowing freshmen to talk at all. Speaker Randall once had this to say about a freshman anxious to address the House in an important debate: "He is a new member and there is no telling what he will say, and he had better not speak." Allen got similar treatment; he was refused time to speak. He thereupon asked permission "to print some remarks in the *Record,* and insert 'laughter' and 'applause' in appropriate places." Allen's jest caught the fancy of the House and he was allowed to make his speech, a long series of humorous sallies. "Now, Mr. Speaker," Allen said, as he concluded, "having fully answered all the arguments of my opponents, I will retire to the cloakroom for a few moments to receive the congratulations of admiring friends." [33] The speech set the House wild with delight and made Allen immediately one of its best-known members.

The natural reluctance of the House to listen to freshmen members has broken down in the modern era. However, an able young man coming into the House for his first term, if he were wise, hesitated to push himself forward unduly. The House of Representatives revered its concepts of seniority, and the new man did best by remaining patient. The leaders of the House in recent years, however, have taken a somewhat different attitude toward the freshmen than had their predecessors. In the last century the newcomers were regarded as fit to be heard only when they voted. Sam Rayburn of Texas, however, closely watched the new men in his party's ranks. He was known for his protégés in the House and helped them when he could to House promotions. So did Charles Halleck of Indiana and John McCormack of Massachusetts, who scrupulously made a point of meeting and getting to know every new member of the House.

During the period when it was more difficult to attract the attention of the leaders, one group of freshmen in 1902 found a clever way to do so. They had formed a club, the Tantulus Club, for the purpose of giving each other united support. David Foster of Vermont was the first of the group to make a speech on the House floor. By advance agreement, the other members of the club clustered around Foster as he spoke, seemingly hanging on his words; when he completed his speech, they gave him an ovation. They pushed forward to shake his hand and congratulate him effusively on his speech. The older members of the House had ignored Foster's speech, but they were taken aback by the ovation he received. Thinking that he had made a great speech, many of them rushed up to compliment Foster, too, among them Sereno Payne of New York, the majority floor leader, and John Dalzell of Pennsylvania, the chairman of the Rules Committee. The freshman had tricked the old-timers by a simple ruse.

Occasionally, a Representative, by a humorous approach, has been able to cajole the House of Representatives into allowing passage of a measure the members might have otherwise ignored or rejected. D. R. Matthews of Florida did so, in a notable instance, in 1960. Matthews wanted the House to add an amendment to an appropriations bill to provide $500,000 to build an entomology laboratory in his Congressional district. The key man for Matthews to woo was Albert Thomas of Texas, floor manager of the bill. Matthews fairly engulfed Thomas in formal courtesies during the debate. He called Thomas his beloved, distinguished, and intellectual leader and offered to "bestow upon him the highest accolade of all and call him my spiritual leader" if he would support Matthews' amendment. Begging forgiveness at every turn for intruding on the attention of the House, apologizing profusely to all the members in almost every sentence, Matthews appealed to his colleagues to let him have this one item in the bill after "some of you have received so much." [34] The members of the House were amused by Matthews' deliberate clowning and mock fawning, none more than Albert Thomas. Other Representatives came to Matthews' support. Wayne Hays of Ohio said the House should vote the money for Matthews' insect laboratory "for I am in favor of getting rid of insects." [35] Thus humored, the House adopted the amendment.

With the special emphasis placed on floor tactics and lobbying activities, little credit has been given to House debate as a means of influencing important House votes. Indeed, it has been almost traditional for the members of the House themselves to argue that no debate has ever changed a vote in the House of Representatives. They have justified debate normally only in terms that it set a legislative record for the bill at hand, and the House debates usually have been dreary events. Frequently, the House has found it difficult to keep even the semblance of a quorum of the House present for its formal debates; most of the members have preferred to spend their time in more useful ways than listening to the *pro-forma* arguments for and against the legislation under consideration. They have preferred to use the time meeting constituents, answering their mail, or even playing a round of golf at one of the nearby courses. "In the twenty-eight years that I have been a member of one or the other branches of Congress," said Carter Glass of Virginia in the 1930's, "I have never known a speech to change a vote." [36] Many a senior member of the House, with a jaundiced view of the effectiveness of House debate, would agree with Glass; but, all the same, House votes have been altered from time to time by the speech of an able and respected member. Perhaps the greatest single example of such an occurrence came in 1894 on the tariff bill of that year. In closing the debate, Thomas Reed of Maine attacked the bill

324

and William L. Wilson of West Virginia, chairman of the Ways and Means Committee, defended it. Wilson began quietly to a packed House, but he ended with a passionate plea for passage of the bill. "This is not a battle over percentages, over this or that tariff schedule," Wilson shouted. "It is a battle for human freedom. . . . This is a roll of honor. This is a roll of freedom, and in the name of honor and in the name of freedom, I summon every Democratic member of this House to subscribe his name after it." [37] The speech electrified the House, and the wildest confusion followed as Wilson tried to take his seat. He was seized by Henry St. George Tucker of Virginia, William Jennings Bryan of Nebraska, and John Sharp Williams of Mississippi; they lifted him to their shoulders. They paraded him thus out of the Hall in a personal triumph without precedent in the history of the House. The bill had been under severe criticism from many Democratic delegations; but, as the roll was called, these delegations fell into line behind the bill. John DeWitt Warner of New York stood near Champ Clark of Missouri as they listened in astonishment to the members voting. "An hour ago," said Warner, "those men had no more idea of voting for that bill than flying." [38] Clark said he never again would doubt that a speech could change votes.

In the modern House, speeches by able and articulate Representatives have also influenced the vote of the House's members. Perhaps no better example was there than that of Hale Boggs of Louisiana, defending the reciprocal trade bill of 1958. Boggs, who had made a specialty of foreign trade, canvassed the whole range of the bill. Arrayed against him were some of the most powerful men of the House, Daniel Reed of New York, Carl Vinson of Georgia, Richard Simpson of Pennsylvania, and Clarence Brown of Ohio. Boggs accused them of trying to take the country back to the protectionist Smoot-Hawley tariff of 1930; and 1958, like 1930, was a time of national economic distress. "Did the Smoot-Hawley tariff bring us the prosperity its supporters said it would bring?" Boggs asked, his voice rising to a shout. "Did it 'protect' those industries that were supposed to be protected? Quite the contrary. We went into the worst depression the United States has ever known—despite the enactment of that tariff." Boggs told the

House that the protectionists wanted to sell exports to foreign countries without permitting imports. International trade, he said, was like breathing. "The trouble, here, however, is that they simply want to exhale," Boggs said. "They do not want to inhale." [39] Boggs's speech played a crucial role in shaping the House's judgment of the bill. Speaker Rayburn, who had come on to the floor to listen to Boggs, said later that Boggs had spoken so effectively that members of the House who had opposed the bill actually changed their minds and voted for it.

A similar case came in 1962, when Wilbur Mills of Arkansas presented a tax bill to the House of Representatives. Mills had been chairman of the Committee of Ways and Means for four years and a member of the committee for sixteen years before that. His colleagues knew him to be both a master of tax law and a sure-footed judge of the political temper of the country. Mills asked the House to pass a bill that increased taxes in nineteen of its twenty-one sections and stiffened tax collections in still another section. It was March, only eight months from the November elections, a difficult time to persuade the Representatives to vote for tax increases. Mills stood in the well of the House and explained the bill and the need for it in detail to his colleagues. Then he answered a series of hostile questions from the opponents of the measure. Throughout the explanation and the onslaught against the bill, Mills did not so much as consult a note; it was a performance of remarkable deftness and mastery of the complex bill. "No other member of Congress," said one House colleague, "would have dared to do that." [40] Noah Mason of Illinois, one of the leading opponents of the bill, felt compelled to take the floor when Mills was through and compliment Mills as the "most capable" chairman of Ways and Means that he had ever known in his twenty-five years in the House. Mills's performance, his colleagues agreed, played a major role in persuading the House to pass the bill.

On purely partisan questions, the party floor leaders frequently have moved into the center of the debate to exhort their party ranks to remain loyal to the party's position. On closely divided questions, the Speaker himself often has taken the floor to appeal for or against the legislation. In the modern House, this has generally been easier for the Democratic leaders than the Republican. Normally the great divisive questions have involved economic questions, thus shoving the liberals and the conservatives into opposite camps. The conservative Republican leaders have not been able to plead on the floor with their Republican rank and file to vote "Republican." To do so would risk losing the Democratic conservatives from the South, their allies in the conservative coalition. The progressive Democratic leaders, however, have appealed directly to those same Southern Democrats to vote "Democratic"—for they had a chance of persuading them on the basis of party loyalty. Joseph Martin of Massachusetts, for twenty years the leader of the House Republicans, confessed in his autobiography that whenever the House debated liberal-conservative issues, he let the Southern Democrats make the speeches on the floor, while he worked behind the scenes to persuade his Republicans to vote with the conservative coalition. Charles Halleck of Indiana, who succeeded Martin as leader of the House Republicans in 1959, followed much the same course. On such questions, Halleck tried to play down party loyalty as an aspect of the vote and to emphasize instead the economic issue involved. It was the obvious way to encourage the largest vote for the conservative position. How much such tactics affected the voting of the members of the House was impossible to determine. So many influences played on each Representative on each vote—his friends, his constituents, the lobbyists, the White House, and his own party loyalty—that no one could be sure, not even the Representative himself, about the precise reason for his voting the way he did.

The party floor leaders frequently in modern years have carried the brunt of the debate on the most partisan of political questions coming before the House. Before John McCormack became Speaker, he was, as Democratic floor leader, perhaps the most bruising of debaters on his side of the center aisle of the Hall of the House. McCormack was master of what Daniel Webster once called an essential prerequisite for a Representative: "An acquired readiness in debate, which is a precious thing in the hour of need." McCormack had the ability to confound his opponents when he held the best of the argument and to confuse them when he did not. Clare Hoffman of Michigan, one of the most articulate and taunting of modern Republicans in debate, tangled with McCormack in 1953 in a long-remembered encounter. Hoffman was belaboring the Democrats in the House, when McCormack stood up to combat Hoffman's assault. He interrupted Hoffman to say, apropos of nothing that Hoffman had said, that he held Hoffman in "a minimum high regard." The clever phrase caught the fancy of the House. Forgotten was Hoffman's speech in the laughter at McCormack's sardonic jest. It was a classic example of McCormack's success with what he called "diversionary" tactics in debate.

"I believe in fighting hard," McCormack said of his participation in House debates, "but I don't like personal fights. I go down on the floor of the House and take on my Republican friends." [41] For Charles Halleck, the Republican leader, McCormack had the maximum high regard. Halleck, said McCormack frequently, was "a foeman worthy of your steel." For Halleck, there was a similar appreciation of McCormack. "John McCormack always was a worthy and formidable antagonist who fought hard—but always fair," Halleck said. "We're both lawyers raised in the tradition of differences to be fought out, but as in the law business, so is it here: these fights are not carried over off the floor. We can fight without malice or rancor." [42] Their attitude toward each other marked a profound change in the House of Representatives from the years in which Representatives boldly announced in the Hall of the House that they were prepared to answer "here and elsewhere" for what they said in debate.

Despite the ill repute of House debate, no legislative strategist has ever dared to ignore formal debate on the House floor. To do so would hazard the very outcome of the vote. Neither camp in any floor fight could risk yielding the debate by default to the opposition. On the contrary, both camps—whether Republican or Democratic, conservative or liberal, farm or city, labor or management, or any of the other competing forces in American society—on every question have brought forward their ablest and most articulate spokesmen to argue their causes on the floor. That House debate for decades has been more chaff than wheat, no member of the House would deny; but, here and there across the history of the House, men have risen on the floor and swung the House to their views, with an apt phrase, an emotional appeal, or a brilliant analysis of the problem at hand. From time to time, the House itself has witnessed great debates, when equally able Representatives argued the merits of the views of the contending forces. At such times, the House has listened to the debaters with far more attention than the normal disinterest. At such times, the members have known that they were hearing a debate, as they themselves have then said, "in the highest traditions of the House of Representatives."

CHAPTER THIRTEEN

The Yeas and Nays

THE yeas and nays have been ordered. The clerk will call the roll."

With those words, for generations, the Speaker has announced a roll-call vote of the members of the House of Representatives. Thereupon a House clerk has called off the names of the Representatives, one by one, in alphabetical order, and then called again the names of the absentees. Each of the Representatives, when his name was called, has responded either "aye" or "no" to signify his approval or disapproval of the measure under consideration. This has been the ultimate point to which a legislative proposition could be brought in the House of Representatives. The vote itself has pronounced the judgment of the House.

Before the vote began, the Representatives already had heard the debate, a debate that frequently has merely reiterated perfunctorily the formal arguments of the contending sides. More important than debates in the proceedings of the House, however, have been the strategy and tactics by which each opposing floor leader has contrived to give his side the advantage in the vote. To triumph in a roll-call vote, a floor leader has had to persuade a majority of the members voting to take his point of view. By parliamentary maneuver, by skillful use of House rules, by amendments adroitly conceived to attract wavering Representatives, by myriad tricks and schemes and stratagems, the contending leaders have plotted to sway the judgments of the House. Even at the very moment that the clerk has been calling the roll of the members, the contest has not ended; for, even at the very end of a roll call, even after the very last name has been called by the clerk, a minority of the House could be abruptly transformed into a majority—if just the right parliamentary situation had arisen and the skillful floor manager had anticipated it.

Above all other qualities, the legislative strategist in the House has had to have the facility to judge, and judge accurately, the mood of the House of Representatives. Without such a sense of the House, no legislative leader could begin to work effectively with all the members. All other tactical and strategic skills in managing a bill on the floor have been dependent on the essential skill of determining how far the members would go on a given question or how far they could be carried. Implicit in this ability has been a profound knowledge of the House itself: its many power blocs, the districts from which the Representatives have come, the House's sense of itself, its sense of justice and fair play, the mystique of the House's own inner life as a living institution of national government. Sam Rayburn of Texas had a grasp of the House's many moods perhaps unmatched in modern times. For almost a half century, he served in the House of Representatives. For six of these years, he chaired the important Committee on Interstate and Foreign Commerce; for nine years he was his party's floor leader; for seventeen years he was Speaker. Rayburn devoted his whole energies to the House. He once said it had been most of his life. Above all he wanted to sense the moods of the House, "those rolling waves of sentiment" as he called them. That was the reason he operated the "Board of Education" as did Speakers John Nance Garner and Nicholas Longworth before him and John McCormack after him. The "Board of Education," actually a private evening meeting of the leaders of the House, served as intelligence headquarters for Rayburn's grand strategy. There, with the help of his ablest lieutenants, he charted the agenda of the House's operations. Rayburn, like other effective House leaders, used other means as well to reckon the consensus of the House. The door of his office, as he freely told members of the House, was always open. "If you hear anything," he habitually said to visitors, "let me know." He wanted information about the House, precise information about the members themselves, the power blocs, the lobbyists, and the Administration's operations. If an influential man failed to stop by to see Rayburn for an abnormally long period, Rayburn invited him to come by for a quiet talk. In time, Rayburn developed an intuitive sense of the House of Representatives. This intuitive sense was the secret of his mastery of the House. "If you can't see and hear and *feel*," he said, "why you're lost." [1]

What made so important an accurate sense of the House's mood was that with such a sense as a basis of operation, a skillful parliamentary leader like Rayburn could then best calculate how to alter that mood, or how best to draft the particular legislation he wanted to fit that mood of the House. The 1961 session of the House of Representatives offered many precise examples of this technique in practice, and examples have been frequent in every session of the House. The new President, John F. Kennedy, had asked the Congress for a broad legislative program that included a farm bill, a depressed-areas bill, a school-construction bill, a bill to increase minimum wages, and a new foreign-aid bill. The House of Representatives, as a whole, appeared hostile to every one of those bills; the critical problem for Rayburn and his lieutenants was to figure out how much of that requested program they could induce the Representatives to approve. The first attempt to pass the minimum-wage bill failed by a single vote. Opposition to this bill was strong among the Southern delegations. Redrafted, with an amendment to disqualify laundry workers and employees of resort hotels, both important objections by Southern Representatives to the original bill, a revised bill was approved 230 to 196. The House leaders, alerted by both Carl Albert of Oklahoma and Richard Bolling of Missouri, knew that the farm bill as submitted by Agriculture Secretary Orville Freeman could not pass. They struck from the bill its most controversial section, one that would have let the Agriculture Secretary appoint committees of farmers to set farm law subject only to a veto by Congress. The bill, as amended, was passed by the House, 224 to 170. The depressed-areas bill also seemed to be in deep trouble, in need of major legislative surgery; or at least so thought its chief sponsor, Daniel Flood of Pennsylvania. Carl Albert, then the House majority whip, quietly sounded out the Southern delegations where the Democratic opposition was believed most prevalent. Albert reported back to Rayburn that this opposition had been exaggerated; a large number of the Southerners would vote for the bill. That bill was left intact as a result of Albert's calculation and the House approved it 251 to 167. The school-construction bill prompted opposition from many quarters. By blocking any financial aid for parochial schools, the House leaders cracked the opposition of thirty-four of ninety-nine Southern Democrats but provoked opposition among many of the House's eighty-eight Roman Catholics. This forced a delay in bringing the bill to the House floor, and the delay proved fatal. The 174 House Republicans froze into almost united opposition to the bill. The House leaders on this measure first reduced the scope of the bill, trying to gain votes for the bill by so doing, then slashed the bill once more. When the bill finally reached the House floor for a vote, it was by then but a shell of its former self. Even so, the House rejected it 242 to 170.

The foreign-aid bill of 1961 provided an exceptional example of a miscalculation by the House leaders. Sam Rayburn had become ill with cancer and had been flown home to Texas to die. John McCormack, the majority leader, had been appointed acting Speaker in Rayburn's absence. The House Appropriations Committee, under the leadership of Otto Passman of Louisiana, had severely cut the foreign-aid bill, reducing the amount for foreign military aid by $400 million. McCormack met privately with Passman, and argued with him that he ought to restore to the bill at least $150 million of that money. "You just cannot please everybody," Passman said. "If you get it too low, then some want it higher. If you go too high, some want it lower." Passman knew, from his own sense of the House, that he indeed had set the military funds too low. He not only agreed to increase the sum by the $150 million McCormack requested, but he added an extra $25 million as well. "Now I want to be generous,"

Passman told McCormack, "because there is some opposition on the floor. Let me recommend $25 million more than the figure on which you have reached an agreement." [2] Even that increase did not satisfy the House. The times were dangerous: Russian Premier Nikita Khrushchev was threatening Berlin. McCormack and Passman watched in embarrassment while the House rejected their compromise agreement and set the military fund a full $125 million higher than they had privately decided. The miscalculation by McCormack on just how far the members of the House would go in granting military funds to United States allies hurt McCormack's standing in the House. McCormack had worked hard to wring from Passman an extra $175 million dollars, but because he had mistaken the exact mood of the House he was humiliated publicly by the formal action of the House.

Such a humiliation has awaited every House leader in command of every major House bill. If he failed to judge aright the temper of the House, if the House rejected his bill or added important amendments to it that he opposed, that House leader suffered a major loss of prestige among his colleagues. "No chairman of a committee wants to take a bill to the House floor and be beaten," said John Byrnes of Wisconsin,[3] a skillful parliamentary tactician. This has always been a matter of the gravest consequence in the proceedings of the House, in the formulation of parliamentary strategy, for frequently this concern for success on the floor has tempered and even killed legislation that otherwise might have been offered for a House vote. Wilbur Mills of Arkansas, a skilled legislative negotiator and cloakroom operator, became chairman of the Ways and Means Committee in 1958 and lost the first bill—an extension of unemployment benefits—that he took to the floor as chairman. A naturally cautious man, Mills was hurt by the loss; and it apparently tempered his action in the years that followed. In the next five years, Mills did not suffer a single floor defeat. He was charged at times with overcaution, as in 1959 when he refused to take to the House floor a bill to raise government interest rates. A majority of Mills's committee, including all ten Republican members, favored the bill, but Mills could not persuade more than five of the fifteen committee Democrats to support it. As an influential Democratic leader in the House, Mills declined to take the bill to the House floor without the support of a majority of his fellow committee Democrats even though he and the committee were upbraided for their inaction. The committee was dubbed the "No-Ways and by No-Means Committee." In other instances, however, Mills was scarcely less than daring in taking controversial measures to the House floor. Such was the trade agreements bill of 1962, a measure that recast and reshaped the basic structure of the American tariff system. Mills deliberately took his time with this Kennedy administration bill to allow the Administration and the organized lobbyists to drum up nationwide support for the bill. This support gradually was reflected in the attitude the members of the House took toward the bill. Mills resisted all major changes in the bill, but he judiciously added some minor amendments to assuage Representatives politically skeptical about this bill. Mills carefully calculated the mood of the House both in adding amendments to the bill and in scheduling it for floor action. When his judgment told him the time had come for action, he took the bill to the floor and won there the House's endorsement of the bill precisely as he had drafted it. President Kennedy's admiration for Mills's skill in the parliamentary management of this bill was summed up in one word: "Magnificent."

Few members of the House at any time have had the almost intuitive skill of Sam Rayburn, or Wilbur Mills, or Carl Albert of Oklahoma in sensing the changing moods of the House. Many members, particularly those with little seniority, have often merely been confused by the complex interplay of almost inexplicable maneuvering that has taken place on some bills in the attempt to win approval of them by the House. Such a bill was H.R. 5, a bill sponsored in 1960 by Hale Boggs of Louisiana to ease United States taxes on American foreign investments. The bill was called up for House action on March 8, 1960. Presumably, the House was to have voted on it that day. Instead, the House leaders did not permit a vote on the bill until May 18, ten weeks later. Without explanation, the leaders simply withdrew the bill for that length of time. What had happened was that Boggs and the Democratic leaders had in March miscalculated the mood of the House. They discovered only after the bill reached the House floor on March 8 that the AFL-CIO, one of the most influential lobby groups, was stiffly opposed to the bill. The labor union feared that the bill would encourage American capitalists to invest abroad where labor was cheaper than in the United States and that this in turn would cost some American workers their jobs. Andrew Biemiller, the AFL-CIO's chief lobbyist, had been notified only belatedly that the bill was up for floor action. He quickly drafted a memorandum on the union's position and dispatched copies to Capitol Hill. John Dent of Pennsylvania read the memorandum to the House: "The AFL-CIO . . . urges the members of the House to vote against H.R. 5," it said, in part. Speaker Rayburn ranged around the House floor, testing the temper of the members as the debate proceeded. Then he went to Boggs, who was floor manager of the bill. "Hale," said Rayburn, "your bill is in trouble." Boggs had already reached the same conclusion. "I know it," he replied.[4] At Rayburn's suggestion, Boggs simply called off further debate on the bill that day. The House leaders postponed further action indefinitely. Boggs went to work to draft amendments to the bill that would placate at least some of the labor opponents of the bill. He drafted two such amendments and drafted them with exquisite care. On May 18, the House again took up the bill and voted on it. The vote demonstrated how carefully Boggs had calculated the concessions he had made in the amendments. The House adopted the bill by the extremely narrow vote of 195 to 192. H. R. Gross of Iowa, an ardent opponent of the bill, taunted Boggs for making the concessions, but Boggs had the last word and the legislative victory. "The gentleman from Louisiana," Gross said to Boggs on the House floor, "had to go back to his committee in order to get some amendments to this bill, to make it palatable enough to sell to the members of the House. He was hanging on the ropes when the bill was before the House previously, so he went back to the committee to get this monstrosity sweetened up and sugar-coated." "He who fights and runs away," replied Boggs, "may live to fight another day."[5]

Not always have the floor managers of House bills been that successful in switching the outcome of a House vote. Not always has it been possible to ameliorate the opposition with minor amendments, as did Hale Boggs, or even with major amendments. Not always have the House leaders been able to read precisely the often fickle moods of the House. The majority party leaders of the House, by the nature of the rules, have long held distinctive parliamentary advantages in controlling action on bills coming before the House. They have many ways to juggle legislation. Their control of the scheduling of legislation itself has always been a major advantage. Their ability to amend bills and by so doing weaken the opposition to those bills could prove an enormously effective parliamentary weapon. And there were many other methods the majority leaders could utilize to serve their advocacy of bills. They have never had the power, however, to force the House to approve a bill that a majority of the members adamantly opposed.

The House of Representatives, since it was first organized in 1789, has processed its legislation on the floor in a parliamentarily complex manner. The House, for all major legislation, has transformed itself by formal resolution into a Committee of the Whole House. In the Committee of the Whole House, the formal debate on the bill at hand has been held, followed in due course by a formal reading of the bill at which time amendments could be offered. When the committee has completed its work on the bill, it has ceased to exist, and the decisions it has made have been then presented to the House itself for ratification. The Committee of the Whole House, a form adopted from the British House of Commons, was a convenience and, in effect, a parliamentary fiction, for the Committee of the Whole House was but the House of Representatives in mild disguise. All members of the House were automatically members of the Committee of the Whole House. The committee met in the same Hall as did the House, and, in general terms, similar parliamentary rules applied. There were, however, distinct differences, and these were the reasons for using this ancient technique for processing legislation. The Speaker, for example, did not preside over the Committee of the Whole House, but selected a chairman from the ranks of the House members who temporarily took over the Speaker's chair and gavel. This was a heritage from the English system, where in the early years the Speaker too often was an agent and spy of the king. There was no such suspicion of the American Speaker, who not only was not required to leave the Hall of the House, as was the British Speaker, but could freely take part in the debate and voting. As developed in its modern use, the Committee of the Whole House had distinctive procedures of its own that facilitated the processing of legislation. The quorum required to be present in the committee was only 100, as against 218 required in the House itself. No roll-call votes could be held in the committee, and that saved time, for a call of all the members of the House normally took a full twenty-five minutes. Votes in the committee were by voice, in which all those favoring the amendment shouted in unison, followed by those opposed, with the chairman deciding which group was louder; by division, in which the members favoring and then those opposing stood to be counted by the chairman; or by teller, in which those favoring and then those opposing marched up the center aisle to be counted by "tellers" appointed by the chairman of the Committee of the Whole. This prohibition of roll-call votes in the Committee of the Whole House not only saved the time of the House, but on occasions, it let members vote freely without thought of political retaliation from the voters back home. Without a roll-call vote, no one could tell how any Representative had voted. No amendment defeated in the Committee of the Whole House could be offered again in the House, except as part of a motion to recommit the bill. No amendment adopted in committee was binding unless confirmed by the House. The procedures used in the Committee of the Whole House allowed strict limitations on debate and even limitations on the amendments that could be offered. The procedures, as well, profoundly influenced the quality and effect of debate in the House and could give to the skillful parliamentary tactician a decided advantage in shaping the decisions of the House.

Under normal procedures, major legislation in the House first

338

has had to be processed by both a legislative committee and then the Rules Committee. The legislative committee normally has held hearings on the bill, adopted such amendments to the bill as its members saw fit, and then recommended the bill for approval by the House. The Rules Committee has then set the number of hours for the House debate on the bill and perhaps even limited the amendments that could be offered. The Rules Committee, when responsive to the majority party leaders, could prove an instrument of great power to those leaders. The committee, for example, could limit formal debate to but a few hours. It also could severely limit the right of members of the House to offer amendments. Under a so-called open rule—a resolution from the Rules Committee allowing any amendments to be offered, provided only that they be germane to the subject matter of the bill—the opponents of the bill have had almost complete freedom to try to alter the bill with amendments. They could attack the bill from many directions. Under a so-called closed rule—one forbidding amendments—the opponents normally had only one chance to alter the bill, and that at the last moment when they could offer a motion to recommit the bill to its sponsoring legislative committee with instructions to make specific changes in the bill. In either case, the resolution from the Rules Committee had to be approved by a majority of the Representatives before it was binding on the House. The House submitted to this process, which gave the Rules Committee vast powers over its proceedings, primarily because the House had to economize its time.

Occasionally this system of processing major legislation has been frustrated by the refusal of a legislative committee, the Rules Committee, or even the majority leaders themselves to let a bill come to the floor for a vote by the Representatives. A majority of the Representatives, however, under House rules, could then force the bill to the House floor either by signing a formal Discharge Petition or by insisting on the utilization of Calendar Wednesday. Calendar Wednesday, adopted in 1909, was a technique that gave every legislative committee the right to bring stymied legislation to the attention of the House. Both it and the Discharge Petition, however, have proved difficult to execute. The Discharge Petition, for example, although specifically provided for in the House rules, has often offended the House's special sense of "orderly procedure." Many members of the House have followed a strict practice of never signing a Discharge Petition, no matter how much they may have approved the legislation that had been blocked; they have felt strongly that legislation should go through normal channels and be first approved by its legislative committee, the committee presumably most expert on that legislation. As mentioned earlier, only two bills brought to the House floor by Discharge Petition have ever been enacted into law. Using Calendar Wednesday has had a different hazard. A bill so brought to the floor always has risked prompting a filibuster, even in modern times. Although formal debate on the bill, by the House rules, has been limited to two hours, the opponents of bills brought to the floor under Calendar Wednesday have frequently filibustered the bills by demanding almost endless roll-call votes on such technicalities as approval of the previous day's journal, motions to adjourn, and the offering of dilatory amendments. Because the sponsors of the bill have had only one legislative day to push the bill through the House, a filibuster could prove effective on such a bill. This was the rare instance in which dilatory tactics, as a filibuster, could be used to kill a bill in the modern House.

Both of these parliamentary forms, technically, were created to protect the majority of the Representatives from the exercise of arbitrary power by the Speaker and the other leaders of the House. Occasionally, however, the House leaders themselves have been forced to use either the Discharge Petition or Calendar Wednesday to overcome the recalcitrance of a committee chairman or even an entire committee. More often, however, the scheduling of bills for floor action has been fully in the control of the party leaders. Indeed, the party leaders even have parliamentary powers that permit them so to control the members of the House that they have been able to prevent them from voting into law extravagant and irresponsible, but politically popular, bills.

The most frequently used technique to accomplish this end has been the "closed" rule for handling controversial and complicated bills. Under the "closed" rule, the average Representative has been denied the right to offer any amendment to the bill in question. In recent years, almost all major bills that have come from the Ways and Means Committee have been so handled. These encompass all bills dealing with taxes, social security, tariffs, unemployment compensation, government interest rates, and the national debt. The House has taken the position by approving these "closed" rules, that these bills have been much too technical in their language to risk the hazards of floor amendments that have not been adequately studied. Such hazards have been real. In the House's action on a minimum-wage bill in 1960, the members adopted an amendment offered by Frank Smith of Mississippi that was designed to exclude from the coverage of the proposed law a few thousand agricultural workers. A day later, after the amendment had been adopted and the bill itself approved by the House, the House was informed that it had made a serious blunder. A freshman Representative, Roman Pucinski of Illinois, a member of the Education and Labor Committee, had suspected the legislative language of Smith's amendment. He checked the language with the legislative experts at the Department of Labor. Sure enough, the Smith amendment did far more than merely exempt a few thousand farm workers from the law; it took away from 14 million of the 24 million workers already covered by the law their protection of their minimum wages and hours. This drastic action had not been Smith's intention or the intention of the House in approving the amendment. The House had to depend on the Senate to correct this mistake.

The House leaders have had still another technique, besides the "closed" rule, to prevent floor amendments on bills. That has been the special provision for suspending the House rules to pass a bill. Normally this technique has been used merely to expedite relatively noncontroversial legislation. Occasionally, however, as on legislation involving war veterans, the technique has been used to block any floor amendments. The practice of suspending the rules, as a technique to pass legislation, has been used since the earliest years of the House of Representatives. In 1794, the first limitation on the practice was imposed. In 1822, the House voted that it would thereafter require a two-thirds vote, rather than a simple majority, to enact legislation by this method. In 1880, the House set aside the first and third Mondays of each month as "suspension" days, when such motions were in order. Prior to the compilation by Asher Hinds, the House's official Parliamentarian, of the precedents of the House in 1907, suspension of the rules proved a genuine help in avoiding awkward parliamentary situations. "When things got into a tangle," wrote De-Alva Alexander of New York, a distinguished historian of the House as well as a member, "it was easier to suspend the rules than to untie the knots." [6] Suspension of the rules, however, as perfected, has even greater advantages than that. It automatically limits debate on the measure in question to forty minutes, forbids all amendments, and can be invoked only if the Speaker of the House approves the bill and recognizes the Representative to make the motion. The leaders of the House discovered that it was not only a convenient method of saving the House's time, but it also proved effective in restraining the House itself. The technique was used to process legislation granting bonuses to war veterans, building public buildings and highways, increasing the salaries of federal employees, and improving rivers and harbors. On such bills, unless the members of the House were restricted, the House leaders could expect an orgy of amendments to increase the bills' provisions. The temptation to do so was always prevalent with such politically popular legislation. At the same time, the House leaders sometimes found that, by using this technique, they could induce the House to pass a politically unpopular measure. They simply coupled it with one certain to delight most of the Representatives. Such was the case in 1925, when unusually heavy pressures came on the House to increase the pay of postal employees. The House leaders tied to the bill increasing the salaries a general increase in postal rates to pay for the pay increases. Then they brought the combined bill to the floor under the provisions of suspension of the rules. No amendments could be offered; the postal-rate increases could not be struck out of the bill. The Representatives had to agree to the postal-rate increases to grant the pay raises for the postal employees. They did.

In more recent years, suspension of the rules has proved particularly effective in controlling the demands of veterans organizations. These groups have maintained one of the most effective and active lobbies in Washington, and their requests for new benefits for the veterans have seemed insatiable to the House leaders trying to protect the United States Treasury from their periodic raids. Veterans' groups like the American Legion and the Veterans of Foreign Wars have long operated posts in almost every community in the United States. In many of these communities, the veterans have been politically active, so active that they composed a powerful "bullet vote" dangerous to heedless politicians, and as a result their legislative demands have normally received the closest attention by Representatives anxious not to offend them. To yield to their full requests, however, could risk disaster to the government. In 1956, for example, the American Legion asked for a veterans pension plan that would have cost the government $183 billion in the course of forty years. In 1959, Olin "Tiger" Teague of Texas, chairman of the House Committee on Veterans Affairs, maneuvered adroitly to reform a part of the veterans' program, placate the veterans themselves, and block their demands for larger pensions. With the support of the Eisenhower administration he proposed a bill that would have limited the pension a veteran could receive in accordance with his other income and that also would have equalized the pensions of widows of veterans of World War II and the Korean War with those of veterans of World War I. The changes would have given some immediate increases in pensions, but eventually would have saved the government more than $18 billion. Teague had still another goal in mind. The House members then were undergoing an organized campaign from veteran groups to grant the survivors of World War I monthly pensions of $100 each, a proposal that would have cost many billions of dollars. Teague wanted to circumvent any chance of the House approving this pension plan. He offered his bill, which ignored

343

this demand, as a means of giving his House colleagues a chance to vote that year on a veterans pension bill—and thus avoid the charge that they had neglected the veterans. Teague called committee hearings on his bill on a Wednesday and had his committee approve it the next day. Then, with the cooperation of Speaker Rayburn, he arranged for the bill to be approved by the House on the following Monday under suspension of the rules. Teague's swiftness in moving the legislation to final House passage was deliberately designed to prevent the veterans' lobbies from mounting a counterassault against the bill. His reason for using suspension of the rules, of course, was to prevent any amendments, particularly one to give $100 a month to the veterans of World War I, which most Representatives would not have wanted to oppose. Teague's strategy was completely successful. His reform bill was approved by the House, 226 to 34, with only scattered protests on the parliamentary procedures he used.

Essentially, the task of the parliamentary tacticians in the House of Representatives has been to produce enough votes to win on the House floor. On some occasions, the members of the House have been deliberately prevented from "working their will" on the substance of a bill—by the imposition of the "closed" rule or by the use of suspension of the rules. Even more rarely, a skillful parliamentary tactician has been able to trap his opponents by effectively making use of the rules of the House. A remarkable case of this occurred in 1961 when the House was acting on a far-reaching housing bill endorsed by the Kennedy administration. Albert Rains of Alabama, who long had made housing his special hobby in the House, acted as floor manager for the bill. The most controversial section of the bill was Title I, which proposed a new federal program of insuring mortgages on low-cost, no-down-payment homes. The Republicans in the House directed their principal assault on the bill at this section. Just as the Republicans were about to begin their attack on this section, Rains volunteered to meet one of their demands by offering an amendment to require down payments on such houses and slightly higher interest rates. His amendment was drafted in the form of a complete substitute for Title I; it was promptly ac-

344

cepted by the House. The Rains amendment, however, encompassed only a part of the complaints the Republicans had against this section of the bill. When a Republican tried to offer another amendment to Title I, it was promptly ruled out of order. Only then did the Republicans discover that Rains had executed a brilliant tactical maneuver. Under the rules of the House, a section of a bill once amended on the floor cannot be amended again. In offering his amendment as a substitute for all of Title I, Rains had prevented the Republicans from offering any other amendments to this section of the bill. The Republican tacticians had carelessly assumed that Rains had merely offered an amendment affecting only a few words of Title I and not the entire section of the bill.

More frequently, however, the floor managers of bills in the House and the other parliamentary tacticians have had to depend on much more obvious methods of protecting their bills from defeat. Often this has meant compromising the substance of the legislation. Usually this has meant the drudgery of endlessly soliciting support for the bill among the House members, sometimes with the promise of making amendments to the bill. And frequently this has meant the harassing chore of making certain that those Representatives committed to one or the other side of a legislative fight actually show up to vote on the bill. "I'm a progressive who believes that the road to progress is, in moments of contest, reasonable compromise," said John McCormack of Massachusetts, in explanation of his floor strategy on controversial bills. "You don't compromise principles, but you harmonize tactics to preserve unity." [7]

Harmonizing tactics to preserve unity—in other words, finding the means of producing a majority of the members of the House—has long been a problem for the House leaders. The struggles to woo Representatives' votes for bills were begun in the earliest weeks of the history of the House. By the time Henry Clay of Kentucky left the Speaker's chair for the last time in 1825, the practice already had become something of a parliamentary art. In the great House fight over the tariff of 1824, for example, Clay's partisans had obviously been at work soliciting advance commitments for the bill. When the bill was put to a vote on April 16 of that year, it was passed by the narrow margin of 107 to 102. Clay, however, was somewhat disappointed that two members of the House, Samuel Foote of Connecticut and Charles Foote of New York, whom Clay believed had been won over, had voted against the bill. Their defection, however, gave Clay a chance to coin a pun. "Yes," said Clay, after the vote, "we made a good stand, considering we lost both of our Feete." [8]

In the modern House, similar hustling for votes has accompanied the floor action on every controversial bill. Sometimes the efforts have been coupled with the open blandishment of special treatment for the individual Representative's home district. In the 1949 struggle to enact a rent-control bill, for example, Wright Patman of Texas during House debate on the bill announced that the federal housing expediter would decontrol rents in from 150 to 200 small communities if the bill were approved with a provision allowing him to recontrol these communities in case the local landlords raised rents unduly. In the 1961 fight over a depressed-areas bill, the proponents of the legislation placed in the Speaker's lobby, where every Representative could see it, a large map of the United States that showed the specific Congressional districts—many of them in the South—that would receive federal help under the provisions of the bill. In the 1962 attempt to pass a farm bill, Harold Cooley of North Carolina, chairman of the Agriculture Committee and floor manager of the bill, desperately and openly bargained for votes for the bill by accepting amendments to his bill. In all Cooley agreed to more than thirty amendments, and he made no pretense at hiding his intent. The House debate itself was marked with unusual candor and clearly showed Cooley's maneuver. At one point William Avery of Kansas challenged Cooley to explain why he was willing to accept a particular amendment. Cooley answered candidly. "The membership probably might be softened up by this amendment," Cooley said.

Avery was startled. "What was that?" he asked. "Will the gentleman restate that?"

Cooley began to reply. "Do you want me to tell you the truth?" he asked. Cooley, however, did not get the chance to

346

explain. Frank Chelf of Kentucky, one of the Representatives who had demanded the amendment, interrupted him. "It is because he needs fellows like me to vote for the bill," Chelf said bluntly. "That is why. I cannot vote for it unless you adopt this amendment."

"That," said Avery, having made his point, "clears that up." [9]

Many bills have had similar histories, although only rarely have the members of the House been as candid as Cooley and Chelf in acknowledging the tactics they were employing. In the 1958 struggle to pass an extension of the Trade Agreements Act, Frank Ikard of Texas worked for many weeks, on behalf of the sponsors of the bill, to draft an amendment that would soften the opposition of Representatives from districts worried about the import of foreign oil. His success played a major role in enactment of that bill. In 1961, the sponsors of Kennedy administration bills consistently made efforts to placate the opposition of the Southern delegations to those bills. They blocked any benefits to parochial schools from the proposed school-construction bill. They eliminated laundry workers from the minimum wage bill. The Kennedy administration itself courted the Southerners for these bills by declining to ask Congress for any civil-rights legislation that year, in spite of President Kennedy's specific campaign promise in 1960 to request such legislation from the incoming Congress. By 1962 these efforts at wooing Southern Representatives had been extraordinarily successful. The Kennedy administration, when it came to office in January, 1961, could scarcely count on the support of more than twenty of the ninety-nine Southern Democrats then in the House. A year later, on most bills, a clear majority of those Southerners were consistently voting for the Kennedy administration's bills. On a controversial tax bill, only fifteen of the Southern Democrats voted "no." On a bill to increase the national debt, only thirty-two of the ninety-nine Southern Democrats opposed it with their votes.

On that same bill to increase the legal limit on the national debt, the Defense Department played a role that caused deep resentment among the House Republicans. President Kennedy had asked Congress to increase the debt limit to $308 billion, and the Republicans in the House opposed the request on the grounds that granting it would only encourage further deficit spending by the government. The Defense Department notified many of the contractors for defense items that unless the Presidential request was approved, they would lose their contracts. This, the departmental spokesman said, would be necessary because the government would not have the legal power to pay for them. Cancellation of these contracts, of course, would have thrown thousands of defense workers out of work—and the defense contractors promptly so notified their various Representatives in the House. Gerald Ford of Michigan and John Byrnes of Wisconsin, both influential Republicans in the House, angrily brought this legislative tactic by the Defense Department to the attention of the House during the debate on the bill. "I say," Byrnes shouted, "that it smacks of blackmail." [10]

A principal part of the floor struggle for votes long has been the delivery of those votes when the House has been ready to decide the question at hand. For a Representative to add his vote to the House's judgment on a bill, he has to be present in the Hall of the House and there answer to his name. It serves no purpose at all for the supporters or opponents of a bill to persuade a Representative to their side of the question if he fails to show up to cast his vote. This infighting for partisan advantage has been at times so fierce that the contending leaders have persuaded even seriously ill Representatives to turn up to vote on those bills. As early as 1790, with the House of Representatives not quite a year old, this technique was used on Alexander Hamilton's bill to have the federal government assume the states' debts. Senator William Maclay of Pennsylvania wrote in his diary that Theodoric Bland of Virginia and Daniel Huger of South Carolina, both Revolutionary War veterans, were carried into the Hall of the House to vote, "the one lame, the other sick." On the same vote, wrote Maclay, George Clymer of Pennsylvania, a signer of the Declaration of Independence, was prevented from leaving the chamber—although he had received formal permission to do so—so that he would be present to vote. In 1824, on the tariff bill that Henry Clay narrowly won, several Representatives so ill they were confined to bed were carried into the Hall of the House "upon their sick couches." In the modern House, similar instances have not been unusual. Charles Halleck of Indiana, chosen Republican leader in 1959, even had a personal slogan for the intensity with which he tried to deliver the Republican votes on bills. "I walk," he often said, "with my walking wounded." The job of the House whips, the party leaders responsible for persuading all their party colleagues to show up for votes, has never been completely done. Never in modern times has every member of the House voted on any piece of legislation. From 1789 through the 1962 session of the House, the highest total vote was cast during the bitter labor legislation fight in 1959. On the critical vote then, 430 answered to their names. There were five absentees.

The House all through its history has been plagued by the unauthorized absence of at least some of its members. With so large a number of members, almost always there were at least a few who were ill. Usually there were far more who simply had gone home to campaign for re-election. The absenteeism of Representatives from Atlantic seaboard states, particularly New York, has always been high. The railroads provided a convenient and inexpensive means to reach their home districts. In the 1920's the New Yorkers already were notoriously negligent in attendance, so much so a Tammany boss had to pledge to the Democratic House leaders that he personally would keep the New York Democrats on the job. The House Democrats held formal negotiations with the Pennsylvania Railroad and arranged for the railroad to run a special train every Monday morning from New York to Washington. The railroad promised to get this train, appropriately named "The Legislator," to Washington before the noon meeting time of the House. Later, in the 1930's, when the Democrats held massive majorities in the House, the New Yorkers and other Northeast Representatives simply refused to come to Washington so early in the week. They began, as well, to leave for their home districts earlier each week. Soon, the other members of the House, the members from Congressional districts

349

too far and too expensive to reach frequently during a session of Congress, scornfully nicknamed those perennially absent on Mondays and Fridays as members of the "Tuesday-to-Thursday Club." They arrived Tuesday and left Thursday. The House leaders had little choice but to accommodate the members absent on these days. If it were possible, they never scheduled any roll-call votes on either Mondays or Fridays, days that in the earlier years of the House had been fully used for legislating. If they feared that an important bill might be closely contested in the House, they carefully scheduled the vote on that bill for Tuesday, Wednesday, or Thursday. The best day of all for a controversial bill has been Wednesday, when the House leaders could expect maximum attendance. Occasionally, an annoyed colleague has demanded a quorum call on a Monday simply to embarrass all those who were absent by officially recording their names. H. R. Gross of Iowa, who frequently criticized the members of the "Tuesday-to-Thursday Club," more often than other members demanded these quorum calls on Mondays. Gross did so, for example, on June 6, 1960. When the roll was called, 143 Representatives—almost exactly one out of every three members of the House—were recorded as absent. Gross repeated this tactic on Monday, July 9, 1962, and the quorum call revealed 144 Representatives absent.

In the early years of the House, to be absent from a roll-call vote was to hazard the formal censure of the House and the imposition of a fine. In the 1840's, the House occasionally simply refused to adjourn until the House clerk had brought in all the absentees, and the members in these instances hugely enjoyed the embarrassment of their fellows so caught neglecting their duties. One such occasion was recorded by an early historian of the House in 1848. The doors of the Hall were locked, as they still are, when the House voted. It was late at night. As each of the absent members was brought by the House clerk to the well of the House, in front of the Speaker's chair, the Speaker asked him whether he had an excuse. "You have been absent from this House without its leave and contrary to its order," the Speaker intoned at the offender. "If you have any excuse to offer, you will now be heard." A Representative from Maryland said he was paid by the day, not by the night—the members then received per diem salaries—for his services in the House. He was promptly fined. A Georgian said he had gone to the house of a valued friend whose child was dying. He was excused. A Virginian next was called to give his excuse. "The gentleman over the way was addressing the Committee [of the Whole House]," he said, "and the usual hour for refreshment had passed. I preferred the arguments of the stomach to the arguments of the gentleman, and so I went home." He was fined. A Tennessean was then called. "I left the Hall at ten o'clock, and, in accordance with the custom of all orderly men, went to bed," he said. "I have no favors to ask of this House, and particularly in the condition in which I find some of its members." He, too, was fined. The recorder of this scene was more alert than the Speaker or the House clerk. An Alabaman was listed as absent when he failed to answer to his name. Yet there he was on the floor now. He had slipped into the chamber, then the old Hall, through a window behind the Speaker's chair, risking his life in the attempt to avoid humiliation before his colleagues. Another Representative, at similar hazard, slid down one of the marble pillars from the gallery and so gained access to the Hall despite the locked doors. Neither could be fined, for they had not been arrested by the clerk and they were in their assigned seats. The writer questioned the value of this insistence by the House on the presence of its absentees. The entire night was wasted in the process of rounding them up. "Daylight looks upon faces pale with watching and sleepless eyes that scarce take note of its approach," he wrote, describing the scene at dawn. "What have the public interests gained? Nothing." [11]

In later years other attempts were made to enforce the attendance of members in the Hall. Speaker Charles Crisp in the 1890's tried to force the Representatives to attend the sessions of the House by threatening to dock their pay for each day's absence. Only illness, and that illness certified by a formal statement from the Representative, was to be valid as an excuse. The prompt shower of certificates indicated that an epidemic had swept the ranks of the House of Representatives, and Crisp's maneuver collapsed.

In the modern House, the House leaders have simply ignored the failure of members to show up for not even fines and personal humiliation could keep all the members in attendance at the House all the time. The twentieth-century practice, even though the absentees under the rules still were technically required to explain their failure to appear, has been to dismiss automatically the imposition of this rule. "By unanimous consent," the Speaker normally has said after the roll call, "further proceedings under the call will be dispensed with." The Representative who has run up a poor attendance record, however, has stood the risk of having it used against him by an energetic opponent in the next election campaign.

Although the House leaders long ago gave up trying to force their colleagues to stay in attendance, they have by no means given up the ever-necessary struggle to keep their supporters on the floor. Indeed, the development of the formal party whip system since the 1890's has had this single goal in mind. The whip, who in the 1960's also acts as assistant floor leader for his party, has had a score of assistant whips dedicated to the same task. They had to keep track of all their party members and keep these party members informed as to when they would be needed on the House floor for specific votes. The floor leaders and the Speaker himself often engaged in this needed work. John McCormack of Massachusetts, even after he became Speaker, sometimes spent the entire evening before an important vote telephoning absent colleagues all over the country to plead with them to return to the House in time to cast their votes. In response to such appeals, members of the House, home campaigning, have frequently flown back to Washington to help their party leaders on a close vote.

Leslie Arends of Illinois, the Republican whip in the 1950's and 1960's, often sat in the Speaker's lobby to watch for any of his party members who might drift away from the chamber before an important vote. If he saw one leaving, he tried to make him stay. "Hey, where are you going?" he shouted at one Republican in 1961. "I'm just going downstairs to get a bite of lunch," his colleague replied. "All right," said Arends, "but come right back. We need you today." [12] In 1962, Arends tried hard to persuade an injured Republican to come to Washington to vote on an important bill. "What if you have a few broken ribs," Arends said to him by long-distance telephone. "Take a couple of shots of whiskey, climb on a plane, and get down here." [13]

The House whips have a clever device for locating their absentees on the day of a critical vote. A Representative would make a routine point of order in the House that the House lacked a quorum—in the modern House, the presence of 218 Representatives. Under a provision of the United States Constitution, the House must have a quorum present to transact the public business. Normally the demand for a quorum has been merely technical. Sometimes it has been used as a dilatory tactic designed to delay the House's proceedings, for it took the House clerk about twenty-five minutes to complete the call of the roll. On the day of an important vote, however, the quorum call could prove an invaluable instrument for the party leaders. As soon as the call had been completed, they had a full list of those absent. They thereupon could telephone, or have aides telephone, the offices of the missing Representatives to find out where they were and remind them that they were needed on the floor to vote.

Not always have the members of the House even known the question being put to a vote on the House floor. Frequently, on relatively minor bills, many of the Representatives have not cared which way they voted. They have just gone along with their parties. In these instances the party whips have bluntly told their rank-and-file members how to vote as they came streaming into the Hall of the House to answer to their names. "Vote 'no,' vote 'no,' ", one party whip has shouted to his men as they came in. His opposite number, shouting at his own man, had a similar plea: "Vote 'aye,' vote 'aye.' " Occasionally, a state delegation, well disciplined by their party leaders back home, have caucused right on the House floor to receive instructions on how they should vote on such pending questions. In the contemporary

House, the Illinois Democrats frequently did so, with the members waiting for Thomas O'Brien, their dean and boss, to arrive to tell them how to vote. O'Brien's arbitrary control of the Illinois Democrats, based on his political proxy from the Democratic party machine in Cook County, Illinois, has long been known to the members of the House, although only rarely has this control been publicly revealed. One such instance, however, came on March 8, 1962, when the House was about to vote on a bill to increase the size of the House to 438 members. John Kluczynski of Illinois, one of the Representatives from Chicago, took the floor to explain his position on the bill. While Kluczynski spoke, O'Brien sat listening to him only a few feet away. Kluczynski told the House that he had been deeply worried about this bill, so worried about it, that he had not been able to sleep the night before. Then, he said, that morning, while he was pacing back and forth, still troubled over the bill, O'Brien had come to him. "We're for the bill," Kluczynski said O'Brien informed him. That was why Kluczynski was for the bill. The members of the House burst into laughter at Kluczynski's frank confession. Kluczynski later removed his statement from the *Congressional Record*.

Sometimes, the floor managers of a bill have overestimated the support among the Representatives for their bill, and permitted their party members a certain laxity in attendance in the Hall of the House. Such was the case in 1959 when the House was acting on a depressed-areas bill, legislation that had deeply divided the House's conservatives and liberals. Oren Harris of Arkansas, chairman of the Interstate and Foreign Commerce Committee, was floor manager for the bill. On the day of the voting, the President of Ireland was in Washington and many of the Irish-American Representatives, including John McCormack of Massachusetts, then Democratic floor leader, had been invited to lunch with him in downtown Washington. The vote on final passage would not come until later in the afternoon, and the Democratic leaders assumed that meanwhile they would have enough voting strength on the floor to defeat any amendments offered. They believed that they could safely spare those who had been invited to the lunch. The first vote confirmed that belief.

354

It came on a Republican amendment offered by William Springer of Illinois, and the Democrats won by a safe margin, 181 to 144. Then, however, James C. Davis of Georgia offered an amendment to slash the bill's money authorization to the $200 million President Eisenhower had requested. Davis, in effect, offered the amendment on behalf of the conservative coalition in the House. Howard W. Smith of Virginia, leader of the Southern conservatives in the House, formally endorsed the Davis amendment in a brief speech; the Republican members of the House did not need encouragement to support President Eisenhower's position. The House, then in Committee of the Whole, adopted the Davis amendment 168 to 157 on a teller vote. The Democratic leaders had not imagined that this could happen. Oren Harris, surprised by the result, took alarm at what was happening to his bill. He quickly summoned William "Fishbait" Miller, official Doorkeeper of the House and an invaluable aid to the House Democrats. Harris asked Miller to telephone McCormack and the other Democrats at the lunch. "Tell them," Harris ordered, "to get the hell back here."

Even as Harris dispatched "Fishbait" Miller to hurry his missing Democrats back to the House floor, John Bell Williams of Mississippi offered another amendment to alter the bill radically. Williams' amendment would have required direct appropriations from Congress to finance the proposed program and forbid any "back-door" loans from the Treasury. This amendment also was adopted, by a teller vote of 169 to 154. Harris' bill abruptly had been shredded in Committee of the Whole. The amendments adopted in Committee of the Whole, however, were not final; Harris still had the right to challenge each of them when the Committee of the Whole completed its work and formally reported the bill back to the House. This Harris did, and with his missing Democrats now returned to the Hall of the House, both amendments were rejected. The House defeated the Davis amendment 214 to 194 and the Williams amendment 216 to 191. The Democratic leaders had been temporarily embarrassed by losing control of the bill on the floor, but they had retrieved the bill safely at the last moment.

The inevitable absence of at least some of the Representatives on every vote prompted the growth of an informal method of accommodating those who were absent, an accommodation so customary in modern times that the Representatives long have assumed that it was a natural prerogative of their office. That was the custom of "pairing off." It was designed simply to protect absent Representatives from criticism for their absences. Technically, under this system, a Representative who was going to be absent for a formal House vote arranged with another Representative who took the opposite side on the vote to make a "pair" with him. They agreed not to vote and thus canceled each other's vote. They then could feel free to be absent from the House. On occasions, members who have disagreed on just about everything have arranged to be paired "until further notice." James Mann of Illinois once made such an arrangement with a seriously ill colleague and as a result scarcely cast a single vote in one annual session of the House. As early as 1824, the practice of "pairing off" had come into use in the House of Representatives. Henry Dwight of Massachusetts on May 17 of that year formally asked the House that he might be excused from voting, a request that was granted, on the grounds that he had a pair with a Virginia Representative then out of the city. The use of pairing steadily increased over the years, even though it was severely criticized by many Representatives for many years. In 1840, for example, John Quincy Adams of Massachusetts formally submitted a resolution to the House condemning pairing as a specific violation of the United States Constitution, the rules of the House, and the duties of the Representatives. Adams' resolution, however, was not put to a vote. Thomas Hart Benton of Missouri, writing in 1856, denounced pairing in the same harsh terms as did Adams and further stated that the practice could lead to the "grossest abuses." The "reprehensible" practice even then had become "common, and even inveterate," Benton reported. "Members pair off, and do as they please—either remain in the city, refusing to attend to any duty, or go off together to neighboring cities; or separate; one staying and one going; and the one that remains sometimes standing up in his place, and telling the Speaker of the House that he had paired off, and so refusing to vote. There is no justification for such conduct, and it becomes a facile way for shirking duty and evading responsibility." [14] Benton noted acidly that the offending members did not deduct their pay for the time of their absence. From the beginning, under the rules of the House, no member of the House could legally absent himself from the House without the formal permission of the House. There was even a time in the earliest years of the House, Benton wrote, when the formal Journals of the House published a list of those Representatives who were "absent without leave."

The House has never directly condoned the practice of "pairing off," although the 1880 revision of the rules of the House provided that the House clerk should announce the names of those Representatives "paired" after each roll-call vote. In 1890 an unsuccessful attempt was made to abolish the custom entirely, but the practice still grew. Thus, by the early years of the twentieth century, both the Democratic and Republican parties in the House had assigned special patronage employees, paid by the House, to act as "pair clerks." Pairing had become so active in the House that the members felt they needed these clerks to facilitate the chore of finding the absentees other Representatives willing to make pairs. Normally, it had been the custom for Representatives to request in writing that they be paired, but these pair clerks soon were "pairing off" all the absent members of the House, with or without a formal request to do so. The clerks did not even bother to determine at times whether the members they paired actually differed on the vote, as technically they were supposed to do. They merely lumped all the absentees together, and they were thus officially listed in the *Congressional Record*. From time to time, a Representative protested this practice, and in the modern House this casualness has been abandoned. In the contemporary *Congressional Record* the pairs listed have recorded which member has paired "for" and which member "against" the legislative proposal at issue. The Speakers of the House and the House as an institution have always regarded the practice of pairing as an unofficial arrangement indulged in by the members

357

for which the House itself took no responsibility. "Neither the Speaker nor the House has anything to do with pairs," Speaker Champ Clark ruled in 1917. "It is a kind of excrescence that has grown up on the body politic." [15]

For the parliamentary tacticians of the House, however, the practice of pairing could prove a useful weapon, particularly in those cases when they expected a close vote on a pending question. If the parliamentary tactician could persuade a Representative opposed to his own position to take a "live" pair with an absent member, that reduced the opposition's vote by one. The difference between a "live" pair and an ordinary pair was that one of the "live" pair was actually present in the Hall of the House at the time of the vote. In this instance, the member present announced his pair to the Speaker and withdrew his own vote. In the furious struggles to produce a majority vote, even this tactic could prove useful. Why would a Representative agree to this tactic that injured the side he favored? Most often out of party loyalty. If he felt he could not politically vote with his party, he might be willing to take this maneuver to minimize the damage he did to his party's cause. Indeed, the floor tacticians carried this tactic even a step further. On rare occasions, they persuaded members to agree to take a "live" pair with absent members if—and only if—by so doing they would actually change the outcome of the House vote. In the great parliamentary battle on extending the draft in August, 1941, this was a tactical safeguard employed by John McCormack of Massachusetts, the Democratic floor leader. That roll-call vote, at its completion, stood 203 to 202 in favor of extending the draft. In the well of the House, ready to withdraw their votes and take "live" pairs, if that would alter the result, stood two Representatives. McCormack had persuaded them to do so. Had the vote stood 203 to 202 against extending the draft, their withdrawal of their votes would have made the official count 202 to 201 for extending the draft. Because this action was not needed, McCormack did not signal them to make the switch.

A more effective tactic than persuading a Representative to agree to take a "live" pair, and thus cost the opposition one vote,

358

was to persuade the Representative to switch his vote entirely if his vote meant the difference between defeat or passage of the bill at hand. This technique long has been employed by the leaders of both parties in the House of Representatives, and scarcely a single controversial bill has come to the House floor in modern times without both party floor leaders having at least two or three such "pocket" votes ready for switching. The Representatives willing to agree to such terms normally have come from safe political districts where the particular bill has had little political impact. They had rather vote the way they originally planned, but they could afford politically to vote the opposite way if their party leaders really needed their votes. Such floor tactics, of course, took exquisite care, for the last thing a party floor leader wanted to do was to ask a rank-and-file member to switch his vote unnecessarily. Both party leaders had to watch the mounting totals as the roll-call vote proceeded and be ready to act at the precise moment after the roll call had been completed and before the Speaker announced the result. They had, as well, to be on guard lest the opposing floor leader try to execute precisely the same tactic on them. In 1950, when the House was considering the natural-gas bill, this tactic was used. The roll call had been completed, but Speaker Rayburn hesitated to announce the result. On signal, a group of Representatives swarmed into the well of the House and began to inquire how they had just voted. This was simply a delaying tactic. While this was going on, Rayburn informed Charles Halleck of Indiana that the bill was defeated unless Halleck could immediately switch at least two of his Republicans to favor the bill. Halleck did better than that: he persuaded three Republicans to switch their votes and the bill was passed 176 to 174. In that fight, Rayburn and Halleck were united in wanting to pass the bill. In 1959, when the House attempted to override President Eisenhower's veto of a $1,200,-000,000 rivers and harbors bill, they were leading the opposing forces. Halleck then commanded but 153 Republicans in the House against Rayburn's 283 Democrats, but to override the veto Rayburn's Democrats had to provide a two-thirds majority of those voting. Halleck had summoned his absentee Republicans to Washington from all over the country, but even so he doubted that he could block so politically popular a bill. "Either you go along with the President," he rasped at his party rank and file, "or you don't." Halleck's campaign began to bear fruit. Two Republicans who had been far distant rushed into the Hall of the House, fresh from the airport, even as the roll-call vote was under way. Carefully tallying the vote on the House floor for the Republicans was Walter Judd of Minnesota. Halleck watched intently, and when the roll call was completed, Judd whispered to him, "We're one vote ahead." The Democratic leaders, however, had planned for just this eventuality; they signaled their three waiting Representatives to switch their votes. Clarence Cannon of Missouri, chairman of the powerful Appropriations Committee, promptly changed his vote from "no" to "aye." Two other Democrats followed. That gave the Democrats a clear lead. Halleck responded immediately. "Get the hell down there and ask about your votes," he ordered a group of Republicans. While they did so and thus delayed the announcement of the vote, Halleck rounded up three Republicans to switch their votes.[16] They were Ivor Fenton and Willard Curtin, both of Pennsylvania, and Edgar Chenoweth of Colorado, all party stalwarts. That placed the final vote at 274 to 138, just one shy of the number needed to override the President's veto.

Only rarely has this tactic been used on the House floor, because only rarely have the House votes been so close that a handful of switch votes could alter the outcome. Even when used, the tactic has had small advantage because usually each party leader has had enough men in his ranks willing to switch their votes to counter any switches attempted by the opposing floor leader. That has not discouraged the making of such advance arrangements, if only to be used as a defensive parliamentary maneuver. On the passage of the 1958 bill that made Alaska a state, Leo O'Brien of New York had the pledges of two Republicans formally opposed to the bill who were willing to switch their votes if it meant passage of the bill. "Those two votes were the only ones I had in the bank," said O'Brien,[17] chief sponsor of the bill. O'Brien and his allies worked hard persuading their colleagues to support the bill—Hale Boggs of Louisiana came to the House to vote for it, even though he was suffering from a virulent attack of streptococcus in his throat—and O'Brien mustered a large enough majority so that he did not have to ask his Republican friends to change their votes.

In the 1962 session of the House, almost on every major bill the floor leaders sought and gained such pledges from members of their parties. All such advance planning was merely precautionary, against the possibility that a vote might be so close that switching a few Representatives at the last moment might alter its outcome. When the House voted in June on President Kennedy's controversial farm bill, it was defeated 215 to 205. On that vote, Carl Albert of Oklahoma had four Democratic Representatives ready to switch their votes from "no" to "aye." They could have changed the final vote, if Albert had signaled them to do so, to 211 to 209, but the bill still would have been defeated. Albert, therefore, did not give the signal. Later that year, on September 20, the Democratic leaders of the House made another attempt to pass a similar farm measure. By the time this bill came up for a vote, however, the Democratic leaders had already despaired of any chance of passing it. Some of their rank-and-file members were deeply worried about the election they had to face in six weeks and, therefore, were unwilling to vote for the bill. Others, a full two dozen of them, had already left Washington for their home districts to campaign and many of these members refused to return. Secretary of Agriculture Orville Freeman continued to lobby for the bill, and President Kennedy had invited John Fogarty of Rhode Island, an influential Representative, to the White House for a private meeting in the hope of persuading him to vote for the farm bill. Fogarty refused. Carl Albert and his lieutenants tried to talk some of the opposition Democrats into supporting the bill but their efforts were only halfhearted. There were other critical bills in trouble as well, and this was no time to waste energy on a bill that had no real chance of approval. On this farm bill Albert made no attempt to line up in advance any "switch" Democrats.

The Democratic leaders, however, had not read the House

aright. There had been a slight alteration, not immediately perceptible, in the Democratic ranks. It was psychological. This was an election year; election day was only a few weeks away, and the Democrats and Republicans had been belaboring each other with the usual campaign vehemence. The effect was to make members of both parties more conscious of their party loyalties. Adding to this, all the House Republicans except one had voted against the earlier farm bill, and the debate on this bill had revealed their continued party unanimity. The vote had taken on extra dimensions as a party issue. This change in the Democrats, however, was not obvious even as the clerk called out the Representatives' names on the vote for final passage. The vote at one point stood 153 for the bill, 167 against. That margin was expected. Albert and Democratic whip Hale Boggs sat dejectedly at the leadership desk, listening as the margin mounted against the bill. There was no activity either by the Republican leaders. The margin against the bill rose to twenty-one. The bill seemed doomed, as predicted. That, however, was the high point of the opposition's margin. The clerk still was calling the roll, and the margin that had been steadily growing against the bill began to shrink, vote by vote. It fell to eighteen votes, then to seventeen, sixteen, fifteen. When it fell to fourteen votes, Albert and Boggs came alive. They perceived that there was a chance to save this bill yet. Both began pleading with Democrats on the House floor, the Democrats known to be in opposition to the bill. "If you come with us," Albert was saying to them, "we can carry this thing." "Please come with us," Boggs pleaded.[18] Speaker McCormack, presiding over the House, beckoned a couple of Representatives to come to the Speaker's chair, where he asked them, desperately, to support the President's bill. Representatives were still coming into the Hall to cast their votes, but time was running out and the Democrats still did not have a majority on the vote. The margin of opposition had continued to shrink, down to eight, to seven, to six. Albert, bargaining for time, begged a group of rank-and-file Democrats to question their own votes to give him a few extra minutes. These Democrats broke from their seats and hurried into the well of the

House, at the foot of the Speaker's dais, to ask, each in turn: "Mr. Speaker, how am I recorded?" The clerk looked up each Representative's vote and told him how he had voted. It was a delaying tactic.

The Republican leaders, Charles Halleck and Leslie Arends, were on their feet, enraged at the Democratic tactics. They had no "aye" votes that they could switch to "no," for all their members, except two who would not switch, had already voted "no." John Taber of New York, senior Republican in the House, rose to his feet. "Clear the well," he bellowed angrily.[19] Halleck tried to stop the Democratic maneuver by making a point of order against the Democrats' dilatory tactic.

"I make the point of order," he said, "that members are asking how they are recorded for obvious purposes of delay."

"The Chair cannot look into the minds of members," replied Speaker McCormack, overruling the point of order, "and determine their motives."

All the while, the margin against the bill was shrinking as Albert and Boggs persuaded late arrivals to support the bill and persuaded as well three of those who had already voted against the bill to switch their votes. Don Magnuson of Washington changed his vote from "no" to "aye." So did J. T. Rutherford of Texas and Hugh Carey of New York. The margin had shrunk to zero, and then the Democrats had gone ahead, one vote at a time. The Republicans were helpless to counteract the Democrats' maneuver. John Byrnes of Wisconsin, from the Republican side of the Hall, shouted sarcastically at the Democratic leaders: "Have you got them? Can we go ahead now?"

Hale Boggs grinned at him. "We've got them," he shouted back.[20] They did. The final vote was 202 to 197, and the bill was passed. The Democratic leaders had executed one of the rarest of parliamentary coups; they had at the last moment plucked victory out of seemingly certain defeat with a few half-spoken words and great tactical skill.

Now and then, in the proceedings of the House of Representatives, the strategists have arranged to have Representatives take action deliberately contrary to their known positions to

363

achieve an ulterior goal. This was the case in the 1870's when Shelby Cullom of Illinois, a Republican, was trying to persuade the House to adopt a bill outlawing polygamy in Utah. The bill was attacked for not originating in the Judiciary Committee, and Cullom feared that if his bill was sent back to that committee, it would be killed. Samuel Cox of New York, a Democratic leader, came to Cullom and asked him to yield him time on the bill and he would help Cullom pass it. "When I did," Cullom recorded, "Cox took the floor, and to my utter astonishment he denounced the bill as the most outrageous bill that had ever been brought before the House, declaring in the most spirited manner that of course it ought to be referred to the Judiciary Committee, because everyone knew that such a reference would kill it." [21] Cullom soon realized, however, what Cox had done for him. The House then had a large Republican majority, but the Republicans were divided over this bill. By denouncing the bill and stating boldly that it ought to be killed, Cox, the Democratic leader, had effectively united the Republicans in favor of it. With their votes united, the bill was easily passed.

In 1960, while the House was legislating on a bill to build public schools, a more complicated tactic was employed by some of the Southern Democrats who wished to defeat the measure. The bill, a Democratic substitute for similar legislation recommended by President Eisenhower, had been under severe attack. A critical amendment was offered by Adam Clayton Powell of New York, a Democrat. Powell's amendment, a variation of an amendment he frequently offered to major bills, would have forbidden the use of any of the money provided in the bill in areas practicing racial segregation. The Powell amendment long had harassed the Democratic party, for it divided the party members neatly, with almost all the Northern Democrats favoring it and all the Southerners opposing it. If adopted, it automatically would force all the Southerners to vote against the entire bill. The amendment had several times been used by Republican leader Charles Halleck in attempts to divide the Democrats in the House. Only a few weeks before, Halleck had had one of his Republicans offer a similar amendment to the housing bill.

That time the amendment was defeated, for Powell himself led the united Democratic opposition to it. "The amendment," Powell explained, "was being used to kill the housing bill." In the school-bill fight, Powell took an opposite view, for he wanted to use it to abolish segregation in the schools of the South. When Powell offered his amendment, Frank Thompson of New Jersey, sponsor of the school-construction bill, knew it threatened ultimate passage of his bill. Not only would it prevent any Southerner in the House from voting for the bill, it also would prompt a filibuster when that bill reached the Senate. Thompson tried to rally the Northern Democrats against the amendment, but his argument failed. When the amendment was put to a teller vote, most of the Northern Democrats voted for it, against Thompson's wishes. The Southern Democrats who wanted ultimately to kill the school-construction bill took an ingenious maneuver to assure the passage of the Powell amendment. Politically, they could not afford to vote for it, but on a teller vote—a vote on which no record could be kept—they could afford not to vote. About thirty of the Southerners ducked into the Democratic cloakroom of the House floor as the vote was about to begin; another dozen or so slipped into the Speaker's lobby and so also got off the House floor. Among those in the Speaker's lobby were James C. Davis, Elijah "Tic" Forrester, and Prince Preston, all of Georgia, Richard Poff of Virginia, and William C. Cramer of Florida. All normally would have fought hard to defeat any antisegregation proposal. When the vote was completed—the Powell amendment carried 151 to 103—an aide rushed into the Speaker's lobby. "They agreed to it," he said. "Good," said Forrester, and the Southerners walked back onto the House floor. The adoption of the Powell amendment ultimately killed the school-construction bill for that year.

Under House rules, the opponents of legislation have had three direct means of killing that legislation: a motion to strike out the enacting clause of the bill, a motion to recommit the bill to the legislative committee from which it came, and the vote on final passage. By far the most brutal of the three, indeed the most brutal act that a legislative body could take, has been the motion to strike out the enacting clause. That motion, if adopted, literally decapitated the bill by striking the language—"Be it enacted . . ."—that gave the bill the force of law. The motion, if adopted, made meaningless all the rest of the words of the bill. To recommit a bill to its sponsoring committee has been to send the bill into indefinite exile. To defeat a bill on final passage has been merely to reject it. To strike out the enacting words has been to place the bill on a legislative guillotine and strike off its head. Although in use since 1812, this treatment of a bill has been so harsh that the House long has shrunk from using it. The motion, applicable only in Committee of the Whole House, has been given high preferential priority since 1822, and when carried, has immediately ended further consideration of the bill until the House itself, by formal vote, has decided whether to let the action of the Committee of the Whole stand as the judgment of the House. During almost every annual session of the House, the motion has been offered against bills up for consideration, but usually only as a means for the opponents of the bills to harass the proponents. The motion was the favorite of Clare Hoffman of Michigan, a legislative gadfly during his twenty-eight years in the House. Hoffman frequently used it to show his own hostility to pending bills and to gain time to speak on them to the House. During the House's deliberations on the Alaskan statehood bill in May, 1958, Walter Rogers of Texas abruptly offered a motion to strike out the enacting clause of the bill. "As yet," he told the House, "I have not heard one sound reason why Alaska should be granted statehood." The supporters of the bill tried to turn back Rogers' motion, but the Committee of the Whole, by teller vote, adopted it, 144 to 106. This action, the action of the Committee of the Whole, was only tentative, subject to ratification by the House. The House suspended its consideration of the bill until the next day. Rogers, of course, knew the House's long hesitancy to behead bills by striking out their enacting clauses, and so he then offered another motion with higher priority, a motion to recommit the bill to the Committee of Interior and Insular Affairs. The effect on the bill would have been the same, with the adoption of either motion; either would have killed the bill. In pressing for a motion to recommit the bill, Rogers in effect was asking the House to kill the bill more gently than by decapitating it. When the House voted on Rogers' motion to recommit the bill, the members rejected it 199 to 174. Rogers knew he could not muster even that many for the harsher motion to strike out the enacting clause, and so he did not bother to ask for a roll-call vote on it.

The opponents of bills have been able to use the motion to recommit in two distinctive ways. The first, called a straight motion to recommit, has killed the bill by simply sending it back to its committee. The second, a motion to recommit with instructions, has had an entirely different purpose. This motion has been to send the bill back to its originating committee with instructions to report the bill back to the House "forthwith" with the changes directed in the instructions. Actually, when this motion has been adopted, its formalities have been treated as mere technicalities; the House has treated the action just as though it had been amended in the normal fashion. By the nature of things, the straight motion to recommit has been a parliamentarily weaker weapon than the motion to recommit with instructions, for it has meant the death of the bill and not merely the adoption of a substitute bill or amendments. In either case, the choice has been of great concern to the legislative tacticians in the House. Under the rules of the House, the motion to recommit could be made only by a Representative opposed to the bill, and he has had so to state at the time. By the House rules, also, the motion to recommit has been a prerogative of the minority political party in the House. The rules have even specified the individuals with priority to offer it, starting with the ranking minority member of the legislative committee from which the bill originated. All of these considerations were critically important in the House's action on the Trade Agreements Act of 1958. The bill had been considered under a "closed" rule that permitted only one amendment to be offered, and that amendment, a protectionist substitute bill, had been defeated. Wilbur Mills of Arkansas, floor manager of the bill, feared that the main assault on his bill would come on the motion to recommit, and so be maneuvered carefully to emasculate that motion. The bill proposed a five-year extension of the reciprocal-trade program, the longest extension ever attempted since the program had been initiated in 1934. The protectionist members of the House, led by Richard Simpson of Pennsylvania, agreed among themselves to offer a motion to recommit the bill with instructions to limit the extension for three years and to permit the Congress to override the President's decisions on whether low tariffs were truly hurting a domestic industry. Simpson, although the leader of the protectionist bloc and an influential Republican member of the Ways and Means Committee, did not have the prerogative to make the motion to recommit. That prerogative, by the rules of the House, belonged to Daniel A. Reed of New York, the most senior Republican on Ways and Means and just as opposed to the bill as Simpson. Simpson, however, assumed that Reed would go along with the decision of the protectionist bloc on how best to weaken the tariff bill. Mills, a master cloakroom operator, privately visited Joseph W. Martin of Massachusetts, the Republican floor leader. Martin, as a supporter of the Eisenhower-sponsored bill, wanted to help Mills in any way he could to protect the bill. Reed and he had long been intimate friends. Mills asked Martin to persuade Reed, if he could, to offer a straight motion to recommit the bill to the Ways and Means Committee. Martin went right to work on Reed. For three days, off and on, he conferred with Reed trying to encourage him to offer the straight recommit motion. Martin appealed to Reed's self-esteem: why let Simpson, whom he ranked in seniority, carry the lead in this fight? He appealed to Reed's fundamental opposition to low tariffs: why not try to kill the bill entirely rather than try merely to limit its scope? Reed gave way and pledged Martin that he would do what Martin, his old friend, had asked. Reed's decision was of the utmost significance to the fate of the bill. Simpson's proposed motion, carefully designed to appeal to a majority of the House's members, had a real chance for success. Mills seriously doubted whether he could defeat it. The motion for a straight recommittal was a far weaker proposal, for it would kill the bill outright. It would be more difficult to adopt. Many Representatives who were willing to limit the program would hesitate to vote to kill so significant a bill. When Reed offered the straight recommittal motion, it was roundly defeated, just as Mills had planned, by a vote of 268 to 146.

Out of such parliamentary maneuvering have the decisions of the House of Representatives been shaped. A knowledge of the rules and precedents of the House, an inner sense of the changing moods of the House, and a willingness to work hard and faithfully have always given the skillful House tacticians a decided parliamentary advantage in determining the nature and the direction of American law.

CHAPTER FOURTEEN

The Other Body

THE House of Representatives, of course, has not alone held the power and the responsibility for Congressional enactment of national law. These legislative prerogatives the House has shared with the United States Senate, a coordinate and coequal branch of the Congress. No law could be enacted without the approval of both, and these two branches of the federal legislature, in a natural competition for prestige and power, have fought for primacy over the federal domain from the very first years of the American Republic. Each chamber, granted high privileges of its own by the United States Constitution, has constantly encroached on those of the other, and as constantly been rebuffed, often amid angry words and bitter incriminations. Each has been narrowly jealous of its own perquisites; yet each essentially has been an aggressive, ambitious assembly anxious to enhance its ascendancy. Both have engaged for seventeen decades in a high rivalry that touched the lives of all Americans. At times, the formal relationships between the two chambers have seemed cordial and even chivalrous, but immediately beneath the veneer of courtesy and seeming mutual deference has raged a furious institutional competition often marked with bitterness and sometimes touched with ridicule and mutual contempt.

Vice President Thomas Jefferson, as presiding officer of the Senate from 1797 to 1801, drew up a manual of parliamentary practice designed deliberately to mollify the instinctive hostilities between the Senate and the House of Representatives. Jefferson's rules specifically forbade members to criticize the other chamber or its members, or even, in fact, to refer in debate to the other chamber or its members. To do so, Jefferson wrote, "might beget reflections lending to a misunderstanding between the two Houses," something to be avoided for the good of the Republic. Jefferson suggested that the Speaker of the House "interfere immediately" to silence any Representative who might condemn or vilify the Senate or the Senators. Such remarks, if made, said Jefferson, would "introduce proceedings and mutual accusations between the two Houses, which can hardly be terminated without difficulty and disorder." [1] Jefferson drafted his manual to meet a specific need, already obvious in the eighteenth century, and that manual's proposals were accepted by both the House and the Senate as binding on their procedures. The responsible members of both chambers recognized from the very beginning the absolute necessity for the safety of the government itself that the two houses of Congress act cooperatively in the great matters that concerned them both. To permit institutional hostilities to permeate their necessary relations invited chaos in the legislative process. Yet the adoption of rules and the formal acceptance of them scarcely resolved the instinctive institutional quarrels inevitable in a bicameral legislature. Over the years, these institutional hostilities have erupted periodically, as they did notably in 1961 and 1962, demonstrating that the antagonisms were still as strong as they were in Jefferson's day.

Speakers of the House, relying on Jefferson's manual and their own discretionary powers, have silenced members of the House and even the House's greatest leaders when words they were speaking cast unseemly reflections on the Senate or its members. Thus, John Randolph of Virginia, a master of vituperation, was called to order in 1807. John Quincy Adams of Massachusetts, "Old Man Eloquent," similarly was silenced in 1836, and so was Thaddeus Stevens of Pennsylvania in 1868, all for remarks reflecting on the character of the Senate and its members. John Quincy Adams' violation of the strict rule brought a reprimand from James K. Polk of Tennessee, then Speaker of the House and later to be President, as Adams had been. Polk, in silencing Adams, told the House that the Jefferson rule had to be enforced if harmony was to be preserved between the House and the Senate. In 1890, the House itself took formal action to uphold the rule. A Representative from Ohio, Robert P. Kennedy, had spoken disparagingly of the Senate in formal House debate. The House officially condemned his words and directed that they be stricken from the *Congressional Record,* an action that denoted severe censure of Kennedy. In so doing, the House formally resolved that "the utmost courtesy and decorum . . . should mark the mutual relations of the two houses of Congress."

Despite the seeming strictness of this rule, the members of both chambers have had little difficulty bypassing its severe limitations to convey in debate what they felt about the other chamber. Normally no point of order has been raised if the member made a passing reference to the other chamber by name that was not in itself offensive. Very early in Congressional history, however, they devised euphemistic phrases and niceties to escape the strictures of the formal rule so that they could say what they wanted to say in debate. The most frequently used of these was the technique by Representatives of calling the Senate "the other body" or "another body" thereby at least seeming to be referring to some remote and perhaps even imaginary institution. By so doing they could refer freely to the Senate in debate and not be confined to silence or meaningless and fatuous pleasantries. In 1903 a revealing incident in the long and often violent rivalry between the Senate and the House took place, and Joseph Cannon of Illinois then did not hesitate to assault the Senate in formal House debate, utilizing the appropriate euphemisms to stay technically within the letter of the strict Jefferson rules. Senator Benjamin "Pitchfork Ben" Tillman of South Carolina touched off the incident by boldly refusing to allow passage by the Senate of a House civil-appropriations bill. Tillman demanded that his state, South Carolina, receive a larger share of the federal funds than provided in the bill, and he backed up his demand with the threat to filibuster against the bill and thus kill it. Cannon, then chairman of the House Appropriations Committee, went to the House floor and savagely denounced Tillman and the Senate itself for this "legislative blackmail." He furiously criticized the Senate's most treasured parliamentary usage, the unlimited Senate debate that permitted Tillman to filibuster against the House bill. Cannon's denunciation of Tillman and the Senate clearly violated the spirit of Jefferson's rule, but Cannon was not called to order. His speech, in fact, enhanced his position in the House and helped elect him Speaker later that same year. Cannon skillfully avoided an open breach of the specific rule by referring to the Senate only as "another body" and by couching his own threats against the Senate in oblique but obvious language. "Another body," Cannon said of the Senate, "under these methods must change its methods of procedure, or our body, backed by the people, will compel that change; else this body, close to the people, shall become a mere tender, a mere bender of the pregnant hinges of the knee, to submit to what any member of another body may demand of this body as a price for legislation." [2] No member of the House, certainly not the Speaker, could have doubted for a moment but that Cannon referred specifically, if obliquely, to Senator Tillman and the Senate; that he accused Tillman of blackmail and that he condemned the Senate for permitting it. By using the House's stylized euphemisms, however, Cannon not only launched a biting attack on the Senate and the Senator but escaped even a token reprimand himself.

Such technical niceties, required in debate on the floors of the House and Senate, have given way entirely in the private conversations of the members and even, occasionally, in sessions of House and Senate committees. One member of the House Judiciary Committee, Samuel Hobbs of Alabama, perpetually opened sessions of that committee with this demand: "Mr. Chairman, I move to abolish the Senate." William Redfield of New York, in his memoirs, repeatedly mocked the United States Senate. "The Senate of the United States is said to be the greatest deliberative assembly in the world," this former member of the House wrote. "There ought to be no doubt about this. The Senators admit it. The burden of its greatness is visibly borne upon some Senatorial shoulders." [3] This type of ridicule of the Senate by members of the House has always been common, and members of the Senate have responded in kind to their colleagues of the House. The testiness between the members of the two legislative bodies has sprung automatically from the natural political rivalry between them. In the cauldron of legislative and political contest, this rivalry has been fomented and encouraged. The natural jealousy of the Representatives for their Constitutional prerogatives over the nation's purse strings and the natural jealousy of the Senators for their Constitutional prerogatives over foreign affairs and patronage have frequently embittered the formal relations between the two Houses. More than this, these institutional jealousies have built institutional pride in the members of both chambers; and this pride has tended to acerbate their personal dealings. Members of the Senate have long assumed that the height of every Representative's ambition has been to win a seat in the United States Senate. With it, the Representative would receive, as automatic perquisites of office, a larger staff, a greater personal prestige, a six-year term in office in place of the Representative's two years, a wider influence over patronage, and a national notoriety denied to the rank-and-file members of the House of Representatives. Members of the House, in response to this Senatorial condescension toward them, have regarded the Senators as an arrogant and pompous breed of politicians. Otto Passman of Louisiana called them "stuffed shirts." [4] Senators long have prided themselves on the "freedom" of Senate debate and compared that freedom invidiously to the controlled and limited debate of the House. In response, the Representatives have contemptuously regarded the Senate as an inefficient, blundering, and undemocratic legislative assembly that was incapable of action except by the unanimous consent of every Senator. The Representatives regarded the Senate's unrestricted debate as conducive to blathering and anarchy, not statesmanship.

These antagonistic attitudes have played an enduring and subtle role in shaping the course of American politics and American law. As a result, the Senate, over the decades, has tended to be more sympathetic to the President than the House of Representatives. Sharing with him responsibility for foreign policy and for the composition of the executive and judicial branches of the government, the Senate normally has been more internationally minded and cosmopolitan than the more provincial House of Representatives. The House, highly sensitive to its original jurisdiction and responsibility for federal taxes and appropriations, has tended to be more parsimonious than the Senate with taxpayers' money, more insistent on reducing the President's requests for higher taxes and larger spending. Representing smaller and more homogeneous districts than the Senators, the members of the House as a group have tended to be less responsive to "bullet-vote" activist pressure groups than their Senate colleagues. That has made the House reflect, less than the Senate, labor unions, ethnic and urban minorities, and the liberal causes these groups have normally espoused.

These inherent differences should prompt no surprise; for conflict between the House and the Senate has been inevitable from the moment the delegates at the 1787 Constitutional Convention in Philadelphia decided to create a bicameral legislature and to give each separate and distinct powers. The intent of the Founding Fathers was plain: they wanted a House of Representatives and a Senate that would be natural rivals and opponents, that would check not only any tyrannical tendencies in the President, but any such tendencies in either branch of Congress. The Senate was designed to be a more mature and responsible body of men to curb the natural impetuousness expected of the House of Representatives. The Philadelphia delegates established distinct and obvious differences in the qualifications for membership in the two chambers to accomplish this. They provided that Senators had to be at least thirty years old and citizens of the United States for at least nine years, while Representatives needed to be but twenty-five years old and citizens of the United States for seven years. The Representatives were to represent the *people* and were to be elected directly by them. Senators were to be ambassadors from their states, elected by the state legislatures, and expected to represent their states in the federal government.

The Senate was to serve as an executive council for the President in deciding grave questions of foreign policy and Presidential appointments to the federal establishment. The House of Representatives was given the power to impeach the President, but not the power to remove him from office. Representatives were to serve terms of but two years' length, to make certain they were responsive to the people. Senators were to serve terms of six years' length, to make certain they were not immediately responsive to every changing mood of the American people and their Representatives.

The differences that the Philadelphia delegates wrought between the House and the Senate were profound, and these differences translated into the actuality of the two great arms of the Congress created profoundly different legislative assemblies. The differences were not alone in institutional formalities but in institutional attitudes as well. The parliamentary procedures of the Senate and the House have always differed radically. The stately calm of the Senate, almost anachronistic in modern times, has stood in sharp contrast to the hubbub and seeming confusion of the House floor. The Senate has gloried in its unlimited debate, and the House has prided itself on its ability to act. Senators have actually believed that their speeches were, in fact, action, and of the most significant kind, a curious confusion of word and matter. Senator Ellison "Cotton Ed" Smith of South Carolina, for example, claimed that his speeches in the Senate literally increased the price of cotton for his farmers back home. "When I started my last speech in the Senate," Smith told his constituents, "cotton was ten cents. When I finished speaking four hours later, cotton was twelve cents. I will continue to serve you in that manner." [5] Revered by the Senate have been its greatest orators: Daniel Webster, Henry Clay, and John C. Calhoun. Revered by the House have been its leaders, those who could persuade or force the House to act, Henry Clay, Thomas Reed, Joseph Cannon, Nicholas Longworth, and Sam Rayburn. Entirely different types of leaders have been required for the House and for the Senate, and only rarely, as in the case of Henry Clay, have these differing qualifications existed in the same men.

"There is no harder place in the world of men, of contest and labor, to make a reputation, win a place, than in the American House of Representatives," said James A. Garfield of Ohio, one of the ablest of the House's leaders. "Less ability and tact will win fame in the Senate. Of all the distinguished men now in that body, there are not five, not educated in the House, who, if transferred to it, would ever again be heard of." [6]

If the delegates to the Philadelphia Convention set the Senate and the House of Representatives deliberately at odds, by the very differences they created in the two chambers, the House and the Senate had to work out for themselves the methods for reconciling those differences. Most pressing of all was the need to find the means of resolving the specific differences in the legislation adopted by the two assemblies. From the very first session of the First Congress, the members of the House and Senate agreed that they would resolve their legislative differences in especially created conference committees. For each bill in dispute the House and Senate each have appointed a special group of managers to represent its chamber and to defend its version of the legislation. These conference committees, through the decades, have negotiated compromises or settlements on these disputed bills by finding common ground acceptable to both the House and the Senate. Frequently, these compromises have not pleased the majority of either chamber. In time, the House-Senate conference committees took on a great importance of their own, for the decisions made in these conferences produced the actual law to be enacted. Not always have these conference committees been successful, for they became arenas of partisan wrangling, often igniting the natural hostilities between the House and Senate. In the event of the failure to reach an accord, the legislation in question—even though approved in differing versions by the House and the Senate—failed of enactment because the differences, even though minor, could not be resolved.

In a real sense, the Senate has successfully claimed the major prerogatives on Capitol Hill. The Senators had an automatic advantage to do so. There always have been fewer Senators than Representatives, and this by itself has given a wider promi-

377

nence and influence to the Senators. In the First Congress 1789-90, there were twenty-six Senators and sixty-five Representatives. In the Eighty-eighth Congress, 1963-64, there were 100 Senators and 435 Representatives. The individual Representative often disappeared in the sheer numbers of his colleagues, while the individual Senator more frequently was flatteringly noticed by both the press and Washington's curiously myopic society. The result has been that the Senators have received more invitations to dinner and more headlines. In the early 1950's the charges by Senator Joseph McCarthy of Wisconsin that Communists had infiltrated the federal government touched off an extraordinary national clamor. In the 1940's similar charges by Representatives, including Martin Dies of Texas, chairman of the Un-American Activities Committee, had largely been ignored. The fact that McCarthy spoke as a Senator automatically gave his accusations a significance that they did not have in the mouth of a Representative. The Senators' six-year terms of office have given them, as well, a sense of permanence far greater than that of most Representatives, many of whom have scarcely felt safe enough politically in their seats in the House ever to stop campaigning for re-election. Almost every vote cast by a Representative could influence his chances at re-election, while a Senator could presume that many of his would be forgotten long before he came up again for re-election. The length of the Senatorial terms has long been among the most attractive features of the Senate in the eyes of harassed and ever-scrambling Representatives.

The Senate's power over patronage and the individual Senator's standing with his political party in his home state added power to his prestige that normally was denied to the Representative. The Senate very early in its history informally agreed to a method of controlling the President's constitutional right to appoint federal officers that gave many Senators the President's actual power of appointment. This was the agreement by members of the Senate to vote against the confirmation to any federal office of anyone obnoxious to the senior Senator from the state from which the nominee came. This was known as "Senatorial courtesy," and it effectively prevented the President from naming whom he chose for office unless he first cleared the appointment with the appropriate Senator. The Senators, out of kindly deference to their colleagues in the House, permitted the Representatives to control the appointments to minor federal offices in their Congressional districts, such as postmasters and United States attorneys. A comparable power of the individual Senator over the Representative from his home state has existed in the political party back home. In the early years of the Senate, the state legislatures tended to send to the Senate the most illustrious men they could find in the state. The development of political parties radically altered this, and by the 1870's the state legislatures were sending to the Senate the state party's political leaders. These Senators, lamented one contemporary, often were "not fit either by reason of intellectual gifts or the admiration and confidence of the people to represent the great States of the Union." These Senators, however, normally carried more influence in their own states than the Representatives. In at least some cases, the Representatives actually owed "their political life and prominence almost entirely to the sufferance of the Senator." [7] In the later years of the nineteenth century, this was true of the Pennsylvania delegation in the House, whose real leader was Senator Matthew Quay of their state. In the modern Congress, a similar influence has been exercised by Senator Harry Byrd of Virginia over the Virginia Representatives.

The deference paid to Senators has long been a byword of American politics. Many members of the Senate have believed themselves more than qualified to be President. Indeed, ever since the golden age of the Senate when Webster, Clay, and Calhoun lifted the stature of the Senate by their eloquence, the Senate has abounded with members who believed themselves fully fit to serve as President of the United States. The list of the Senatorial hopefuls for the Presidency has read like a list of the Senate's prominent members. In the Senate of 1960 there were thirteen members who had either run for the Presidency or had been prominently mentioned for the post: Harry Byrd of Virginia, Everett Dirksen and Paul Douglas of Illinois, Barry Goldwater of Arizona, Hubert Humphrey of Minnesota, Lyndon

379

Johnson of Texas, Estes Kefauver of Tennessee, John Kennedy of Massachusetts, Robert Kerr of Oklahoma, Wayne Morse of Oregon, Richard Russell of Georgia, Stuart Symington of Missouri, and Strom Thurmond of South Carolina. Not a single Representative in 1960 qualified for that distinction. In the earlier years of the Senate, particularly those immediately after the Civil War, Senators were inclined to regard themselves as superiors even of the President. "The most eminent Senators," wrote George Hoar of Massachusetts of his Senate colleagues in the 1870's, "would have received as a personal affront a private message from the White House expressing a desire that they should adopt any course in the discharge of their legislative duties that they did not approve. If they visited the White House, it was to give, not to receive, advice." [8] Despite the long-held ambitions of Senators to become President, despite their conviction of their own eminent qualifications, only two—Warren Harding of Ohio and John Kennedy of Massachusetts—ever achieved the Presidency from the Senate; and neither of them was a leader of the Senate. In terms of the House, the fact that the pretensions of Senators for the Presidency were seriously considered, that the Senate itself was regarded as a natural forum for the incubation of Presidents, added a luster to the Senate that the House of Representatives could not match. It was not strange, in these terms, that many a Representative set his sights on membership in the United States Senate.

In the Senate of 1811, sixteen of the thirty-four Senators had served in the House of Representatives. In the Senate of 1861, there were seventeen of the forty-four Senators who had previously been Representatives. In the Senate of 1911, thirty-three of the ninety-two Senators had been members of the House, and in the Senate of 1961, there were forty-three of the one hundred Senators who had been Representatives—among them majority leader Mike Mansfield of Montana and minority leader Everett M. Dirksen of Illinois. All through the history of Congress members of the House have sought seats in the United States Senate. Those Representatives who were successful, or hoped to be, normally considered the change a "promotion" from the House.

James G. Blaine of Maine, who moved to the Senate after serving thirteen years in the House, six of them as Speaker, frequently spoke of such "promotions." William B. Allison of Iowa, Blaine wrote, "was promoted to the Senate." [9] Richard Yates of Illinois, he wrote in another instance, was "promoted from the House." William S. Vare of Pennsylvania, who won election to the Senate in 1926, expressed his ambition this way: "Having served fourteen years in the lower house of Congress, it was to my way of thinking only a natural impulse to aspire for a promotion to the United States Senate." [10] Others spoke of "graduating" from the House to the Senate. Still others regarded a Representative's transfer to the Senate as a "well-earned reward" for the Representative's faithful service in the House. Dispassionate observers of national politics, like Lord Bryce, long have regarded the House of Representatives "as a stepping stone" [11] to the more important office of Senator. Woodrow Wilson, observing the Congress in the 1880's, saw the caliber of the Senate then as similar to the House from which so many of the Senators came. "No stream can be purer than its sources," Wilson wrote. "The Senate can have in it no better men than the best men of the House of Representatives; and if the House of Representatives attracts to itself only inferior talent, the Senate must put up with the same sort." [12]

The able men of the House, those dedicated to the House as a political institution, have not agreed at all that the best men of the House necessarily have been promoted to the Senate, nor in fact that the transfer has been a promotion. Champ Clark of Missouri, who gave his entire adult life to the House, denied the thesis that the Senate was a superior body to which Representatives should aspire. On describing the transfer of Henry Cabot Lodge of Massachusetts to the Senate in 1893, Clark said Lodge had been "translated" to the Senate. "I do not say promoted," Clark explained, "for I am not sure that it is a promotion to go from House to Senate." [13] A half century before Clark wrote, John Sherman of Ohio described his own transfer to the Senate from the House as "not for a time agreeable." "However conspicuous the member may have been in the House," said

381

Sherman, who had been one of the House's most prominent members, "he must take his place in the Senate at the bottom of the ladder, and, according to Senatorial usage, must be reasonably modest in expressing his opinions." [14] There were pitfalls for the Representative who moved to the Senate, as Sherman did in 1861. Those pitfalls were still evident in the Senate a century later. By Senate usage still, the new junior Senator, no matter how experienced and tested in his years in the House of Representatives, had to restrain his temptation to join freely in Senate debate and had to defer to senior Senators actually far less experienced than he. For these reasons, not all Representatives who moved to the Senate enjoyed the change. James Frear of Wisconsin cited a score of Representatives he had known who had moved to the Senate in the 1920's and 1930's. They were attracted to the Senate, he said, by the six-year terms enjoyed by Senators. "Yet I have known from personal statements," Frear went on, "that several so transferred from the House to the Senate regretted having made the change. They told me so. Smothered in the Senate by details and the ambitions of older Senators inclined to expect especial consideration through long service, the so-called promotion was disappointing." [15] Thomas B. Reed of Maine, one of the House's most brilliant members and for six years its Speaker, regarded the Senate with cold contempt. "The Senate," he said caustically, "is a nice, quiet sort of place where good Representatives go when they die." [16]

Not all Representatives have automatically sought a seat in the Senate even when the opportunity to do so has been given them. "Some very able men, indeed, prefer to stay in the House," [17] wrote Robert Luce of Massachusetts in the 1920's. The same could be reported of the House in the 1960's. Indeed, the Senate has not received the most capable of the House's members by automatic political osmosis. Members like Carl T. Curtis of Nebraska, Jennings Randolph of West Virginia, Winston Prouty of Vermont, and Francis Case of South Dakota had but minor rank in the House before moving to the Senate. Some of the House's ablest members have categorically refused to accept seats in the Senate; they preferred their seats in the House. Among these in the modern House have been John Fogarty of Rhode Island, influential in the House's decisions on medical research; Gerald Ford of Michigan, influential in military appropriations; and Richard Bolling of Missouri, a legislative strategist and parliamentary tactician. There were many able members of the modern House who simply would not have considered serving in any other political office. These were men who had come, over their years of service, to identify themselves with the House itself, men like Howard W. Smith of Virginia, John Taber of New York, Clarence Brown of Ohio, Albert Rains of Alabama, and Charles Halleck of Indiana. Sam Rayburn of Texas felt as strongly as any of them the high calling and honor it was to serve in the House of Representatives. A young Representative and friend of Rayburn, Stewart Udall of Arizona, once tried to persuade Rayburn to encourage the political future of a young Representative from Texas who wanted to run for the Senate. With Speaker Rayburn's help, Udall suggested, the young Texas Representative could have a great political career. Rayburn did not care for the suggestion. "The House of Representatives," he said, "should be high enough for any man's ambition." [18]

Only rarely has a former Senator run for a seat in the House of Representatives, and then, normally, only because he had lost his seat in the Senate. The most extraordinary example of a sitting Senator deliberately switching to the House of Representatives was Henry Clay in 1811. Clay gave up his seat in the Senate to run for the House, because he believed it a more likely forum from which to give play to his national ambitions. He was right, for the House elected him Speaker on his first day as a Representative. In the decades that followed the prestige of the Senate increased, and Clay returned to that chamber. In the modern Senate, no member would consider willingly yielding his seat to become a member of the House. This has long been the attitude of United States Senators. "Is there today," asked a writer in 1909, "any member of the Senate who would imitate the example of Henry Clay who had been elected to that body and might have remained there throughout his life, and yet preferred the House?" [19] The answer then obviously was "No." This disparity of prestige and personal power between individuals serving in the two chambers has itself aggravated the natural irritation between the Senate and the House of Representatives.

There were other causes for irritation as well, not the least of which were the pretensions of at least some of the Senators. In the first years of Congress, the Senate cloaked its operations with an air of mystery by holding all its meetings in secret. "Its members strutted about in purple," said Samuel McCall of Massachusetts, "and sought to emphasize by their conduct and appearance the awful dignity of their office." [20] In those first years, the Senate debated seriously the formal title that should be used in addressing the President—one title suggested was *His Highness, the President of the United States of America, and Protector of the Rights of the Same*—and whether Senators should receive higher salaries than mere Representatives. The House then showed its egalitarian spirit not only by insisting that the President be called simply "Mr. President," as befitted an antimonarchial government and people, but also by denying the Senators higher pay. In the years that followed, the proliferation of the federal patronage system automatically increased the standing of Senators over that of Representatives. The Senators controlled the federal appointments and with that control they assumed political influence second only to the President's. "Many a state governor has been eager to lay down his gubernatorial honors to don the Senator's toga," wrote a political scientist in 1904. "Indeed, as an object of ordinary political ambition, the Senatorship stands next to the Presidency itself. It is accounted more to be desired than a Cabinet post and is scarcely less coveted than a seat on the bench of the Supreme Court." [21] Not until the creation of the Civil Service system were the Senators shorn of this great power over patronage. Before that took place, however, the Senate's awesome power so affected the members of the Senate that even *employees* of the Senate looked down scornfully on the members of the House of Representatives. In 1889, the House itself engaged in a heated debate over the "insolence with which they were treated by the employees of the Senate."

In these years also were developed institutional habits in the dealings between the Senate and the House that came in time to be assumed as automatic prerogatives of the Senators. When the House and Senate created a joint Congressional committee, for example, a Senator always acted as chairman. When the House and Senate disagreed on the language of a bill and appointed a conference committee to settle differences, not only did the senior Senator preside over the meetings of the conference committee, but the House managers for the bill had to troop over to the Senate side of the Capitol for those meetings. The Senators would not deign to walk so far as the House wing of the Capitol to meet with the Representatives. These privileges, so galling to Representatives sensitive to the institutional prestige of their own chamber, have been under assault for decades, with only scattered successes achieved by the House by the 1960's. The creation of the Joint Congressional Committee on Atomic Energy broke one of these traditions: the chairmanship of the committee has been alternated in every Congress between a member of the House and a member of the Senate. Even this break with the past, however, was not achieved without a fight with the Senate. When the committee convened in 1953, with the Republicans newly in control of Congress, the question of who would be chairman was so bitterly contested that there was some doubt whether the Joint Committee could continue to operate at all. In the previous Congress, the chairman had been a Senator, Brien McMahon of Connecticut. The House members insisted that the new chairman be the ranking House Republican on the committee, Sterling Cole of New York. The Senate members of the committee refused to concede the post to Cole, and Cole finally informed Speaker Joseph Martin that he was personally embarrassed by the fuss and intended to withdraw as a candidate for the chairmanship. Martin, backed completely by Sam Rayburn, then the minority floor leader, told Cole that the question was not his to resolve, that it affected the prestige of the House itself and not just Cole's personal feelings. Martin and Rayburn insisted that Cole, by right, should be chairman; the Senate members of the committee finally retreated and yielded to Cole as chairman.

Institutional wrangling between the House and the Senate, inevitable by their very natures, always has been fiercest in matters of foreign relations and government spending. There were sound reasons why this was so. Both involved the gravest questions of national policy and the most significant factors of the institutional powers of the House and the Senate. The Constitution assigned Congressional primacy in foreign affairs to the Senate by giving the Senate the power to advise on and consent to treaties with foreign governments. To the House, the Constitution gave original jurisdiction to all bills "for raising revenue." Both specific powers have been under assault from the earliest years of the Congress. The House of Representatives, while necessarily yielding to the Senate the power to ratify treaties, has from the beginning claimed discretionary powers of its own to determine whether these treaties, once ratified by the Senate, should be put into effect. Normally, to effect a treaty, government money had to be appropriated, and in this area the House of Representatives claimed not only jurisdiction but absolute discretion. This was the kernel of the great House debate over the Jay Treaty in 1796, in which the speech of Fisher Ames of Massachusetts proved decisive. The treaty had been ratified by the Senate, but the House threatened to nullify the document by refusing to appropriate the funds to carry it out. In like fashion, the Senate has challenged the House's great original powers over the raising of public revenues. The Senate normally has yielded to the House, as the Constitution specified, original jurisdiction over tax measures; but the Senate has denied the House's claim that the Constitution's language gave the House also original jurisdiction over appropriations bills. For Senate strategists, bills "for raising revenues" meant only tax bills; they did not include bills for the spending of those revenues. For House strategists, their jurisdiction obviously included both types of bills. Over the decades the Senate consistently has defended its priority in foreign affairs, and the House with equal diligence has defended its claims to originate all money bills. The House usually has shrunk from repudiating United States treaties ratified by the Senate, and the Senate has hesitated to press to a showdown its own claims to original powers in appropriating federal funds. The long quarrel doubtlessly has had a profound psychological effect on both chambers and on the instinctive attitudes of their members. Senators, by and large, have felt more competent and cosmopolitan in foreign affairs than their colleagues in the House of Representatives. Members of the House, on the other hand, traditionally have felt more qualified and more economy-minded in spending the American taxpayers' money.

As early as 1792, the rivalry between the House and Senate over foreign affairs and governmental appropriations took on a serious aspect. President Washington then was considering a treaty with Algiers for the ransom of Americans captured by the Barbary pirates. The question arose: Where could Washington get the money to pay the ransom? Thomas Jefferson, then Secretary of State, opposed using any system of raising the money without the sanction of both the House and the Senate. Jefferson sounded out members of the Senate and the House and learned that the Senate was willing to approve an annual bribe for Algiers but unwilling to let the House take part in the transaction. The House, Jefferson discovered, might well refuse to appropriate the money. "The President had wished to redeem our captives at Algiers and to make peace with them on paying an annual tribute," Jefferson recorded. "The Senate was willing to approve this, but unwilling to have the lower house applied to previously to furnish the money. They wished the President to take the money from the Treasury, or open a loan for it. They thought that to consult the Representatives on one occasion would give them a handle always to claim it, and would let them into a participation of the power of making treaties, which the Constitution had given exclusively to the President and the Senate." [22] President Washington himself consulted with a committee from the Senate on the question, and did eventually submit a treaty to the Senate to make peace with Algiers. Despite Jefferson's fears, the House did appropriate this tribute money needed to placate the Barbary pirates.

In 1796, the House acted to protect its prerogatives over appropriations. Behind the leadership of Albert Gallatin of Pennsylvania, the House challenged the system of Congressional appropriations initiated by Treasury Secretary Alexander Hamilton and supported by the Senate. Until then, the House and the Senate appropriated the money to run the new government under a single bill that made no attempt to specify how that money was to be spent. The gross amount could be allocated at the discretion of the President and his Cabinet officials. Gallatin argued that this was a dangerous principle for the government of a free people, and he insisted that the House of Representatives possessed the discretionary power to determine how the appropriations would be expended. That power, Gallatin said, was vested in the House of Representatives to permit the House to check the other branches of the government whenever necessary. Gallatin, in making this first declaration in Congress of the supremacy of the House of Representatives, stated that Hamilton's appropriating system, endorsed by the Senate, threatened great fiscal abuses and denied Congress, and specifically the House, its Constitutional control of the nation's purse. Gallatin lost this fight in 1796, but he won the principle of specific appropriations five years later when he was appointed Secretary of the Treasury by President Jefferson. As Secretary, and with the full support of Jefferson, Gallatin submitted to the House an itemized budget that specified precisely how the Jefferson administration proposed to spend the appropriations requested, a system ever since followed by succeeding administrations.

These early instances of House and Senate hostilities over their respective primary jurisdictions were but the beginning of a long and continuing struggle between the two chambers. The House repeatedly attempted to gain a foothold in foreign affairs, primarily the Senate's concern, and the Senate, with equal determination, tried to invade the House's jurisdiction over revenue measures. In 1818, the House tried to force the President to recognize the new South American republics. Eight years later, the House tried to instruct the American delegates to an international conference at Panama. The House in 1837 attempted to force United States recognition of the Republic of Texas, and in 1842 the House tried to downgrade the American minister to

Mexico. When the United States, by treaty with Russia, purchased Alaska, the House of Representatives voted the price of $7,200,000 only after adopting an amendment that declared first that the purchase was invalid without approval of the House as well as the Senate, and then gave that approval. In 1876, the House directed that certain American embassies and consular offices be closed, and the action brought a protest from President Grant that this was "an invasion of the Constitutional prerogatives and duty of the President." In the years after World War I, the House approved other directions for the conduct of United States foreign policy. In 1940, the House of Representatives narrowly defeated, 108 to 105, an amendment to an appropriations bill to sever diplomatic relations with Russia. The amendment, sponsored by John McCormack of Massachusetts, prompted a debate on the House's power to take part in United States foreign policy. McCormack argued that the House could so take part through its power to appropriate or not to appropriate money. "Congress," he said, "has the power not to appropriate money for any particular purpose." [23] Emanuel Celler of New York denied McCormack's thesis, a thesis proffered as early as during the debate on the Jay Treaty in 1796. "Since when do we in this chamber, or in the cloakroom," Celler asked his House colleagues, "conduct the foreign affairs of this nation?" [24]

Over these same years when the House was intruding in foreign affairs, the Senate was straining and even overstepping the Constitutional limits on its powers over tax measures. The Constitution empowered the Senate to amend revenue measures, but it forbade the Senate to initiate such bills. In 1831, a proposal by Senator Thomas Hart Benton of Missouri to abolish a tariff was challenged by Benton's Senate colleagues on Constitutional grounds, and Benton withdrew it. In 1833, Senator Henry Clay of Kentucky argued that his tariff bill properly originated in the Senate because it lowered tariffs rather than raised them, an argument denied by Senator Daniel Webster of Massachusetts. In 1837, another Senate proposal, this time to authorize an issue of Treasury notes, touched off an angry House debate in which one Representative bitterly spoke of the Senate's dictation to the

House and John Quincy Adams said acidly that for the previous five years not a single of the many revenue bills had originated in the House. The Senate bill was withdrawn. During the Civil War, a Senate bill providing for a five per cent income tax was also withdrawn after Thaddeus Stevens of Pennsylvania denounced it as a violation of the House's Constitutional prerogatives. After the Civil War, the Senate became even more bold. In 1872, the Senate tacked onto a minor bill a general revision of all tariffs. Despite the strong opposition of James Garfield of Ohio in the House, the Senate's bill was enacted into law. In 1883, the House passed a bill cutting internal taxes only to have the Senate add another entire revision of the tariff law. That revision also became law despite angry protests from the House. In 1901 the Senate repeated the tactic, this time killing a House bill to repeal stamp taxes and substituting a new bill to cut taxes on beer and tobacco. In 1905, the House called a temporary halt to these incursions on its prerogatives by voting 263 to 5 to return to the Senate a bill passed by the Senate that again affected United States tariffs.

The claim of the Senate to amend freely any House bill, and by so doing to add revenue provisions that had not originated in the House, has had a checkered career in the twentieth century. As late as 1962, the Senate attempted to pass a medical-insurance plan for the aged, to be financed by social security taxes. A similar bill had been stalled in the House Ways and Means Committee, and the House had therefore failed to act on it. At the urging of President Kennedy and his aides, his Senate adherents tried to pass the bill as an amendment to a relatively insignificant tax bill already approved by the House. The Senate itself, by a 52 to 48 vote, rejected the proposal. By contemporary vote counts, a clear majority of the Senate appeared to favor the medical plan, but the method of adopting it—by bypassing the House on a major tax measure—brought enough resentment in the Senate itself to swing a majority of the Senate against the bill.

The hostilities engendered between the House and the Senate over foreign policy and taxes were, by their nature, somewhat restrained. After all, the Constitution did give specific jurisdiction over them to one or the other chambers. There was, however, no restraint in the animosities fomented during the quarrels over Congressional appropriations. The House of Representatives, from the beginning, insisted that its members held the power to originate all appropriations bills on the grounds that these bills, money bills, were bills "raising revenue." The Senate acquiesced in the House's actually originating these bills, but always denied the validity of the House's claim that these bills could properly be defined as raising revenue. The Senate denied that the House originated these appropriations bills as a matter of Constitutional right. The Senate's claim to coequal power with the House of Representatives on appropriations also rested on the action of the Constitutional Convention in 1787. At that convention, Edmund Randolph of Virginia proposed that all "money bills" originate in the House of Representatives and that the Senate be denied the right to amend them. This proposal was rejected. The Senate has read the rejection of Randolph's proposal as *prima facie* evidence that the Founding Fathers intended the Senate to have coequal powers here with the House. The House's members, however, could quote the view of the Founding Fathers to the House's advantage. James Madison, Alexander Hamilton, and James Wilson in formal statements all agreed that the Constitution gave the House of Representatives the sole right to originate all "money bills." Hamilton even said that "this power over the purse may in fact be regarded as the most complete and effectual weapon with which any constitution can arm the immediate representatives of the people." [25] President Washington also appeared to accept this same construction. In his first Inaugural Address, Washington made a personal request, which, he said, he "most properly addressed to the House of Representatives." That request was that the House, in appropriating money for the supply of the government, delete any appropriation for his salary. Washington had never accepted compensation for serving his country, and he did not want compensation for serving as President.

Before the Civil War, the Senate largely refrained from pressing its claim to originate appropriations. Most of the appropriations in those years were carried as part of tax measures and automatically fell to the House's jurisdiction. Only once, in 1857, did the Senate actually originate a general appropriations bill, but that bill did not precipitate a Constitutional quarrel between the two chambers. The House simply ignored it. In 1881 the question again rose, and this time the House referred the Senate appropriations bill to its Judiciary Committee with a request that the committee investigate the Senate's authority for originating the bill. That committee, under the chairmanship of Proctor Knott of Kentucky, reported that the Senate did indeed have the power to originate the bill and that "the power to originate bills appropriating money from the Treasury of the United States is not exclusive in the House of Representatives." The committee's report, approved by a majority of the committee, however, brought a sharp rebuff from five dissenting members of the committee. They issued formal "minority views" in which they reached an exactly opposite conclusion. The Knott Committee's findings did not settle the question. Three decades later, in 1912, a Senator, John Sharp Williams of Mississippi, who had served with distinction in the House of Representatives, took up the matter once more. He, as a member of the Senate, denied the validity of the Knott Committee's decision, even though by so doing he rejected the Senate's old claim. A bill to raise revenue, Williams argued, was any bill that turned money "into an active instrumentality for carrying on the government." [26]

Now why were these institutional arguments significant? Why were they conducted with such acrimony on both sides? Involved was the most fundamental and most powerful of all the ingredients of government: money. The power to originate legislation appropriating money, the jurisdiction to initiate the spending of money gave the chamber with that power an enormous if subtle advantage in determining the course of the federal government and thereby affecting the very history of the United States and the well-being of its people. Here was the root force of the national government. Here, as Alexander Hamilton said, was a weapon with which the House of Representatives could claim pre-eminence in the American government just as did the House of Commons in the British government. Armies could be raised or discharged, navies built or scuttled, dams, canals, bridges, highways, even cities, all the multitudinous works of an energetic people inhabiting a magnificent continent could be encouraged or thwarted by the decisions of those with basic control of the nation's purse. That the Senate had unquestioned right to amend and so alter the House's basic decisions on appropriating funds to run the government begged the fundamental question. The Senate, in exercising its power of amendment, had to start with the decisions of the House, and those House decisions permeated the entire spirit of the appropriations being enacted. The Senate could try to increase or decrease the dollars appropriated for any given project by the House of Representatives. The Senate could try to persuade the House to reject a given program or start another one. The Senate, in short, could tamper with the basic work of the House, but could do no more than that so long as the House successfully defended its right to priority over the consideration of these appropriations. It was for these reasons that the Senate and House quarrelled bitterly over the right to originate appropriations bills. As political institutions with differing heritages and often opposing philosophies of government, the House and the Senate did not agree on how to run the American government, on what path that government should take, or on the goals to be sought by the American people. It was but natural that they should fight for supremacy over appropriations.

The Senate claimed early in the nineteenth century two specific prerogatives over the Representatives in the appropriating process. The Senators acquiesced, reluctantly, to the House's originating appropriations bills, claiming for themselves only the lesser power of amending those bills; but the Senators were able to win two concessions for their chamber's legislative prestige. The first of these was that the meeting place for all House-Senate conference committees on appropriations bills was the Senate Appropriations Committee's rooms in the Senate wing of the Capitol. The other was that a Senator always presided at these meetings. These meetings were of great importance, as conference committee meetings on all other legislation were; for at these meetings the final decisions on the legislation were made. Only rarely did the House and Senate agree on appropriations bills. Normally the Senate did exercise its right to amend the work of the House, and normally, in amending, the Senate increased the money to be appropriated in these bills. Even in the 1790's, when Albert Gallatin was fighting to protect the House's rights on appropriations, the Senate was increasing the appropriations sent to it by the House. By the 1860's Representatives already were angrily condemning the Senate's constant additions to the House's appropriations bills. In the 1880's Woodrow Wilson recorded the then time-tested pattern on appropriations: the House cut the estimates submitted by the executive branch and sent the bills to the Senate, where the Senators "usually propose grants of many additional million." [27] In the early 1900's, a political scholar examined the processes of Congressional appropriations and reached this conclusion: "The Senate is not . . . as the Constitution intends it to be, a check on the House, but habitually increases the appropriations made by the latter." [28] In 1919 Joseph Cannon of Illinois quoted Senator Reed Smoot of Utah as saying that only once in eighteen years of his experience had the Senate ever reduced an appropriations bill.

In the institutional war between the Senate and the House over appropriations, the House in the 1880's gravely weakened its own cause. The House, with the consent of the then Speaker John Carlisle of Kentucky, took from its Appropriations Committee jurisdiction for many of the appropriations bills and distributed them among seven legislative committees. This was done to weaken the power of the then chairman of the Appropriations Committee, Samuel Randall of Pennsylvania. Inadvertently, the House also weakened its own strength in combating the Senate and the President on appropriations. Randall himself predicted the action would prompt unprecedented government "extravagance." The House's own inner restraints had been removed. Joseph Cannon of Illinois, who succeeded Randall as Appropriations Chairman, said this action by the House marked "the beginning" of Presidential interference in legislation and enfeebled the House in its long struggle to protect the interests of taxpayers. John Fitzgerald of New York, also a chairman of the House Appropriations Committee, blamed the change for tripling the government's expenditures in a quarter of a century. The Senate did become dominant in appropriations, and World War I dramatized the House's loss of power. In 1920, to regain control over appropriations the House took three major steps. It passed legislation creating the Budget Bureau to help the cause of government economy. It restored all appropriations bills to the Appropriations Committee. And it adopted a rule that forbade acceptance of any Senate amendment to an appropriations bill without specific approval of that amendment by a separate vote of the House itself. Within a decade the House had again assumed its dominance over the Senate on appropriations, to the annoyance of the Presidents whose budgets the House continued to cut. In 1926, Nicholas Longworth of Ohio proudly reported that "today the House of Representatives stands firmly entrenched in the control over the nation's purse strings." [29]

This dominance was not to go unchallenged. In 1932, in creating the Reconstruction Finance Corporation, a government agency to lend money to businesses, the Congress authorized the agency to finance its operations by borrowing funds from the Treasury. Normally in the past, government agencies had received their operating funds by direct appropriations from the Congress. The new financing scheme permitted the agency to borrow directly from the Treasury and thus bypass the House of Representatives and its economy-minded Appropriations Committee. The members of the House's economy bloc promptly labeled the new debt transactions thus provided as "back-door" spending and they argued that these conflicted with the Constitution's requirement that money could not be drawn from the Treasury except by "appropriations made by law." The technique, devised during President Herbert Hoover's administration, was adopted by the Franklin Roosevelt administration and those of Harry Truman, Dwight Eisenhower, and John Kennedy as an easier financing method than direct appropriations. A score of federal programs were given the same financing technique in the next decades, among them commodity-credit loans, slum clearance, housing loans, small-business loans, foreign aid, the Tennessee Valley Authority, rural electrification, and highway- and airport-construction programs. In the course of three decades, the government financed programs costing more than $109 billion through these debt transactions. The "back-door" spending method divided those favoring these programs against those opposing them; and the old argument over institutional prerogatives between the House and Senate became confused in the battle between the "economizers" and the "spenders," between the "isolationists" and the "internationalists." The advocates of "back-door" spending credited it with the success of the programs on which it was utilized. "All of this important, progressive legislation," said John McCormack of Massachusetts in 1961, "is successful in operation only by reason of the public debt transaction policy and the contract authority being granted." [30] Senator J. William Fulbright of Arkansas in 1959 candidly told the Senate in formal debate that public debt transactions were being used to finance the International Monetary Fund deliberately to bypass the "penny-pinching" on the House Appropriations Committee. Advocates in the House of various economic programs argued that "back-door" spending was necessary if these programs were to be created. "If you vote against it," said Wright Patman of Texas in 1961 during debate on the depressed-areas bill, "there will be no depressed-areas bill this season." [31] In vain did the economy-block members argue that the programs could as well be financed by direct appropriations. The arguments cut through the ranks of the House and Senate, with advocates and opponents arrayed against each other in both chambers. Although the House institutionally disliked voting to bypass its own Appropriations Committee, instinctively aware that this damaged the strength of the House itself, normally enough Representatives feared that a vote against "back-door" spending as the financing method for a given program would be interpreted by their voters back home as a vote against the bill itself. The depressed-areas bill of 1961, financed by "back-door" spending, passed the House by a 223 to 193 vote. "What a way to run a business—any business from a peanut stand to a bank," exclaimed Clarence Cannon of Missouri, chairman of the Appropriations Committee. "And yet that is the way we are running the greatest government on earth. Let us close the back door." [32]

Cannon and his fellow economy advocates in the House had their revenge on the Senate later that year. In the final bill of the 1961 session of Congress, a supplemental appropriations bill, they wrote in provisos that wiped out "back-door" spending not only for the depressed-areas bill but for three other programs already in operation. The House debated the bill and approved it, September 27, and then adjourned for the year. Even as the House adjourned, the Senate was debating the bill; and many of the Senators were angered by the House's action in altering the financial arrangements on these four programs, alterations they believed threatened the successful continuance of these programs. When the Senators discovered that the House had adjourned for the year, they were enraged. The House had not waited to learn whether the Senate would agree to the provisos; and, in failing to wait, the House gave the Senate the choice of either accepting the bill as it was or denying $573,000,000 in the bill's appropriations needed to operate many of the government's important agencies. In institutional terms, the House had violated the normal courtesy assumed to exist between the House and the Senate. By its formal act of adjournment with so major a bill still unpassed and in disagreement, the House had profoundly insulted the Senate, and insulted the Senate at one of its most sensitive points, its own prestige.

"We shall have to give in to what the other body wishes," Senate majority leader Mike Mansfield angrily told his colleagues. "So far as the Senate is concerned, we have taken a shellacking and I think it is outrageous. I certainly do not agree that this is something we should swallow and smile while we do it. We have no choice. . . ."[33] Senate minority leader Everett Dirksen was equally angered. There was dark talk on the Senate floor of retaliation on the House in 1962. "An outrage is being perpetrated upon the Senate," Dirksen said. "Are we a coordinate branch of the legislative establishment, or are we not?" The House's action, said Dirksen, was "an affront to the Senate" [34] that the Senate should not tolerate. Senator Karl Mundt of South

397

Dakota described the House's action as "a shotgun held at the head of the Senate. . . . This is not the kind of comity which should exist between the two Houses." [35] Given no choice and in a sullen mood, the Senators reluctantly approved the bill.

The 1962 session of Congress had scarcely begun before the internecine warfare between the House and the Senate again broke out. Again Representatives were maneuvering to take from the Senate some of the Senate's powers over appropriations. Chairman Cannon of the House committee telephoned Senator Carl Hayden of Arizona, chairman of the Senate Appropriations Committee in February to inform Hayden that the House Appropriations Committee planned to alternate the meeting places of the House-Senate conference committees on appropriations between the House committee rooms and the Senate committee rooms. The House committee, in short, had decided to abrogate the century-long arrangement under which these meetings were invariably held on the Senate side of the Capitol. Hayden called his committee into session on February 9, and the committee voted unanimously to accept the House committee's proposal provided the House yielded to the Senate the right to originate half of the appropriations bills adopted each year. On April 10, the first appropriations conference committee met on the Senate side of the Capitol under the chairmanship of a Senator. At the conclusion of that meeting, the House members informed the Senators that the next meeting of the conference committee would be held on the House side of the Capitol. They indicated that they intended to have a House member preside at that meeting. This, to the Senators, was institutional aggression, unilateral abrogation by the House of a traditional and, therefore, hallowed privilege of the Senate. Their tempers flared, and they refused categorically to yield to the House committee's ultimatum. The House continued to pass its annual appropriations bills; and the Senate continued to approve them, too, with amendments. The impasse continued, however, on the conference committee. As a result, the appropriations needed to run the government were not being finally adopted. April drifted into May and May into June, and still the Senators and Representatives refused to yield their

398

adamant positions. The institutional quarrel was growing into a government crisis: many of the government's agencies would have no funds to operate once the new fiscal year began on July 1. Negotiations continued between Hayden and Cannon. The Senators agreed to move the meeting place of conference committees to the Old Supreme Court Chamber, almost halfway between the House and the Senate but still part of the Senate wing of the Capitol. Chief James Rowley of the Treasury's Secret Service had no funds to pay his agents and he asked them to volunteer to continue their work without pay. Almost 2,000,000 government workers were faced with similar work without pay. The Defense Department's massive appropriations bill had been approved by both chambers but still had to be adjusted by a House-Senate conference committee. On June 22, Chairman Cannon wrote a stinging letter to Chairman Hayden, telling him that "the country at large" was greatly concerned about the continuance of the existing system of appropriations under which the Senate "invariably increased every appropriation bill passed by the House." In the previous ten years, Cannon said, the Senate's increases had amounted to $32 billion. In the previous twenty-three years, these Senate increases had totaled $60 billion. The House committee, said Cannon, was only trying to remedy "this situation" by its proposals. The implication was that with a Representative presiding over the conference meetings, the increases in appropriations could be resisted.

The Senators took grave offense at Cannon's letter. Hayden addressed the Senate to inform his colleagues that a "crisis" was at hand. Senator Richard Russell of Georgia denounced the "unfair and vicious attacks" on Chairman Hayden. Senator Willis Robertson of Virginia, in an emotional speech to the Senate, declared that the House committee's "unfounded" accusations were "the most insulting . . . that one body has ever sent to another" and in clear violation of the rules of the House. The House committee, said Robertson, was "subtly charging the Senate committee with wasting public funds." [36]

Robertson detailed the processes by which the Senate and the Senate Appropriations Committee handled appropriations bills.

He acknowledged that the Senate did indeed increase the House bills, but there were sound reasons for this. The Senate committee, for example, usually received additional appropriations requests made by the Administration after the House had already enacted appropriations bills. Invariably, also, the heads of federal departments and agencies appealed to the Senate committee to reverse damaging cuts in their appropriations made by the House. More than that, Robertson said in his revealing speech, House members themselves often pleaded personally with the Senate committee to approve appropriations rejected by the House committee and the House. "Get the Senate to adopt your amendment," Robertson quoted members of the House committee, "and we will agree to it in conference." [37]

The Senate debate raged on, with other Senators joining Robertson in denouncing the House committee's behavior. Robertson, who had served fourteen years in the House before his election to the Senate, spoke acidly of the House's pretensions to superiority in the appropriation process. The Senate, he said, merely asked its full rights as a "coequal" branch of Congress "although no sitting member of the Senate ever ran for election to the House of Representatives." Robertson's slur on the House's prestige, his implication of the higher rank of the Senate, was immediately welcomed by Senator Spessard Holland of Florida. "The Senator from Virginia brings up an interesting point," Holland said. "Certainly I have never heard of a sitting Senator's running for election to the House of Representatives, but I have heard of many members of the House who have run for election to the Senate."

This was the climax of the 1962 quarrel between the House and the Senate over appropriations. Negotiations continued between Cannon and Hayden, and eventually the House committee reluctantly agreed to continue for another year the traditional practices of the House and Senate in processing appropriations bills. Clearly, however, the quarrel was not over; nor probably would it ever be over. The House and the Senate had been created with a natural rivalry here as in many other areas of their operations, and the natural result of that rivalry was competition for legislative primacy.

The delegates at the Philadelphia Convention, in drafting the Constitution that created the Senate and the House, made no provision at all for the settlement of differences between the two bodies. That differences would arise was obvious, for both had the power to amend the bills adopted by the other. The question arose immediately on the formation of the First Congress. On April 7, 1789, the day after the Senate finally acquired its first quorum, the Constitutional majority necessary for the Senate to transact business, the Senate appointed a special committee to draft rules for working out such disagreements as inevitably would arise between the Senate and the House. That committee shortly afterward met with a similar committee appointed by the House's first Speaker, Frederick Muhlenberg of Pennsylvania. The two committees agreed that in such cases the differences should be resolved by special conference committees appointed by both chambers. There was no other practical way for such disagreements to be settled. Even then, the Senate and the House had too many members for the two chambers to sit jointly to work out their legislative disagreements. The conference committees established in the First Congress set the pattern for all the Congresses to follow.

Technically, these conference committees could only resolve the actual differences and disagreements between the House and Senate versions of the pending bills. They had no authority to add new matter to the legislation, nor to alter language identical in both versions of the bill. As early as 1790, however, a House-Senate conference committee did change a decision made by both the House and the Senate, and that, too, became a precedent to be followed. Both the House and the Senate had agreed to spend $30,000 for the pay of United States ministers to foreign nations. The conference committee nevertheless arbitrarily increased this sum to $40,000. In the decades that followed, conference committees similarly altered bills committed to their care, inevitably raising furors in both the Senate and the House, and sometimes even in the nation at large. These conference committees gradu-

401

ally were given greater and greater powers. By 1862, both the House and the Senate adopted the practice of passing entirely new bills as substitutes for the bills approved by the other chamber. This left the conferees free to write an entirely new bill in conference. Ten years earlier the conference committees were immensely strengthened by rulings that required the House and the Senate to accept or reject the conference agreements as a whole, without amendment. Thus the members of the Senate and the House had to accept amendments not wanted or kill the entire bill. Other rulings gave conference agreements on bills the highest legislative priority: they could be called up for floor action at any time. These great powers brought the charge that the conference committees constituted, in effect, a third house of Congress, more powerful than the other two. As early as the 1860's, Speaker Schuyler Colfax stated, the conference committees, not the House and Senate, determined the real substance of federal law. In 1883, a conference committee on a tariff bill, in a notable instance, radically altered many of the nation's tariff schedules in violation of the provisions of both the House and Senate bills. One change made by the conference committee brought the charge of unconstitutionality. Not until a conference committee in 1917 wrought a scandalous alteration in legislation committed to its members was a major limitation imposed on conference committees. That conference committee was considering differing versions of tax legislation. Only after both the House and the Senate had approved the committee's agreement was it discovered that the committee had actually added special provisions to the bill that exempted Senators and Representatives and all government employees from taxes on their salaries. The disclosure created a national sensation, and the following year the Senate adopted a rule that formally made such additions of new material to a bill by a conference committee a direct violation of Senate rules.

Over the years, conference committees have engaged in often epic struggles on bills committed to them. Sometimes the conference committees have been able, on noncontroversial bills, to complete their work within a few minutes. At other times the conference committees have met for weeks, day in, day out, trying to find common ground for agreement. Such a struggle took place, for example, on the enactment of the housing bill of 1937. Jesse Wolcott of Michigan, one of the House conferees, described the difficulty. "When I first came to Congress," he said, "I was told that all major legislation was a matter of compromise. I did not know quite what that meant until I took part in some conferences with the Senate on legislation. I did not fully realize what it meant until a conference on this bill, when, after spending eleven and a half hours yesterday giving and taking, adding and subtracting, sparring for advantage back and forth, we finally succeeded in coming to an agreement." [38] Sometimes the conferees lost their argument simply from sheer exhaustion. Carter Manasco of Alabama described such an instance in the conference on the surplus property bill of 1944. "For three weeks the conferees sat in session from ten o'clock in the morning until five-thirty and six o'clock every afternoon," Manasco said. "About nine o'clock Friday night the conferees reached an agreement. We did not want to stay in session all night. We realized that there were quite a few members who wanted to go home. . . . We thought that the bill as it passed the House was a much better bill than the bill we agreed to, but in three weeks' time, when you go up against men who have ideas different from your own, you finally get worn down. I have talked surplus property all day. . . . I am tired of it and I want to get rid of it." [39]

Senators, by virtue of the Senate's rules that have allowed filibustering, have often had a decided advantage in at least one aspect of House-Senate conferences: they have been able to fight successfully for or against special amendments or "pet" projects in these bills. The Senators have simply threatened to filibuster against the bill unless they have had their way. This was the threat Senator Ben Tillman made in 1903 that so angered Joseph Cannon of Illinois. Oscar Underwood of Alabama once described the difficulty of resisting such a threat in conference committees. "I have gone to the conference table with Senate amendments on many bills," Underwood said, "and convinced a conference—the representatives of the Senate in conference—that their amendments were wrong, and they would calmly tell me that they would not yield because a Senator So and So would talk the bill to death if I did not accept his amendment. And with great governmental issues at stake, I have been compelled to accept minor amendments to great bills that I will not say were graft, but they were put there for the purpose of magnifying the importance of one man with his constituency at the point of jeopardizing good legislation in America." [40] In 1938, Senator Royal Copeland of New York described how Senate conferees defeated a House amendment in a conference committee. "I told the House conferees," he said, "that some of the most able filibusterers in the Senate were so opposed to that amendment that we could not accept it, and it was stricken from the bill." [41] In 1962, Senator Frank Church of Idaho was running for re-election and he felt he could not afford politically to fail to win for his home state Congressional approval of funds for the $186 million Bruces Eddy dam. It had been added by the Senate to a House appropriations bill. "If they strike out Bruces Eddy," Church threatened the House-Senate conference committee, "I shall hold the Senate floor as long as God gives me the strength to stand." [42] The conference committee yielded to Church's threat and approved $2 million that year for the dam.

On occasion, the House's own leaders have deliberately maneuvered to help the House-Senate conference on a bill to overturn the decision of the House on a question these leaders believed of fundamental national importance. In recent years, this has been a common practice in handling the foreign-aid appropriations bill. Repeatedly the House Appropriations Committee has deeply cut the Administration's request for funds for this program. The House itself has normally sympathized with those cuts made by the committee, even though the House's formal leaders have tried to prevent them. With no real chance of persuading a majority of the House to reverse the Appropriations Committee decisions, the House's leaders have simply permitted the House to adopt those bills as amended without even trying to restore the funds denied by the committee. This has been part of an over-all strategy to regain at least some of those denied funds,

404

not an abject surrender by the House leaders. They have known that the Senate was much more sympathetic toward foreign aid than their House colleagues. Invariably, the Senate has increased the amount of money voted for foreign aid by the House. The strategy followed by the House leaders has been to allow the House-Senate conference committees the widest freedom in reaching an accord, hoping this accord would be more generous to foreign aid than the bill the House originally approved. With no formal record of the House's precise judgment on the various sections of the foreign-aid bill, the conferees automatically have had a freer hand in raising these amounts closer to the totals approved by the Senate. Thus, if the House leaders forced a vote, for example, on increasing the economic-aid section of the bill and been roundly defeated, the House conferees necessarily would have felt bound by that House vote to resist the Senate increase. They therefore would be much more reluctant to increase the money for economic aid in the conference. Even without specific votes by the House to challenge the cuts taken by the House Appropriations Committee, the House conferees—all chosen, of course, from the Appropriations Committee—have been exceedingly difficult to persuade to increase the dollars in these bills. The House conferees, normally led in recent years by Otto Passman of Louisiana, have instinctively felt hostile to foreign aid; repeatedly they have uncovered examples of wasted funds in this program and examples of administrative blundering. These have only increased their suspicions of the program itself, and those suspicions have made them harsh negotiators in conference with the Senate. In 1958, for instance, the House conferees stubbornly resisted adding as much to the foreign-aid bill as the Senate conferees wanted. Speaker Sam Rayburn pleaded personally with Passman to yield further to the Senate conferees than the $220 million Passman had offered as a compromise. "If they get $220 million, they'll be damn lucky," Passman said of the Senate conferees.[43] They can have the $220 million in a half hour, or they can get it in ten days." Faced with such an adamant opponent, the Senate conferees capitulated and accepted the additional $220 million.

In the course of every annual session of Congress, almost every major bill has had to pass the scrutiny of a House-Senate conference committee. Of the 936 bills enacted into law by the Eighty-fifth Congress, 1957-58, 106 went through conference, of which thirty-odd were appropriations bills. All were of major legislative governmental importance. The conference on these disputed bills often takes on significant institutional complexities involving the ancient rivalry for primacy between the House and the Senate. Frequently the members of the Senate, on disputed bills, have pleaded emotionally to their fellow Senators not to yield to the demands of the House. They have stated that the very prestige of the Senate was endangered. Members of the House have as frequently spoken of their fears for the prestige of the House if their conferees yielded to the demands of the Senate. Senator Theodore Francis Green of Rhode Island made one such an appeal to the Senate when he insisted that if the Senate yielded to a certain House amendment "we shall be groveling at the feet of the House of Representatives." [44] This was an argument obviously intended to excite Green's fellow Senators to resist the House amendment by appealing to their institutional sense of vanity. In 1939, Robert Rich of Pennsylvania made a like appeal to his House colleagues. "The question is, will the House continue to yield?" Rich said. "Will the House stiffen its backbone, or will you continue to be jelly-fish, wishy-washy representatives of the people or tweedledees or tweedledums?" [45]

In their struggles for primacy over national legislation and federal appropriations, the question has arisen: Which is stronger, the House or the Senate? The question has had no ready answer, and those seeking to answer it have not agreed. Roland Young, after long study of Congress, reported that Senators as a rule were "better bargainers than the Representatives in securing both appropriations and legislation." [46] That might be demonstrable over the long course of Congressional history, for contemporaries of the late nineteenth century and early twentieth appear agreed on the Senate's dominance of the conference committees. That, however, was before the House itself strengthened its appropriations conferees by the institutional changes made in 1920. That was also before the Senate lost most of its power over patronage and before its power over foreign affairs was seriously impaired by the modern substitution of economic and military programs for the traditional treaties. Gilbert Steiner in 1951 published his findings of the relative power between the Senate and the House in a remarkable book, *The Congressional Conference Committee*. Steiner carefully examined the Congressional consideration of fifty-six major pieces of legislation over a twenty-two year period, from 1927 through 1948. He found clear evidence that the House of Representatives held a "pronounced superiority" over the Senate on these bills. He found thirty-two instances, out of the fifty-six, in which "House influence dominated the final version of a bill." There were only fifteen instances in which the Senate's influence so predominated, and nine of the final bills Steiner judged were the product of mutual compromise. In every bill examined by Steiner that affected taxes or appropriations, the House's area of primary Constitutional jurisdiction, the House's views clearly dominated those of the Senate. On bills affecting fiscal policy, however, the views of the Senate largely predominated. The House also clearly dominated farm legislation. In summing up his findings, Steiner generalized that the House of Representatives, in contests with the Senate over legislation and appropriations, "is more likely to prevail."

There have been sound reasons why the House of Representatives should dominate the Senate in legislative and appropriations quarrels. As noted earlier in this book, the House for many decades has more intensely studied legislative problems and appropriations than the Senate. As early as the 1880's, Woodrow Wilson invidiously compared the Senate's relatively casual hearings on bills to the "painstaking" work of House committees. The result of the more exhaustive and careful hearings by the House has been to create genuine experts in the various fields of legislative concern. Men like Wilbur Mills of Arkansas and Gerald Ford of Michigan in the modern House of Representatives have spent almost their entire Congressional careers in deep study of specific fields of legislation and appropriations. The fact that the Senate has always had far fewer members than the House of

Representatives has always given the Senators a greater individual prestige over the rank-and-file members of the House. The very fewness of Senators, however, has handicapped the Senate as an institution in the legislative wars with the House of Representatives. In the House, all the major committees have been "exclusive." A Representative serving on an "exclusive" committee, like Ways and Means or Appropriations, has not been allowed to serve on any other House committee. That gave the Representative the opportunity at least to become an expert in the field of jurisdiction of his committee, by concentrating his energy and intelligence on that single field of legislation. In the Senate, no such arrangement has been possible, and every Senator— even the chairmen of powerful committees—have had to serve on at least two, and as many as six, committees. With his responsibilities and attention thus scattered, the individual Senator has often not even been able to attend regularly the committee hearings on important bills, no less keep up with the detailed study required to make him a legislative authority on any given bill. He had too many committees demanding his time and attention. When these Senators have presented themselves as managers for Senate bills in conference with the House managers for a rival bill, they frequently have discovered that they confronted arguments they could not answer, demonstrations they could not refute. They have not had the easy facility with their bills that permitted them to present their strong points, nor the expertness to show the weaknesses of House bills. The effect has often been to produce what Gilbert Steiner found: a pronounced superiority by the House in its quarrels with the Senate. The House conferees normally have known more about legislation at hand than their Senate counterparts and that has given them a greater opportunity to prevail.

"It's as simple as this," Thomas Curtis of Missouri explained. "They're trying to man the same positions with 100 men that we are with 435. They can't master the subjects. The House imposes its view on the Senate most of the time because the House knows more about most subjects than the Senate." [47]

This has been, this power of the House in contest with the

Senate, the solace of the Representatives who have had to submit to the greater political and social pretensions of Senators. They have often had to troop humbly across the Capitol to the Senate wing to confer with Senators, although in recent years this snobbish insistence of superiority by the Senators has been breaking down. In recent decades, all conferences on taxes, tariffs, and the other subjects under the jurisdiction of the Ways and Means Committee, have been held in the House wing of the Capitol. Other House-Senate conferees, like those on banking and currency questions, have been alternating between the House and Senate wings. Although the Representatives have had to take second place to Senators in the public's opinion of their worth, they could claim, however, with justice that the House of Representatives dominated the nation's legislative processes, that the House stamped its impress on national law to a far greater degree than did the Senate, that the House gave talented Representatives with the willingness to work almost unlimited opportunity to shape and direct the course of American history. Those who left the House for seats in the Senate, those who remained behind could say, sought the greater personal prestige that the office of Senator automatically offered. Those who remained behind, however, could also say that they preferred the near anonymity of the House of Representatives and control of its great political power.

CHAPTER FIFTEEN

The Ordeal of Decision

OVER its long history, the House of Representatives has periodically been convulsed by mighty struggles that have wrenched
apart the orderly routine of its ways and tested the mettle of
every member. Wars and the threats of wars, and the House's
response to them, have divided the House and the country at
large. Elemental political questions of gravest consequence—
three times the House has been confronted with crises on the election of a President—have driven the Representatives into angry
and partisan quarrels. Great social questions, profoundly acer-
bating racial, religious, and ethnic disagreements, have had to be
faced, however violent the antagonists became. From the beginning, the nature of the federal government's intrusion into the
nation's economic life has harassed and often perplexed the
members of the House, dividing them in modern times in struggles over labor law and welfare legislation much as they were
divided in the 1790's by Alexander Hamilton's proposals to
establish the fiscal credit of the United States.

These legislative battles, reflecting as they did great divisions
in the American people, have helped shape the course of American history. They have been fought with great verve and determination, and at times with great bitterness, by the contending
forces. Their outcomes have determined American law, and

American law in large measure has determined the character of the nation. There was cause for the ferocity of these conflicts, for their significance to the country was transparent. Perhaps not so transparent have been the consequences of the battles, often fought with even more bitterness, over the rules and procedures that have governed the House's own inner operations. On the surface, these quarrels have seemed to involve merely technical problems, scarcely of a character to be compared with the great national questions of taxation, appropriations, and other fundamental law. Yet the House's consideration of these parliamentary questions has been marked with a violence often unequaled in its legislative contests. The early conflicts over filibustering, the imposition of stringent limits on debate, the near rioting against Speaker Reed's revolutionary rulings, and the great revolt against Speaker Cannon, all were crises for the House of Representatives. All went to the heart of the House of Representatives as a political institution—and all had a profound and enduring effect on American law, for they deeply influenced the House's essential role in writing that law. In the throes of these crises, as in the struggles over basic law, the members of the House have undergone an ordeal of pressure politics, parliamentary maneuver, and intrigue that pitted the ablest strategists of the House against each other.

In the pages to follow here, one such struggle—the conflict in 1961 over the Rules Committee—has been described. Superficially, the Representatives seemed to be quarreling about next to nothing: the membership of the committee. In reality, however, the question raised had grave import for the House and for the United States. The House's answer to it affected the tenuous balance of power between the great conservative and liberal blocs within the House. And, doing so, the House's answer seriously affected the response of Congress to the sweeping legislative proposals of the newly elected President, John Kennedy. Not all parliamentary fights in the House have had this double incitement for high passion, and no struggle in the House has ever exactly duplicated any other. This contest has been chosen to illustrate the processes by which the House of Representatives has made its decisions.

On Saturday afternoon, December 31, 1960, Sam Rayburn of Texas returned to Washington to prepare for the opening of the new Congress, the Eighty-seventh, on the following Tuesday. This was to be for Rayburn his forty-ninth year as a member of the House of Representatives and his seventeenth year as Speaker of the House. He arrived in Washington just a week before his seventy-ninth birthday. Deeply weighing on his mind lay a political crisis that was to erupt over the weeks that followed into a momentous struggle for control of the House of Representatives.

In Palm Beach, Florida, the President-elect of the United States, John Kennedy, was still feverishly putting together the administration he was to bring to power when he took the oath of office on January 20. Rayburn, only ten days before, had flown to Palm Beach to visit Kennedy and to discuss candidly with him the difficulties confronting them both in the House of Representatives.

Their difficulties were more complex and subtle than a glance at the political labels of the new Representatives would have suggested. The new House contained 261 Democrats and 174 Republicans, a massive Democratic majority for the new Democratic President. Those party labels, however, did not give the orientation of these Representatives in the political spectrum. Most of the ninety-nine Democrats from the Southern States were conservatives, as were almost all of the 174 Republicans. They formed an actual majority hostile to the liberal legislative program that Presidential candidate John Kennedy had pledged, if elected, to enact. More than that, the conservatives in the House controlled the Rules Committee, which held primary jurisdiction over the House's legislative agenda. Under the chairmanship of Howard Smith of Virginia, titular leader of the Southern conservatives, the Rules Committee posed a portentous threat to the Kennedy administration's entire legislative program; for the committee held broad discretionary power to decide what legislation could go to the House floor for a vote by the Representatives. Ostensibly, the Rules Committee was committed to the Democratic party. Eight of its twelve members were Democrats. Two of these, however, "Judge" Smith of Virginia and William Colmer of Mississippi, were conservatives, opposed in principle to just about every item of the Kennedy welfare and economic program. In the 1960 election, Smith had not endorsed Kennedy, and Colmer had actually supported a rival slate of independent Presidential electors in Mississippi. Colmer, indeed, with three other Mississippi Democrats in the House, had helped prevent Kennedy from receiving the eight electoral votes of Mississippi. Smith and Colmer normally joined the four Republican members of the Rules Committee in opposition to all welfare legislation. The other six Democratic committee members—Ray Madden of Indiana, James Delaney of New York, James Trimble of Arkansas, Homer Thornberry of Texas, Richard Bolling of Missouri, and Thomas O'Neill of Massachusetts—normally supported such legislation. This equal philosophical division of the committee members on economic questions resulted usually in tie votes, six to six. Without the assent of a clear majority of the committee, no major bill could be sent to the House floor for action under the House's normal procedures. Not only that, but "Judge" Smith as committee chairman had his own discretionary powers. He possessed nearly arbitrary power, for example, over the committee's agenda, determining which bills to call up for committee discussion. He had also great power in deciding when the committee should meet, or even whether the committee met at all. The total effect was to give Smith and the committee's conservatives the means to thwart almost any legislation they chose.

For Sam Rayburn, the hostility of the Rules Committee to the progressive legislation he favored was no new thing. The very year he first became Democratic floor leader—1937—the committee had gone into revolt against the New Deal legislation of Franklin Roosevelt. Rayburn had been a member of the House since 1913, and he had seen the obstruction of Rules Committee chairmen Philip Campbell and Bertrand Snell in the 1920's. He had participated, over the years, in various attempts to restrain

413

the arbitrary powers of the committee, and, as Speaker, he had long been forced to negotiate with the Rules Committee chairmen and its members to arrange for at least some of the bills he wanted to be cleared for floor action. For Rayburn, these negotiations had never been entirely satisfactory, nor had they been for the Democratic liberals, for inevitably at least some of the major bills had to be surrendered as ransom for the others.

Only two years before, as the Congress was about to convene in January, 1959, Rayburn had pledged to the liberals in his party that he would not permit "Judge" Smith and the Rules Committee to block the welfare legislation they wanted to pass. The Rules Committee had stymied most of the important Democratic bills, however, and Rayburn had been humiliated by his inability to fulfill his pledge. At a meeting of the Rules Committee in August, 1960, Ray Madden of Indiana and Thomas O'Neill of Massachusetts tried hard to force Smith to release all the Democratic bills then pending before the Rules Committee. Smith refused. "The only legislation I will agree to consider," he said, "is the minimum-wage bill. You can tell your liberal friends that they will get that—or nothing. If you try to bring up anything else, I'll adjourn the meeting." [1]

Even before the 1960 Congressional session ended, the Democratic liberals began to prepare for a full-scale assault on the Rules Committee. The conservatives and the liberals had already deeply polarized their views of the committee. By June, 1960, the disagreement was clearly irreconcilable. "These radicals are bad enough now," said a Republican leader in the House, "but without the Rules Committee to throw a few road blocks they'd be uncontrollable." Edith Green of Oregon, a supporter of the school-construction bill, had precisely an opposite view. "Here we are in the third year of the space age," she said, "and the Rules Committee goes on record against increasing man's knowledge." Chet Holifield of California, Frank Thompson of New Jersey, Stewart Udall of Arizona, and Richard Bolling of Missouri began a series of strategy meetings. In early July, they were already discussing the available alternatives for action against the Rules Committee when the Eighty-seventh Congress convened in Jan-

414

uary, 1961. They wanted to take control of the Rules Committee to help enact their own liberal program. Bolling, who was to become one of the liberals' chief strategists in the coming fight, was a member of the Rules Committee who well knew the difference between controlling the committee and having it controlled by the opposition. "It's the difference," he said, "between pushing a car uphill and stepping on the gas on a straightaway." The liberals' strategy encompassed more this summer than merely talking about the reforms they might advocate for the Rules Committee the following January. They began in earnest to build even then a powerful coalition of outside interests to help them fight for the reforms they wanted. The committee had alienated many significant political pressure groups by its hostility to the liberals' bills. The liberals, led by Bolling, informed each of these groups why the legislation they wanted had been hampered or killed in the House: it was the fault of the Rules Committee. More than that, the liberals brought forward several less important bills to the Rules Committee, not so much to try to get them cleared for the House floor as to have the conservatives on the Rules Committee veto them and thus alienate those interested groups, too. This was a tactic to enlist new allies in the fight. Thus used were such measures as a fair-trade practices bill and a library-services bill. Bolling, as a member of the Rules Committee, handled this strategy. Thompson, who had been one of Senator John Kennedy's earliest supporters for President, meanwhile adopted for use in the House of Representatives a campaign technique used by Kennedy's forces at the Democratic National Convention in Los Angeles to capture the votes of convention delegates. This was a card catalogue on every delegate to the convention. Each card systematically bore pertinent information about each delegate. Thompson and the staff of the Democratic Study Group began the tedious chore of preparing similar cards on the members of the House of Representatives. These cards, measuring three by five inches, contained the Representative's name and Congressional district, his wife's name, his college, his profession, his family relations and the family relations of his wife, his hobbies, and any other information that might prove useful. The

415

concept behind the compiling of these cards was simply to collect as much information about each Representative as possible. The cards would tell, when the time came, who best could influence each and every member of the House of Representatives on how to cast his vote.

"Everyone around here is reachable," Frank Thompson said. "All you have to do is find out how."

November 8, 1960, election day, came and went, and John Kennedy and a Democratic House of Representatives were elected. The new House was to have 261 Democrats and 174 Republicans. The Democrats had lost a score of their members, mostly from the North, and this had almost imperceptibly shifted the political bent of the House. The Eighty-sixth House had been marginally liberal; the Eighty-seventh would be marginally conservative. That meant not only that the liberals would have a far more formidable task in enacting the programs that Kennedy had pledged in his campaign; it also meant that it would be far more difficult for them to seize control of the Rules Committee. Bolling had conferred at length with Kennedy during the campaign on the problems Kennedy would face with the Rules Committee if he were elected President. He reiterated those explanations to Kennedy and Kennedy's brother Robert after the election.

A few days after the election, the liberal leaders passed the word that they planned to capture control of the Rules Committee by "purging" William Colmer of Mississippi from the committee. That would eliminate one conservative from the committee and break the "tie" between liberals and conservatives on the committee that had so long stymied liberal legislation. The excuse for purging Colmer, a Democrat, was that he had "disloyally" opposed Kennedy's election as President and had supported insurgent Democratic Presidential electors. The reason for purging him was to take control of the committee and by the least controversial method. To remove Colmer from the committee would require, ostensibly, only a favorable vote by the Democratic House caucus; it could be restricted to a Democratic party question in the House. To change the rules of the House

416

would require a vote of the entire House, Republicans as well as Democrats.

Right after the election, the leaders of the conservatives in the House began to maneuver to head off the gathering liberal assault. On the Friday after the Tuesday election, "Judge" Smith announced that he would fight any attempt to change the Rules Committee. The committee, he said, was "all right as it is." Besides, he argued, the conservative control of the committee matched the views of the new House of Representatives that had just been elected. "The new House," he said, "will be more conservative than the House elected in 1958." Two weeks later, Smith came to Washington to confer with Charles Halleck of Indiana, the Republican floor leader. Attending the conference was William Colmer, the principal target of the liberals' attack. The meeting was devoted to preliminary preparations for the conservative coalition in the fight over the Rules Committee. Halleck declined to reveal at the time the details of the discussion. "We've seen eye to eye in the past," Halleck said, "and I expect we'll see eye to eye in the future."

For a month, both sides worked anxiously to build their strength for the coming power struggle. The Democratic Study Group staff, under the direction of William Phillips, had already compiled a series of monographs on the Rules Committee. They included a fourteen-page analysis of proposals to "overcome legislative obstruction by the Rules Committee," a thirteen-page paper on opposition in the House to altering the House rules, and a six-page paper on the "refusal of a committee post for party disloyalty." These papers were distributed to members of the House to make the liberals' argument. Thompson flew to Palm Beach to brief the President-elect on the maneuvers of the Democratic liberals. "Judge" Smith's House lieutenants, meanwhile, began to poll the members of the House on how they stood on the question of altering the Rules Committee. Word came to Washington that Kennedy favored purging Colmer from the committee. Burr Harrison of Virginia, one of Smith's ablest supporters, reported that seventy-two of the ninety-nine Southern Democrats in the House had given pledges to stand by Smith in any fight. On December 30, in Washington, thirty-four members of the Democratic Study Group, the liberal bloc, caucused and then issued a statement that it was an "absolute necessity" to break the conservatives' control of the Rules Committee. The liberal caucus appointed three of its members, Chet Holifield of California, Frank Thompson of New Jersey, and John Blatnik of Minnesota, as a committee to meet with Speaker Rayburn as soon as they could secure an interview. Rayburn returned to Washington the next afternoon, and the drama of a great internal fight in the House, one that was to be a severe trial for just about every Representative, began to unfold. It would not be resolved until exactly one month later.

Rayburn returned to Washington determined to alter the Rules Committee, to take arbitrary control of it away from "Judge" Smith. He had so pledged to President-elect Kennedy at their meeting in Palm Beach. Rayburn, however, had not decided what means he could use. That he had to act, he did not doubt. The previous session of Congress had convinced him that he could no longer depend on his annual negotiations with Smith to clear bills for floor action. Rayburn had another reason for deciding to act against the Rules Committee: without such action, the legislative hopes of the young Democratic President would be wrecked by the certain obstruction of Smith's committee. Rayburn had known Kennedy casually when Kennedy had been a member of the House from 1947 to 1953. The Speaker had supported Senator Lyndon Johnson of Texas for the Democratic Presidential nomination, but he had campaigned hard for Kennedy when Kennedy had been nominated. Rayburn had held one conference with Kennedy during the campaign; he had conferred again with him in Palm Beach. Earlier Kennedy had seemed too young to Rayburn to be President, but the two conferences with Kennedy had altered his view. Rayburn had been deeply impressed. Later, when Kennedy took the oath of President on the Capitol steps, Rayburn had been captivated by Kennedy's inaugural address. Its eloquence surpassed, said Rayburn, the inaugural addresses of Franklin Roosevelt and even of Abraham

418

Lincoln. "He's a man of destiny," Rayburn said of Kennedy. Rayburn intended to help him enact his program.

On Sunday, January 1, 1961, Rayburn invited Smith to call on him in his office in the empty Capitol. Smith came and the two old antagonists talked earnestly for two hours about the Rules Committee. Rayburn did not suggest that Colmer be purged from the committee. Instead, he asked Smith to agree to add three new members to the Rules Committee. Two of the three would be Democrats, and one of those would be a Southerner. Smith knew perfectly well that Rayburn's suggested change of the committee would swing the balance of the committee to the liberal cause. Not even the appointment of a Southerner would help, for Rayburn would pick a Southerner who was an economic liberal, perhaps one of Alabama's liberal Representatives. Smith flatly rejected Rayburn's proposal; he would agree to nothing that would strip him of his power over the Rules Committee.

On the same day, Speaker Rayburn also met with Bolling and Thompson. Bolling, one of Rayburn's intimates, and Thompson argued the liberals' cause, and told Rayburn of the work they had already done. They both knew that the liberals could not win a House fight of this kind, unless Rayburn backed their cause. They told him, nevertheless, that the Democratic liberals intended to fight it out with the conservatives over the Rules Committee even if Rayburn decided to do nothing. Too many of the liberals, said Bolling, had committed themselves too far to back off now.

On Monday, January 2, Rayburn called a conference at his Capitol office to let the liberals and his own party leaders know his decision. Attending the session were John McCormack of Massachusetts, then majority leader; Carl Albert of Oklahoma, then majority whip; Bolling, and the three-man committee from the liberal Democratic bloc: Holifield, Thompson, and Blatnik. They met at nine o'clock in the morning, and the conference took less than a half hour. Rayburn told the six men he had summoned, all Democratic liberals, that he had decided to purge Colmer from the committee for his "disloyalty" to the Democratic party in the 1960 Presidential election.

Rayburn's decision was precisely the one the Democratic liberals wanted. They wanted to punish Colmer, to make an example of him to other Southern Democrats who had, since 1948, been straying from the party's folds in Presidential campaigns. Yet the precedents for punishing Colmer were weak. The most recent example of such discipline that even the Democratic Study Group could cite had been in 1925. Then the Republican regulars, under Speaker Nicholas Longworth, had deprived thirteen Republicans of their committee posts for supporting Robert La Follette's Presidential candidacy. In 1948, thirty Southern Democratic Representatives had supported Strom Thurmond's Presidential candidacy. They had gone unpunished. So had the Southern Democrats who had bolted against Adlai Stevenson in 1952 and 1956. In 1956, Adam Clayton Powell of New York, a Democrat, had openly supported Dwight Eisenhower for President; and he had not been punished, either. The failure previously to punish members for party disloyalty in effect had condoned their action. Besides, until now Rayburn had always taken the position that a Representative's party loyalty in the House of Representatives was determined solely by his vote in the House for the election of a Speaker. If he voted for the Democratic candidate for Speaker, he automatically was a Democrat. If he voted for the Republican candidate, he was a Republican. It did not matter what he had done or how he had been designated in the election campaign.

Rayburn's decision to purge Colmer reversed his long-standing position on the question of party loyalty. This was unlike Speaker Rayburn. Besides, he normally shrank from punishing Democratic Representatives whatever their offenses. In 1958, Thomas Lane of Massachusetts had been sent to prison for a federal income-tax offense: he was re-elected that year and Rayburn ignored the federal crime, permitting Lane to resume his position on the House Judiciary Committee. Rayburn took the position that this was not a question to be noticed by the House; it was a question only for the voters in Lane's Congressional district. Not only did it appear unlike Rayburn to change his mind on so important a question, it also conflicted with Rayburn's real desire to resolve the problem of controlling the Rules Committee by simply increasing its membership. This was his original position, the one he tried to persuade "Judge" Smith to accept just the day before. To those intimate with Rayburn and privy to his methods of operation, there appeared firm evidence that the Speaker was executing a skillful maneuver to crack the resistance of the Southern conservatives. Rayburn kept his own counsel. Richard Bolling, a Rayburn intimate, however, doubted that Rayburn intended to carry the threatened purge of Colmer to fulfillment. "We are still open to an accommodation," Bolling said privately, on the day Rayburn let known his decision. "We are not bloodthirsty."

Although Rayburn had enjoined secrecy on those attending the Monday morning conference with him, it was only a matter of hours before Rayburn's decision had been leaked to the newspapers. By midafternoon, the decision was known all over Capitol Hill. It had a shock effect on many members of the House, particularly those with great seniority. Rayburn's decision, in one sense, undercut the House's revered seniority system. If a Representative could be punished this way for an "offense" committed outside the House, no member with seniority was safe. When Clarence Cannon of Missouri that afternoon heard Rayburn's decision, he was enraged. Cannon was chairman of the Appropriations Committee, a conservative Democrat, and, with thirty-eight consecutive years of service in the House, he was third in seniority only to Rayburn and Carl Vinson of Georgia. He rushed to Rayburn's office to denounce the decision to Rayburn. Vinson also was deeply disturbed by Rayburn's decision: he was chairman of the Armed Services Committee with forty-six years of seniority. So was Francis "Tad" Walter of Pennsylvania, chairman of the House Un-American Activities Committee with twenty-eight years' seniority. Both were influential men in the House. Vinson ranked unofficially as second to "Judge" Smith in command of the Southern Democratic conservatives. Walter, although from Pennsylvania, had the respect of the Southern delegations in the House. Cannon and Vinson both had important additional reasons for wanting to dissuade Rayburn from following through on his decision to remove Colmer from the Rules Committee. Colmer had not been alone among the Mississippi

Democrats to campaign against John Kennedy. There were three others: John Bell Williams, Jamie Whitten, and Arthur Winstead. Whitten was a member of Cannon's Appropriations Committee and chairman of an appropriations subcommittee. Winstead was a high-ranking member of Vinson's Armed Services Committee. If Colmer was to be denied his membership on the Rules Committee, Winstead, Whitten, and Williams could not be excused for the same offense. Neither Cannon nor Vinson wanted his committee raided.

Speaker Rayburn listened to the protests from his most senior colleagues, but gave no indication that he did not intend to drive Colmer from the Rules Committee. He waited for "Judge" Smith to come to him to offer terms of settlement. To allow time for this, Wilbur Mills of Arkansas played a crucial role. Mills, as chairman of the Ways and Means Committee, was automatically the chairman of the Democratic Committee on Committees. It was that committee's task at the beginning of each new Congress to assign every Democrat in the House to a committee. It would be the job of Mills's Committee on Committees to remove Colmer from the Rules Committee, if he were indeed removed. Discreetly, Mills declined to call the Committee on Committees into session. He wanted to allow a "cooling off" period in which Rayburn and Smith could reach an accommodation. Mills, a practiced hand in power-bloc negotiations, knew that Rayburn's lieutenants and Smith's lieutenants would be working hard for a compromise less harsh on individual members of the House and less dangerous to the House's system of seniority. These lieutenants and the senior men of the House like Vinson, Cannon, and Walter would act as mediators between the two Democratic camps. In this stage of the struggle for control of the Rules Committee, there was no function for the members of the Democratic Study Group, the liberal bloc, to perform. They simply had to wait for the outcome of the negotiations between Rayburn and Smith and be ready for the next round of the fight.

Rayburn had well chosen his ground. In deciding to purge Colmer, he had confined the quarrel to the Democratic ranks in the House. By long tradition, each party in the House had the right to fill its own committee assignments. The other party had no right to interfere in the selections. Rayburn, by choosing to purge Colmer, eliminated the Republicans from the decision. "Judge" Smith's power depended on the united conservative coalition, the Republicans and Southern Democrats. He had no chance of controlling the decisions of the Democrats in the House. Rayburn was supreme there. Of the 261 Democrats in the House, only seventy-two—all Southerners—were committed to Smith's position. With no chance of victory in the caucus for the Southern conservatives, Rayburn had only to wait for Smith's Southern bloc to crack.

For a full week, Smith ignored Rayburn entirely. He did not so much as deign to call on the Speaker. The House had formally reconvened on January 3 and Rayburn had been formally elected, for the tenth time, as Speaker of the House. Smith consulted with many of his Southern allies, and Rayburn consulted with his lieutenants, but neither made the slightest gesture to the other at an accommodation. Several of Smith's lieutenants, however, tried to act as intermediaries. One told Rayburn that he thought Smith might be willing to make a token concession to the Speaker, in deference to party harmony. Smith might accept a new House rule that would withdraw the Rules Committee's control over sending bills to conference with the Senate. Another reported to Rayburn that Smith might be willing to make a gentleman's agreement to clear five of President Kennedy's major bills for floor action. The intermediaries insisted that they did not speak for "Judge" Smith, that they merely thought Smith might accept such terms. It made no difference; Rayburn rejected them out of hand and insisted that he intended to purge Colmer from the Rules Committee. Smith's lieutenants spent a week testing Rayburn's resolve, and Rayburn did not budge. Instead, Rayburn let slip the word that not only Colmer would be purged; so would the other three Mississippians who had bolted the Democratic party in 1960, Williams, Winstead, and Whitten.

"Judge" Smith could hold off no longer. His own Southern ranks were wavering under this severe threat Rayburn had made to the seniority system, the seniority system that for generations

423

had given Southern Representatives their committee chairman-ships and principal power in the House of Representatives. On Monday afternoon, January 9, Smith took the elevator down one flight from his gallery-level office in the Capitol and walked into the Speaker's office. In a forty-minute conference, Smith formally offered to give his pledge that he would clear five major Kennedy bills for House passage and would also surrender the Rules Committee's control over sending House bills to conference with the Senate. Under the circumstances, these were but token concessions from Smith. Rayburn knew that President Kennedy would have far more than five major bills he wanted passed in 1961, and there would be other bills in the years that followed. Rayburn also knew that Smith was in danger of losing control of the Southern conservatives. He rejected Smith's offer and insisted that either Colmer be removed from the committee or that the committee's membership be enlarged. Either would cost Smith his control of the committee. Smith refused to agree to either the purging of Colmer or the "packing," as he called it, of his committee. A Rayburn lieutenant tried to shake Smith's adamant position. "Judge," he said, "be reasonable."

Smith would not yield. "No purgin'," he said, "no packin'."

When Smith left Rayburn's office without reaching agreement with the Speaker, he lost control of his Southern conservatives. Vinson, known as the "Old Swamp Fox" in the House for his tactical skill, had tried to work out an accommodation with Rayburn for Smith. Now he acted to save the situation for the Southerners most concerned about endangering the seniority system in the House. For Vinson, Smith's failure to find a compromise with Rayburn decided the issue at hand: the conservatives had lost control of the Rules Committee. Rayburn not only had the votes in Mills's Committee on Committees to force Colmer's removal, he also had the votes to do so in the Democratic caucus, which had to ratify the action of the Committee on Committees. The fight was lost; now Vinson, as second in command of the Southern conservatives, acted to change the terms of surrender. Rayburn had shown plainly in his January 1 conference with Smith that he really wanted to increase the Rules Committee's membership, not to purge anybody, and Vinson maneuvered to have Rayburn return to his original position. To do so, Vinson had to be able to assure Rayburn that enough Southern Democrats would vote for this change to make certain of its adoption by the House. Vinson called a caucus of the Southern conservatives for Tuesday afternoon, January 10.

Vinson acted with unusual discretion in summoning this caucus of Southern conservatives. He invited only some of the Southern Democrats; he excluded those known to be supporting Rayburn and others whose allegiance was in doubt. The Southerners had a severe security problem, and he restricted those invited to try to keep the proceedings secret. Both the liberal and the conservative camps had infiltrated each other's ranks with Representatives acting as espionage agents. There were several such agents of the liberals in the ranks of the Southern Democrats. The question of security was significant to both sides, for neither wanted their plans betrayed to the opposition. A security breach could undermine the most carefully calculated plans. Despite Vinson's precautions—he had limited the caucus to less than half of the Southern Democrats—the meeting was penetrated by the Southern agents of the liberal camp. Shortly after the caucus had ended, two Southern Representatives telephoned full reports of the session to one of the leaders of the liberal Democratic camp. The information thus reported was relayed to Rayburn.

The Southern caucus was attended by "Judge" Smith and a scattering of Representatives from Virginia, North Carolina, South Carolina, Mississippi, Georgia, Texas, and some of the other Southern states. Vinson told the assembly that the fight to keep the Rules Committee in the hands of the conservatives had been lost. They could not defeat Rayburn's plan to purge Colmer. Olin Teague of Texas supported Vinson's position at the meeting, and Vinson urged the members that they try to settle the quarrel on Rayburn's original terms of enlarging the Rules Committee's membership. That alone would spare Colmer and a breach in the seniority system. Smith adamantly refused to agree to Vinson's argument, even though it was obvious that he no

425

longer could hold the support of the seventy-two Southerners committed to him.

Rayburn had won on the terms that he had wanted: he had cracked the South's resistance to his seizing control of the Rules Committee from the conservative coalition. Vinson had joined Rayburn and could, he believed, assure Rayburn adequate Southern votes to enlarge the Rules Committee. He had carried with him, according to the immediate estimates, about half of "Judge" Smith's hard-core Southern conservatives. With this assurance in hand, Rayburn confidently altered his announced plan. He would not press for Colmer's ouster from the Rules Committee. He called a special news conference and made that announcement on Wednesday afternoon, January 11. "I decided," he said, "that the painless way and the way to embarrass nobody who didn't want to be embarrassed was to raise the committee from twelve to fifteen." He scheduled a special party caucus for the following week to instruct the Democratic members of the Rules Committee to send to the House floor the necessary resolution to increase the committee's membership by three.

During this period and for another week, the Republicans in the House could do nothing. Rayburn had, up to this point, confined the argument and the fight within the Democratic party by proposing to purge Colmer from the committee. Charles Halleck of Indiana was unable to act; he could not help his ally "Judge" Smith, for Colmer's was a committee assignment question that only the Democrats could decide. The Republican rank-and-file members were divided. The hard-core conservatives were angered by this attempt by Rayburn to seize control of the Rules Committee, long a bastion of the conservatives in the House. Other conservative Republicans argued they had no right to interfere in this Democratic quarrel. The small contingent of Republican progressives wanted Rayburn to take over the committee, by whatever method he chose. Joseph Martin of Massachusetts, the Republican leader before Halleck, openly acknowledged that he supported Rayburn's decision to remove Colmer or to increase the size of the committee. Martin denied that he had taken this position out of vengeance against Halleck, who two years earlier had defeated Martin for the Republican leadership. Martin had been getting particular attention from John McCormack of Massachusetts, the Democratic floor leader. McCormack maneuvered to split the Republicans by persuading Martin to support Rayburn in the fight over the Rules Committee. Martin had made up his mind to do so, and this still further strengthened Rayburn's position.

The Democratic caucus was held Wednesday morning, January 18, two days before John Kennedy was to take the oath as President. On Tuesday afternoon, the members of the Democratic Study Group held their own caucus. They had no choice but to support Rayburn's change of plan.

Rayburn clearly had the votes to win, and he acted to temper the hostilities that had been bred in his party by the quarrel over the Rules Committee. "I have no room for hate," he told his fellow Democrats at the caucus. "I have no malice in my heart." He told them that he would ask them to purge no one, and that he had no intention of "stacking" any House committee. He then asked them to instruct the Democratic members of the Rules Committee to report to the House floor a resolution to increase that committee's membership to fifteen. "Judge" Smith followed Rayburn and he acknowledged that he had no chance of defeating the Speaker's motion. "I went to school in a little red school house," Smith told his colleagues, "and I learned how to count. And I have never forgotten how." Smith thus acknowledged that he could not defeat Rayburn in the Democratic caucus, and he asked Rayburn to withdraw from his motion the "instructions" to the Rules Committee to report the resolution to the House floor. He wanted to be spared the humiliation of being ordered to act by the caucus. "It will be reported," said Smith. "I give you my word. . . . I will fight it on the floor." McCormack quickly accepted Smith's request. "Any time the gentleman from Virginia gives his word," McCormack said, "I accept it as his bond." With a great shout the assembled Democrats approved the proposal to increase the Rules Committee's membership.

That seemed to end the conflict over the committee and its control. Rayburn had won. This, however, was merely a lull before an even greater storm in the House of Representatives. Up to this point, the House Republicans had not been able to take part in the struggle. Halleck had met with the Republican Policy Committee on Friday, January 13, to discuss the question; the party leaders at that time had decided to do nothing until after the Democratic caucus. The Democratic party's decision to increase the size of the Rules Committee had radically altered the political situation. This was a question to be decided by the House itself, for it meant a change in the House rules, and not just an intraparty decision for the Democrats. The Republicans were now free to join the fight, and the day after the Democratic caucus, January 19, Halleck again met with the Republican Policy Committee. The chief Republican leaders—Halleck, Leslie Arends of Illinois, the party whip, Clarence Brown of Ohio, the ranking Republican member of the Rules Committee, and John Byrnes of Wisconsin, chairman of the Policy Committee—were agreed on their course of action: they would join "Judge" Smith's flagging cause. Unanimously, the thirty-four members of the Policy Committee endorsed their leaders' decision and approved this resolution: "Be it resolved that the Policy Committee go on record in opposition to the proposed packing of the Rules Committee." Byrnes spoke for the Republican leadership when he said that Rayburn's proposal smacked of Franklin Roosevelt's "packing plan" for the Supreme Court in 1937. He said the Republicans would fight to prevent Congress from becoming a "rubber stamp" for President Kennedy or an "annex" of the White House. "Republicans," he said, "will always fight to preserve the integrity of the Congress."

The Republican leaders, even as they entered the fight, doubted that they had any chance of winning. "Mr. Sam wouldn't move this way without the votes," one of the House Republican leaders said. "We assume he has the votes." This assumption was based on their belief that Carl Vinson of Georgia had pulled about half of the Southern conservatives away from Smith and handed them to Rayburn. Rayburn could not have been stopped from purging Colmer from the committee; the Republicans in the House assumed he still could not be blocked. Even so, however,

428

they believed they owed it to their own best interests to make the attempt. In this attempt, they had their own insurgents to worry about, for not all the Republicans opposed giving control of the Rules Committee to Rayburn. These were almost entirely Republican progressives who had disliked the Rules Committee's past actions in blocking progressive legislation. Republicans like John Lindsay of New York and James Fulton of Pennsylvania refused to follow the Republican leaders in opposition to the Rayburn proposal. Lindsay said that "conscience and common sense" should keep the Republicans from coalescing with the Southern Democrats of "Judge" Smith. Thomas Curtis of Missouri, a Republican, took a different position; he believed that the Democrats had cynically created a "phony" issue over the Rules Committee which, he said in an almost unique interpretation of that committee's function, "does not possess the power and has not possessed the power to keep legislation off the floor of the House."

All during this period, the lobbyists had been at work. They split over the question of controlling the Rules Committee just as did the conservatives and liberals in the House. The great conservative lobbies—the American Farm Bureau Federation, the U.S. Chamber of Commerce, the National Association of Manufacturers—clearly recognized the danger to their own legislative interests if the Rules Committee were to be made responsive to Rayburn and the Kennedy administration. The great liberal lobbies—the AFL-CIO, its member unions, the National Education Association—recognized as well the danger to themselves if the Rules Committee were left in the hands of the conservative coalition. Both camps signaled their field offices to send a gigantic flood of mail and telegrams to the members of the House. The conservative lobbyists normally have the advantage in these mail campaigns; their members traditionally have responded more readily to such appeals than the members of labor unions. Bolling and the liberal strategists, however, had long before made plans to arouse the liberal groups for this fight. They not only received the normal response from labor unions; they also had the mayors of cities, schoolteachers, and all the other groups interested in progressive legislation excited about the outcome. The response to the conservative lobbyists' appeals stung Sam Rayburn. Telegrams poured into the House Office buildings, many of them simply reading: "Don't pack the Rules Committee." Rayburn argued to his Democrats that most of them came from Republicans. "Eighty per cent of them come from people who voted for Richard Nixon," he said. Rayburn feared that these telegrams and letters would frighten Southern Democrats into opposing the change in the Rules Committee.

Once Vinson broke with "Judge" Smith, Rayburn felt confident of winning the parliamentary fight. The switch of Rayburn's tactics—from purging Colmer to increasing the membership of the committee—had an unforeseen result, however. Not only did Halleck and his conservative Republicans now join in the fight, but the Southerners Vinson pledged to Rayburn drifted away. During the week end after Kennedy's inauguration, the strategists for the conservative coalition compared notes. Smith's lieutenants rechecked the Southern delegations and discovered that Vinson had not dealt Smith as mortal a blow as had been feared. They counted sixty-seven Southerners who still favored Smith's cause. Smith and his lieutenants relayed this information to the Republican high command of Charles Halleck and Leslie Arends. Smith conceded, however, that he was not entirely certain of all sixty-seven. "They claim sixty-one of these are signed in blood," Arends said at the time. Halleck and Arends were counting their own ranks. They calculated that they could not lose more than 24 of the 174 Republicans in the House. That meant they had at least 150 Republicans ready to support Smith against Rayburn, and these added to Smith's 67 Southerners could total 217 votes—just one shy of a Constitutional majority of the House. Admittedly, the conservative coalition's calculations were somewhat uncertain, but even so the conservatives obviously had a real chance yet to keep control of the Rules Committee.

On Monday, when he returned to the House, Rayburn realized the sudden change. Where Halleck and his Republicans had assumed they were backing a lost cause on the previous Thursday, they now sensed victory. Rayburn and his lieutenants discovered not only that most of the Southern votes that Vinson had promised had vanished, but also that some of the border-state Democrats were restless. The ranks of the Northern and Western Democrats were unbroken, but they were not enough to give Rayburn the victory. Even added to the certain border-state and Southern Democrats, they would not be enough. Rayburn had to have Republican votes as well to win.

The discovery that the issue was clearly in doubt prompted a new and massive inside struggle in the House. Both camps had hard-core supporters; but both camps also had defectors. Among the Southerners, the battle areas were the delegations of Texas, Tennessee, Alabama, Arkansas, Georgia, and Louisiana, with lone Representatives in Virginia and Mississippi in doubt. The border-state Democrats in West Virginia and Kentucky were committed hard for Rayburn, but some of the Democrats in Maryland, Missouri, and Oklahoma were uncertain. The Republicans had similar problems. The GOP delegations from Massachusetts, Pennsylvania, New Jersey, and New York were under fire and wavering, and there were defections also likely in the Ohio, California, Wisconsin, Washington, and Nebraska delegations. In all these delegations were Representatives still not totally committed either way. With some there would be doubt about their votes until they were actually cast. The leaders and chief lieutenants of both camps unleashed on them all the personal pressure and argument they could devise. Frank Thompson of New Jersey now made full use of his carefully prepared card file of his colleagues, checking the cards of all the doubtful Representatives to find some new way to influence those members to join Rayburn's cause. Both camps alerted their allies among the lobbyists, and they swarmed to Capitol Hill to do their best to sway the Representatives to one or the other side.

Both sides kept detailed reports on every member of the House, and both struggled to win hard commitments from at least 218 members of the House, the number that would make victory certain. On Monday, January 23, both camps knew that neither camp had that many committed votes. Still at large and uncommitted were thirty-odd Representatives. How they swung would decide the struggle. Rayburn, as Speaker, announced that

431

the House would vote on the question on Thursday, January 26. That left less than four days for campaigning. Both sides, liberal and conservative, not only had to try to win over the undecided members but they had to make certain that the opposition did not raid their own ranks. Many Representatives were politically nervous on how to vote; many from divided Congressional districts knew they would be hurt politically at home no matter which way they voted, for to vote either way would offend at least some of their constituents. The question of increasing the size of the Rules Committee, a seemingly insignificant technical matter in the inner workings of the House of Representatives, had been so dramatized by the struggle itself and the implications of its outcome that it had become the major national issue of the hour. The marginal Representatives from close districts were unsure where political safety lay, and many of them squirmed under the intense buffeting they received from the lieutenants of Rayburn, Smith, and Halleck, the lobbyists, and the constituents back home who were writing massive quantities of letters and telegrams telling them what to do. Frank Thompson of New Jersey, now chief counter for Rayburn's forces, called these Representatives "shaky legged," for they were afraid to commit themselves to either camp. Almost hopelessly undecided was Frank Boykin of Alabama. Boykin was a friend of Rayburn and a conservative; he was pulled emotionally to vote both ways. He committed himself to Rayburn; then under pressure from Smith's camp, he changed his mind and committed himself to Smith. Rayburn's lieutenants applied new pressure to Boykin and again he switched. Smith's lieutenants fought back hard for Boykin's vote, and once more he switched. Again Rayburn's people won Boykin back, only to lose him again. At this point—Boykin had been on both sides three separate times—Thompson called off further attempts to woo Boykin until the actual day of the vote. The fight for Boykin's vote—he voted finally against increasing the Rules Committee— illustrated the desperation of the struggle. It was so close that every single vote was of crucial importance. The decision of the House might well rest on a single Representative's vote.

Rayburn had difficult problems; so did Smith and Halleck.

Rayburn had assumed that the Southern Democrats would flock to him, once he called off the purging of Colmer. When they drifted back to Smith's camp, Rayburn was both disappointed and hurt. With some of the Southerners, Rayburn tried to argue. Many of the Southern Democrats who admired Rayburn were deeply worried about the telegrams pouring in from their constituents. "I've got fifteen or twenty telegrams about this," one nervous Southern Democrat told Rayburn.

"How many voters in your district?" Rayburn asked him.

"About 50,000."

"Well," argued Rayburn, "how do you know but that 49,000 of them don't want you to use your own judgment?" With other Southerners, Rayburn felt they owed it to him personally to support him now, and he was grieved to find they were supporting Smith. He refused to try to make them change their minds. "I won't call them up," said Rayburn, "and have them tell me 'no.' "

Halleck had similar defections among his Republicans; and Halleck, often angry, argued furiously with some of them to return to their party ranks. One of these was Glen Cunningham of Nebraska. Halleck grabbed him on the House floor, both hands on Cunningham's coat, and literally shook him as he spat out arguments against "packing" the Rules Committee. Cunningham wrenched himself free of Halleck's grasp and staggered away from him. "That bastard!" Cunningham muttered. Some of Halleck's Republicans from Pennsylvania were bolting; and Halleck sent Ivor Fenton, the dean of the Pennsylvania Republicans, to try to talk party sense to them. These Republicans, representing depressed economic areas, were under heavy pressure from the labor unions who had equated a vote against increasing the Rules Committee with a vote against the economic legislation needed to rebuild their local industries. When Fenton could not persuade them to return to party ranks, Halleck himself went after them. James VanZandt had given his pledge personally to Rayburn; he succumbed to Halleck's drill-sergeant expletives and arguments. William Scranton, a freshman from Scranton, Pennsylvania, refused to yield to Halleck's pleas. The Massachusetts Republicans also were defecting heavily to

433

Rayburn's camp; they had similar economic problems in their Congressional districts. Joseph Martin, the House Republican leader whom Halleck had deposed just two years before, had openly joined Rayburn, and he was trying to line up other Republicans for Mr. Sam against Halleck and Smith. Halleck's people alerted the Massachusetts business community to put pressure on the wavering Massachusetts Republicans, and Halleck himself argued the issue with them. Lawrence Curtis switched back to Halleck's cause; but three others—William Bates, Bradford Morse, and Silvio Conte—resisted Halleck's pleas to the end.

In the Democrat camp, all the influential men were struggling hard for the votes of their colleagues. John McCormack, who had helped persuade Martin to back Rayburn, was trying for more converts. Carl Albert of Oklahoma was quietly ranging the Southern delegations on behalf of Rayburn. Carl Vinson, dean of the Georgians, was arguing with them to follow Mr. Sam. He was also trying with Francis Walter of Pennsylvania, to work out a compromise between Rayburn and Smith that would avert a showdown vote and thus prevent the otherwise inevitable wrenching of the Democratic ranks in the House.

Frank Thompson's office in the New House Office Building had become headquarters for the Rayburn nose-counters. Thompson kept a master list of those committed to Rayburn and those who yet might be won, the Representatives still listed as doubtful. Reporting to Thompson were a corps of liberal leaders, several lobbyists including Andrew Biemiller of the AFL-CIO, and a pair of Republican defectors, Thomas Curtis of Missouri and Frank Osmers of New Jersey. Thompson, with the guidance of all these agents, was directing the fire on the Representatives still hesitating to commit themselves. He dispatched as many as twenty different persons to pressure a single hesitating Representative. "It's like a firing squad," said Richard Bolling. "You don't know which bullet killed him."

By noon Wednesday, the day before Rayburn had scheduled the House vote, Thompson had marked on his tally sheet, actually a pamphlet-sized list of every member of the House, a total of 209 Representatives firmly committed to Rayburn. The Speaker was nine votes short of a full majority of the House. By coincidence, at that same hour, the conservative coalition had counted precisely the same number, 209, committed hard to Smith and Halleck. Both tallies, of course, were jealously guarded by each camp, and neither knew precisely how strong the other side actually was, although each could accurately guess approximately the strength of the other. Both tallies listed eighteen members of the House as "uncertain" or "doubtful." Halleck had lined up 148 Republican votes for Smith, and Smith still could only count as certain 61 Southerners.

The Representatives still listed as doubtful were Southerners hesitating between loyalties to Rayburn and Smith and to home district pressures, a handful of border-state Democrats, and a few Republicans from urban and industrial Congressional districts.

On Wednesday, Thompson received a telephone call from one of his field men that he had just rechecked the Maryland delegation. He found that Richard Lankford, a Democrat, who represented the Annapolis district, was beginning to weaken on his commitment to Rayburn. "Tell him," Thompson said into the telephone, "that if he doesn't come with us, we'll move the Naval Academy."

Thompson and Richard Bolling had met in Thompson's office to go over once more the list of Representatives. They had to find nine more than they had, and the vote was only twenty-four hours away. They had invited to the conference Robert Jones of Alabama to help with the Southerners.

Thompson ran through the list of Southerners. He came to the name of a freshman member from a Southern delegation whom Carl Vinson had been unable to persuade to support Rayburn. "How can we reach this guy?" Thompson asked Jones. "Who knows him?" Jones said he knew a man in the freshman's home district. Thompson picked up his telephone and put through a long-distance call to Jones's friend. Then he handed the telephone to Jones as Jones's friend came on the line.

"Hello, you old rascal," Jones shouted into the telephone. "This is Bob Jones in Washington." Jones asked what his friend knew about the freshman Representative.

"Yes, a reputable guy, able, competent." This was no help to Jones, and the conversation dragged on.

"What's that?" Jones interrupted, "a dam in your district? What's the name of it? Can you spell it for me? Yes, Yes. Is there much excitement about it down there in the district. Yes, yes. Has it been authorized yet? Fine, fine—it will be by nightfall, and thanks a million."

The Rayburn lieutenants had found a new route to apply pressure to the freshman Representative: to offer their support to get the federal government to build this dam in his district.

Thompson continued down the list of Representatives. He came to a Republican in his own state of New Jersey. He dialed his office on the telephone and asked the Representative for his vote. "I'm sorry," said the Republican, "I'm committed."

"Well, I'm sorry," Thompson said, "but I hope we can still be neighborly." Thompson came to another Southerner, and he asked Jones whether he knew of any way to apply new pressure on him. "The Air Force can take care of him," Jones said. Thompson asked Jones about another Southerner. "If you can get the Post Office to issue the stamp he wants," Jones said, "you've got him." They went through the list that way, searching for new pressure that could be applied on the doubtful members.

In Smith's camp and Halleck's, much the same kind of operation was under way. They were having just as much trouble as Rayburn's men in winning over the still doubtful men. The conservatives received heartening news Wednesday afternoon: Speaker Rayburn announced abruptly that he had postponed the vote on the Rules Committee from Thursday until the following Tuesday, January 31. Rayburn, doubtful about the outcome of the vote, had used his prerogative as Speaker to delay the vote. He wanted to give his own men more time to try to line up an absolute majority of the members. "I don't think we'll be in worse shape Tuesday than we would be tomorrow," Rayburn said, "and I still think we'll win." Smith and Halleck both read Rayburn's maneuver correctly: Rayburn did not have a certain victory. "They must be afraid they don't have the votes," Smith said. Halleck phrased the same thought with more imagery. "It looks," said Halleck, "as though the New Frontier is having trouble with its first roundup."

Rayburn had another motive in mind—to let the House hear President Kennedy make his first State of the Union Address before they voted. Kennedy was to make that address on Monday, January 30. Rayburn had specifically asked the new President to stay out of this House fight. He feared that obvious White House interference would drive the Southerners into opposition; Rayburn had already been angered by Stewart Udall's attempts to help. Udall had resigned from the House on January 18 to accept the Cabinet position of Secretary of the Interior. Udall telephoned several Western Republicans—among them Ben Reifel of South Dakota and Edgar Chenoweth of Colorado—and asked them to vote for Rayburn's proposal. To such Representatives, the Interior Department had special influence, for much of the activities in their Congressional districts came under the jurisdiction of the Interior Department. Halleck protested that Udall had been calling Representatives "particularly sensitive" to Interior Department influence, and Udall denied doing anything improper. He said he was only playing by the usual "rules of the game." President Kennedy himself was keeping fully informed on the fight for votes in the House, frequently telephoning Capitol Hill to get the latest vote count. His brother, Attorney General Robert Kennedy, was even more deeply involved, meeting the Rayburn lieutenants at breakfast at his home for detailed discussion on the strategy to win the doubtful Representatives. Lawrence O'Brien, the President's liaison chief with Congress, also was trying to help Rayburn, but he was still new to his post and not as effective as he later became in persuading Democratic Representatives to back the Administration's bills.

On Wednesday evening, President Kennedy at his first news conference as President, endorsed Rayburn's attempt to increase the membership of the Rules Committee. In doing so, Kennedy tried to avoid the appearance of interfering in the House's private affairs. "The Constitution states," Kennedy said at his news conference, "that each House shall be the judge of its own rules, and, therefore, the Speaker of the House, Mr. Rayburn, has been extremely anxious that the House be permitted to settle this matter in its own way." Kennedy added, however, that "it is no secret," that he, the President, wanted to see Rayburn win this fight and clear the way for the House to consider the Administration's coming legislative proposals. "Shouldn't the members of the House themselves and not merely the members of the Rules Committee have a chance to vote on those measures?" Kennedy asked rhetorically. "But the responsibility rests with the members of the House," he said, "and I would not attempt to infringe upon that responsibility. I merely give my view as an interested citizen."

The President, however, was too deeply involved to keep himself entirely out of the fight. He learned that the North Carolina Democrats were opposing Rayburn's plan to enlarge the Rules Committee. Of the ten North Carolina Democrats, only one—Herbert Bonner—was committed to support Rayburn. Kennedy had been particularly generous to North Carolina in selecting men for high positions in his new administration. Among them was Luther Hodges, the former governor of the state, whom Kennedy named as Secretary of Commerce. Kennedy decided to try to persuade at least some of the North Carolinians to support Rayburn; and he picked Harold Cooley, dean of the North Carolina delegation, as the Representative to call. Cooley was listed on Frank Thompson's tally as doubtful; but he was, unknown to Thompson, already committed to and working for "Judge" Smith. Speaker Rayburn pleaded with the President not to call Cooley. "If you call him," Rayburn said, "he will tell his friends, and it will be all over the House." Nevertheless, Kennedy did call Cooley to ask him to support Rayburn, and the President telephoned two other Democrats as well.

The five-day delay in the vote that Rayburn ordered gave both camps that much additional time to try to collect enough vote commitments to win. Both camps intensified their badgering of the uncertain and doubtful Representatives. Richard Bolling, in the thick of Rayburn's campaign, summed up the ferocity of the struggle. "This," he said, "is the moral equivalent of war." By Saturday afternoon, Bolling and Thompson had added five more men to Rayburn's side. They had 214 "hard" commitments, just

438

four short of the unbeatable 218 needed. Thompson received a telephone call from one of his lieutenants. "It's good news," Thompson announced, as he hung up the telephone. "Jennings is solid." This was Pat Jennings of Virginia, who represented a depressed district in the western part of the state. Jennings had been wavering for days, undecided whether to stick with "Judge" Smith or vote to enlarge the Rules Committee as a means of assuring House consideration of the economic legislation his district wanted. The intelligence systems of both camps were of comparable excellence. At almost the same moment that Thompson got the news that Jennings had committed himself finally to Rayburn, a telephone in "Judge" Smith's office rang: it was a Smith lieutenant reporting Jennings' defection to Rayburn. At that hour, on Saturday afternoon, Smith had increased his committed Southerners to 63. Halleck had informed Smith that he had either 151 or 152 Republican votes for blocking Rayburn's plan. That meant that the conservative coalition had 214 or 215 votes altogether, against Rayburn's 214. There were still Representatives wavering back and forth between the two groups. Among these were George Huddleston of Alabama, William Mailliard of California, Floyd Breeding of Kansas, Charles Mathias of Maryland, Frank Smith of Mississippi, George Wallhauser of New Jersey, Arch Moore of West Virginia, and Omar Burleson and Lindley Beckworth of Texas. The very closeness of the vote made an ideal situation for both sides to try to bargain with the doubtful members for "pocket" votes. The Democrats of the Texas delegation had swung behind Rayburn, their dean, in unprecedented numbers, and Burleson and Beckworth disliked opposing the Speaker, a fellow Texan. Both privately committed themselves to vote for Rayburn, but only if their votes meant the difference between victory or defeat for the Speaker.

The closeness of the vote—and the doubt of its outcome—also encouraged the senior men of the House to try to negotiate a truce between the two camps. Vinson and Walter tried hard to find an accommodation between Rayburn and Smith that would spare the House, and the Democratic party, from its ordeal. Rayburn himself, on Friday, tried to find a compromise with Smith.

He called on Smith and asked him whether he, as chairman of the Rules Committee, would agree to send to the House floor every bill approved by a House legislative committee and specifically requested by the Speaker. Smith refused Rayburn's proposal. Then Rayburn asked Smith whether he would agree to clear any Administration bill that was approved by a legislative committee. Again Smith refused. Smith offered only the compromise terms he had offered on January 9: he would agree to clear the five major Kennedy bills already announced. "Why," exclaimed Rayburn, "the President may have forty bills!" Rayburn left the conference angry. "He won't give an inch," Rayburn snapped. "He won't give an inch."

Word of Rayburn's attempted compromise with Smith sent a chill through the ranks of the Democratic liberals. This was what they most feared, an accommodation between Rayburn and Smith that would not alter the Rules Committee's basic hostility to liberal legislation. The liberals behind Bolling, Thompson, Holifield, and Blatnik preferred to go through with the vote on Tuesday and lose, rather than withdraw under an unsatisfactory compromise. Vinson and Walter were still striving for an accord. They could not persuade Smith to reduce his terms, and they could not persuade Rayburn to settle for less than clearance of the entire Kennedy legislative program. Walter proposed a middle-ground solution: a change in the House rules that would allow any bill receiving a tie vote in the Rules Committee to be sent to the House floor anyway. That proved unsatisfactory to the two camps. On Saturday afternoon, Rayburn called a news conference and announced that the vote would be held on Tuesday, as already announced. Rayburn did this partially to quiet the fears of the Democratic liberals and partially to counteract editorials in Southern newspapers. These editorials indicated that the change in the Rules Committee was being advocated by "radicals" from the North, and Rayburn wanted the newspapers to know that it was he, Rayburn, who wanted the change.

In the final days, there were dark reports of threats coming from both sides to retaliate on party members who voted "wrong." One Rayburn lieutenant approached a freshman Democrat, who had not yet received a committee assignment. He warned him what a "wrong" vote could mean. "If Rayburn loses this vote," he said, "you can go to 'Judge' Smith for your committee assignment." Rayburn, of course, not Smith, had a controlling voice in such assignments; and the threat was plain. John Flynt of Georgia, who had committed himself to vote with Smith, angrily protested that he had been threatened with a denial of assignment to the House Appropriations Committee, unless he voted with Rayburn. "Without a moment's hesitation," Flynt said, "I sent word that neither Jack Flynt nor Georgia wanted any assignment that badly." There were similar reports about the Republicans. The freshmen Republicans had not yet been assigned committees, and there were rumors that Halleck was subtly suggesting that those who voted with Rayburn would receive poor assignments when they were made. William Scranton of Pennsylvania received by telephone a threat to cut off future campaign funds.

Perhaps the most unique tactics used in the entire struggle were those devised for two members of the House noted for excessive drinking. Both Representatives were committed to vote against changing the Rules Committee. A Rayburn lieutenant plotted to use their weakness for alcohol against them. He tried to arrange to get the two members so drunk that they would not be able to show up on the House floor to vote. One, a Southern Democrat, was known to go on drinking binges, which sometimes lasted a full week. The liberal Democrats sent to his home on the Sunday before the vote a full case of bourbon in the hope that he would be tempted to get drunk and stay drunk. The other, a Republican, was a steady and heavy drinker. The Rayburn lieutenant arranged for a lobbyist friend to take the Republican out on the town the night before the vote and try to get him so drunk that he would not appear in the House the next day. Neither arrangement worked, for both Representatives cast their votes on Tuesday. The Rayburn lieutenant who had thought up the plan found that the conservative coalition leaders had frustrated it. "They knew their weaknesses, too," he explained.

All day Monday, the struggle for votes continued. Almost imperceptibly, a slight advantage began to show on Rayburn's side. "Judge" Smith conferred with the lobbyists from the U.S. Chamber of Commerce, the American Medical Association, the Farm Bureau, and the National Association of Manufacturers Monday afternoon to check on last-minute strategy. Sam Rayburn likewise called a meeting of the "Board of Education." There, Rayburn met with his closest allies, among them John McCormack, the party floor leader; Carl Albert, the party whip; Bolling; and Thompson. For an hour and a half, they scrutinized Thompson's list of Representatives committed to Rayburn. Thompson detailed the vote, state by state, as he had it calculated on his tally sheet. Thompson's calculations had been checked, rechecked, and rechecked again to make certain that every member listed as committed to Rayburn really would stand firm. Thompson's final total for Rayburn stood at 217, just one short of a Constitutional majority and certain victory. They knew there would be a few absentees. Joseph Martin, who had been ill, had flown to Nassau in the Bahamas and would not be back. Martin, however, had arranged to have a "live" pair with Edgar Chenoweth, one of the Republicans Interior Secretary Udall had telephoned, and that would kill one of the conservative coalition's votes. Louis Rabaut and John Bennett, both of Michigan, were ill and were not expected to vote. The Thompson total of 217 included Rayburn himself, who would not vote except to break a tie, and the Democratic leaders believed that they would certainly win provided every one of their committed men showed up.

At his regular news conference just before the House met on Tuesday, Speaker Rayburn told the reporters: "I think we're in." One of the reporters, William Arbogast of the Associated Press, asked Rayburn, teasingly, whether he had made up his own mind on how he would vote in case of a tie. Rayburn replied by playfully mimicking one of the "shaky-legged" Representatives deeply troubled by the decision. "I'm worried about it," Rayburn said, with a laugh, "praying over it—I haven't made up my mind!" The reporters burst into laughter at Rayburn's jest.

Rayburn, just before the hour of noon, took his accustomed place by a door in the Speaker's lobby, ready to enter the chamber at precisely noon. The House floor was already crowded, and so were the galleries. At the moment the House clock showed noon, Rayburn swept through the side door and mounted the rostrum to the Speaker's chair. Every Representative in the chamber rose to his feet as did the spectators in the galleries, and they gave Rayburn a standing ovation. It was a unique and spontaneous gesture. The ovation, however, did not indicate the vote to come. It was, instead, a mark of respect for Rayburn, a token of affection for him that was almost choking in sentimentality.

Rayburn struck his gavel on the desk. "The House will be in order," he mumbled. He introduced the chaplain for the daily prayer, and then H. R. Gross of Iowa made a point of order that a quorum was not present. McCormack moved a call of the House. Normally a quorum call would be only a nuisance, but on this day it was a strategic necessity for both camps. It told both camps which Representatives were missing and gave both the opportunity to find their men and bring them to the House floor. Only eight members were missing, and of these three were known not to be coming: Martin, Bennett, and Rabaut. Of the others, four were committed to vote for Smith, one was committed to vote with Rayburn. The party whips quickly located these men and hastened them to the floor.

One Representative, Thor Tollefson of Washington, a Republican, answered to the quorum call and then left the chamber for the rest of the day. He had committed himself to vote to change the Rules Committee, and he had been subjected to a bitter counterassault from his own Republican leaders. He found himself in the position of either voting against what he believed or voting to hurt his own Republican leaders. He chose not to vote at all.

James Trimble of Arkansas formally opened the debate on the resolution to enlarge the Rules Committee. Trimble, a member of the Rules Committee's liberal bloc, was the formal sponsor of the resolution. "I am a Democrat," he told the House. "I have always fought my battles in the battle-scarred uniform of the Democratic party and ... I have a firm belief in the position that with the majority rests the responsibility." He asked that the resolution be adopted so that the majority party leaders could assume their full responsibility for the bills brought to the House floor.

Clarence Brown of Ohio, senior Republican on the Rules Committee, asked that the resolution be defeated. "If the Rules Committee can be packed to obtain political decisions," he said, "other committees of the House can likewise be packed." As the debate proceeded, the lieutenants of the principal leaders tried to bolster their men. William Colmer threw an arm over the shoulder of Porter Hardy of Virginia, who had been under heavy pressure to bolt from Smith's camp. In the back of the Hall, behind the rail, Bolling and Albert Rains of Alabama were quietly talking to Lankford of Maryland, assuring him that he had chosen correctly for Rayburn.

Rayburn, seemingly unconcerned, presided over the House, calmly listening to the speeches. He tilted back on his leather chair and surveyed the chamber over which he had presided for more than sixteen years. The House itself was hushed, and the tension mounted as the time to vote grew near.

"Judge" Smith was recognized at twelve fifty. He told the House that he had no quarrel with Speaker Rayburn. "If there is any quarrel between the Speaker and myself," Smith said, "it's all on his side." That momentarily broke the tension. Everyone laughed, including Rayburn, at Smith's suggestion that there was no real quarrel. Smith grew deadly earnest. "I will cooperate with the Democratic leadership of the House of Representatives —just as long and just as far as my conscience will permit me to go." The Democratic liberals burst into laughter, and Smith sharply reprimanded them. "Some of these gentlemen who are laughing maybe do not understand what a conscience is," he said. Smith asked that the vote on the resolution be postponed, this time until the House had proceeded along through the session long enough to determine whether the Rules Committee in fact was not reflecting the majority will of the House. He again offered to clear the five major Administration bills, and he offered more than that.

"There has been some talk about my going out and milking

444

cows once or twice," he said, referring to his occasional end-of-session disappearances from Washington that prevented the Rules Committee from meeting and acting on pending bills. He pledged that he would not delay committee consideration of any bill requested by the House's Democratic leaders.

Halleck supported Smith with a slashing speech against the Administration's expected bills. "I have had an avalanche of mail, most of it handwritten, from people opposed to this resolution," Halleck said. "As I read that mail from the people of this country, right-thinking people by the millions, I am convinced that they are afraid that this effort signals a collapse of the opposition to such unwise measures. They are afraid the floodgates will be let down and we will be overwhelmed with bad legislation."

Speaker Rayburn left the rostrum as Halleck spoke, and took a seat on the floor, after assigning Carl Albert to preside over the House temporarily in his place. When Halleck finished, Rayburn was recognized to close the debate. Again, Rayburn received a standing ovation from his colleagues and the galleries. Only a few Southerners, among them "Judge" Smith, did not join in this tribute. Rayburn thanked his colleagues for their kindness and courtesy, and then he proceeded to attack Smith's argument that he intended to "pack" the Rules Committee. The suggestion, he said, was insulting. He conceded, however, that he had once packed the Rules Committee, long before he had become Speaker. It was back in 1933, he said, when he, in opposition to the then House leaders, fought successfully to put "Judge" Smith on the Rules Committee. Smith conceded the point by nodding agreement to Rayburn's statement. Rayburn then appealed for passage of the resolution, which he said was a necessity to the Kennedy program. "Let us move this program," he said. "Let us be sure we can move it."

Rayburn, to a storm of applause, mounted the rostrum to his chair and the debate was over. The clerk began to read the roll of the House, calling out each name, and the members responded "aye" or "no" as they were called. The House was hushed as the roll was called. Smith walked to the back of the chamber and stood behind the rail to listen to the vote. Bolling, off the floor, lit

445

a cigarette and puffed at it nervously. Thompson sat at the Democratic leader's desk on the floor and carefully checked the votes against his master talley sheet, to spot any defections from those committed to Rayburn. Many of the members were keeping count of the yeas and nays, and when Osmers voted "aye," almost two thirds of the way through the roll, the count was exactly even. Henry Reuss of Wisconsin so signaled his colleagues, with a sweeping gesture of his arms. Now the Hall was silent except for the clerk calling the names and the staccato replies.

When the clerk completed the first call of the roll, Rayburn leaned forward and in a whisper asked Lewis Deschler, House Parliamentarian, how the vote stood. "Two hundred and fourteen to 209," Deschler whispered back. It was still exquisitely close and not yet over. Eleven members had failed to answer the first call, and now the clerk called out their names again. Clarence Cannon of Missouri was called, and he voted "aye." Rayburn had 215 votes. Another member was called, and he voted "no." The people in the galleries sucked in their breath at this, making a low, whistling sound. George Fallon of Maryland was called, and he voted "aye." Rayburn had 216 votes. Then came another "no" vote, and then another. At each, the people in the galleries again made that same low, whistling sound, an involuntary response. It was obvious that the galleries were for Mr. Sam. Fred Marshall of Minnesota was called, and he voted "aye." Rayburn had 217 votes. Now he could not be beaten, for even if the conservatives could tie this vote, Rayburn's vote would break that tie. In effect, Rayburn had exactly an absolute majority of the House. Still one more name was called, and the Representative voted "no." The vote stood 217 to 213, only four votes apart. A switch of two votes would make it a tie.

From the well of the House, Edgar Chenoweth asked Rayburn for recognition. Rayburn snapped at him, suspecting apparently a last-minute tactic by Halleck to alter the vote. Chenoweth, however, merely announced that he had a "live" pair with absent Joseph Martin and he therefore withdrew his "no" vote and voted "present."

It was just 2 P.M. by the House clock. Rayburn, standing, announced the House's decision. "On this vote," he said, "the yeas are 217 and the nays are 212 . . ." A great roar of triumph came up from the House floor and out of the House galleries, drowning Rayburn's words that the resolution had been passed.

"Judge" Smith left the floor, walking out through the Speaker's lobby. "Well," he said, smiling wanly, "we done our damnedest."

Rayburn was delighted as he left the chamber. He had scored a great personal victory. His eyes were dancing.

"We won," he said, "and I am satisfied."

With the victory won, Rayburn informed Wilbur Mills and the members of Mills's Committee on Committees that he wanted Carl Elliott of Alabama and B. J. Sisk of California, both liberals, to be named as the new Democratic members of the Rules Committee. Halleck and the Republican Committee on Committees named William Avery of Kansas, a moderate conservative. The additional three members shifted the balance of power in this crucial committee from conservative to liberal. Where the conservatives had held vast obstructive powers under the six-to-six conservative-liberal stalemate, the newly added members gave the liberals an eight to seven preponderance over the conservatives. With that liberal dominance of the Rules Committee, the Kennedy administration's bills had a far better chance of success than they would have otherwise had.

The Rules Committee in 1961, without delay, cleared for formal House action many of Kennedy's controversial bills, bills that otherwise would have been buffeted and harassed by the Rules Committee. Among these were a depressed-areas bill, a minimum-wage bill, legislation providing unemployment benefits, and a far-ranging housing bill. Even with the committee deliberately orientated to favor Kennedy's bills, however, the committee members did not automatically ratify every Administration bill. Indeed, the Rules Committee voted to kill in 1961 Kennedy's domestic bill of highest priority: the school-construction bill. In 1962, the same committee refused to send Kennedy's plan to create a Department of Urban Affairs to the House floor for a vote. These actions played the principal role in the ultimate Congressional rejection of both measures. Neither, however, was rejected by the Rules Committee primarily on the lines of the normal conservative-liberal conflict. The school-construction bill would have denied federal funds for parochial and private schools, and James Delaney of New York, a political liberal, joined the committee conservatives in opposition to it because he, a Catholic, regarded the bill as discriminatory. The proposal to create an Urban Affairs Department raised a racial question when President Kennedy indicated that he intended to appoint a Negro to the Cabinet post, if adopted; the Southern liberals on the Rules Committee felt compelled therefore to vote against it. Even so, for the House supporters of President Kennedy, the change in the Rules Committee's political attitude was more than worth the effort to get it.

The 1961 struggle for control of the Rules Committee, in the long history of the House of Representatives, was but another skirmish in the never-ceasing political war that has raged in the House ever since its very first session. There have been other parliamentary fights of equal or even greater vehemence and violence. There have been other such struggles over the Rules Committee. On every major bill that has divided liberals and conservatives, labor and management, the city and the farm, there have been similar battles for the power to write the law. There will be others in the future. In these struggles the very intensity of those pitted against each other marked, in part, the vitality of the House of Representatives as a political forum, and, in part, the importance of the House as a legislative assembly.

CHAPTER SIXTEEN

The Consent of the Governed

W HO are to be the electors of the federal representatives?" an author of *The Federalist Papers* asked rhetorically in 1788. "Not the rich, more than the poor; not the learned, more than the ignorant; not the haughty heirs of distinguished names, more than the humble sons of obscurity and unpropitious fortune. The electors are to be the great body of the people of the United States." [1]

And who, he asked, were to be those chosen as Representatives? Again he answered his own question: "Every citizen whose merit may commend him to the esteem and confidence of his country. No qualification of wealth, of birth, of religious faith, or of civil profession is permitted to fetter the judgment or disappoint the inclination of the people."

The government established for the United States in 1787 was, admittedly, an experiment in freedom. The government, as Abraham Lincoln later described it, was "dedicated to the proposition that all men are created equal," and at the time of its establishment that was not a proven proposition. It was, instead, a revolutionary doctrine that declared the nation's sovereignty rested in the people and that no government was valid without the consent of the governed. The peoples of the earth, almost without exception, were enthralled in the varied tyrannies of absolute monarchs and privileged aristocracies. To create a government of law, predicated on the theory that the governed should govern the gov-

449

ernors, as an experimental substitute for the government of benevolent and not-so-benevolent despots, was to test, in Thomas Jefferson's phrase, whether "man can . . . be trusted with the government of himself." There was no assurance that the experiment would succeed. Indeed, the historical record indicated plainly that it would more likely fail.

On no branch of the new government did the responsibility for the success of the experiment fall more heavily than on the House of Representatives. The House had been created deliberately to be the arm of that government most intimately responsible to and responsive of the people. Elected directly by the people and with no artificial discriminations against the election of any citizen, the Representatives clearly were intended to draw their sustenance and their strength immediately from the people. There could be no guarantee—indeed there were grave doubts—that such a system of selecting officials could produce competent and responsible men fit to run a government. Such doubts were expressed openly in debates at the Philadelphia convention that drafted the Constitution. There were fears that free elections would produce nothing but demagogues, but the doubts and fears proved unfounded.

Fisher Ames of Massachusetts was a member of the First House of Representatives in 1789, and he wrote that his colleagues on the whole were "very good men, not shining, but honest and reasonably well informed." [2] The same could be said of the House of Representatives in the 1960's, and of all the years in between. There were in the House that Ames knew a few "shining" members—Ames himself was one of these—and there have been such exemplary members all through the history of the House. The rank-and-file Representatives, however, have more nearly resembled the people back home that they represented. That could not be surprising; that was the intention of the Founding Fathers and they so designed the House of Representatives that it would be *representative*. Over its many decades, the House of Representatives has reflected the whole people, their weaknesses as well as their strengths, their foolishness as well as their wisdom, their prejudices as well as their tolerances, their fears as well as their courage. "This body," said Dewey Short of Missouri, "is a mirror in which America can see herself." [3] The House of Representatives, said William Redfield of New York, is "probably a fair cross section of the people, showing us very much as we are and throwing faults and virtues into high relief." [4]

There was a precise and exact reason why this was so, a reason perfectly known by every member who ever sat in the House of Representatives. He could violate the sensibilities and the views of his constituents only at the imminent peril of being forced into political retirement by those constituents. He depended on the consent of the people of his Congressional district for his continued career in the House of Representatives.

The representative character of the House, however, has never been a perfect copy of the nation at large. It could not be. The House's representative character has been flawed, for example, by discrepancies in the Congressional districts themselves. Ideally, each Representative should speak and act for exactly the same portion of the American people. The actual number of constituents in Congressional districts, however, have varied widely. In the Eighty-eighth House, 1963-64, for example, Bruce Alger of Texas, representing Dallas, has 951,527 constituents, and John Bennett of Michigan, representing eight rural counties, has but 177,431. In 1962, twenty Congressional districts had more than 621,000 constituents each, while twenty others had less than 253,000. In large measure, these wide discrepancies were caused by the failure of state legislatures to reapportion their Congressional districts in accordance with the never-ceasing movements of the state populations. For more than a century and a half, that movement in the main has been from the farm to the city, and the failure to reapportion the districts has long given the rural areas of the country an unwarranted overrepresentation in the House. The effect of this lag has been aggravated as well by the deliberate actions of rurally dominated state legislatures of so gerrymandering those Congressional districts they have altered to favor rural voters. The extent of this malapportionment could be argued; a judgment on it depended on how rural and urban

451

Congressional districts were defined. Some were obviously rural, some obviously urban, but others had varying proportions of farmers and city people and could not easily be classified. In the 1940's, by one estimate, the House of Representatives contained a dozen more Representatives from rural areas than the actual populations of these areas warranted. By another estimate, the House of Representatives in the 1960's had twenty-seven more rural Representatives than a correct apportionment would have allowed. Interestingly enough, the nation's urban areas were no longer paying the principal cost of such rural overrepresentation as there was. The modern movement of population out of the cities into the suburbs has actually given many cities—New York, Philadelphia, and Chicago among them—larger delegations in the House than they were entitled to by their populations. The areas that have suffered the major loss in recent years have been the new suburbs. The same estimate that calculated rural areas were overrepresented by twenty-seven members of the House also calculated that twenty of these House seats rightly belonged to the nation's suburbs and only seven of them to the urban centers.

Whether this gave the House itself an unnatural rural bias could be debated. It has long been assumed, for example, that the rural overrepresentation has given the conservative bloc in the House unjustified additional strength. That assumption has been based on the further assumption that all rural Representatives have been conservatives and all urban Representatives have been liberals. This, of course, has not been so. *Congressional Quarterly,* a nonpartisan research organization, closely examined the voting records and party affiliations of the members of the House of Representatives for the 1960's. How would the temper of the House be altered if the overrepresentation of their twenty-seven Congressional districts were distributed equitably between urban and suburban areas of the country? *Congressional Quarterly* concluded that the liberal bloc actually would gain no new members from urban areas but would pick up nine additional members from suburban areas. The effect of these, however, would be canceled by the loss of that many liberals from rural areas. "The

452

vote studies . . . indicate that rural Democratic Congressmen, especially outside the South, vote only slightly less 'liberally' than their suburban and urban colleagues," *Congressional Quarterly* reported on its findings. "There is no evidence such a reapportionment would increase 'liberal' voting strength in the House." The net result of *Congressional Quarterly*'s investigation indicated that, despite the discrepancies in the urban-rural-suburban distribution of Congressional districts, the House's voting patterns would not be radically altered.

This finding did not, of course, justify the existing inequities in the apportionment of Congressional seats; but, even as *Congressional Quarterly* reported its conclusions, a possible remedy appeared for such malapportionments as there were. In 1962, the Supreme Court handed down a ruling, in *Baker* v. *Carr,* that was hailed as a "historic landmark decision," heralding the end of rural domination of state legislatures. The decision, brought in a case involving the Tennessee legislature, had profound implications for the United States House of Representatives. The Supreme Court had previously declined to enter the "political thicket" of Congressional or state apportionment, but in the 1962 ruling the Court upheld the right of voters to sue to prevent the dilution of their voting rights. The Court ordered lower courts to grant relief to such voters if their claims were founded in fact. The ruling brought a flood of litigation; within five months there were fifty cases pending in thirty-two states and federal and state courts had already invalidated directly or indirectly at least part of the legislative apportionments in sixteen states. With their power to determine the geographic boundaries of Congressional districts, the state legislatures have long had an intimate relationship with the House of Representatives. How great an effect the Court's ruling would eventually have on the House of Representatives was impossible to assess immediately. The decision, however, did prompt the correction of the worst abuse of a popular majority in perhaps the nation's most notoriously gerrymandered Congressional district. That was Georgia's Fifth, the nation's second largest Congressional district, with 823,680 citizens. The district was composed of the city of Atlanta and two neighboring rural and suburban counties. Atlanta contained sixty per cent of the total population, but these voters were in effect disenfranchised by the power the county-unit system gave the rural and suburban voters. Voting under Georgia's county-unit system the two rural and suburban counties outweighed Atlanta. For sixteen years, James C. Davis, a political conservative from one of the outlying counties, represented the district in the House of Representatives despite Atlanta's pronounced liberalism. Twice, in 1946 and 1952, Davis had been elected with less votes than his opponent, but he had won a majority of the county-unit votes. As a direct result of the Supreme Court decision in 1962, Georgia did away with the county-unit system in favor of the popular elections common elsewhere in the country. Davis was promptly defeated by a political moderate.

The House has always had such imperfections in its claim to be a truly representative assembly, as it has had blemishes in the qualifications of some of its members. To point at these imperfections, or at the deficiencies of any individual Representatives, as characteristic of the House as a whole would belie the real standard of the House as a democratic institution. More than this, it would rob the House of Representatives of credit for its historic achievement. The history of republics has been the history of repeated failures. They have fallen, from the ancient republics of the Greeks to those of the modern era—France, Germany, and Latin America—into chaos or tyranny. "Had every Athenian citizen been a Socrates," wrote an author of *The Federalist Papers*,[5] "every Athenian assembly would still have been a mob." The genius of the American Republic, of the men who established the American system of government, was to devise a government by representation of the people, a government in which democracy was restrained from its own excesses. Here, singularly, the House of Representatives has played a unique and extraordinary role. Not only has it borne the most direct responsibility to reflect the views of the country, it has as well borne the closest scrutiny by the people. And the fundamental spirit of the House—in its perhaps most significant historic triumph—has permeated the entire federal government. The House of Representatives was created in the eighteenth century as *the* representative branch of the government. The nineteenth century saw the President claim the same *representative* character. The twentieth century found the once aristocratic Senate making the same claim, and even the Supreme Court had taken on a *representative* quality. The history of the American Republic has been the continuing success of the nation's continuing experiment in freedom through representative government.

In this historic process, the House of Representatives has played a primary and fundamental role, and by so doing, the House has helped create a nation more prosperous, more powerful and more free than the world has ever known. The House has been, in this larger sense, the solemn assembly of which Josiah Quincy spoke a century and a half ago. It has remained what it was then, the representative of the people, the depositary of their power, and the image of their wisdom.

EXPLANATORY NOTE

In the text of this book, the House of Representatives in the twentieth century has generally been assumed to have 435 members, the number set after the 1910 Census. In 1958, Alaska was admitted to the Federal Union as a state, and in 1959, Hawaii also was admitted. Each was immediately allowed a single Representative, and they brought the House's total membership to 437 during the Eighty-sixth and Eighty-seventh Congresses, 1959-60 and 1961-62. After the 1960 Census and the reapportionment of House seats that Census required, Hawaii was granted two Representatives while Alaska continued to have but one. In the Eighty-eighth Congress, 1963-64, the total membership was returned to 435.

NOTES TO CHAPTER ONE

1. Max Farrand (ed.), *The Records of the Federal Convention of 1787*, 1911, Vol. I, p. 48.
2. *Ibid.*
3. *Ibid.*
4. *Ibid.*, p. 57.
5. *Ibid.*, p. 49.
6. Jonathan Elliot (ed.), *Debates on the Federal Constitution*, 1836, Vol. II, p. 103.
7. *Ibid.*, p. 348.
8. *Ibid.*, p. 284.
9. *Ibid.*, p. 8.
10. *Ibid.* p. 167.
11. *Ibid.*, Vol. IV, p. 57.
12. Edmund Quincy, *Life of Josiah Quincy of Massachusetts*, 1867, p. 199.
13. See Thomas Hart Benton, *Thirty Years in the U.S. Senate*, 1854-56, Vol. I, pp. 205-207, for Tocqueville's evaluation of the House and Benton's denunciation of Tocqueville's "error."
14. David Crockett, *Davy Crockett's Own Story As Written By Himself*, 1955, pp. 210-211.
15. Woodrow Wilson, *Congressional Government*, 1885, p. 210.
16. James Bryce, *The American Commonwealth*, 1893, Vol. I, p. 143.
17. Charles Buxton Going, *David Wilmot, Free Soiler*, 1924, p. 56.
18. Paul DeWitt Hasbrouck, *Party Government in the House of Representatives*, 1927, p. v.
19. William Henry Smith, *Speakers of the House of Representatives of the United States*, 1928, p. 261.
20. Melville E. Stone, *Fifty Years A Journalist*, 1921, p. 46.
21. Bascom N. Timmons, *Garner of Texas*, 1948, p. 291.
22. *Congressional Record*, January 3, 1957, p. 46.
23. Henry Cabot Lodge (ed.), *The Federalist*, 1907, p. 338. (*Federalist Paper*, No. LIII, which has been credited to both Alexander Hamilton and James Madison.)

24. George Rothwell Brown, *The Speaker of the House: The Romantic Story of John N. Garner,* 1932, p. 64.

25. Champ Clark, *My Quarter Century of American Politics,* 1920, Vol. II, p. 76, and Vol. II, p. 13.

26. Smith, *op. cit.,* p. 5.

27. Willis Fletcher Johnson, *Life of James G. Blaine,* 1893, p. 337.

NOTES TO CHAPTER TWO

1. Jonathan Elliot (ed.), *Debates on the Federal Constitution,* 1836, Vol. II, p. 301.

2. Max Farrand (ed.), *The Records of the Federal Government,* 1911, Vol. III, p. 133.

3. *Ibid.,* p. 359.

4. Elliot, *op. cit.,* Vol. II, p. 298.

5. *Ibid.,* Vol. III, p. 16.

6. Josiah Quincy, *Figures of the Past,* 1883, p. 284.

7. Quoted by Arthur M. Schlesinger, Jr., in *Age of Jackson,* 1945, p. 6.

8. Robert C. Winthrop, Jr., *A Memoir of Robert C. Winthrop,* 1897, p. 78.

9. Quoted by Telford Taylor in *Grand Inquest, The Story of Congressional Investigations,* 1955, p. 49.

10. Woodrow Wilson, *Congressional Government,* 1885, p. 43.

11. Henry Adams, *The Education of Henry Adams,* 1918, p. 261.

12. Clara Longworth DeChambrun, *The Making of Nicholas Longworth,* 1933, p. 267.

13. DeAlva Stanwood Alexander, *History and Procedure of the House of Representatives,* 1916, p. 358.

14. Lawrence H. Chamberlain, *The President, Congress and Legislation,* 1946, pp. 422-423.

15. Bascom N. Timmons, *Garner of Texas,* 1948, p. 279.

16. Joe Martin (As Told to Robert J. Donovan), *My First Fifty Years in Politics,* 1960, p. 229.

17. *Ibid.,* p. 10.

18. *Ibid.,* p. 6.

NOTES TO CHAPTER THREE

1. Quoted by Joseph P. Chamberlain in *Legislative Processes, National and State,* 1936, pp. 60-61.

2. Paul S. Reinsch, *American Legislatures and Legislative Methods,* 1913, p. 60.

3. Samuel W. McCall, *The Business of Congress,* 1911, p. 65.

4. Woodrow Wilson, *Constitutional Government in the United States,* 1908, p. 88.

5. Asher C. Hinds and Clarence Cannon, *Precedents of the House of Representatives of the United States,* 1907, 1936, Vol. I, p. v.

6. Quoted by Bertram Gross in *The Legislative Struggle,* 1953, p. 355.

7. DeAlva Stanwood Alexander, *History and Procedure of the House of Representatives,* 1916, p. 187.

8. *Bartlett's Familiar Quotations* (13th Ed.), pp. 433-434.

9. Henry G. Wheeler, *History of Congress,* 1848, Vol. I, p. 175.

10. Thomas Hart Benton, *Thirty Years in the U.S. Senate, 1854-56*, Vol. II, p. 247.

11. Hubert Bruce Fuller, *The Speakers of the House*, 1909, pp. 222-223.

12. *Ibid.*, p. 231.

13. Samuel W. McCall, *The Life of Thomas Brackett Reed*, 1914, pp. 167-168.

14. George Rothwell Brown, *The Leadership of Congress*, 1922, p. 88.

15. Hinds and Cannon, *op. cit.*, Vol. VI, p. v.

16. James Bryce, *The American Commonwealth*, 1893, Vol. I, p. 135.

17. Clara Longworth DeChambrun, *The Making of Nicholas Longworth*, 1933, p. 187.

18. Lewis Deschler, *Rules of the House of Representatives*, 1945, p. vi.

19. J. T. Salter, *Public Men In and Out of Office*, 1946, p. 158.

NOTES TO CHAPTER FOUR

1. Ch'ang-wei Ch'iu, *The Speaker of the House of Representatives Since 1896*, 1928, p. 292.

2. *Ibid.*, p. 23.

3. M. P. Follett, *The Speaker of the House of Representatives*, 1896, p. 296.

4. *Ibid.*, p. 297.

5. DeAlva Stanwood Alexander, *History and Procedure of the House of Representatives*, 1916, p. 43.

6. Floyd M. Riddick, *The United States Congress, Organization and Procedure*, 1949, p. 72.

7. Follett, *op. cit.*, p. 95.

8. *Ibid.*, p. 72.

9. Champ Clark, *My Quarter Century of American Politics*, 1920, Vol. I, p. 310.

10. *Ibid.*, Vol. II, p. 443.

11. Transcript of an interview of Sam Rayburn of Texas by William Lawrence on American Broadcasting Company's radio and television network, July 16, 1961, p. 12.

12. Samuel Arthur Bent, *Familiar Short Sayings of Great Men*, 1899, p. 150.

13. Clara Longworth DeChambrun, *The Making of Nicholas Longworth*, 1933, p. 294.

14. Sam Rayburn in conversation with Richard Bolling of Missouri, who repeated the incident to the author.

15. Ben Perley Poore, *Perley's Reminiscences of Sixty Years in the National Metropolis*, 1886, Vol. II, p. 512.

16. Follett, *op. cit.*, p. 288.

17. Joe Martin (As Told to Robert J. Donovan), *My First Fifty Years in Politics*, 1960, p. 181.

18. Sam Rayburn to the author.

19. Interview in *U.S. News and World Report*, October 13, 1950, with Sam Rayburn.

20. *Time*, October 13, 1961, p. 26.

21. Rayburn to the author.

22. Transcript of ABC interview with Rayburn, *op. cit.*, p. 20.

23. Rayburn related the incident to the author.

24. Charles Willis Thompson, *Party Leaders of the Time*, 1906, p. 180.

25. Hubert Bruce Fuller, *The Speakers of the House*, 1909, p. 281.

26. J. Frederick Essary, *Covering Washington,* 1927, p. 204.
27. *Time,* October 13, 1961, p. 27.
28. Bascom N. Timmons, *Garner of Texas,* 1948, p. 260.
29. Garner made the statement to an intimate, now a lobbyist in Washington, who repeated it to the author.
30. Rayburn to the author.
31. Carl Albert of Oklahoma to the author.
32. James E. Watson, *As I Knew Them,* 1936, p. 125.
33. Martin, *op. cit.,* p. 181.

NOTES TO CHAPTER FIVE

1. O. O. Stealey, *Twenty Years in the Press Gallery,* 1906, p. 306.
2. Bascom N. Timmons, *Garner of Texas,* 1948, p. 122.
3. Sam Rayburn to the author.
4. Charles Willis Thompson, *Party Leaders of the Time,* 1906, p. 149.
5. The incident was recounted to the author by one of the Representatives at the meeting of the "Board of Education."
6. Joe Martin (As Told to Robert J. Donovan), *My First Fifty Years in Politics,* 1960, p. 101.
7. Rayburn to the author.
8. Champ Clark, *My Quarter Century of American Politics,* 1920, Vol. II, p. 337.
9. John McCormack of Massachusetts to the author.
10. Joseph Martin of Massachusetts to the author.
11. Martin to the author.
12. Charles A. Halleck of Indiana to the author.
13. Halleck to the author.
14. Carl Albert of Oklahoma to the author.
15. Halleck to the author.
16. Martin, *op. cit.,* p. 183.
17. Albert to the author.
18. DeAlva Stanwood Alexander, *History and Procedure of the House of Representatives,* 1916, p. 128.
19. *Ibid.,* p. 126.
20. Clark, *op. cit.,* Vol. II, p. 338.
21. *Ibid.,* Vol. II, p. 337.
22. *Ibid.,* Vol. II, p. 339.
23. Ch'ang-wei Ch'iu, *The Speaker of the House of Representatives Since 1896,* 1928, p. 128.
24. Hubert Bruce Fuller, *The Speakers of the House,* 1909, p. 271.
25. Clark, *op. cit.,* Vol. I, p. 208.
26. A remark frequently repeated by Howard Smith of Virginia when questioned about his role as chairman of the Rules Committee.
27. Floyd M. Riddick, *The United States Congress, Organization and Procedure,* 1949, p. 123. Riddick's source left a blank for the obvious word "hell."
28. *Ibid.*
29. Clarence Brown of Ohio recounted the episode to the author.
30. *Time,* January 15, 1951, p. 14.
31. Rayburn to the author.
32. Albert Rains of Alabama to the author.
33. Richard Bolling of Missouri to the author.
34. Lee Metcalf of Montana to the author.

35. V. O. Key, Jr., *Politics, Parties and Pressure Groups*, 1942, p. 496.
36. Rayburn to the author.
37. Clark, *op. cit.*, Vol. II, p. 10.
38. Francis Walter of Pennsylvania recounted the incident to the author.
39. David B. Truman, *The Congressional Party, A Case Study*, 1959, p. 204.
40. Rayburn described this incident to the author.
41. Rayburn to the author.
42. William Green of Pennsylvania to the author.
43. Paul DeWitt Hasbrouck, *Party Government in the House of Representatives*, 1927, p. 218.

NOTES TO CHAPTER SIX

1. This remark was made in the presence of the author.
2. Frank G. Carpenter, *Carp's Washington*, 1960, p. 110.
3. Earl Schenck Miers (ed.-in-chief), *Lincoln Day by Day: A Chronology 1809-1865*, 1960, Vol. I, p. 314.
4. Ben Perley Poore, *Perley's Reminiscences of Sixty Years in the National Metropolis*, 1886, Vol. I, p. 300.
5. M. R. Werner, *Tammany Hall*, 1928, p. 508.
6. O. O. Stealey, *Twenty Years in the Press Gallery*, 1906, p. 56.
7. James G. Blaine, *Twenty Years of Congress, From Lincoln to Garfield*, 1883, Vol. I, p. 70.
8. Asher C. Hinds and Clarence Cannon, *Precedents of the House of Representatives of the United States*, 1907, 1936, Vol. IV, p. 276.
9. *Time*, February 2, 1959, p. 12.
10. Miers, *op. cit.*, Vol. I, p. 299.
11. Emanuel Celler, *You Never Leave Brooklyn*, 1953, p. 7.
12. Woodrow Wilson, *Congressional Government*, 1885, p. 62.
13. This was Rayburn's traditional advice to freshmen, many times repeated, and reflected his view of the House of Representatives.
14. Champ Clark, *My Quarter Century of American Politics*, 1920, Vol. I, p. 220.
15. Edward Nelson Dingley, *Life and Times of Nelson Dingley, Jr.*, 1902, p. 484.
16. Bascom N. Timmons, *Garner of Texas*, 1948, p. 112.
17. Henry Cabot Lodge (ed.), *The Federalist*, 1907, p. 329. (*Federalist Paper No. LII.*)
18. George F. Hoar, *Autobiography of Seventy Years*, 1907, Vol. I, p. 268.
19. A remark to the author by a House leader who declined use of his name.
20. See Explanatory Note preceding Notes to Chapter One.
21. DeAlva Stanwood Alexander, *History and Procedure of the House of Representatives*, 1916, p. 6.
22. J. W. Dean, *History of the Gerrymander*, 1892, p. 5.
23. Edmund Quincy, *Life of Josiah Quincy of Massachusetts*, 1867, pp. 133-134.
24. Wayne Hays of Ohio explained his tactic to the author.
25. Joe Martin (As Told to Robert J. Donovan), *My First Fifty Years in Politics*, 1960, p. 73.
26. Jeffery Cohelan of California to the author.
27. Frank A. Flower, *Life of Matthew Hale Carpenter*, 1883, pp. 470-471.
28. Max Farrand (ed.), *The Records of the Federal Convention of 1787*, 1911, Vol. I, pp. 132-134, 142.

NOTES TO CHAPTER SEVEN

1. George F. Hoar, *Autobiography of Seventy Years*, 1907, Vol. I, p. 262.
2. Quoted by James McGregor Burns in *Congress On Trial*, 1949, p. 54.
3. Charles Willis Thompson, *Party Leaders of the Time*, 1906, p. 167.
4. Woodrow Wilson, *Congressional Government*, 1885, p. 69.
5. James Bryce, *The American Commonwealth*, 1893, Vol. I, p. 159.
6. Wilson, *op. cit.*, p. 79.
7. Quoted by Rowland Evans, Jr., in "Louisiana's Passman: The Scourge of Foreign Aid," *Harper's Magazine*, January, 1962, p. 81.
8. *Ibid.*, p. 78.
9. Mahon's remark was made to *Time* correspondent James L. McConaughy, Jr., in December, 1957.
10. Wilson, *op. cit.*, pp. 60-61.
11. Quoted by Holbert N. Carroll in *The House of Representatives and Foreign Affairs*, 1958, p. 92.
12. Quoted in *Washington Star*, January 7, 1962, p. B-3.
13. Quoted in *Congressional Record, Appendix*, June 19, 1941, p. A-3131.
14. Thompson, *op. cit.*, p. 168.

NOTES TO CHAPTER EIGHT

1. Woodrow Wilson, *Congressional Government*, 1885, p. 155.
2. James DeWitt Andrews (ed.), *The Works of James Wilson*, 1896, Vol. II, p. 46.
3. DeAlva Stanwood Alexander, *History and Procedure of the House of Representatives*, 1916, p. 366.
4. Telford Taylor, *Grand Inquest, The Story of Congressional Investigations*, 1955, p. 106.
5. Alexander, *op. cit.*, p. 364.
6. George S. Boutwell, *Reminiscences of Sixty Years in Public Affairs*, 1902, Vol. II, p. 71.
7. Quoted by D. W. Brogan in *Government of the People, A Study in the American Political System*, 1943, p. 170.
8. Ben Perley Poore, *Perley's Reminiscences of Sixty Years in the National Metropolis*, 1886, Vol. I, p. 78.
9. *Ibid.*
10. Ransom H. Gillet, *Democracy in the United States*, 1868, pp. 294-295.
11. Theron Clark Crawford, *James G. Blaine*, 1893, pp. 281-282.
12. Boutwell, *op. cit.*, Vol. II, p. 10.
13. John Sherman, *Recollections of Forty Years in the House, Senate, and Cabinet*, 1895, p. 161.
14. Ida M. Tarbell, *The Tariff In Our Times*, 1912, p. 33.
15. Cleveland Bailey of West Virginia made the statement that President Eisenhower was "a lousy liar" to the author, then a correspondent for the United Press, for use by the United Press in a Washington dispatch.
16. Frank J. Donner, *The Un-Americans*, 1961, p. 3.
17. Emanuel Celler, *You Never Leave Brooklyn*, 1953, p. 187.
18. Robert K. Carr, *The House Committee on Un-American Activities, 1945-1950*, 1952, p. 216.
19. Carl Beck, *Contempt of Congress*, 1959, p. 50.
20. Richard M. Nixon, *Six Crises*, 1962, p. 13.
21. L. A. Gobright, *Men and Things at Washington*, 1869, pp. 14-15.

22. Edward Winslow Martin, *The Life and Public Services of Schuyler Colfax*, 1868, p. 142.

23. Frank G. Carpenter, *Carp's Washington*, 1960, p. 293.

24. J. Frederick Essary, *Covering Washington*, 1927, p. 211.

25. Bascom N. Timmons, *Garner of Texas*, 1948, p. 75.

26. Quoted by the United Press in a dispatch on June 14, 1960.

27. Taylor, *op. cit.*, p. 13.

NOTES TO CHAPTER NINE

1. E. P. Herring, *Group Representation Before Congress*, 1929, p. 274.

2. George F. Hoar, *Autobiography of Seventy Years*, 1907, Vol. I, p. 307.

3. Thomas Hart Benton, *Thirty Years in the U.S. Senate*, 1854-56, Vol. I, p. 21.

4. Frank G. Carpenter, *Carp's Washington*, 1960, p. 281.

5. Ben Perley Poore, *Perley's Reminiscences of Sixty Years in the National Metropolis*, 1886, Vol. II, p. 44.

6. *Ibid.*, Vol. II, p. 513.

7. Kenneth G. Crawford, *The Pressure Boys*, 1939, p. 41.

8. Edward Winslow Martin, *Behind the Scenes in Washington*, 1873, p. 221.

9. James Bryce, *The American Commonwealth*, 1893, Vol. I, p. 681.

10. Poore, *op. cit.*, Vol. II, pp. 48-49.

11. Martin, *op. cit.*, pp. 230-232.

12. Edgar S. Maclay (ed.), *Journal of William Maclay, United States Senator From Pennsylvania, 1789-1791*, 1890, p. 209.

13. Carpenter, *op. cit.*, p. 277.

14. Poore, *op. cit.*, Vol. I, p. 443.

15. James MacGregor Burns, *Congress on Trial*, 1949, p. 44.

16. V. O. Key, Jr., *Politics, Parties and Pressure Groups*, 1942, p. 208.

17. Herring, *op. cit.*, p. 45.

18. *Ibid.*

19. Crawford, *op. cit.*, p. 4.

20. Herring, *op. cit.*, p. 41.

21. Robert Luce of Massachusetts, quoted by George B. Galloway in *The Legislative Process in Congress*, 1953, p. 480.

22. J. Frederick Essary, *Covering Washington*, 1927, pp. 174-175.

23. Herring, *op. cit.*, p. 69.

24. An official of the AMA, who requested anonymity, to the author.

25. The labor lobbyist, who declined use of his name, to the author.

26. Quoted by Bertram Gross in *The Legislative Struggle*, 1953, p. 261.

27. George B. Galloway, *The Legislative Process in Congress*, 1953, p. 476.

28. Crawford, *op. cit.*, p. 37.

29. Stephen Kemp Bailey and Howard D. Samuel, *Congress At Work*, 1952, p. 282.

30. *Ibid.*

31. A veteran lobbyist to the author.

32. McCormick's remark reflected the intimacy of his working relationship, as majority leader of the House, with the AFL-CIO's chief lobbyist.

33. The Representative, who wished to remain anonymous, to the author.

34. The lobbyist, who wished to remain anonymous, to the author.

35. One of the participants recounted the incident to the author.

36. The lobbyist to the author.

37. The lobbyist to the author.
38. A labor lobbyist to the author.

NOTES TO CHAPTER TEN

1. Allan Nevins (ed.), *Diary of John Quincy Adams*, 1928, p. 55.
2. L. A. Gobright, *Men and Things at Washington*, 1869, p. 67.
3. Theron Clark Crawford, *James G. Blaine*, 1893, pp. 222-223.
4. Woodrow Wilson, *Congressional Government*, 1885, p. 260.
5. Joseph P. Tumulty, *Woodrow Wilson As I Know Him*, 1921, p. 173.
6. Edmund Quincy, *Life of Josiah Quincy of Massachusetts*, 1867, p. 220.
7. Ben Perley Poore, *Perley's Reminiscences of Sixty Years in the National Metropolis*, 1886, Vol. II, p. 144.
8. DeAlva Stanwood Alexander, *History and Procedure of the House of Representatives*, 1916, p. 379.
9. *Ibid.*
10. Paul Kilday of Texas to the author.
11. Josiah Quincy, *Figures of the Past*, 1883, p. 74.
12. Jesse Macy, *Party Organization and Machinery*, 1904, pp. 38-39.
13. Frank G. Carpenter, *Carp's Washington*, 1960, p. 120.
14. President Kennedy to the author, August 24, 1961.
15. Bryce Harlow to the author.
16. Harlow to the author.
17. Richard Bolling of Missouri to the author.
18. Ben Jensen of Iowa to the author.
19. One of the participants at the meeting to the author.
20. Lawrence F. O'Brien to the author.
21. John Bailey to the author.
22. O'Brien to the author.
23. Alfred Santangelo of New York and Richard Donohue to the author.
24. O'Brien to the author.
25. O'Brien to the author.

NOTES TO CHAPTER ELEVEN

1. Ransom H. Gillet, *Democracy in the United States*, 1868, p. 203.
2. Charles Willis Thompson, *Party Leaders of the Time*, 1906, pp. 184-185.
3. Clara Longworth DeChambrun, *The Making of Nicholas Longworth*, 1933, p. 273.
4. Bascom N. Timmons, *Garner of Texas*, 1948, p. 136.
5. Theodore Roosevelt, *Thomas H. Benton*, 1899, p. 309.
6. The Representative, who wished to remain anonymous, to the author.
7. Joe Martin (As Told to Robert J. Donovan), *My First Fifty Years in Politics*, 1960, p. 84.
8. *Ibid.*, p. 85.
9. The Representative to the author.
10. John Sherman, *Recollections of Forty Years in the House, Senate, and Cabinet*, 1895, p. 178.
11. Nathan Sargent, *Public Men and Events*, 1875, Vol. II, p. 55.
12. Quoted in *Washington Star*, March 18, 1960, p. A-14.
13. Edmund Quincy, *Life of Josiah Quincy of Massachusetts*, 1867, p. 387.
14. Theron Clark Crawford, *James G. Blaine*, 1893, p. 161.

15. *Congressional Record,* February 16, 1949, p. 1289.
16. *Congressional Record,* June 21, 1960, p. 12622.
17. Samuel Leland Powers, *Portraits of a Half Century,* 1925, p. 236.
18. *Ibid.,* p. 237.

NOTES TO CHAPTER TWELVE

1. Thomas Hart Benson, *Thirty Years in the U.S. Senate,* 1854-56, Vol. II, p. 247.
2. William A. Robinson, *Thomas B. Reed, Parliamentarian,* 1930, p. 255.
3. James A. Frear, *Forty Years of Progressive Public Service,* 1937, p. 226.
4. *Congressional Record,* May 1, 1956, p. 7317.
5. Ben Perley Poore, *Perley's Reminiscences of Sixty Years in the National Metropolis,* 1886, Vol. I, p. 75.
6. Nathan Sargent, *Public Men and Events,* 1875, Vol. II, p. 256.
7. O. O. Stealey, *Twenty Years in the Press Gallery,* 1906, p. viii.
8. Robert Luce, *Legislative Assemblies,* 1924, p. 303.
9. Stealey, *op. cit.,* p. 319.
10. *Washington Merry-Go-Round,* 1931, p. 220.
11. James Bryce, *The American Commonwealth,* 1893, Vol. I, p. 144.
12. Samuel W. McCall, *The Business of Congress,* 1911, p. 108.
13. Woodrow Wilson, *Congressional Government,* 1885, p. 89.
14. Hubert Bruce Fuller, *The Speakers of the House,* 1909, p. 121.
15. Howard Zinn, *LaGuardia in Congress,* 1958, p. 126.
16. John Austin Stevens, *Albert Gallatin,* 1898, pp. 120-121.
17. Champ Clark, *My Quarter Century of American Politics,* 1920, Vol. II, p. 183.
18. Earl Schenck Miers (ed.), *Lincoln Day by Day: A Chronology 1809-1865,* 1960, Vol. I, p. 302.
19. George F. Hoar, *Autobiography of Seventy Years,* 1907, Vol. II, pp. 178-179.
20. George Rothwell Brown, *The Speaker of the House: The Romantic Story of John N. Garner,* 1932, p. 48.
21. For a comparison of the two statements by Bryan, see Burton Stevenson's *The Home Book of Quotations, Classical and Modern,* 1958, pp. 1551-1552.
22. Horace Greeley, *The Life and Public Services of Henry Clay,* 1860, p. 47.
23. Edmund Quincy, *Life of Josiah Quincy of Massachusetts,* pp. 297-298.
24. Henry Adams, *John Randolph,* 1882, p. 286.
25. Poore, *op. cit.,* Vol. I, p. 294.
26. Theron Clark Crawford, *James G. Blaine,* 1893, pp. 144-145.
27. *Ibid.,* pp. 146-147.
28. Clark, *op. cit.,* Vol. I, p. 359.
29. Henry G. Wheeler, *History of Congress,* 1848, Vol. I, p. 426.
30. Donald W. Riddle, *Congressman Abraham Lincoln,* 1957, p. 107.
31. Ida M. Tarbell, *The Tariff In Our Times,* 1912, p. 66.
32. Frank G. Carpenter, *Carp's Washington,* 1960, p. 213.
33. Clark, *op. cit.,* Vol. II, p. 201.
34. *Congressional Record,* June 23, 1960, p. 13043.
35. *Congressional Record,* June 23, 1960, p. 13046.
36. Bertram Gross, *The Legislative Struggle,* 1953, p. 366.
37. Festus P. Summers, *William L. Wilson and Tariff Reform,* 1953, p. 185.
38. Clark, *op. cit.,* Vol. I, p. 355.

39. *Congressional Record,* June 10, 1958, pp. 10716-10723.
40. A Representative to the author.
41. John McCormack to the author.
42. Charles Halleck to the author.

NOTES TO CHAPTER THIRTEEN

1. Sam Rayburn to the author.
2. *Congressional Record,* September 5, 1961, p. 17037.
3. John Byrnes of Wisconsin to the author.
4. Sam Rayburn to the author.
5. *Congressional Record,* May 18, 1960, p. 9813.
6. DeAlva Stanwood Alexander, *History and Procedure of the House of Representatives,* 1916, p. vi.
7. John McCormack to the author.
8. Horace Greeley, *The Life and Public Services of Henry Clay,* 1860, p. 88.
9. *Congressional Record,* June 21, 1962, p. 10532.
10. *Congressional Record,* June 13, 1962, p. 9468.
11. Henry G. Wheeler, *History of Congress,* 1848, Vol. I, p. 429.
12. The author witnessed this episode.
13. Leslie C. Arends of Illinois related this conversation to the author.
14. Thomas Hart Benson, *Thirty Years in the U.S. Senate,* 1854-56, Vol. II, p. 178.
15. Asher C. Hinds and Clarence Cannon, *Precedents of the House of Representatives,* Vol. VIII, pp. 629-630.
16. *Time,* September 14, 1959, p. 24.
17. Leo O'Brien of New York to the author.
18. Carl Albert later related to the author the pleas he and Hale Boggs of Louisiana made to their rank-and-file members.
19. John Taber's remark did not appear in the *Congressional Record.*
20. The Boggs-Byrnes exchange, although shouted, also was not recorded in the *Congressional Record.*
21. Shelby M. Cullom, *Fifty Years of Public Service,* 1911, p. 141.

NOTES TO CHAPTER FOURTEEN

1. Lewis Deschler, *Rules of the House of Representatives,* 1945, pp. 156-158.
2. Nathanial Wright Stephenson, *Nelson W. Aldrich, A Leader in American Politics,* 1930, p. 215.
3. William C. Redfield, *With Congress and Cabinet,* 1924, p. 22.
4. Otto Passman of Louisiana to the author.
5. Allan A. Mitchie and Frank Ryhlick, *Dixie Demagogues,* 1939, p. 274.
6. A. G. Riddle, *The Life, Character and Public Services of Jas. A. Garfield,* 1881, p. 83.
7. Paul S. Reinsch, *American Legislatures and Legislative Methods,* 1913, p. 122.
8. George F. Hoar, *Autobiography of Seventy Years,* 1907, Vol. II, p. 46.
9. James G. Blaine, *Twenty Years of Congress, From Lincoln to Garfield,* 1883, Vol. II, p. 539.
10. William S. Vare, *My Forty Years in Politics,* 1933, p. 152.

11. James Bryce, *The American Commonwealth,* 1893, Vol. I, p. 116.
12. Woodrow Wilson, *Congressional Government,* 1885, p. 195.
13. Champ Clark, *My Quarter Century of American Politics,* 1920, Vol. II, p. 154.
14. John Sherman, *Recollections of Forty Years in the House, Senate, and Cabinet,* 1895, p. 205.
15. James A. Frear, *Forty Years of Progressive Public Service,* 1937, p. 145.
16. Hubert Bruce Fuller, *The Speakers of the House,* 1909, p. 215.
17. Robert Luce, *Legislative Assemblies,* 1924, p. 312.
18. Stewart Udall of Arizona related the conversation to the author.
19. Fuller, *op. cit.,* p. 282.
20. Samuel W. McCall, *The Business of Congress,* 1911, p. 148.
21. Jesse Macy, *Party Organization and Machinery,* 1904, p. 47.
22. *Annals of the American Academy of Political and Social Science,* September, 1953, p. 147.
23. *Ibid.,* p. 157.
24. *Ibid.*
25. Henry Cabot Lodge (ed.), *The Federalist,* 1907, p. 365 (*Federalist Paper No. LVIII*).
26. *Senate Document No. 872,* Sixty-second Congress, Second Session, 1919.
27. Wilson, *op. cit.,* p. 156.
28. Reinsch, *op. cit.,* p. 111.
29. W. F. Willoughby, *Principles of Legislative Organization and Administration,* 1934, p. 512.
30. *Congressional Record,* February 20, 1961, p. 2309.
31. *Time,* May 5, 1961, p. 16.
32. *Ibid.*
33. *Congressional Record,* September 26, 1961, p. 20192.
34. *Ibid.*
35. *Ibid.,* p. 20193.
36. *Congressional Record,* July 9, 1962, pp. 12012, 12014.
37. *Congressional Record,* July 9, 1962, p. 12028.
38. Bertram Gross, *The Legislative Struggle,* 1953, p. 324.
39. Gilbert Y. Steiner, *The Congressional Conference Committee, Seventieth to Eightieth Congresses,* 1951, p. 123.
40. Willoughby, *op. cit.,* p. 497.
41. Steiner, *op. cit.,* p. 101.
42. *Washington Post,* October 12, 1962, p. 1.
43. Otto Passman to the author.
44. Steiner, *op. cit.,* p. 71.
45. *Congressional Record,* May 1, 1939, p. 4974.
46. Steiner, *op. cit.,* p. 71.
47. *New York Times,* Magazine Section, May 20, 1962, p. 93.

NOTES TO CHAPTER FIFTEEN

1. The author collected the information used in the narrative of this chapter at first hand. He observed the struggle on a daily basis from its beginning to its end, and he enjoyed throughout the confidences of leaders in both camps. On several occasions he attended, as a nonparticipating observer, the private meetings of those most intimately involved in the fight to cajole the votes of a majority of the Representatives.

1. Henry Cabot Lodge (ed.), *The Federalist,* 1907, p. 356. (*Federalist Paper* No. LVII, which was attributed to both Madison and Hamilton.)

2. Ralph V. Harlow, *The History of Legislative Methods in the Period Before 1825,* 1917, p. 125.

3. Volta Torrey, *You and Your Congress,* 1944, p. 174.

4. William C. Redfield, *With Congress and Cabinet,* 1924, p. 15.

5. Lodge, *op. cit.,* pp. 346-347. (*Federalist Paper* No. LV, which was attributed to both Madison and Hamilton.)

BIBLIOGRAPHY

ACHESON, SAM HANNA. *Joe Bailey, the Last Democrat.* New York: Macmillan Co., 1932.

ADAMS, CHARLES FRANCIS. *Charles Francis Adams.* Boston: Houghton Mifflin Co., 1900.

ADAMS, HENRY. *John Randolph.* Boston: Houghton Mifflin Co., 1882.

————. *The Education of Henry Adams.* Boston: Houghton Mifflin Co., 1918.

————. *The Life of Albert Gallatin.* New York: Peter Smith, 1943.

ALEXANDER, DEALVA STANWOOD. *History and Procedure of the House of Representatives.* Boston: Houghton Mifflin Co., 1916.

ANDREWS, JAMES DEWITT (ed.). *The Works of James Wilson.* 2 vols. Chicago: Callaghan & Co., 1896.

ARNETT, ALEX MATHEWS. *Claude Kitchen and the Wilson War Policies.* Boston: Little, Brown & Co., 1937.

ATKINSON, C. R. *The Committee on Rules and the Overthrow of Speaker Cannon.* New York: Columbia University Press, 1911.

BAILEY, STEPHEN KEMP. *Congress Makes a Law, the Story Behind the Employment Act of 1946.* New York: Columbia University Press, 1950.

————, and SAMUEL, HOWARD D. *Congress at Work.* New York: Henry Holt & Co., Inc., 1952.

BARNES, WILLIAM H. *The Fortieth Congress of the United States.* 2 vols. New York: George E. Perine, 1869.

BARRY, DAVID S. *Forty Years in Washington.* Boston: Little, Brown & Co., 1924.

BARTH, ALAN. *Government by Investigation.* New York: Viking Press, 1955.

BARTHOLDT, RICHARD. *From Steerage to Congress.* Philadelphia: Dorrance & Co., 1930.

BECK, CARL. *Contempt of Congress.* New Orleans: Phauser Press, 1959.

BENTON, THOMAS H. *Thirty Years in the U.S. Senate.* 2 vols. New York: D. Appleton & Co., 1854 and 1856.

BERMAN, DANIEL M. *A Bill Becomes a Law.* New York: Macmillan Co., 1962.

Biographical Directory of the American Congress, 1774-1961. Washington, D.C.: Government Printing Office, 1961.

BLAINE, JAMES G. *Twenty Years of Congress, from Lincoln to Garfield.* 2 vols. Norwich, Conn.: Henry Bill Publishing Co., 1884.

————. *Political Discussions.* Norwich, Conn.: Henry Bill Publishing Co., 1887.

BONE, HUGH A. *Party Committees and National Politics.* Seattle: University of Washington Press, 1958.

BOUTWELL, GEORGE S. *Reminiscences of Sixty Years in Public Affairs.* 2 vols. New York: McClure, Phillips & Co., 1902.

BOWERS, CLAUDE G. *The Party Battles of the Jackson Period.* Chautauqua, N.Y.: Chautauqua Press, 1923.

BOYKIN, EDWARD. *Congress and the Civil War.* New York: Robert M. McBride Co., Inc., 1955.

————. *The Wit and Wisdom of Congress.* New York: Funk & Wagnalls Co., 1962.

BROGAN, D. W. *Government of the People, a Study in the American Political System.* New York: Harper & Bros., 1943.

————. *Politics in America.* New York: Harper & Bros., 1954.

BROWN, DAVID WALTER. *The Commercial Power of Congress.* New York: G. P. Putnam's Sons, 1910.

BROWN, GEORGE ROTHWELL. *The Leadership of Congress.* Indianapolis: Bobbs-Merrill Co., Inc., 1922.

————. *The Speaker of the House: The Romantic Story of John N. Garner.* New York: Brewer, Warren & Putnam, 1932.

BRYCE, JAMES. *The American Commonwealth.* 2 vols. New York: Macmillan Co., 1893.

BUCKLEY, WILLIAM F. (ed.). *The Committee and Its Critics.* New York: G. P. Putnam's Sons, 1962.

BURNHAM, JAMES. *Congress and the American Tradition.* Chicago: Henry Regnery Co., 1959.

BURNS, JAMES MACGREGOR. *Congress on Trial.* New York: Harper & Bros., 1949.

————. *John Kennedy: A Political Profile.* New York: Harcourt, Brace & World, Inc., 1960.

BUSBEY, L. WHITE. *Uncle Joe Cannon.* New York: Henry Holt & Co., Inc., 1927.

CALDWELL, ROBERT G. *James A. Garfield.* New York: Dodd, Mead & Co., 1939.

CANNON, CLARENCE. *Cannon's Procedure in the House of Representatives.* Washington, D.C.: Government Printing Office, 1944.

CARPENTER, FRANK G. *Carp's Washington.* New York: McGraw-Hill Book Co., Inc., 1960.

CARR, ROBERT K. *The House Committee on Un-American Activities, 1945-1950.* Ithaca, N.Y.: Cornell University Press, 1952.

CARROLL, HOLBERT N. *The House of Representatives and Foreign Affairs.* Pittsburgh: University of Pittsburgh Press, 1958.

CELLER, EMANUEL. *You Never Leave Brooklyn.* New York: John Day Co., Inc., 1953.

CHAMBERLAIN, JOSEPH P. *Legislative Processes, National and State.* New York: D. Appleton-Century Co., 1936.

CHAMBERLAIN, LAWRENCE H. *The President, Congress and Legislation.* New York: Columbia University Press, 1946.

CH'IU, CH'ANG-WEI. *The Speaker of the House of Representatives since 1896.* New York: Columbia University Press, 1928.

CLARK, CHAMP. *My Quarter Century of American Politics.* 2 vols. New York: Harper & Bros., 1920.

CLAY, HENRY. *The Life and Speeches of Henry Clay.* 2 vols. New York: Greeley & McElrath, 1843.

CONNALLY, SENATOR TOM. *My Name Is Tom Connally* (as told to Alfred Steinberg). New York: Thomas Y. Crowell Co., 1954.

COX, SAMUEL S. *Eight Years in Congress, from 1857-1865.* New York: D. Appleton & Co., 1865.

————. *Three Decades of Federal Legislation, 1855-1885.* Washington, D.C.: J. M. Stoddart and Co., 1885.

CRAWFORD, KENNETH G. *The Pressure Boys.* New York: Julian Messner, Inc., 1939.

CRAWFORD, THERON CLARK. *James G. Blaine.* N.P.: Edgewood Publishing Co., 1893.

CRISSEY, FORREST. *Theodore E. Burton: American Statesman.* Cleveland and New York: World Publishing Co., 1956.

CROCKETT, DAVID. *Davy Crockett's Own Story As Written By Himself.* New York: Citadel Press, 1955.

CULLOM, SHELBY M. *Fifty Years of Public Service.* Chicago: A. C. McClurg & Co., 1911.

DEAN, J. W. *History of the Gerrymander.* Boston: Privately printed, 1892.

DECHAMBRUN, CLARA LONGWORTH. *The Making of Nicholas Longworth.* New York: Ray Long & Richard R. Smith, Inc., 1933.

DEPEW, CHAUNCEY M. *My Memories of Eighty Years.* New York: Charles Scribner's Sons, 1923.

DESCHLER, LEWIS. *Rules of the House of Representatives.* Washington, D.C.: Government Printing Office, 1945.

DICKSON, HARRIS. *An Old-Fashioned Senator, a Story-Biography of John Sharp Williams.* New York: Frederick A. Stokes Co., 1925.

DIMOCK, MARSHALL EDWARD. *Congressional Investigating Committees.* Baltimore: Johns Hopkins Press, 1929.

DINGLEY, EDWARD NELSON. *Life and Times of Nelson Dingley, Jr.* Kalamazoo, Mich.: Ihling Bros. & Everard, 1902.

DONNER, FRANK J. *The Un-Americans.* New York: Ballantine Books, Inc., 1961.

DURHAM, KNOWLTON. *Billions for Veterans.* New York: Brewer, Warren & Putnam, 1932.

EBERLING, ERNEST J. *A Study of the Origin and Development of the Power of Congress to Investigate and Punish for Contempt.* Columbia University Studies in History, Economics, and Public Law. New York: Columbia University Press, 1928.

ELLIOT, JONATHAN (ed.). *Debates on the Federal Constitution.* 4 vols. Washington, D.C.: Privately printed for the editor, 1836.

ELLIS, EDWARD S. *The Life of Colonel David Crockett*. Philadelphia: Porter and Coates, 1884.

ESSARY, J. FREDERICK. *Covering Washington*. Boston: Houghton Mifflin Co., 1927.

EWING, CORTEZ A. M. *Congressional Elections, 1896-1944*. Norman, Okla.: University of Oklahoma Press, 1947.

FARRAND, MAX (ed.). *The Records of the Federal Convention of 1787*. 4 vols. New Haven: Yale University Press, 1911-37.

FOLLETT, M. P. *The Speaker of the House of Representatives*. New York: Longmans, Green & Co., Inc., 1896.

FORD, PAUL LEICESTER (ed.). *Essays on the Constitution of the United States*. Brooklyn: Historical Printing Club, 1892.

FREAR, JAMES A. *Forty Years of Progressive Public Service*. Washington, D.C.: The Associated Writers, 1937.

FULLER, HUBERT BRUCE. *The Speakers of the House*. Boston: Little, Brown & Co., 1909.

GALLOWAY, GEORGE B. *Congress at the Crossroads*. New York: Thomas Y. Crowell Co., 1946.

————. *The Legislative Process in Congress*. New York: Thomas Y. Crowell Co., 1953.

————. *History of the House of Representatives*. New York: Thomas Y. Crowell Co., 1961.

GELLERMANN, WILLIAM. *Martin Dies*. New York: John Day Co., Inc., 1944.

GILLET, RANSOM H. *Democracy in the United States*. New York: D. Appleton & Co., 1868.

GOBRIGHT, L. A. *Men and Things at Washington*. Philadelphia: Claxton, Remsen & Haffelfinger, 1869.

GOING, CHARLES BUXTON. *David Wilmot, Free Soiler*. New York: D. Appleton & Co., 1924.

GRIFFITH, ERNEST S. *Congress, Its Contemporary Role*. New York: New York University Press, 1956.

GROSS, BERTRAM. *The Legislative Struggle*. New York: McGraw-Hill Book Co., Inc., 1953.

HALSTEAD, MURAT. *Life and Distinguished Services of Hon. Wm. McKinley*. N.P.: Edgewood Publishing Co., 1896.

HAMILTON, GAIL. *James G. Blaine*. Norwich, Conn.: Henry Bill Publishing Co., 1895.

HARLOW, RALPH V. *The History of Legislative Methods in the Period before 1825*. New Haven: Yale University Press, 1917.

HASBROUCK, PAUL DEWITT. *Party Government in the House of Representatives*. New York: Macmillan Co., 1927.

HAYNES, GEORGE H. *The Senate of the United States*. 2 vols. New York: Russell & Russell, Inc., 1960.

HELLER, ROBERT. *Strengthening the Congress.* Washington, D.C.: National Planning Association, 1945.

HERRING, E. P. *Group Representation before Congress.* Baltimore: Johns Hopkins Press, 1929.

HINDS, ASHER C., and CANNON, CLARENCE. *Precedents of the House of Representatives of the United States.* 11 vols. Washington, D.C.: Government Printing Office, 1907 and 1936.

HOAR, GEORGE F. *Autobiography of Seventy Years.* 2 vols. New York: Charles Scribner's Sons, 1907.

HORN, STEPHEN. *The Cabinet and Congress.* New York: Columbia University Press, 1960.

HOUSTON, DAVID F. *Eight Years with Wilson's Cabinet.* 2 vols. Garden City, N.Y.: Doubleday, Page & Co., 1926.

HULL, CORDELL. *The Memoirs of Cordell Hull.* 2 vols. New York: Macmillan Co., 1948.

JAMES, MARQUIS. *Mr. Garner of Texas.* Indianapolis: Bobbs-Merrill Co., Inc., 1939.

JENKINS, JOHN S. *The Life of John Caldwell Calhoun.* Buffalo and Auburn, N.Y.: John E. Beardsley, 1850.

JOHNSON, WILLIS FLETCHER. *Life of James G. Blaine.* Philadelphia: Atlantic Publishing Co., 1893.

JOSEPHSON, MATTHEW. *The Politicos, 1865-1896.* New York: Harcourt, Brace & World, Inc., 1938.

KEFAUVER, ESTES, and LEVIN, JACK. *A Twentieth-Century Congress.* New York: Duell, Sloan & Pearce, Inc., 1947.

KEY, V. O., JR. *Politics, Parties, and Pressure Groups.* New York: Thomas Y. Crowell Co., 1942.

————. *Southern Politics in State and Nation.* New York: Alfred A. Knopf, Inc., 1949.

KIPLINGER, W. M. *Washington Is Like That.* New York: Harper & Bros., 1942.

KOFMEHL, KENNETH. *Professional Staffs of Congress.* Lafayette, Ind.: Purdue University Press, 1962.

LA FOLLETTE, BELLE CASE, and LA FOLLETTE, FOLA. *Robert M. La Follette.* 2 vols. New York: Macmillan Co., 1953.

LEWIS, STUART. *Party Principles and Practical Politics.* New York: Prentice-Hall, Inc., 1928.

LIEF, ALFRED. *Democracy's Norris, the Biography of a Lonely Crusade.* New York: Stackpole Sons, 1939.

LINDSEY, DAVID. *"Sunset" Cox: Irrepressible Democrat.* Detroit: Wayne State University Press, 1959.

LODGE, HENRY CABOT (ed.). *The Federalist.* New York: G. P. Putnam's Sons, 1907.

LONGWORTH, ALICE ROOSEVELT. *Crowded Hours.* New York: Charles Scribner's Sons, 1933.

Lowi, Theodore J. (ed.). *Legislative Politics, U.S.A.* Boston: Little, Brown & Co., 1962.

Lowry, Edward C. *Washington Close-Ups.* Boston: Houghton Mifflin Co., 1921.

Luce, Robert. *Legislative Procedure.* Boston: Houghton Mifflin Co., 1922.

————. *Legislative Assemblies.* Boston: Houghton Mifflin Co., 1924.

————. *Congress: An Explanation.* Cambridge, Mass.: Harvard University Press, 1926.

————. *Legislative Problems.* Boston: Houghton Mifflin Co., 1935.

McCall, Samuel W. *Thaddeus Stevens.* Boston: Houghton Mifflin Co., 1899.

————. *The Business of Congress.* New York: Columbia University Press, 1911.

————. *The Life of Thomas Brackett Reed.* Boston: Houghton Mifflin Co., 1914.

McConachie, L. G. *Congressional Committees: A Study of the Origin and Development of Our National and Local Legislative Methods.* New York: Thomas Y. Crowell Co., 1898.

McCown, Ada C. *The Congressional Conference Committee.* New York: Columbia University Press, 1927.

McCune, Wesley. *The Farm Bloc.* Garden City, N.Y.: Doubleday, Doran & Co., 1943.

McGeary, Nelson. *The Developments of Congressional Investigative Power.* New York: Columbia University Press, 1940.

McGurrin, James. *Bourke Cockran, a Free Lance in American Politics.* New York: Charles Scribner's Sons, 1948.

Maclay, Edgar S. (ed.). *Journal of William Maclay, United States Senator from Pennsylvania, 1789-1791.* New York: D. Appleton & Co., 1890.

Macy, Jesse. *Party Organization and Machinery.* New York: Century Co., 1904.

March, Charles W. *Reminiscences of Congress.* New York: Baker & Scribner, 1850.

Marshall, Thomas R. *Recollections of Thomas R. Marshall.* Indianapolis: Bobbs-Merrill Co., Inc., 1925.

Martin, Edward Winslow. *The Life and Public Services of Schuyler Colfax.* San Francisco: H. H. Bancroft & Co., 1868.

————. *Behind the Scenes in Washington.* Philadelphia: Continental Publishing Co. and National Publishing Co., 1873.

Martin, Joe (As Told to Robert J. Donovan). *My First Fifty Years in Politics.* New York: McGraw-Hill Book Co., Inc., 1960.

Mazo, Earl. *Richard Nixon, a Political and Personal Portrait.* New York: Harper & Bros., 1959.

Michie, Allan A., and Ryhlick, Frank. *Dixie Demagogues.* New York: Vanguard Press, 1939.

MIERS, EARL SCHENCK (ed.-in-chief). *Lincoln Day By Day: A Chronology 1809-1865.* 3 vols. Washington, D.C.: Lincoln Sesquicentennial Commission, 1960.

MILLER, CLEM. *Member of the House.* New York: Charles Scribner's Sons, 1962.

MOORE, JOSEPH WEST. *The American Congress, 1774-1895.* New York: Harper & Bros., 1895.

NELSON, HAROLD L. *Libel in News of Congressional Investigating Committees.* Minneapolis: University of Minnesota Press, 1961.

NEUBERGER, RICHARD L., and KAHN, STEPHEN B. *Integrity, the Life of George W. Norris.* New York: Vanguard Press, 1937.

NEVINS, ALLAN (ed.). *Diary of John Quincy Adams.* New York: Longmans, Green & Co., Inc., 1928.

NICHOLS, EGBERT RAY (ed.). *Congress or the Supreme Court.* New York: Noble and Noble Pub., Inc., 1935.

NIXON, RICHARD M. *Six Crises.* Garden City, N.Y.: Doubleday & Co., 1962.

PECK, HARRY THURSTON. *Twenty Years of the Republic, 1885-1905.* New York: Dodd, Mead & Co., 1926.

PEPPER, GEORGE WHARTON. *Family Quarrels: The President, the Senate, the House.* New York: Baker, Voorhis & Co., 1931.

POORE, BEN PERLEY. *Perley's Reminiscences of Sixty Years in the National Metropolis.* 2 vols. Philadelphia: Hubbard Bros., 1886.

———— (ed.). *Veto Messages of the Presidents of the United States.* Washington, D.C.: Government Printing Office, 1886.

POWELL, FRED WILBUR (ed.). *Control of Federal Expenditures, a Documentary History, 1775-1894.* Washington, D.C.: Brookings Institution, 1939.

POWERS, SAMUEL LELAND. *Portraits of a Half Century.* Boston: Little, Brown & Co., 1925.

PRITCHETT, C. HERMAN. *Congress Versus the Supreme Court 1957-1960.* Minneapolis: University of Minnesota Press, 1961.

QUINCY, EDMUND. *Life of Josiah Quincy of Massachusetts.* Boston: Ticknor & Fields, 1867.

QUINCY, JOSIAH. *Figures of the Past.* Boston: Roberts Bros., 1883.

REDFIELD, WILLIAM C. *With Congress and Cabinet.* Garden City, N.Y.: Doubleday, Page & Co., 1924.

REINSCH, PAUL S. *American Legislatures and Legislative Methods.* New York: Century Co., 1913.

RIDDICK, FLOYD M. *The United States Congress, Organization and Procedure.* Manassas, Va.: National Capitol Pub., Inc., 1949.

RIDDLE, A. G. *The Life, Character, and Public Services of Jas. A. Garfield.* Cleveland: W. W. Williams, 1881.

RIDDLE, DONALD W. *Congressman Abraham Lincoln.* Urbana, Ill.: University of Illinois Press, 1957.

RIGGS, FRED W. *Pressures on Congress.* New York: King's Crown Press, 1950.

ROBINSON, WILLIAM A. *Thomas B. Reed, Parliamentarian.* New York: Dodd, Mead & Co., 1930.

ROOSEVELT, THEODORE. *Thomas H. Benton.* Boston: Houghton Mifflin Co., 1899.

ROSTEN, LEO C. *The Washington Correspondents.* New York: Harcourt, Brace & Co., 1937.

RUSSELL, CHARLES EDWARD. *Blaine of Maine, His Life and Times.* New York: Cosmopolitan Book Corp., 1931.

SALTER, J. T. *Public Men In and Out of Office.* Chapel Hill, N.C.: University of North Carolina Press, 1946.

SARGENT, NATHAN. *Public Men and Events.* 2 vols. Philadelphia: J. B. Lippincott Co., 1875.

SAUND, D. S. *Congressman From India.* New York: E. P. Dutton & Co., Inc., 1960.

SCHATTSCHNEIDER, ELMER E. *Politics, Pressures and the Tariff.* New York: Prentice-Hall, Inc., 1935.

SCHLESINGER, ARTHUR M., JR. *The Age of Jackson.* Boston: Little, Brown & Co., 1945.

SCHMECKEBIER, LAURENCE F. *Congressional Apportionment.* Washington, D.C.: Brookings Institution, 1941.

SCHMUCKER, SAMUEL M. *Henry Clay.* Philadelphia: John E. Potter & Co., 1860.

SCHRIFTGIESSER, KARL. *The Gentleman from Massachusetts: Henry Cabot Lodge.* Boston: Little, Brown & Co., 1944.

————. *The Lobbyists: The Art and Business of Influencing Lawmakers.* Boston: Little, Brown & Co., 1951.

SEWARD, WILLIAM H. *Life and Public Services of John Quincy Adams.* New York: C. M. Saxton, 1859.

SHERMAN, JOHN. *Recollections of Forty Years in the House, Senate, and Cabinet.* Chicago and New York: Werner Co., 1895.

SLOANE, WILLIAM MILLIGAN. *Party Government in the United States of America.* New York: Harper & Bros., 1914.

SMITH, WILLIAM HENRY. *Speakers of the House of Representatives of the United States.* Baltimore: Simon J. Gaeng, 1928.

STANWOOD, EDWARD. *James Gillespie Blaine.* Boston: Houghton Mifflin Co., 1905.

STEALEY, O. O. *Twenty Years in the Press Gallery.* New York: Publishers Printing Co., 1906.

STEINER, GILBERT Y. *The Congressional Conference Committee, Seventieth to Eightieth Congresses.* Urbana, Ill.: University of Illinois Press, 1951.

STEPHENSON, NATHANIEL WRIGHT. *Nelson W. Aldrich, a Leader in American Politics.* New York: Charles Scribner's Sons, 1930.

476

STEVENS, JOHN AUSTIN. *Albert Gallatin*. Boston: Houghton Mifflin Co., 1898.

STONE, MELVILLE E. *Fifty Years a Journalist*. Garden City, N.Y.: Doubleday, Page & Co., 1921.

SUMMERS, FESTUS P. *William L. Wilson and Tariff Reform*. New Brunswick, N.J.: Rutgers University Press, 1953.

TAUSSIG, FREDERICK W. *The Tariff History of the United States*. New York: G. P. Putnam's Sons, 1923.

TAYLOR, TELFORD. *Grand Inquest, the Story of Congressional Investigations*. New York: Simon & Schuster, 1955.

THOMPSON, CHARLES WILLIS. *Party Leaders of the Time*. New York: G. W. Dillingham Co., 1906.

TIMMONS, BASCOM N. *Garner of Texas*. New York: Harper & Bros., 1948.

TOCQUEVILLE, DE, ALEXIS. *Democracy in America*. 2 vols. New York: Alfred A. Knopf, Inc., 1945.

TORREY, VOLTA. *You and Your Congress*. New York: William Morrow & Co., 1944.

TRUMAN, DAVID B. *The Congressional Party, a Case Study*. New York: John Wiley & Sons, 1959.

TUMULTY, JOSEPH P. *Woodrow Wilson as I Know Him*. Garden City, N.Y.: Doubleday, Page & Co., 1921.

TURNER, JULIUS. *Party and Constituency: Pressures on Congress*. Baltimore: Johns Hopkins Press, 1951.

UNDERWOOD, OSCAR W. *Drifting Sands of Party Politics*. New York: Century Co., 1931.

VARE, WILLIAM S. *My Forty Years in Politics*. Philadelphia: Roland Swain Co., 1933.

VOORHIS, JERRY. *Confessions of a Congressman*. Garden City, N.Y.: Doubleday & Co., Inc., 1947.

WALKER, HARVEY. *The Legislative Process, Lawmaking in the United States*. New York: Ronald Press Co., 1948.

WALLACE, ROBERT ASH. *Congressional Control of Federal Spending*. Detroit: Wayne State University Press, 1960.

WATTERSON, HENRY. *"Marse Henry," an Autobiography*. New York: George H. Doran Co., 1919.

WAYLAND, FRANCIS FRY. *Andrew Stevenson: Democrat and Diplomat, 1785-1857*. Philadelphia: University of Pennsylvania Press, 1939.

WEBB, W. L. *Champ Clark*. New York: The Neale Publishing Co., 1912.

WERNER, M. R. *Tammany Hall*. Garden City, N.Y.: Doubleday, Doran & Co., 1928.

WESTPHAL, ALBERT C. F. *The House Committee on Foreign Affairs*. New York: Columbia University Press, 1942.

WHEELER, HENRY G. *History of Congress.* 2 vols., New York: Harper & Bros., 1848.

WHITE, WILLIAM S. *Citadel: The Story of the U.S. Senate.* New York: Harper & Bros., 1957.

WILMERDING, LUCIUS. *The Spending Power, a History of the Efforts of Congress to Control Expenditures.* New Haven: Yale University Press, 1943.

WILSON, H. H. *Congress: Corruption and Compromise.* New York: Rinehart & Co., Inc., 1951.

WILSON, JAMES Q. *Negro Politics: The Search for Leadership.* New York: Free Press of Glencoe, Inc., 1960.

WILSON, RUFUS ROCKWELL. *Washington, the Capital City.* 2 vols. Philadelphia: J. B. Lippincott Co., 1902.

WILSON, WOODROW. *Congressional Government.* Boston: Houghton Mifflin Co., 1885.

————. *Constitutional Government in the United States.* New York: Columbia University Press, 1908.

WINTHROP, ROBERT C. *Addresses and Speeches on Various Occasions.* Boston: Little, Brown & Co., 1852.

WINTHROP, ROBERT C., JR. *A Memoir of Robert C. Winthrop.* Boston: Little, Brown & Co., 1897.

WISE, HENRY A. *Seven Decades of the Union.* Philadelphia: J. B. Lippincott Co., 1872.

YOUNG, ROLAND. *Congressional Politics in the Second World War.* New York: Columbia University Press, 1956.

————. *The American Congress.* New York: Harper & Bros., 1958.

ZINN, HOWARD. *LaGuardia in Congress.* Ithaca, N.Y.: Cornell University Press, 1958.

Index

absenteeism; absent without leave, 356; in early days, censure and fine for absence, 350-351; New York Democrats, special Monday train for, 349; no control of attendance now, 352; a third of House absent, 350; "Tuesday to Thursday Club," 350

Acorn Club, 295

acoustics in House, 309

action, political, of lobbyists, 222-223

Adams, Henry, comments on Senate, 31

Adams, John, on patronage, 248; scrupulous in relationship with House and Senate, 245

Adams, John Quincy, 120-121, 122-123, 156, 157; advice to Speaker, 64; elected to House after Presidency, 25, 27; election engineered by Clay in House, 25; filibustering tactic, refusal to vote, 49-52; on Jefferson and the House, 236; "Old Man Eloquent," 317, 371; reapportionment, 137-138; on Senate's intrusion in revenue legislation, 390; silenced on Senate, 371, 372; on Southern Manifesto, 386

Adams, Sherman, 187-188, 254

"Admiral," 122, 170

AFL, 218

AFL-CIO, 233, 294, 336, 429

aged, medical insurance financed by social security taxes urged on Senate by Kennedy, bypassing House, 390

Agriculture Committee, 161-162, 178, 201, 290, 346

Alaska, purchase of, 389

Albert, Carl, of Oklahoma, 85, 100, 127, 332, 335, 361, 362, 363, 419, 434, 442, 445; on floor leader, 94, 95

Alger, Bruce, of Texas, 139, 451

Allen, John, of Mississippi, 322

Allison, William B., Senator, of Iowa, 381

amendment; added to bill to kill bill, 364-365; as filibustering tactic, 48-49; to make bill passable, 273

American Bankers Association, 227

American Farm Bureau Federation, 223, 226, 227, 289, 429, 442

American Legion, 218, 223-224, 343

American Medical Association, lobbying of, 208, 220-221, 225, 227, 442

American Municipal Association, 227

Americans for Constitutional Action, 223

Americans for Democratic Action, 222-223, 226

Ames, Oakes, of Massachusetts; and Crédit Mobilier, 118; lobbyist, 210

Ames, Fisher, of Massachusetts, 27, 308, 386, 450; eloquence of, 313-314; at Massachusetts convention, 3

Andersen, Carl, of Minnesota, 290, 291

Anderson, Jack Z., 254-255

Anderson, John, 188

Anfuso, Victor, of New York, 264, 296-297

Anti-Nebraska Party, 73

appropriations; money bills, House and Senate disputes over, 386-406; safeguarding of, 151

Appropriations Committee, 155, 158, 163-166, 261, 287, 373, 405, 421, 422; careful study of all bills, 177; foreign aid program, 1962, 178; public works appropriations, 178

Arbogast, William, Associated Press, 442

Arends, Leslie, of Illinois, 86, 100, 127, 352-353, 363, 428, 430

Armed Services Committee, 159, 178, 201, 261, 421, 422

atomic bomb, appropriation for, 91

Autoworkers, 294

479

Buchanan, James, President, 28, 182
Buckley, Charles, of New York, 264
Bucktails, 73
Buckwheat Club, 272
Buffington, James, of Massachusetts, and patronage, 248
"bullet vote," tool of lobbyists, 219, 222-223, 343
Burdick, Usher, of North Dakota, 110, 320
Burgess, Tristam, of Rhode Island, "Bald Eagle of the House," 121
Burleson, Albert Sidney, 37, 252, 253
Burleson, Omar, of Texas, 439
Burr, Aaron, plagiarized, 70
Burrows, Julius Caesar, of Michigan, 321
Burton, Theodore, of Ohio, 171
Butler, Benjamin, of Massachusetts, 12, 322
Butler, Thomas, of Pennsylvania, 172
Butler, Walter, of Iowa, "Pansy," 122
Byrd, Harry, Senator, of Virginia, 379
Byrnes, John, of Wisconsin, chairman Policy Committee, 109, 128, 162, 177, 305, 334, 348, 363, 428
Byrnes, Joseph, Speaker, 65

"Cactus Jack," 122
"Calamity," 122
Calendar Wednesday, 54, 84, 171, 339-340
Calhoun, John C., of South Carolina, 128, 285, 312, 376, 379; eloquence of, before Civil War, 28; transferred from House to Senate, 27-28
Cambreleng, Churchill, of New York, 125, 171; answered all letters, 141
Campaign Committees, 88, 112-113
campaigns, election, 134
Campbell, George, of Tennessee, 309; duel with Gardinier over House debate, 7, 45
Campbell, Philip, of Kansas, chairman Rules Committee, personal pocket veto, 102-103, 413
Campbell, Timothy, of New York, 120
Cannon, Clarence, of Missouri, 91, 167, 177, 311, 360, 396-400, 421, 422, 446; chairman Appropriations Committee, 127, 164; House parliamentarian, 56-57, 66, 83; "Mole," 122
Cannon, Joseph G., of Illinois, Speaker, 41, 59, 72, 74, 85, 89-90, 101, 109, 115, 207, 217, 274, 275, 310, 376, 403, 411, 421; arbitrary action by, 78; caucus restricted, 74; chairman Ways and Means Committee, 171; challenged Theodore Roosevelt, 29; and control of House, 79-81; controlled all legislation and fate of members, 30; denounced Sen-

ate, 372-373; floor leader, 96; and Garner, 80-82; Garner on, 34; kept House in two-day session, 98-99; on lobbyists, 205-206; offered to entertain motion to declare chair vacant, 54; powers denied by House, 80; quoting Smoot on appropriations, 394; rebuffed Theodore Roosevelt's program, 238; revolt of House against, 31, 53-54; on the Speaker, 64; a strong Speaker, 19; "Uncle Joe," 122
Carew, John, Tammany boss, 113
Carey, Hugh, of New York, 363
Carlisle, John, of Kentucky, Speaker and lobbyists, 213; recognition at discretion of Speaker, 30-31, 76
Carnahan, A. S. J., of Missouri, 161
Carpenter, Frank, quoted, 119
Carpenter, Matthew, Senator, 314
Case, Francis, Senator, of South Dakota, 382
Cass, Lewis, 320
Cassiday, George, bootlegger, 10
Catholic vote, 272
caucus; given power to select floor leader, 96; increased division in Democratic Party, 109; party, 72-74; Republican, 274
Celler, Emanuel, of New York, 126-127, 129, 297, 389; bill against gerrymandering, 139
Chambers, Whittaker, 193, 196-197
Chelf, Frank, of Kentucky, 130, 347
Chenoweth, Edgar, of Colorado, 360, 437, 442, 446
Cheves, Langdon, of South Carolina, 27, 121, 126, 171; chairman Ways and Means Committee at thirty-five, 126
Chief Legislator, 238
Chief Lobbyist, 239
Chipman, John S., of Michigan, 9
Chipperfield, Robert, of Illinois, 161
Church, Frank, Senator, of Idaho, threat to filibuster for Bruces Eddy Dam, 404
Church, Marguerite Stitt, of Illinois, 161
Cieplinski, Michael, 251
Cilley, Jonathan, of Maine, 306, 307
CIO Committee on Political Education (COPE), 222
Civic Affairs Association, 223
civil rights legislation, 286, 288, 347; bill, Southern bloc response to, 286-287
civil service, establishment of, reduced Senate patronage, 384
Civil War; destroyed worst of factionalism, 28; restored two-party system, 28-29
Clark, Champ, of Missouri, Speaker, 66, 67, 69, 101, 130, 305, 325; bypassed by Wilson, 32; on freshman members, 129;

on floor leader, 93; on the House, 14; on House and Senate, 381; once overruled, 65; party whip, 98; presiding officer, not rival of President, 33; revolt against Cannon, 53-54; on speeches, 319-320; spoke from floor, 71; and a wheel chair, 99; on whip, 98

Clay, Henry, of Kentucky, Speaker, 7, 31, 62, 64, 66, 81, 121, 126, 128, 309, 312, 316, 317, 345-346, 349, 376, 379, 389; advice to Speaker Winthrop, 66; arranged federally financed highway and canals, 25; and committees, 152; dueler, 306; eloquence of, 28, 316-317; engineered election of President John Quincy Adams in House, 25; forced Missouri Compromise, 25; forced recognition of new South American republics, 25; forced U.S. into War of 1812, 25; "Millboy of the Slashes," 121; motion of the previous question, to cut off filibusters, 45-47; removed House from President's influence, 25; set pattern, 71; Speaker as leader of House his concept, 67-69; Speaker at thirty-four, 123; a strong Speaker, 19

Cleveland, Grover, 120; restricted patronage, 249; tried to lead Congress, 30-31

Clifford, Clark, 253

Clinic, The, 254

Clymer, George, of Pennsylvania, 348

coalition, modern conservative, 283-285

Cobb, Howell, of Georgia, 27, 189, 285

Cobb, Williamson, of Alabama, 319

Cochran, Bourke, of New York, 315

Cockburn, George, Sir, 7

Coffin, Frank, of Maine, 161

Cohelan, Jeffrey, of California, 143-144, 294

Cohen, Benjamin, 253

coinage, weights and measures, 156

Cole, Sterling, of New York, 385

Colfax, Schuyler, of Indiana, Speaker on conference committees, 402; given shares in Crédit Mobilier, 118, 213; great charm but lacked Clay's will, 69; on railroad passes, 198; spoke from floor, 71

Colmer, William, of Mississippi, 281; and Rules Committee, 413, 444; Kennedy said to favor purge of, 416; Rayburn announces purge, fails to do so, 420-428

"Columbian Orator," 321-322

Columbian Reader, 321

Commerce Committee Subcommittee on Legislative Oversight, 187

Committee on Committees; each party, 38, 158, 422, 424, 447; formal assign-

ments to committees, 110-111; influence of Speaker on, 72

Committee of the Whole House, 44-45; defeated amendment may not be repeated except as part of motion to recommit, 338; limitations on debate, 338; no roll-call votes, 338; processing of major legislation, 337-338, 355; quorum required, 338; Speaker selects a chairman, 337-338

committees, conference, of House and Senate, 377

committees; development of standing, 150-151; distribution among states, 157; importance of, 148; major, all exclusive, 408; manipulation of membership, 159; members technically elected, 157-158; work of, 151-154

communism, McCarthy investigation of, 37

conference committees; appeals, emotional, in House and Senate, 406; establishment of, 401; forbidden to add new material, 402; foreign aid, 405; House members more expert, 407-409; powers of, 401; Senate threat of filibuster, 403

Congress; did not pass Truman domestic program, 36; friction between Senate and House, 376-380; graded by percentage of President's program adopted, New Deal, 35; little legislation now originates in, 243; passed labor act over Truman veto, 36; powers of, 22; preferences for House or Senate, 380-384; presidential liaison with, 36-37, 254-255, 256-269

Congressional Conference Committee, The, 407

Congressional Globe, 319

Congressional Government, 30, 152

Congressional Quarterly, 452-453

Congressional Record, 142-143, 144, 268, 290, 295, 303, 319, 320, 322, 354, 372; editing of, 143; not a record of House floor action, 302

Congressman from India, 251

Conkling, Roscoe, of New York, 318-319

Consent Calendar, 54

conservative and liberal, tactics in debate, 327-328

constituents, 140-144

Constitution, approval of by states, 3-4

Conte, Silvio, of Massachusetts, 434

contributions, from organizations, 223

Cooley, Harold, of North Carolina, 346, 347, 438

Coolidge, Calvin, 33

Copeland, Royal, Senator, of New York, on conference committee, 404

Corcoran, Thomas, 253
Cox, Eugene, of Georgia, 103, 106, 107, 282, 283
Cox, Samuel, of New York and Ohio, floor leader, 96, 320-321, 364
Cramer, William C., of Florida, 365
Crawford, Theron; on influence of President on legislation, 237; on investigations, 184-185
Crédit Mobilier, 118, 212-213
crime, Kefauver investigation of, 37
crisis, continuing, of twentieth century nations, new, 18; surpluses and shortages, 18; unemployment, 18
Crisp, Charles F., of Georgia, Speaker, 31, 72, 109, 275, 351-352; increased powers of Rules Committee, 30
Crockett, Davy, of Tennessee, 8, 9, 120, 140; electioneering of, 134-135
Cullom, Shelby, of Illinois, 364
Cunningham, Glen, of Nebraska, 433
Curley, James Michael, of Massachusetts, mail fraud by, 118
Curtin, Willard, of Pennsylvania, 360
Curtis, Carl T., Senator, of Nebraska, 382
Curtis, Lawrence, of Massachusetts, 434
Curtis, Thomas, of Missouri, 408, 429, 434
Cushing, Caleb, of Massachusetts, 5
Cushman, Samuel, of New Hampshire, "Previous Question," 122, 310
Cutting, Francis, of New York, 308

Daly, Charles, 262, 268
Dalzell, John, of Pennsylvania, 81
Dana, Charles A., 246
Davis, Henry Winter, of Maryland, 318
Davis, James C., of Georgia, 284, 355, 365, 454
Dawes, Henry L., of Massachusetts, 312
Dawson, John, of Louisiana, 305
Dayton, Jonathan, of New Jersey, Speaker, 96
debate; *Congressional Record,* speeches not from floor, 302-303; to eloquence, common sense, House listens, 305-306; eloquence in, 312-319; forces destroying, 304; free from libel and slander laws, 303; humor in, 320-324; limited by House rules, 300-302; violence in, 306-312
Defense Department; and debt ceiling, 347-348; and House, 20
Delaney, James, of New York, 93, 297, 412
Democracy in America, 7-8
Democratic cleavages, 277-278
Democratic Party, split in, 74-75
Democratic Patronage Committee, 110

Democratic study group, 272, 293, 422; involved in enlarging of Rules Committee, 417, 418
Dent, John, of Pennsylvania, 294, 336
Deringer, Henry, gunsmith, 307
Deschler, Lewis, House parliamentarian, 60, 66, 446
Dickens, Charles, 311
Dickinson, Lester, of Iowa, 289
Dickson, Cecil, AMA, 208
Dies, Martin, of Texas, 191, 192, 378
dilatory motions, 51, 64
Dillon, Douglas, 261
Dingley, Nelson, of Maine, floor leader, 96, 171; chairman Ways and Means Committee, 124; to freshman member, 129-130
Dirksen, Everett, Senator, of Illinois, 127, 244, 379, 380, 398
Discharge Petition, 54, 84, 339-340
discipline of House members, difficulties of, 110
discomfort, crowding, and chaos, 150 years of, 309
District of Columbia Committee, 201
districts; marginal, 133; variations in, 279, 451
Donohue, Richard, 258, 262, 268
Dorn, Francis, of New York, 223
Dorn, W. J. B., of South Carolina, 281
Douglas, Paul, Senator, of Illinois, 379
Douglas, Stephen, of Illinois, 28; campaign of, 135
Dowse, Edward, of Massachusetts, 287
Driscoll, Denis, of Pennsylvania, 216
dueling, first law against, 306
Dulles, John Foster, 169, 177
Dunne, Peter, quoted, 118
Dwight, John, of New York, whip, developed techniques, 98
Dwight, Henry, of Massachusetts, 356

Edelman, John, 231
Education and Labor Committee, 156, 168, 172-173, 178, 201, 341; changed to liberal by appointments, 159-160
Eisenhower, D. D., 6, 35, 105, 162, 166, 256, 271, 344, 355, 359, 364; and Democratic Congress, 88-89, 186, 187; and Foreign Affairs Committee, 169-170; had formalized Congressional liaison, 36; and Lebanon, 36; liaison and patronage, 254-255; and relationship with House, 20-21; used television, assigned staff member as lobbyist, 239; and use of veto, 244
election and re-election of members, 133-134

483

elections; contested, 135-136; unfairly awarded, 136
Elliott, Carl, of Alabama, 160, 258, 447
eloquence in, 312-319
Emancipation Proclamation, 241-242
Eppes, John W., of Virginia, floor leader, 96, 171, 285; party whip, informal, 97
Essex Junto, 316-317
Estes, Billie Sol, 175
"Everything Is Made for Love," 122

Fallon, George, of Maryland, 446
Farley, James A., 247, 253
farm bloc, 274, 288-291; broken in 1960's, 291; four Southern crops supported, 289; subsidy program under attack, 291
Farmers' Alliance, 289
Fascell, Dante, of Florida, 281
"Father of the House," 126
Federalist Papers, 13-14, 134, 449, 454
Federal Reserve Act, 242
Fenton, Ivor, of Pennsylvania, 297, 360, 433
file, completeness of, on members of Rules Committee, 415-416
filibustering, 42-43, 45-46, 47-52, 340; Senate threat of, conference committee, 403-404
Fillmore, Millard, of New York, floor-leader and chairman Ways and Means Committee, 95, 171
Fish, Hamilton, of New York, 191
fistfights, recent, 311
Fitzgerald, John, of New York, 171
five-minute rule, and amendments, 48, 64
Flood, Daniel, of Pennsylvania, 333
Flynt, John, of Georgia, 441
Fogarty, John, of Rhode Island, 167, 177, 264, 361, 383; bricklayer, foremost House authority on medical research, 117
Foote, Charles, of New York, 346
Foote, Samuel, of Connecticut, 346
Ford, Gerald, of Michigan, 127, 165, 167, 348, 383, 407
foreign affairs, 155-156, 160, 161, 168, 178, 201, 261; cuts in programs, 169-170; House and Senate friction over, 386, 405
foreign aid, House and Senate on, 405
foreign policy, bipartisan, 240
Forrester, Elijah L., of Georgia, "Tic," 286, 365
Foster, David, of Vermont, 323
franking, misused by lobbyists, 217
Frear, James, of Wisconsin, 111, 143, 276, 382
Free-Soilers, 73

Freeman, Orville, 261, 332, 361
Frelinghuysen, Peter, of New Jersey, 161
"Front Porch," 122
Fulbright, J. William, of Arkansas, 128, 160, 296, 298; on backdoor spending, 396
Fulton, James, of Pennsylvania, 429

Gallatin, Albert, of Pennsylvania, floor leader, 27, 95-96, 162, 313, 374, 387-388; made secretary of treasury by Jefferson, 1801, 388
Gardinier, Barent, of New York, 309; duel with George Campbell of Tennessee over House debate, 7, 45; filibusterer, 45
Garfield, James A., 30; chairman Appropriations Committee, 45, 125, 171; chairman Military Affairs Committee, 125; eloquence of, 312-313; floor leader, 95; given shares in Crédit Mobilier, 118; on the House, 14; as House member opposed Senate bill revising tariffs, 390; on House and Senate, 377
Garland, Peter, of Maine, 203
Garner, John Nance, of Texas, Speaker, 65, 89, 91, 101, 108, 143, 160, 276, 297, 331; "Cactus Jack," 122; and Cannon, 80-82; on freshman member, 130; gerrymandered district for himself, 140; graduated income tax, 163; on the House, 12; and Longworth, 81-84; on Ways and Means Committee, 163; Wilson confidential liaison, 253
Gary, Vaughn, of Virginia, 167
Gerry, Elbridge, of Massachusetts, 146; Massachusetts delegate to Philadelphia convention, against excess of democracy, 2
gerrymandering, 138-140; most notorious example, 453-454
Giaimo, Robert, of Connecticut, 160, 203
Giddings, Joshua, of Ohio, 121, 289, 306
Giles, William, of Virginia, 313
Gillet, Ransom, 273-274
Gillett, Frederick, of Massachusetts, 70, 74, 108; on Fitzgerald, 171; on the House, 14; presiding officer not rival of President, 33
Glass, Carter, of Virginia, chairman Banking and Currency Committee, and Federal Reserve Act, 242, 324
"gobbledygook," 291
Goldfine, Bernard, 187-188
Goldwater, Barry, Senator, of Arizona, 379
Goodell, Charles, of New York, 203
Gordon, Thomas, of Illinois, 161, 168
Gould, Jay, lobbyist, Erie Railroad, 214

484

487

Landrum, Philip, of Georgia, 284
Lane, Thomas, of Massachusetts, 420; convicted of tax evasion, 119
language of House debates, provocative, 308
Lankford, Richard, of Maryland, 202, 203, 435, 444
leader, party floor; all speakers since 1919 former party floor leaders, 97; chosen by caucus, not Speaker, 96; different types required by House and Senate, 376; duties, 92; freed from committee responsibilities, 96; tactics, 93, 94
leadership, Rayburn on, 75
legislation, major processing of absenteeism, 349-352; Calendar Wednesday, 339-340; closed and open rule, 341; Committee of the Whole House, 337-338, 354-355; defeat bill by votes, 367; Discharge petition, 339-340; filibuster, 340; killing bill by amendment, 365: manipulation of amendments, 346-348: pairing off, 356-358; parliamentary tactics, 342-345; party whip, 352-353; processed on the floor, 337; recommitting a bill, 366, 367; striking out enacting clause, applicable only in Committee of Whole House, 365-366; suspension of rule, 341; switch votes, 358-365
"Legislator, The," 349
Lewis, Dixon, of Alabama, 126
Lewis, John L., on Garner, 80
libel and slander laws, members free from in House, 303
liberal bloc, 291-294
liberal and conservative, tactics in House debate, 327-328
Lincoln, Abraham, 418-419, 449; creation of Nevada statehood plus patronage for constitutional emancipation amendment, 246-247; on eloquence of Alexander Stephens, 314; Emancipation Proclamation, Congress not involved in, 241; legislation suggested, compensation to slaveholders, 241-242; patronage to control Congress, 32-33, 237, 246; quoted, 119; term in House, 124
Lindsay, John, of New York, 280, 429
lobbyists; American Legion, power of, 223-224; associations of, 224; call girls and bribes, recent, 215; change in lives of House members, 215; changed techniques of, 214; changes in abilities and numbers, 206-208; conservative, work with Halleck, 228; contributions from organizations, 223; difficulties of Presidents with, 225-226; early pressures from public officials, 206; files on representatives, 220; four Kennedy lobbyists,

in addition to federal agencies and departments, working House only, 262, intensified political action, 222-223; Kennedy campaign, 226-227; Kennedy Chief Lobbyist, 239, 264-267; Kennedy lobbyists work from Speaker's office, 268; members of House as, 210; misuse of franking, 217; money lost to members of House by gambling, 213; new groups, labor unions, women's organizations, 219; open hearings, 217; pervade all communications media, 221-222; railroad labor, 224; railroad passes, 210; registration of, 217; rumors of sale of votes, 212-213; Rayburn and McCormack work with AFL-CIO lobbyists, 228; school construction bill, strategy, 230-233; stimulation of grass roots action, 218-219; successes of, 213-214; telegrams, unauthorized, used by, 216; veterans', 343; White House representative works with, 228-229; Wilson investigation, 215-216; women, 210-212
Locofocos, 73
Lodge, Henry Cabot, Senator, 19, 381; revitalized Senate, kept U.S. from League of Nations, 33
logrolling, 273
Longworth, Nicholas, of Ohio, Speaker, 11, 32, 66, 70, 74, 89, 91, 101, 109, 111, 275, 295, 305, 331, 376, 395, 420; and "Board of Education," 81-84; floor leader, 96; and Garner, 81-84; on the House, 11; overruling of, 65; political leader of House, 33; restored political Speakership, 70; on rules of the House, 60; and steering committee, 108
Loud, Eugene, of California, 295
Lowndes, William, of South Carolina, 27; floor leader, 96
Luce, Robert, of Masschusetts, 218, 382
Lumley, John, NEA, 232
Lumpkin, John, of Georgia, answered all letters, 141
Lyon, Matthew, of Vermont, 307

MacArthur, Douglas, and Russell investigation of dismissal, 37
Machrowicz, Thaddeus, of Michigan, 296
Maclay, William, Senator, 212, 348
Macon, Nathaniel, of North Carolina, Speaker, 24; Speaker the elect of the elect of all the people, 64; subservient to Jefferson, 67
Madden, Ray, of Indiana, 413, 414
Madison, James, of Virginia; as delegate to Philadelphia convention, for democratic House, 2; floor leader, 95-96; made almost subservient to House by

Mills, Roger Q., of Texas, 171
Mills, Wilbur, of Arkansas, chairman Ways and Means Committee, 90, 127, 159, 167, 177, 261, 265, 278, 326, 334, 335, 367, 368, 407, 422, 447; Committee on Committees, 422
minorities, vote of activist, 37-38
Mitchell, Clarence, NAACP, 208
Mitchell, James P., 177
"Mole," 122
Mondell, Franklin, of Wyoming, 70, 311; floor leader, 96
money bills, House and Senate friction over, 386-406
Monroe Doctrine, 241
Monroney, Michael, 261
Moore, Arch, of West Virginia, 439
Morrill, Justin, of Vermont, 171-172
Morrissey, John, of New York, 9, 120
Morse, Bradford, of Massachusetts, 434
Morse, Samuel F. B., experiences with House, 8-9
Morse, Wayne, Senator, of Oregon, 380
Moseley, William, of New York, 318
Moss, John, of California, 128
motion; of the previous question, 45-46, 64; and declaration of War of 1812, 46-47; to recommit, 54, 84
Moulder, Morgan, of Missouri, 187
"Mr. Sam," 122
"Mr. Will," 122
Muhlenberg, Frederick, of Pennsylvania, first Speaker, 63, 401
Mundt, Karl, of South Dakota, 160, 397-398
Murphy, Charles, 253
Mussolini, Benito, mistress of, 193

National Association for the Advancement of Colored People, 208, 226
National Council of Churches, 231
National Association of Home Builders, 227
National Association of Manufacturers, lobbying activities, 215, 218, 226, 227, 429, 442
National Association of Real Estate Boards, lobbying of, 225
national defense fully supported, 240
National Education Association, 226, 231, 429
National Farmers Union, 223, 226
National Housing Conference, 226
National Retail Merchants Associations, 227
National Rural Electric Cooperative Association, 226
"Navaho, The," 173
Negro, as political issue, 277, 278, 286, 287, 288

Nelson, John, of Wisconsin, 276
Nevin, Robert, of Ohio, 295
New Deal, 238
New Freedom, 238
New Frontier, 239
newspapermen, as lobbyists, 210
Newton, Thomas, of Virginia, chairman Interstate Commerce Committee at forty-three, 126
New York Times, The, reporter on lobbying, 212
Nicholas, George, of Virginia, 24
Nixon, Richard M. of California, 127, 159, 196-197, 291, 295, 430
Norris, George, of Nebraska, revolt against Cannon, 53-54, 74, 98, 295
Norton, Mary, of New Jersey, 168
notoriety, national, of ineffective members, 15

Oberdorfer, Don, 202
O'Brien, Elva, 261
O'Brien, Lawrence, 36-37, 256-269, 437
O'Brien, Leo, of New York, 360, 361
O'Brien, Thomas, boss of Chicago House Democrats, 113, 162, 354
O'Connor, John, of New York, chairman Rules Committee, 104
O'Hara, James, of Michigan, 160, 231
"Old Man Eloquent," 49, 122, 286, 317-318, 371
"Old Swamp Fox," 122, 424
Oliver, Robert, lobbyist, 228
one-hour rule, 47-48, 64, 100
O'Neill, Thomas, of Massachusetts, 92, 93, 413, 414
"Operation Abolition," 195
Ordinance of Nullification of South Carolina, 26
Osmers, Frank, of New Jersey, 434, 446

Pacific Steamship Company, 212
pairing off; John Quincy Adams on, 356; lists in Congressional Record, 357; live pair, 358; pair clerks, 357; Thomas Hart Benton on, 356-357
"Palace of Fortune," 209
"Pansy," 122
passes, railroad, 210
Passman, Otto, of Louisiana, 20, 165-166, 177, 178, 278, 333, 374, 405; and foreign aid, 20
Patman, Wright, of Texas, 346, 396
patronage; little available to House, 110; used by Presidents to manipulate Congress, 240-241
Patronage Committee, 88
Patton, John, of Virginia, 286
pay and perquisites, House members, 144-145; public attitude toward, 144-145

Payne, Sereno, of New York, 81, 171
Pearce, James, of Maryland, 131
peddlers, influence, investigation of, 37
Pelly, Thomas, of Washington, 130
Pendleton, Edward, lobbyist, 209, 213
Pennington, William, of New Jersey, Speaker, 66
"Perish Credit," 122
Persons, Wilton, 254
Peyton, Balie, of Tennessee, 197-198
Phelps, John, of Missouri, 126
Phillips, John, of California, 311
Phillips, William, 293, 417
Pierce, Franklin, President, 28; prevented duel, 308
"Pig-Iron," 123
Pincus, Walter, 202
pistols, drawn on House floor, 306-307
Poff, Richard, of Virginia, 365
policy, national, depends on interplay of President, Senate, House, 19
Policy Committee, 88
Polish Americans, 272, 296
politics, deterioration of, before Civil War, 28
Polk, James Knox, of Tennessee, 28, 314; did not challenge man who pulled his nose, 308; floor leader and chairman Ways and Means Committee, 95, 171; silenced John Quincy Adams on Senate, 372; "Young Hickory," 320
Poore, Ben Perley; on House investigations, 183-184; quoted, 20; report of financial wrongdoings by House members, 118; on women as lobbyists, 210-211
Populist Party, 289
pork barrel, the, 143-144, 164, 171, 244, 275
Powell, Adam Clayton, of New York, 131, 173, 202, 203, 311, 364-365, 420
Powell amendment, 364, 365
Presidency, President; checks and balances, constitutional, 18-19; compromised by deterioration of politics before Civil War, 28; early, gave own policies in State of Union speeches, 241; effect of World War II on, 36; Eisenhower used television, appointed White House assistant as lobbyist, 239; Harrison avoided leigslative matters, 236-237; holds initiative, 18; Jefferson involved in selection of Speaker, committee chairmen, 236; Kennedy, press conferences and television for New Frontier program, staff of lobbyists, 239; Lincoln, patronage to get legislation, 237; Lincoln and use of Emancipation Proclamation, 241-242; as lobbyist, 239, 260-269; Monroe Doctrine,

241; party's chief legislator, 35; patronage used by, 240-241, 245-252; personal relations with legislators and world stature more important than patronage, 252-253; pushed aside after Civil War, 19; Roosevelt, F. D., press conferences, fireside chats, weekly meetings leaders of Congress, 238; Roosevelt, Theodore, presented Presidential program, Square Deal, 237; Senate, 1960, thirteen had run for or been mentioned for Presidency, 380; strong, 19; Truman Fair Deal, Congress partly rejected, 238-239; Tyler preferred Congress in adjournment, 237; use of veto, 243-245; Washington, John Adams scrupulous about approaching Congress, 235; Wilson presented New Freedom, lobbied personally for it, 238; world stature of President enhances standing with Congress, 239-240
Preston, Prince, of Georgia, 365
"Previous Question," 122
Prouty, Winston, Senator, of Vermont, 382
Public Works Appropriations Bill, 164, 178
Public Works Committee, 178, 201
Pucinski, Roman, of Illinois, 341

Quay, Matthew, Senator, of Pennsylvania, 379
Quie, Albert, of Minnesota, 203
Quincy, Josiah, of Massachusetts, 27, 245, 285, 308-309, 316-317, 455; definition of House, 6
quorum and quorum call, 50, 353

Rabaut, Louis, of Michigan, 442, 443
racketeering, labor, McClellan investigation of, 37
Rainey, Henry, Speaker, 65; favored Steering Committee, 108
Rains, Albert, of Alabama, 106, 128, 261, 278, 344-345, 383, 444
Randall, Robert, 188
Randall, Samuel J., of Pennsylvania, Speaker, 12, 72; floor leader, 96
Randolph, Edmund, of Virginia, 391
Randolph, Jennings, Senator, of West Virginia, 382
Randolph, John, of Virginia, 96, 141, 171, 317, 371; filibusterer, 45, 47
Rankin, John, of Mississippi, 146, 159, 194, 283, 311; on gag rule, 44
Rayburn, Sam, of Texas, Speaker, 44, 62, 65, 67, 69, 70, 72, 85, 86, 88, 89, 90, 91, 93, 104, 105, 106, 107, 108, 109, 110, 111, 126, 127, 128, 132, 139, 156, 157, 159, 160, 169, 170, 178, 187, 194,

493

suspension of rules; limits debate, forbids amendment, can be invoked only if Speaker approves bill and recognizes motion, 342

switch votes, dramatic possibilities of, 358-365

Symington, Stuart, Senator, of Missouri, 380

Taber, John, of New York, 91, 127, 164-165, 297, 311, 363, 383

Taft, William Howard; and Democratic House, 186; presentation of railroad bill drafted by attorney general, 33

Taft-Hartley Law, passed over veto, 243

Tallmadge, James, of New York, 131

Taney, Roger, Chief Justice, 237

"Tantalus Club," 295-296, 323

tariffs, 21; influence of Speakers Clay and Rayburn, 62

Tawney, James, of Minnesota, 171

Taylor, John W., of New York, party whip, 97-98

Taylor, Robert, 192

Taylor, Zachary, 28

Teague, Olin, of Texas, "Tiger," 343-344, 425

Temple, Shirley, 192

Tennessee Valley Authority, 283

Thomas, Albert, of Texas, 167, 177, 261, 323-324

Thomas, J. Parnell, 192-193, 196

Thompson, Frank, of New Jersey, 160, 231, 257, 258, 285, 292, 293, 365, 414, 416, 418, 419, 431, 432, 434, 435, 438, 440, 442, 446

Thompson, John, sergeant at arms, 190

Thornberry, Homer, of Texas, 83, 413

Thurmond, Strom, Senator, of South Carolina, 380, 420

Tillman, Benjamin, Senator, of South Carolina, "Pitchfork Ben," 372-373, 403

Tilson, John Q., of Connecticut, 81, 82; Republican floor leader, 114

Tocqueville, Alexis de, 319; on House, 7; on Senate, 8; on illiteracy in House, 119-120

Tollefson, Thor, of Washington, 443

Townsend, Francis, 190

Tracy, Uriah, of Connecticut, 121

Trimble, James, of Arkansas, 286, 413, 443

Truman, H. S, 35, 83, 105, 225, 256, 271, 284, 395; appointed two liaison representatives with Congress, 36; attempt to throw election of, into House, 23; Congress partially rejected domestic "Fair Deal" program, 36, 238-239; and Hiss investigation, 193-194; and isolationism,

36; Korean War, 36; liaison men, 253; Marshall Plan, 36; people of Turkey and Berlin, 36; and Republican Congress, 88-89, 186; Taft-Hartley labor bill passed over veto, 36, 243

Tucker, Henry St. George, of Virginia, 325

Twenty Years of Congress, 128

"Twister of the Tail of the British Lion," 130-131

Tyler, John, President, pleased when Congress adjourned, 237

"Uncle Carl," 122

"Uncle Joe," 122

Udall, Stewart, of Arizona, "The Navaho," 160, 173, 292, 293, 383, 414, 437; and Barden, 173

Un-American Activities Committee, 159, 191-197, 378, 421

Underwood, Oscar, of Alabama, 69, 171; on conference committee, 403-404; floor leader, 96

Underwood Tariff, 215

United Mine Workers, 226, 233, 277, 294

United Nations, 298

United States Chamber of Commerce, 218, 226, 227, 429, 442

U.S. Conference of Mayors, 226

Van Zandt, James, of Pennsylvania, 433

Velde, Harold, of Illinois, 194

ventilation in House, 309

Veterans Affairs Committee, 201

Veterans of Foreign Wars, 343

veto, use of, 243-245

Vice President, a weak presiding officer, 68-69

Vining, John, of Delaware, 212

violence on floor of House, 306-309

Vinson, Carl, of Georgia, chairman Armed Services Committee, "Admiral," "Old Swamp Fox," "Uncle Carl," 122, 124, 126, 127, 143-144, 159, 170, 259, 261, 266, 281, 282, 325, 421, 422, 424, 425, 426, 428, 430, 434, 435, 439, 440

Vinton, Samuel, of Ohio, 171

Voorhis, Jerry, of California, 291

Vorys, John, of Ohio, 161

votes; big city organizations, 113-114; bills, tailoring of, 332-337; processing of major legislation, 337; rumors of sale of, 212-213

Wage and Hour Bill, 105, 107

Wagner, Robert, 264

Walcott, John, 189

Wallhauser, George, of New Jersey, 439

495

Walker, Felix, of North Carolina, and buncombe, 10-11

Walker, Joseph, of Massachusetts, "Gray Eagle of Quinsigamond," 121

Walker Tariff of 1847, 32

Walter, Francis, of Pennsylvania, chairman Democratic Patronage Committee, chairman Un-American Activities Committee, 107, 110, 127, 421, 422, 434, 440

Ward, Sam, lobbyist, 208-209, 213, 221

Warner, John Dewitt, of New York, 325

Washburn, Cadwallader, of Wisconsin, 308

Washburne, Elihu, of Illinois, 132, 133, 308

Washington, George, 18, 206; asked advice of Senate, 236; and Barbary pirates, 387; House threatened to encroach on treaty-making power of, 24; scrupulous in relationship with House and Senate, 235; on Senate, 23

"Watchdogs of the Treasury," 132, 165

Watson, James, of Indiana, and wooden shoes, 9

Ways and Means Committee, 155, 158, 160, 201, 261, 265, 325, 334, 368, 390, 408, 422; bills from, usually under closed rule, 341; careful study of all bills, 177; conferences held in House wing, 409; created to resist Hamilton, 236; distribution of Democrats in, 162; Trade Agreements Act, 1955, 1958, 177

Weaver, James, of Iowa, 289

Webster, Daniel, 19, 31, 121, 155, 312, 376, 379, 389; eloquence of, 28; sent to House by New Hampshire and Massachusetts, 27; transferred to Senate, 27-28

Weeks, Sinclair, 177

Weller, Luman, of Iowa, "Calamity," 122

whip, 97-100; information on voting strength, 99-100; may substitute for floor leader, 99; Speaker's call, 99; whip's calls, 99

White, John, of Kentucky, Speaker, 100; plagiarism discovered, led to suicide, 70

Whitney, Charles, 188

Whitney, Reuben, 197-198

Whittemore, Benjamin, of South Carolina, sold West Point and Annapolis appointments, 118

Whitten, Jamie, of Mississippi, 287, 422, 423

Whittlesey, Elisha, of Ohio, 132, 133

Wickersham, James, of Alaska, 311

Willard's Hotel, waiter shot and killed at, 307

Williams, John Bell, of Mississippi, 223, 286, 422, 423

Williams, John Sharp, of Mississippi, 325; on Knott Committee, 392

Wilmot, David, of Pennsylvania, 131

Wilmot Proviso, 131

Wilson, Henry Hall, 231, 232, 258, 262, 268

Wilson, James, Pa. delegate to Phila. convention for democratic House, 2; on Supreme Court, 179, 204, 391

Wilson, William, of West Virginia, 171; defeated by lobbyists, 214; chairman Ways and Means Committee, 325

Wilson Woodrow, 67, 154, 218, 239, 253; on appropriations, 394; bypassed Speaker 32; on committees, 152-153; on Congress, 29-30; dealt directly with legislators, 252; and Federal Reserve Banking and Currency Act, 242; on freshman members, 129; on the House, 8; on House investigations, 183; on House and Senate, 381; on leaders of House, 167; lobbying investigation, 215-216; made himself Chief Legislator, 238; offered program, "New Freedom," and carried it to Congress, 22, 238; Postmaster General Burleson his liaison with Congress, 37; a strong President, 19; on study in House and Senate, 407; on veto, 242; world stature as idealist helped prestige with Congress, 239-240

Winchell, Walter, 296-297

Winstead, Arthur, 422, 423

Winthrop Robert, of Massachusetts, Speaker, 38, 64, 66, 123

Wise, Henry, of Virginia, 46, 198

Wolcott, Jesse, of Michigan, 403

Wolverton, Charles, of New Jersey, 135

women, improper involvements with, 119

Woodruff, Roy, of Michigan, 276

Yancey, William, of Alabama, 307

Yates, Richard, Senator, of Iowa, 381

Young, Roland, 406

Zablocki, Clement, of Wisconsin, 296